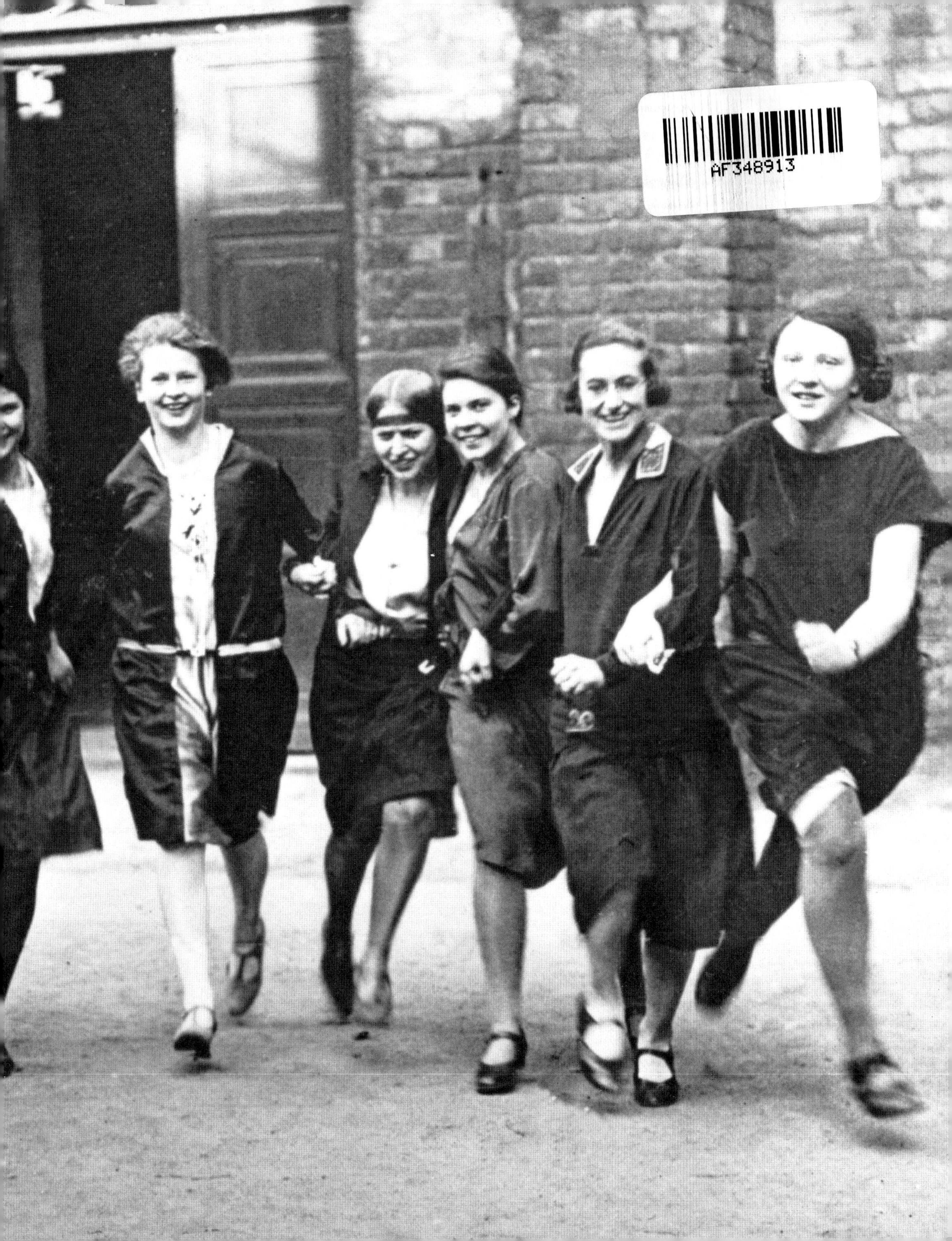

AF348913

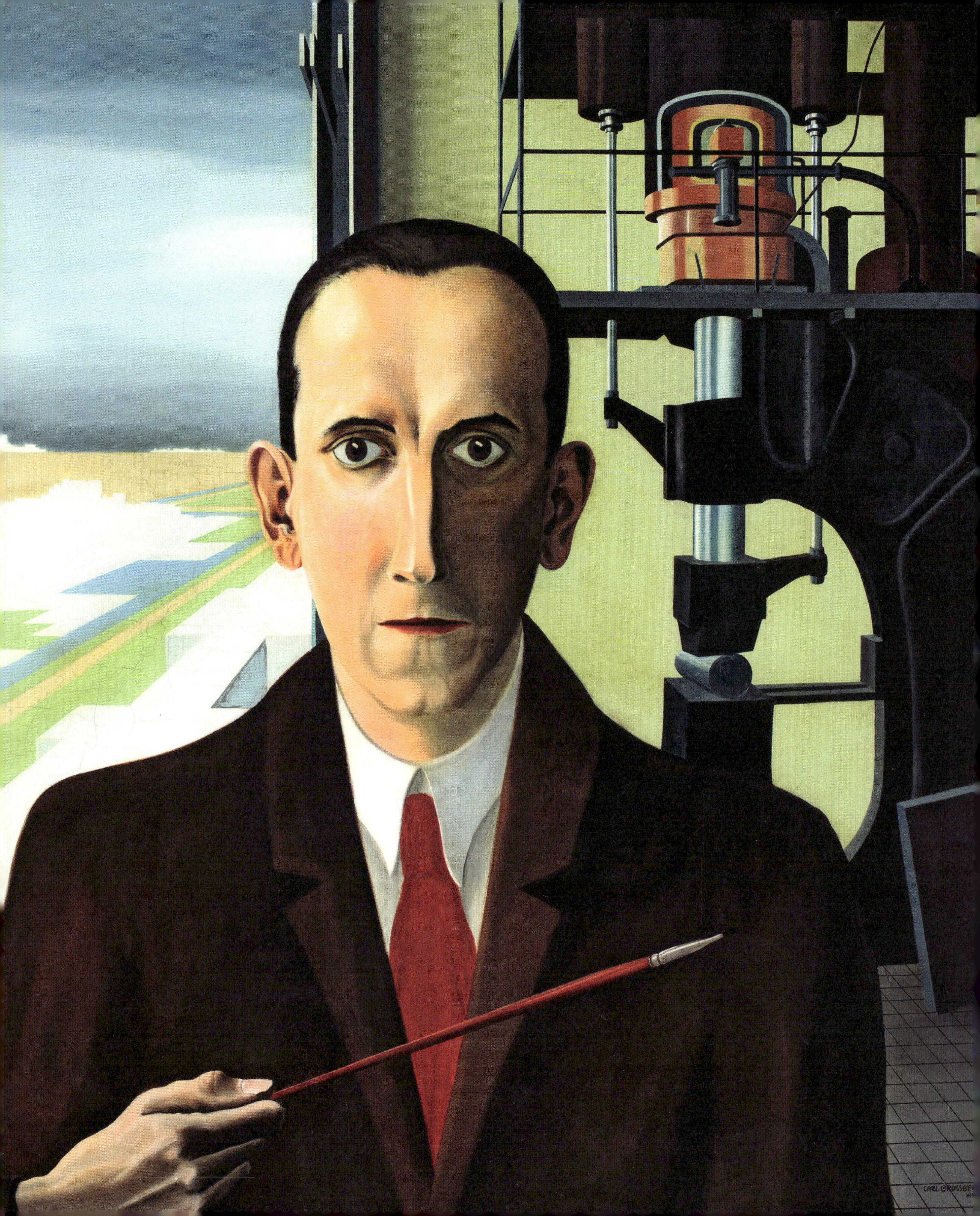

THE COLD GAZE – GERMANY IN THE 1920S

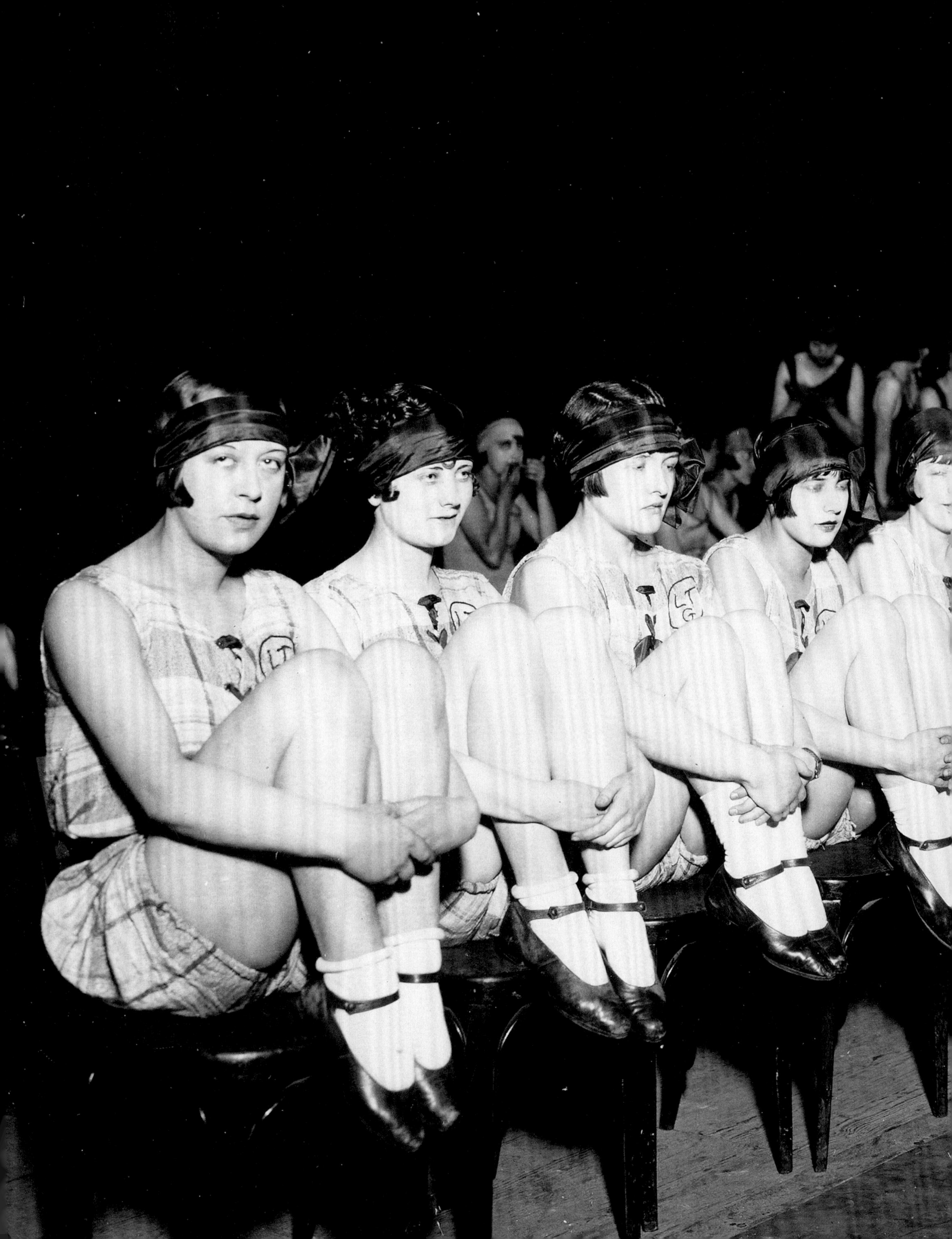

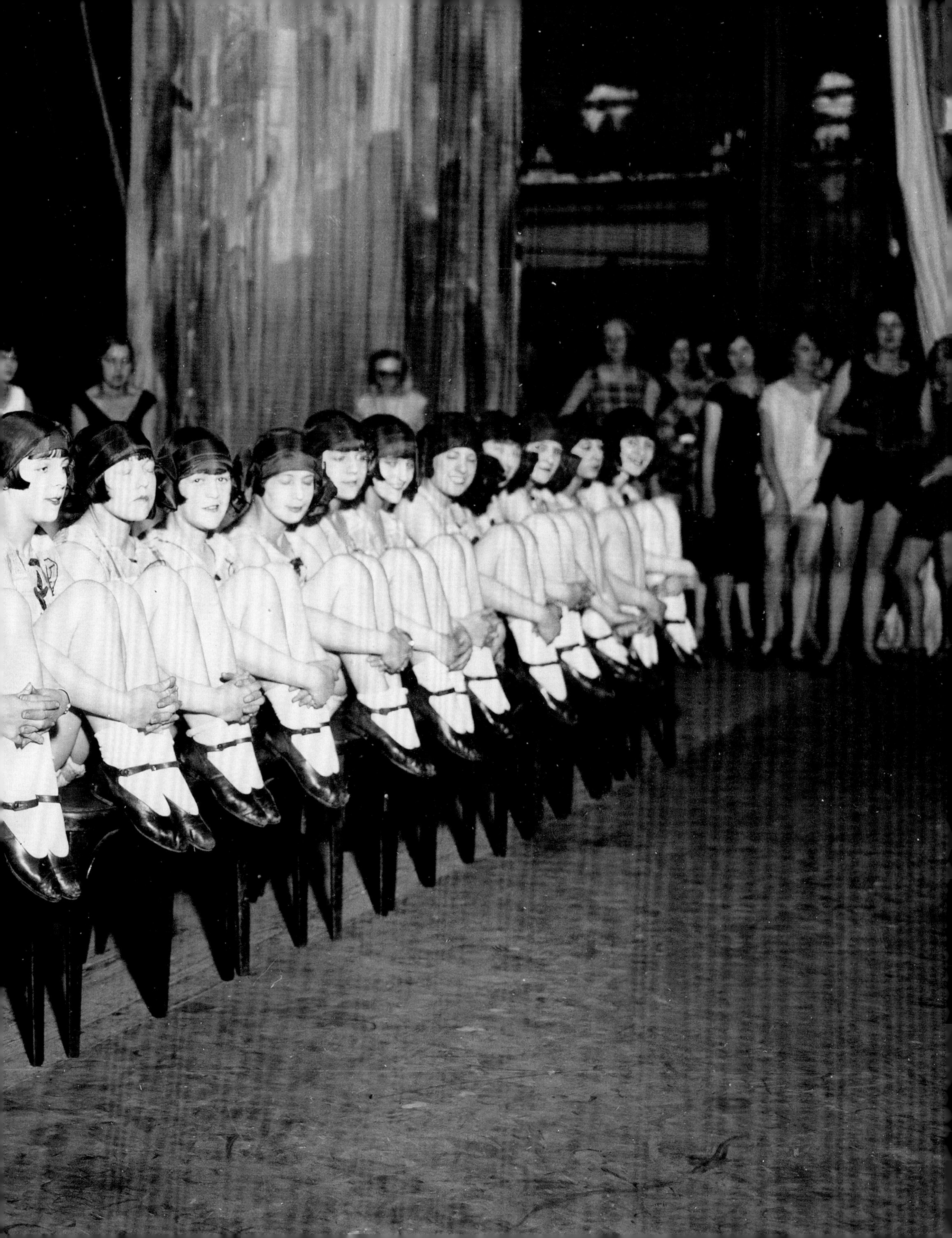

Foreword

The German TV series *Babylon Berlin* was enthusiastically received when it aired in Denmark in 2017. The series paints a sumptuous and enticing picture of 1920s Berlin during the Weimar Republic (1918-1933), replete with conspiracies, shady characters, political intrigue, burgeoning Nazism and sexual escapades in the roaring Berlin nightlife. That this tumultuous epoch speaks to our time is also evident in new film adaptations and Danish translations of novels from the period, including Alfred Döblin's *Berlin Alexanderplatz*, Erich Kästner's *Fabian* and Hans Fallada's *Kleiner Mann – was nun?* (Little Man, What Now?), and in the host of talks and events about the period that are being held across the country.

With the exhibition *The Cold Gaze – Germany in the 1920s*, we invite you on a journey a century back in time to the fascinating and varied art and culture of the 1920s Weimar Republic. At the heart of it all is New Objectivity, the striking art movement known for its sober realism, caustic satire and clinical gaze. In addition to painting, drawing and photography, this lavish exhibition also features architecture, design, film, theatre, literature and music from the period. Moreover, the exhibition takes a special look at the German photographer August Sander (1876-1964) and his pioneering documentary "group portrait" of modern people.

In the aftermath of First World War, Germany goes through a turbulent period of deep poverty and political unrest concurrent with the brief flourishing of democracy during the Weimar Republic, before the culture of freedom is snuffed out with the Nazis' rise to power in 1933. The exhibition charts the outlines of the rich and broadly unfolding cultural life of the years between the two world wars.

In the early 1920s, artists disillusioned by the war turn towards the real world, working in a less expressive style of realistic representation. The movement is dubbed "Neue Sachlichkeit" (New Obejctivity) by the art historian Gustav Friedrich Hartlaub, who, as director of Kunsthalle Mannheim, mounts an exhibition of that title in 1925. In turn, New Objectivity becomes a cultural catchphrase in Germany, appearing in popular plays and cabaret performances as a signifier of the zeitgeist. Severed from its narrow affiliation with painting, the term eventually comes to represent the aesthetic of an entire era. Rooted in objectivity, rationality, standardization and functionalism, it aspires to reach beyond an elitist and individualistic view of art to create a common popular culture.

New Objectivity is less a clearly defined movement than a new way of looking at the world with a cold, exacting gaze. In a society marked by violent upheaval, the movement's artists strive to capture modern everyday living, representing the life and work of ordinary people in a realistic sober style stripped of sentiment and often with a high level of detail. Life in the big city, modern, functionalist architecture, rapid industrialization and technical advances, feverish nightlife with cabarets and night clubs, sexual liberation, promiscuity and prostitution, alongside socially critical depictions of the tough living conditions of the working class, the new role of women and the decadent lifestyle of the upper class – all are central themes and subjects unfolded in the exhibition across artistic expressions, illuminated by a wealth of historical documentation.

Providing photographic resonance to the exhibition's main storyline, we are showcasing a large selection of *People of the 20th Century*, the life's work of the German photographer August Sander. Starting in the mid of the 1920's, Sander portrayed both prominent and anonymous Germans from all walks of life in a simple and sober manner, representing distinct "types" while allowing the unique character of each individual to shine. As a whole, this monumental image atlas of more than 600 black and white photographs, is a classic in the history of European art and photography. While Sander portrays a number of New Objectivity artists, many of the movement's themes are clearly represented in his work. He photographs the underbelly of capitalism, the new liberated woman and the modern city.

This exhibition is organized in partnership with the Centre Pompidou in Paris. Angela Lampe, curator of modern art, and Florian Ebner, head of the Centre Pompidou's photography department, devised the exhibition's concept and carried out the monumental task of organizing and selecting the extensive material. A big collegial thank you to both curators and their team for their huge research effort and exemplary collaboration in bringing the exhibition to Humlebæk.

We are grateful to all the lenders, private and public collections, that generously made works available to this exhibition. Special thanks to Gabriele Conrath-Scholl

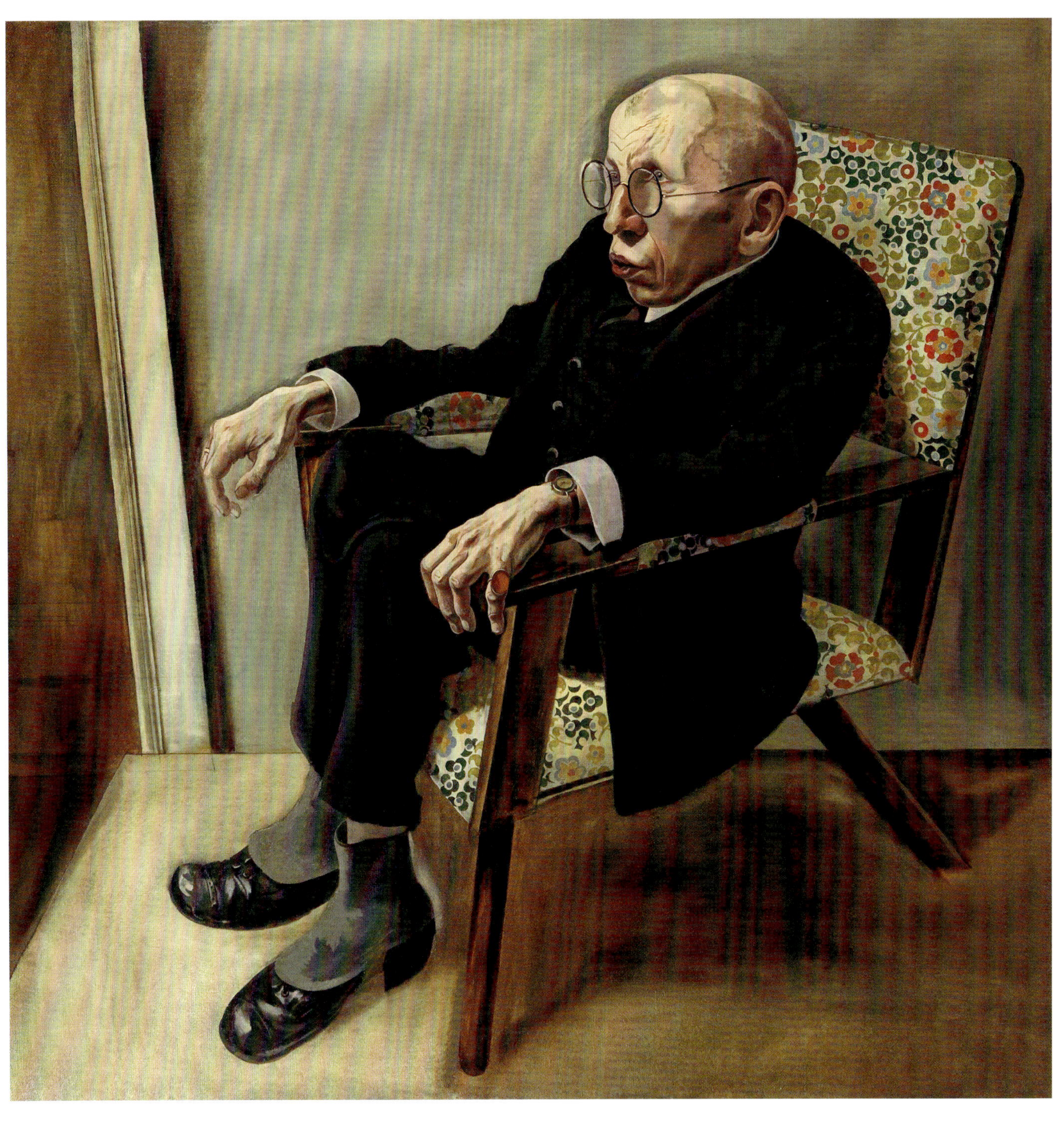

GEORGE GROSZ *Porträt des Schriftstellers Max Herrmann-Neiße (Portrait of the Author Max Herrmann-Neiße)*, 1925

Preceding spread: **KEYSTONE VIEW CO.** *Die Tiller-Girls sind da! (The Tiller Girls Are Here!)*, 1926

and Claudia Pfeiffer of Die Photographische Sammlung/SK Stiftung Kultur in Cologne, which administrates the August Sander Archive, for their tremendous engagement in the project and the extraordinarily large loans to this exhibition that are making it possible to present a selection of more than 250 vintage prints from Sander's life-long project, *People of the 20th Century*, to a Danish audience.

An exhibition like this obviously does not come about on its own. We thank the museum's exhibition team, comprising exhibition coordinators Eva Lund and Marie Mose Hyllested, exhibition producer Jesper Lund Madsen, editor Lærke Rydal Jørgensen, graphic designer Marie d'Origny Lübecker, image editors Sidse Buck and Kim Hansen and the rest of the museum staff, who poured their positive energy and habitual professionalism into realizing this project. A special thanks is due to exhibition designer Maya Lahmy and curatorial assistant Louis Nitze, who followed the creation of the exhibition and helped shape its final form at the Louisiana.

Thanks as well to the Goethe Institute in Copenhagen for productive dialogue and financial support for events held over the course of the exhibition.

Mounting an exhibition of this nature would not be possible without substantial funding. The C.L. David Foundation and Collection has once again enabled the Louisiana to realize a major and important exhibition at an international level. We owe the Foundation a great debt of gratitude.

Poul Erik Tøjner
Director

Kirsten Degel
Curator

Lenders

Akademie der Künste, Berlin / Archiv der Massenpresse Patrick Rössler, Erfurt / Archiv Günter Karl Bose, Berlin / Bauhaus-Archiv Museum für Gestaltung, Berlin / Bayerische Staatsgemäldesammlungen, Munich, Pinakothek der Moderne / Berlinische Galerie – Museum of Modern Art, Photography and Architecture / Bibliothèque Forney / Musée des Arts Décoratifs, Paris / British Pathé, London / Bröhan Design Foundation, Berlin / Bundesarchiv-Filmarchiv, Berlin / Centre Pompidou, Musée national d'art moderne, Paris / Centre Pompidou, Musée national d'art moderne, Blibliothèque Kandinsky, Paris / Collection Frank Brabant, Wiesbaden / Collection Frieder Gerlach, Konstanz / Collection Wortelkamp, Berlin / Collection of Linda Sutton & Roger Cooper, London / Collection Thilo von Debschitz, Wiesbaden / Designmuseum Danmark, Copenhagen / Deutsches Filminstitut & Filmmuseum, Frankfurt / Deutsche Kinematek / Museum für Film und Fernsehen, Berlin / Deutsches Historisches Museum, Berlin / Deutsches Literaturarchiv Marbach / Die Photographische Sammlung / SK Stiftung Kultur der Sparkasse KölnBonn – August Sander Archiv, Cologne / ernst-may-gesellschaft, Frankfurt am Main / Fondation Hindemith, Blonay / Friedrich-Ebert-Stiftung e.V., Bonn / Friedrich-Wilhelm-Murnau-Stiftung, Wiesbaden / Galerie Berinson, Berlin / German National Library, Leipzig / Hamburger Kunsthalle / Hessisches Landesmuseum, Darmstadt / Institut für Theaterwissenschaft der Freien Universität Berlin, Theaterhistorische Sammlungen / Klingspor Museum, Offenbach / Kunsthalle Mannheim / Kunsthalle Rostock / Kunstmuseum Moritzburg Halle / Kunstsammlung Oberschwäbische Elektrizitätswerke (OEW) / Landkreis Sigmaringen / Kunstsammlungen Chemnitz – Museum Gunzenhauser / La Contemporaine, Bibliothèque de documentation internationale contemporaine, Nanterre Landesarchiv Berlin / Lindenau-Museum, Altenburg / LWL-Landesmuseum für Kunst und Kultur, Westfälisches Landesmuseum, Münster / Museum Angewandte Kunst, Frankfurt / mumok – museum moderner kunst stiftung ludwig wien / Musée d'Art Moderne de Paris / Museen der Stadt Aschaffenburg, Christian Schad Stiftung / Museo Nacional Thyssen-Bornemisza, Madrid / Museum Folkwang, Essen / Museum für Gegenwartskunst, Siegen / Städtische Museen Freiburg, Museum für Neue Kunst, Freiburg / Museum Ludwig, Köln / Münchner Stadtmuseum / Oldenburg State Museum for Art and Cultural History / Otto Dix Stiftung, Vaduz / Richard Nagy Ltd., London / Sprengel Museum, Hannover / Staatliche Museen zu Berlin, Preussischer Kulturbesitz, Nationalgalerie / Stiftung Stadtmuseum Berlin / Stiftung Museum Kunstpalast, Düsseldorf / Städtische Galerie im Lenbachhaus und Kunstbau, Munich / Staatsgalerie Stuttgart / Tamasa Distribution, Paris / The George Economou Collection / The Jewish Museum, New York / The Metropolitan Museum of Art, New York / Theatre Collection, University of Cologne / ullstein bild, Berlin / University of Applied Art Vienna / Otto and Marie Neurath Isotype Collection, University of Reading / Vitra Design Museum, Weil am Rheim / Von der Heydt-Museum, Wuppertal / Werkbundarchiv – Museum of Things, Berlin

And private collectors who wish to remain anonymous.

Opposite page: **KARL BERTSCH** Exhibition Poster, *Neue Sachlichkeit. Deutsche Malerei seit dem Expressionismus* (New Objectivity. German Painting After Expressionism), Kunsthalle Mannheim, 1925. MARCHIVUM, Mannheim

BERTSCH 25
DIE NEUE
SACHLICH
KEIT
DEUTSCHE
MALEREI
SEIT DEM
EXPRESSIONISMUS
14. JUNI-
18. SEPT.
EINTRITT 50₰
KATALOG M. 1.-
STÄDT. KUNSTHALLE MANNHEIM
OFFSETDRUCK DER MANNHEIMER VEREINSDRUCKEREI

THE FIRST WORLD WAR AND THE DEFEAT led to a culture in
Germany characterised by a general shame and embarrassment about
pre-war utopias. The 1920s saw the emergence of what German literary
historian Helmut Lethen (born 1939) calls the 'cold persona,' a new social
type seeking to avoid the feeling of humiliation by adopting a mask of
coldness and indifference.

This new behaviour deeply changed the practice of portraiture.
Where before it focused on the models' psychological expression, it
now concentrated on their external markers. Photographer August
Sander (1876-1964) chose 'classes and professions' as one of his groups,
photographing not so much individual characters as occupations. The New
Objectivity artists thus portrayed not so much personalities as social types,
defined by their social class and profession.

In the manner of the artist Julius Bissier (1893-1965), who represents
himself forging his own bust without emotion or affect, the portraits
appear cold, emptied of all feeling, in resonance with their often neutral
and deserted backgrounds. The subjects appear alone, with a detached
expression and an absent, even empty gaze. They seem to be trying to
disguise their feelings behind an impenetrable appearance.

JULIUS BISSIER *Selbstbildnis eines Bildhauers* (Self-Portrait of a Sculptor), 1928

PORTRAITS

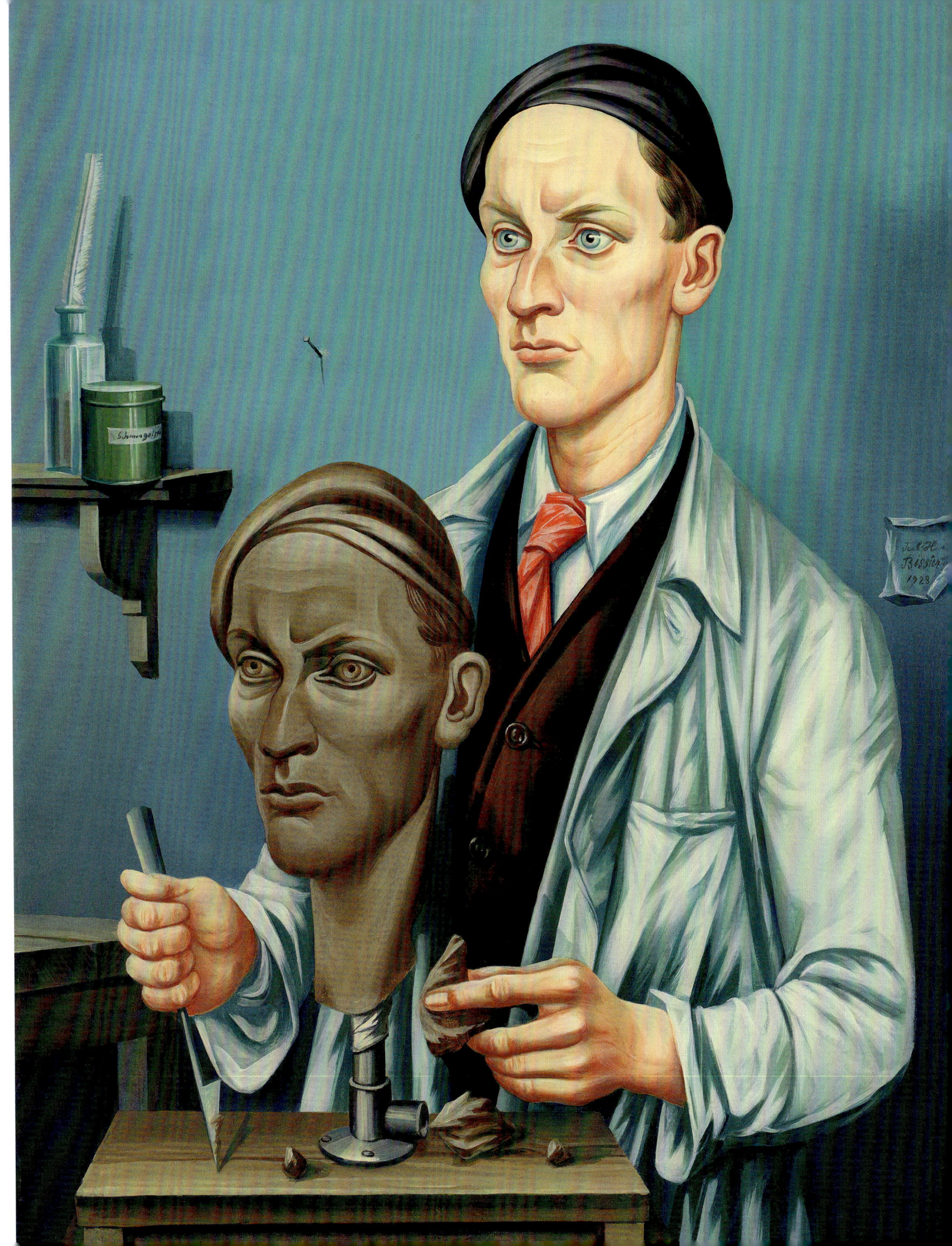
Bissier
1929

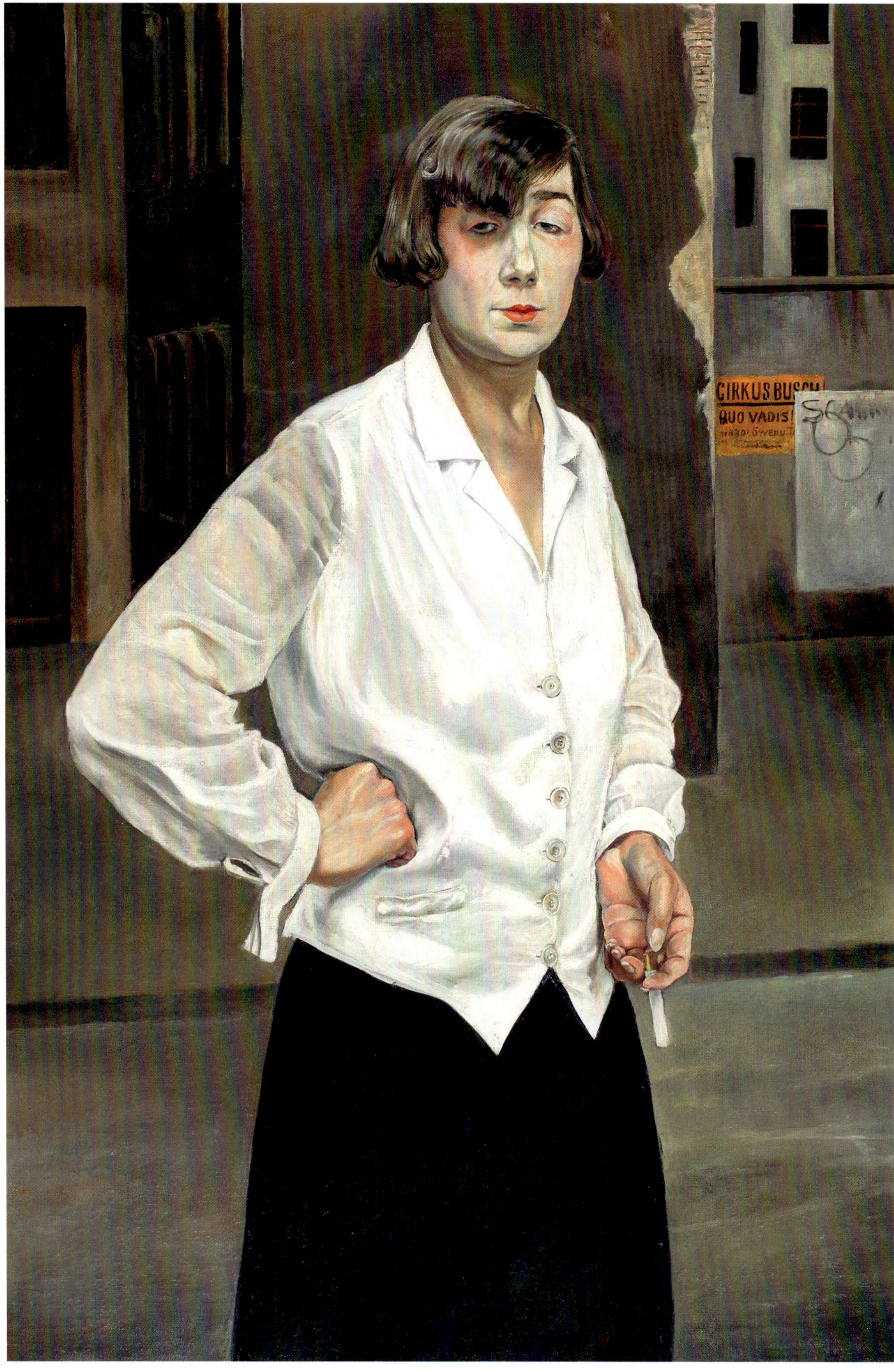
CIRKUS BUSCH
QUO VADIS!
mit 30 Löwen u. Ti

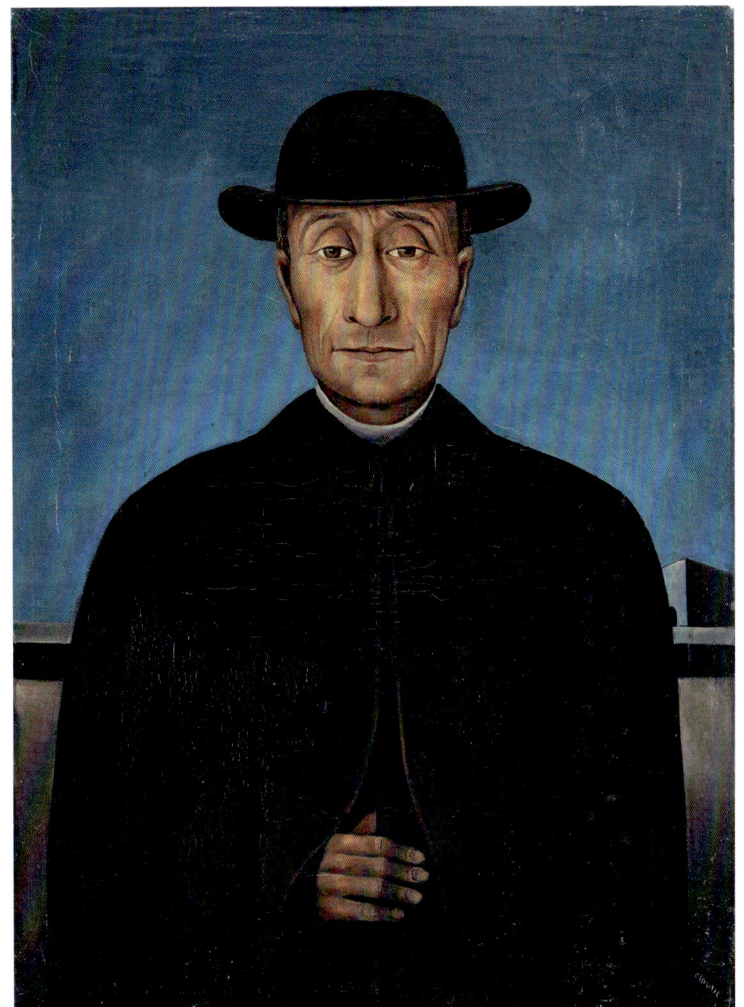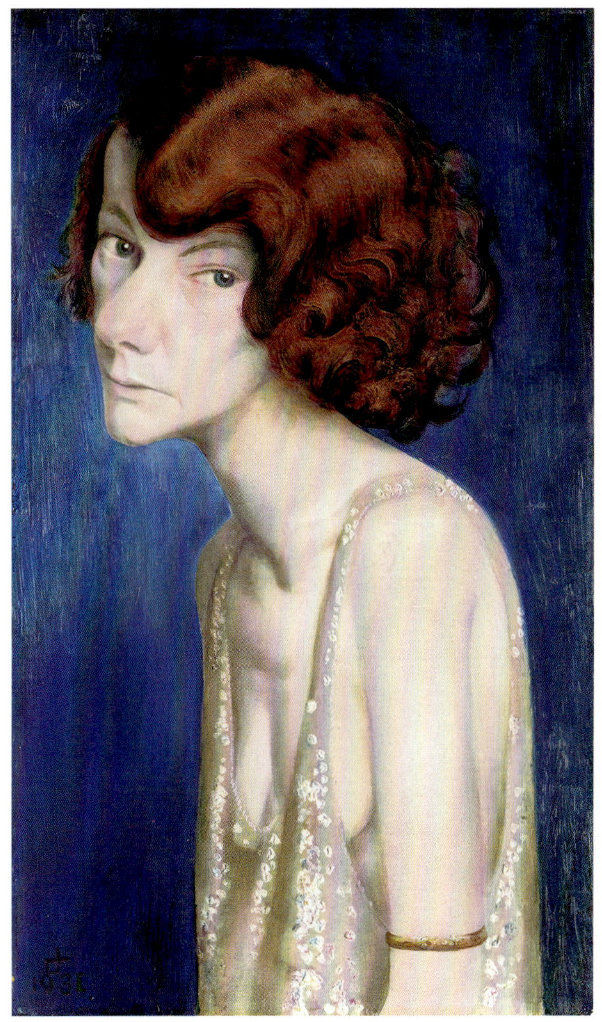

Opposite page: **RUDOLF SCHLICHTER** *Margot*, 1924

CARLO MENSE *Don Pepe*, 1924
OTTO DIX *Rothaarige Frau (Damenporträt)* (Red-haired Lady (Female Portrait)), 1931

11

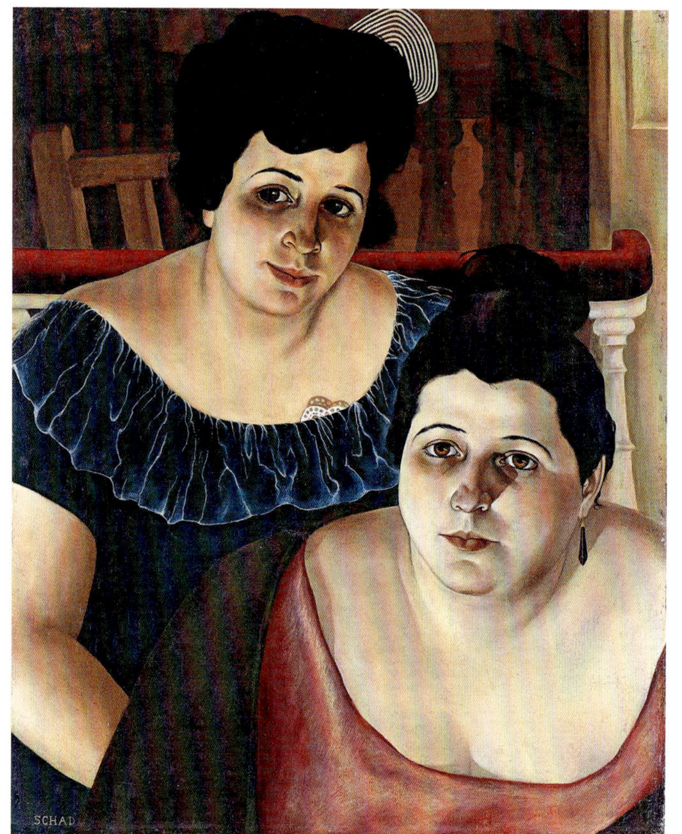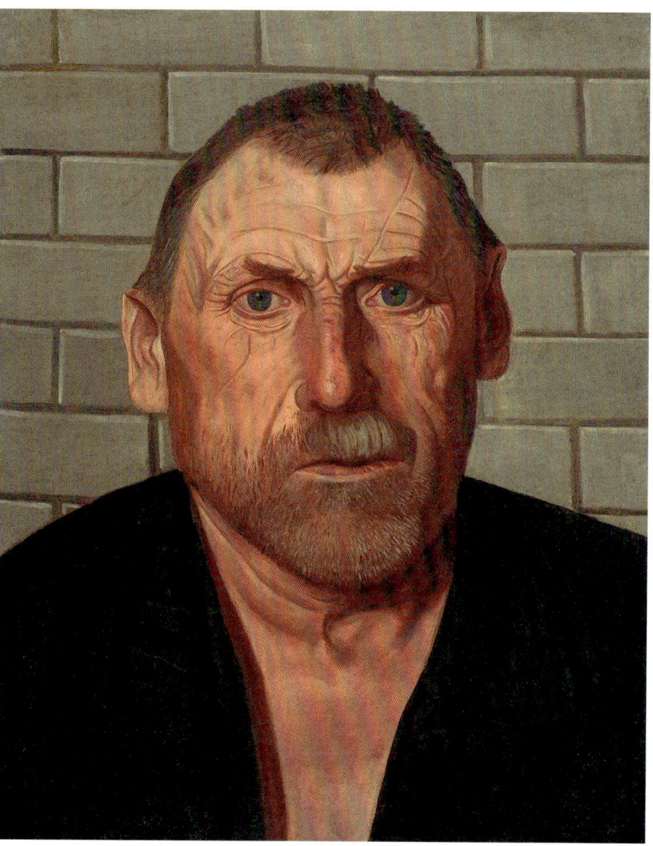

CHRISTIAN SCHAD *Maria und Annunziata 'vom Hafen'* (Maria and Annunziata 'From the Harbour'), 1923
WILLI MÜLLER-HUFSCHMID *Akademiemodell* (Academy Model), c. 1922
Oil on paper on plywood, 67 × 54 cm. Galerie Berinson, Berlin

Opposite page: **CHRISTIAN SCHAD** *Anna Gabbioneta*, 1927

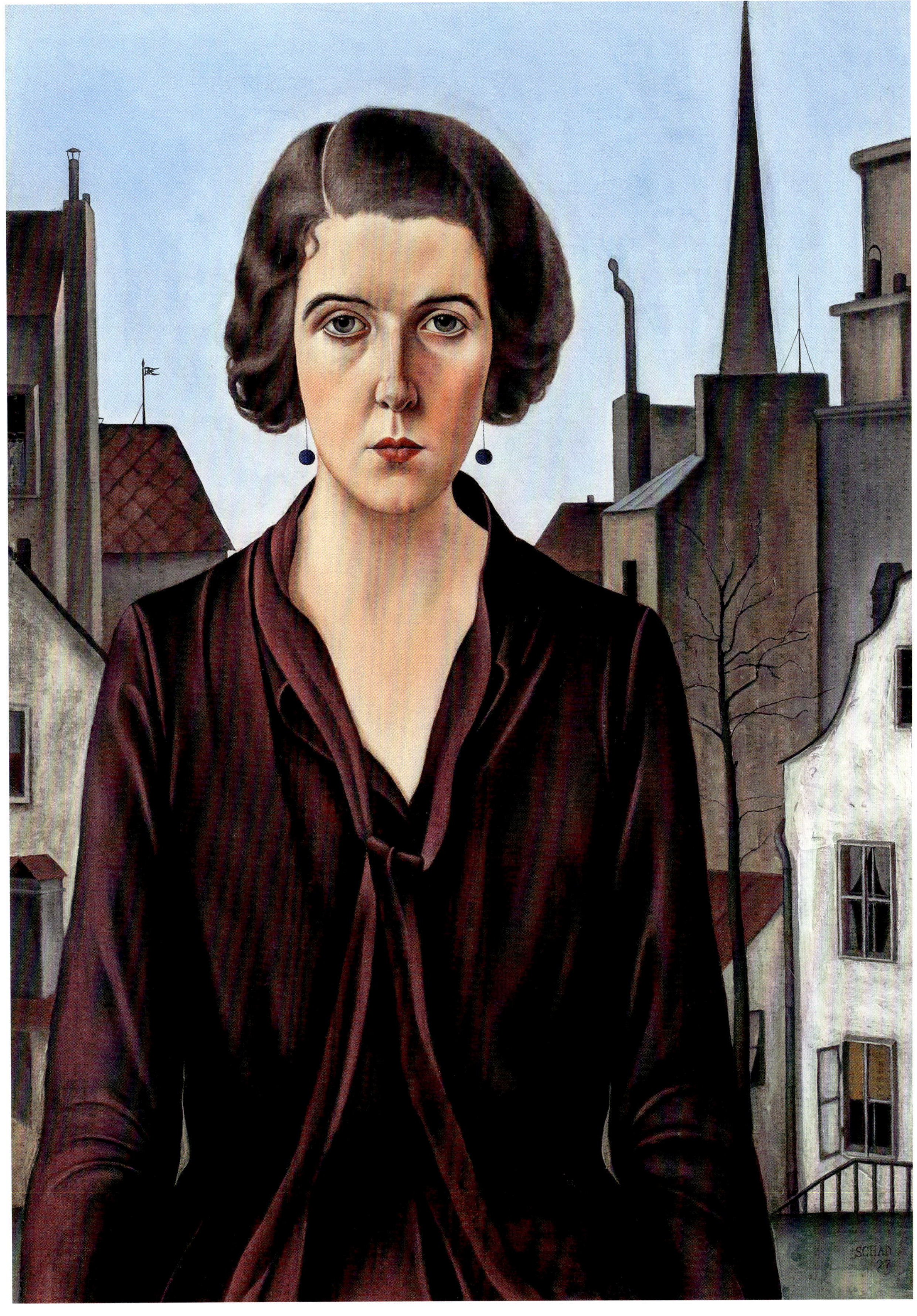

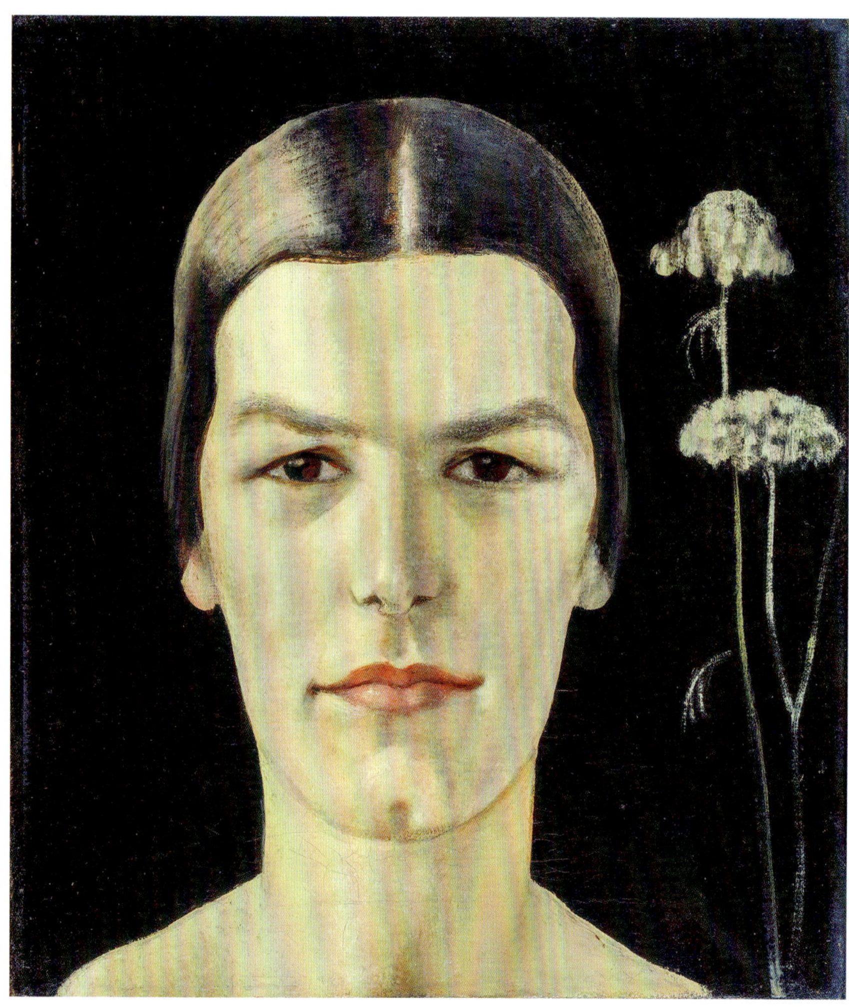

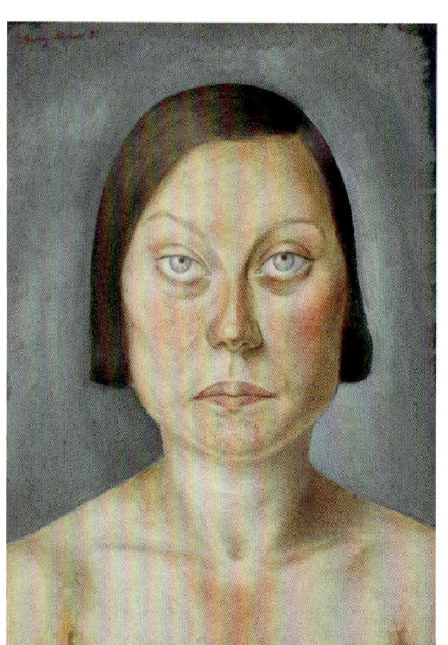

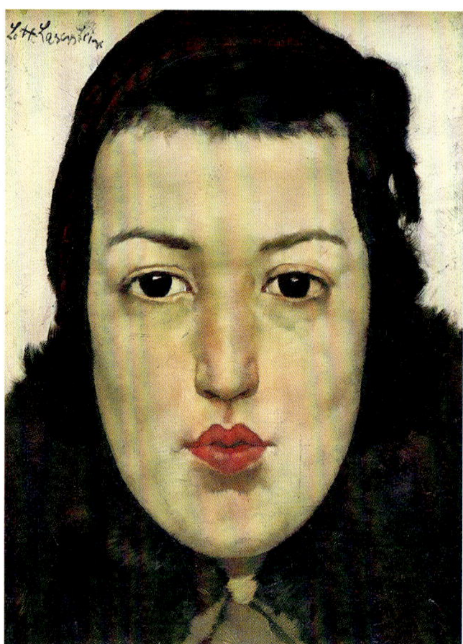

ANITA RÉE *Bildnis Hildegard Heise (Portrait of Hildegard Heise)*, 1927
GUSSY HIPPOLD-AHNERT *Trude (Bildnis der Schwägerin Trude)* (Trude (Portrait of Sister-in-Law Trude)), 1932
LOTTE LASERSTEIN *Russiches Mädchen (Russian Girl)*, c. 1928

Opposite page: **FRANZ RADZIWILL** *Einer von den Vielen des XX. Jahrhunderts (One of the Many from the Twentieth Century)*, 1927

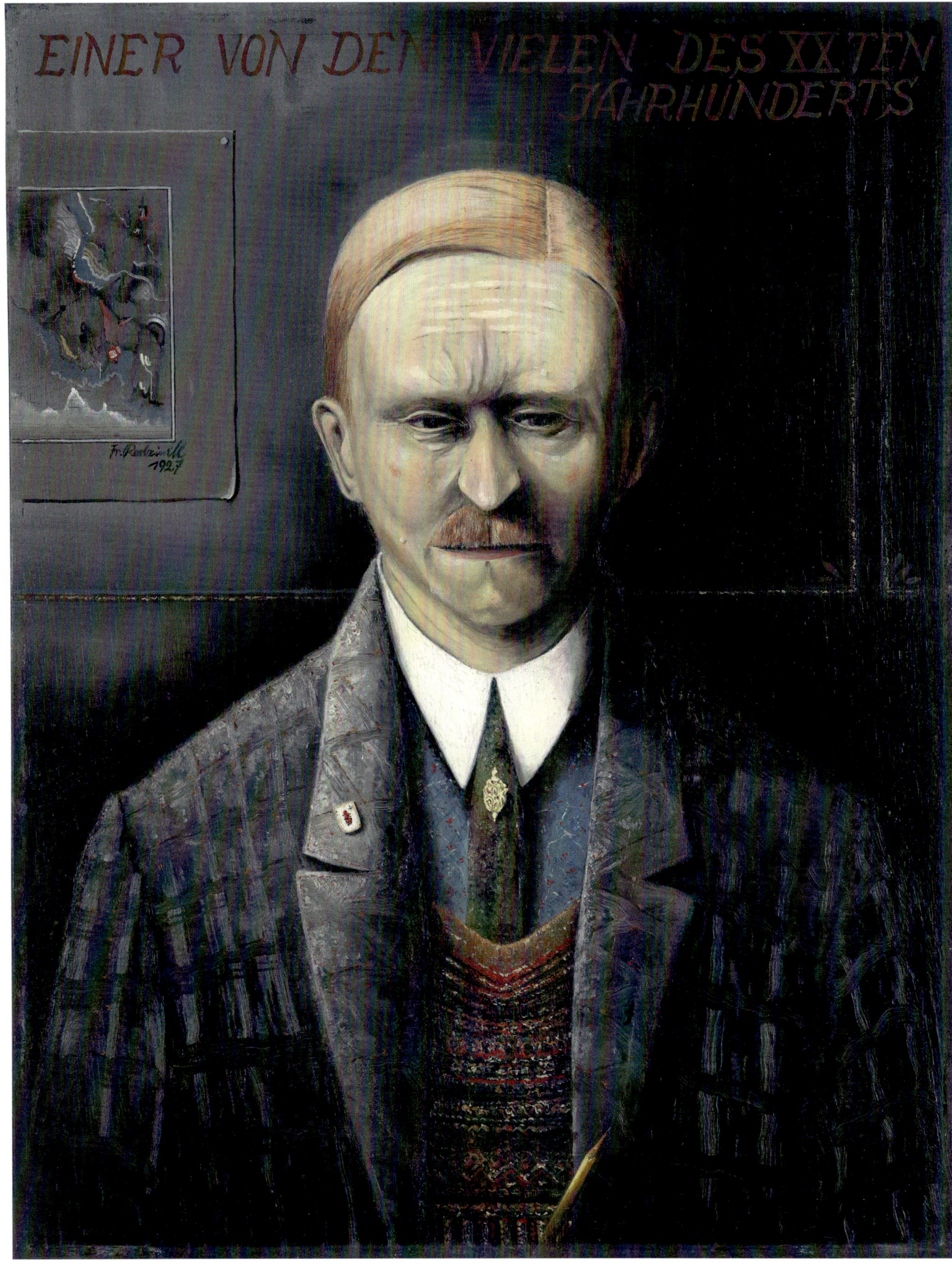

EINER VON DEN VIELEN DES XX TEN
JAHRHUNDERTS
Fr. Radziwill
1927

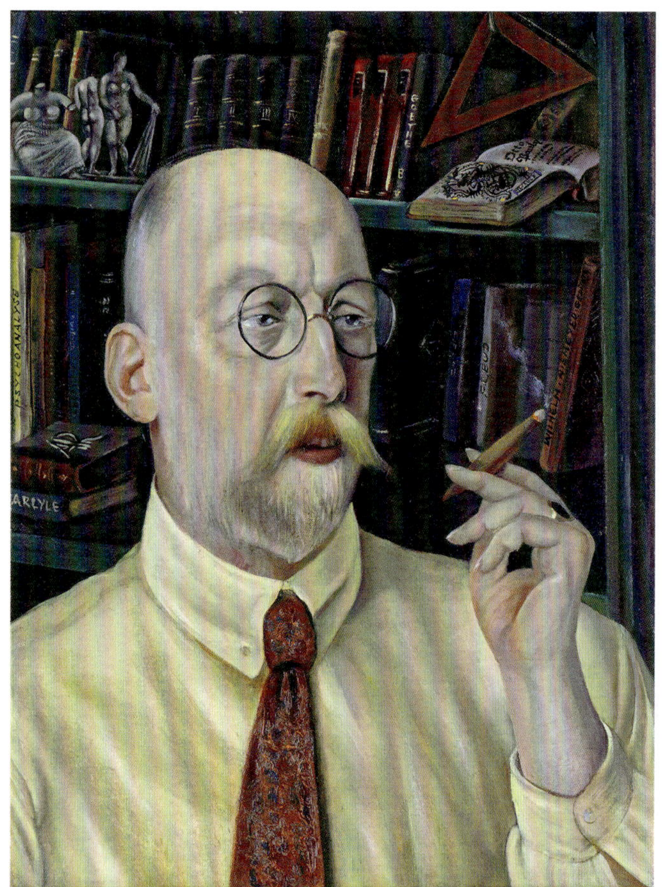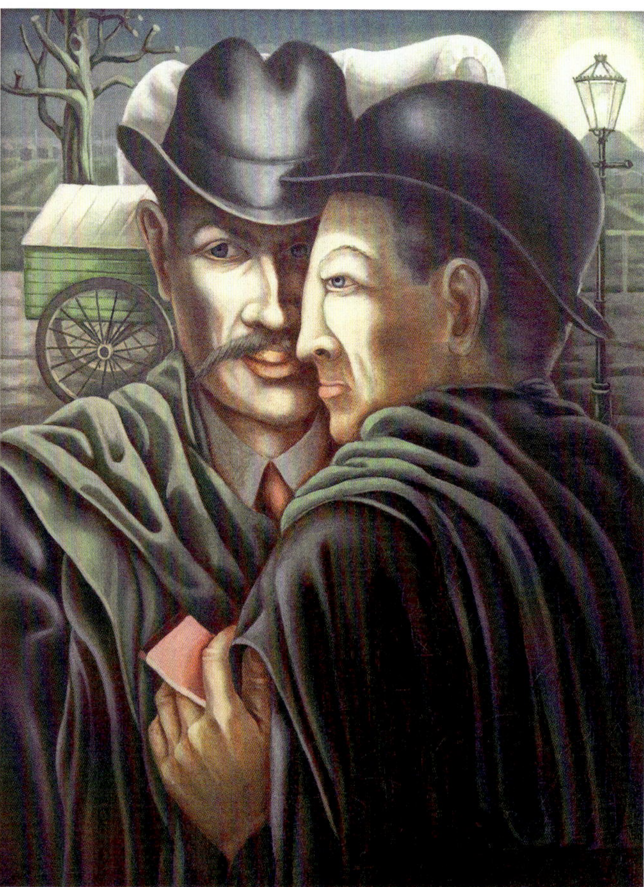

ANITA RÉE *Bildnis Otto Pauly* (Portrait of Otto Pauly), c. 1927
GRETHE JÜRGENS *Stoffhändler* (Textile Merchant), 1932

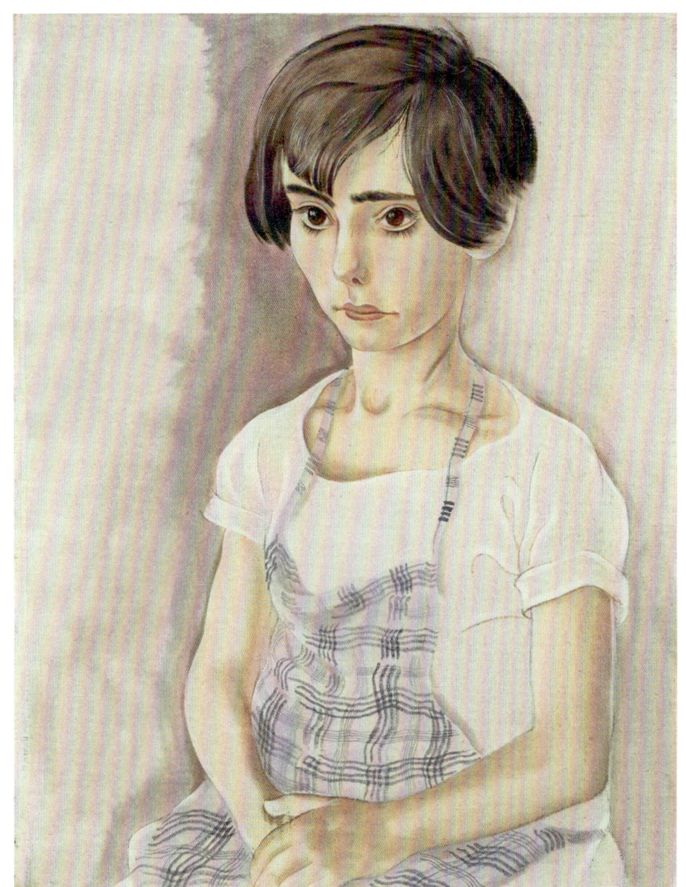 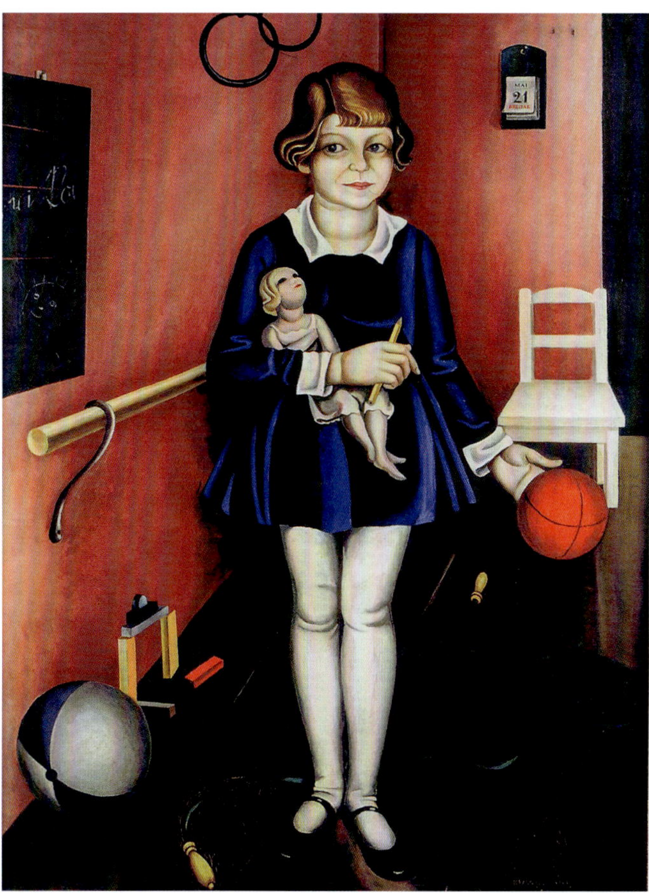

GEORGE GROSZ *Junge Spanierin* (Young Spanish Woman), 1917
ISSAI KULVIANSKI *Mein Töchterchen Kiki* (My little Daughter Kiki), 1927

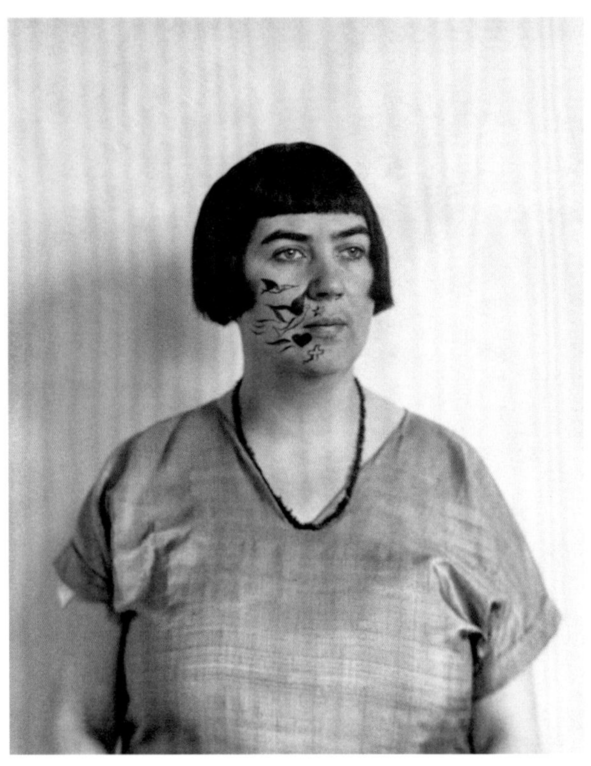

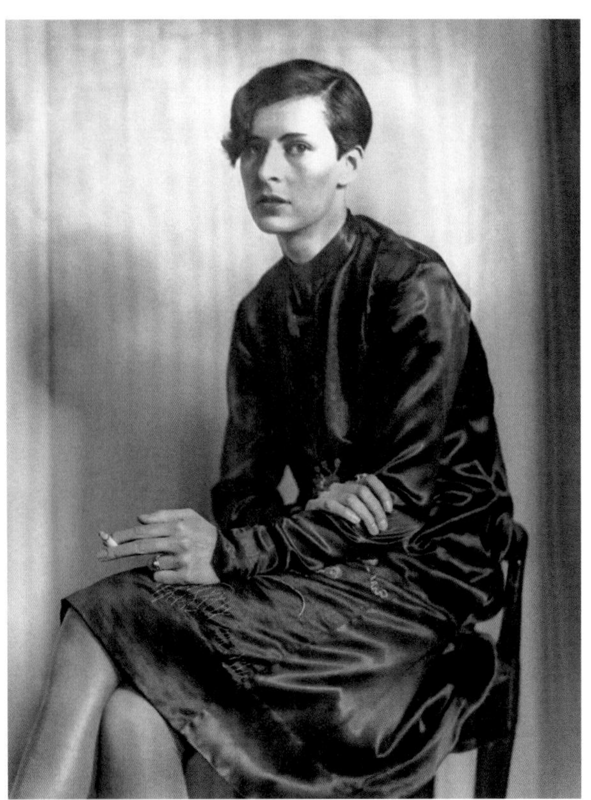

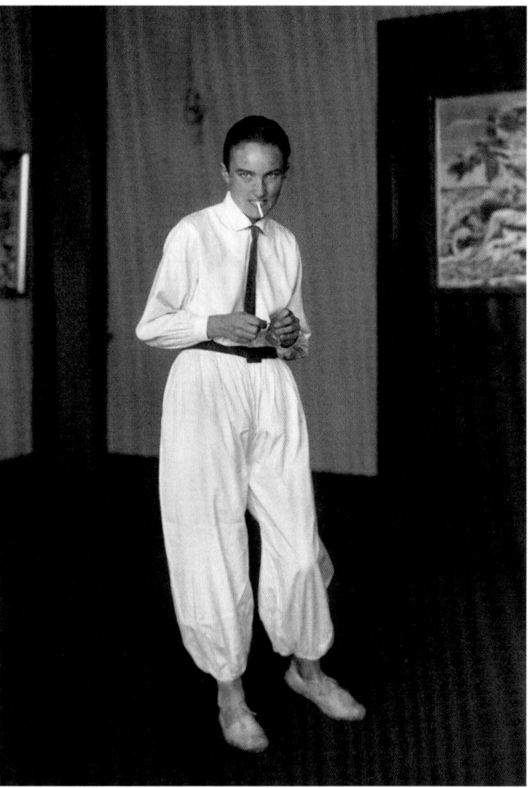

AUGUST SANDER *Malerin [Marta Hegemann] (Painter [Marta Hegemann])*, c. 1925
Sekretärin beim Westdeutschen Rundfunk in Köln (Secretary at West German Radio in Cologne), 1931
Frau eines Malers [Helene Abelen] (Painter's Wife [Helene Abelen]), 1926-1927

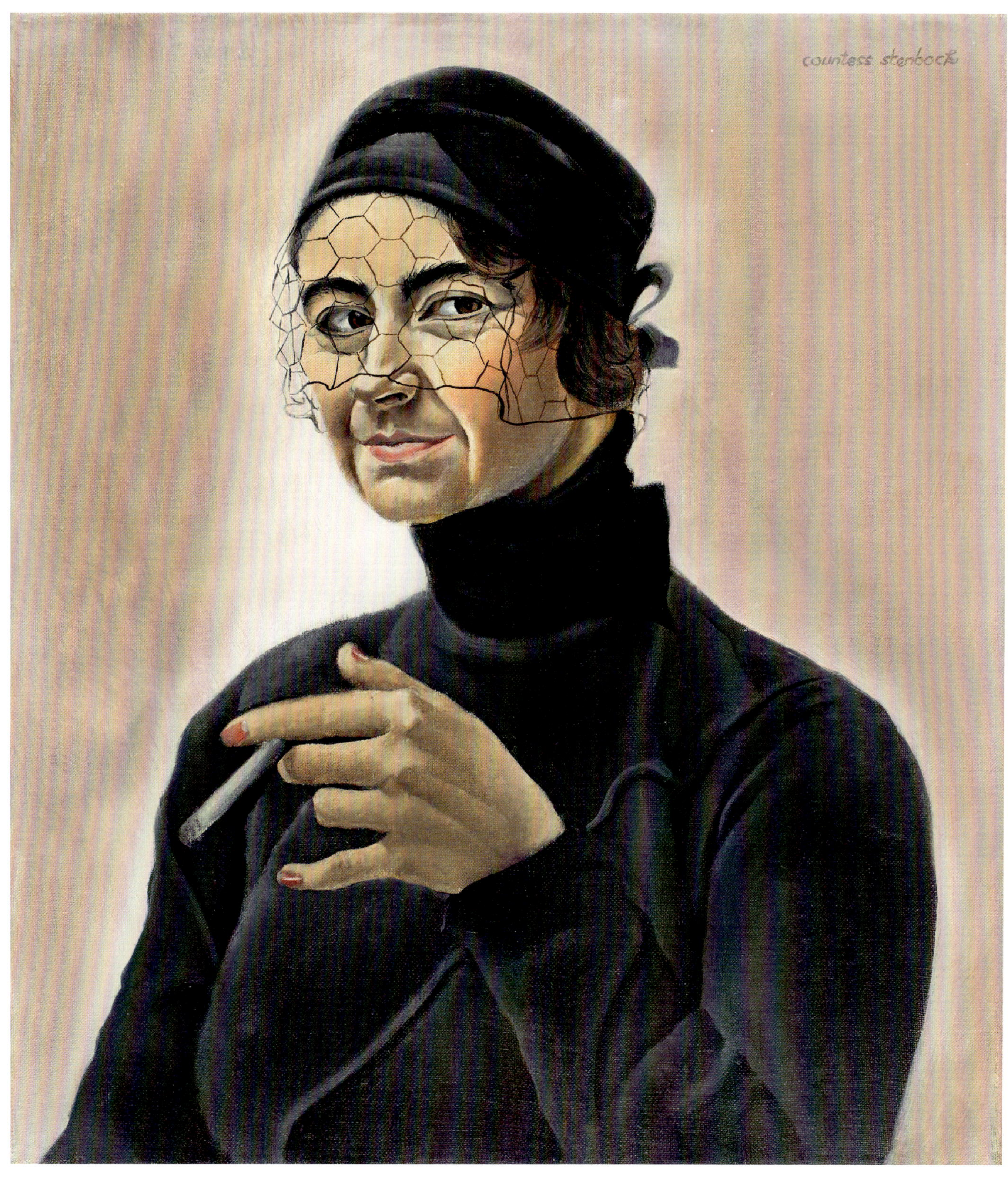

LEONORE MARIA GRÄFIN STENBOCK-FERMOR *Porträt Hildegard Schroeder (Konzertpianistin) (Portrait of Hildegard Schroeder (Concert Pianist)), 1930*

The Cold Persona and Melancholy

By Catherine Wermester

In 1923, the Austrian author Robert Musil wrote: "[...] Our time's lack of faith means: The age believes only in facts. Its conception of reality recognizes only what is, as it were, really real. An unofficial ideology has taken shape."[1] The debate about the facts and the deeper meaning of this new type of conception and relationship to reality, which was far removed from the Expressionist vision, exercised the literary world throughout the Weimar Republic. In 1929, Kurt Pinthus, who in 1920 had edited an anthology of young German expressionist poetry, *Twilight of Humanity*, published "Manly Literature"[2], in which he welcomed the fact that the passionate, enthusiastic teenager of the Expressionist era had been replaced by *a man*, free of pathos and sentimentality, who was more inclined to make facts his creative driving force than to overestimate the power of ideas. In his view, the new literature, the so-called objective literature, which he describes as virile, deserves this title not only because it is without illusion, but even more because it is the enemy of all illusion. Its despair and indifference are "tempered with steel."[3] It speaks to the man who does not cry out, does not lament, as the Expressionists did, to the man who clarifies and notes, and in so doing himself becomes clear and assured.[4] Musil, in 1923, had observed the phenomenon from a greater distance and distinguished the intention from its accomplishment: "'I believe only in facts' means nothing more than: I want to proceed with certainty."[5]

For committed writers and artists, passive recording of the facts was a sign of resignation. For example, Béla Balázs,[6] a Hungarian filmmaker and critic, who was also known at the time as a member of the Bund Proletarisch-Revolutionärer Schriftsteller (Association of Revolutionary Proletarian Writers) in Germany, demanded from his peers a gaze as sharp as that of a person looking through a microscope, a power of analysis unaffected by mood, and a steady hand. For him, literature incapable of going beyond observation was the result of "an inner fatigue,"[7] an "intimate war wound,"[8] typical of this generation which went to the front with its head full of chimeras and which, once there,

stopped believing in anything at all. Musil, for his part, wrote that in order to be satisfied with the facts, it was necessary to have "bad experiences."[9]

Between Expressionism and the New Objectivity, there had been the war. It had devalued everything, trampled everything, ruining the strongest beliefs and certainties, destroying even the hope of an *afterlife*. It had been followed by defeat and a failed revolution. Writing in 1915, Austrian Sigmund Freud did not see the situation as quite so bleak. In his *Thoughts for the Times on War and Death*, he judged positively the disappointment experienced by the citizen of the civilised world, seeing it as an opportunity to break free of illusions. Still, even then, the fears that the psychoanalyst was to express about the human impulses of aggression and self-destruction in 1929[10] were very much there, being directly experienced, day after day, by the soldiers at the front. In the interwar period, the scourges of lies and false values and enemies of idealisation would also assert, like German painter George Grosz, that "Man is not good, he is a beast."

The "cold persona," as the German literary historian Helmut Lethen[11] called it, embodied this state of mind which justified the rules of behaviour in the Weimar era. It was its privileged social mask, the face that one showed the better to hide from the eyes of others what one was determined to keep secret, the doubts, weaknesses and fears. As a defence against the danger of public humiliation and social discredit, the modus vivendi of the cold persona was, according to Lethen, part of a "culture of shame."[12] In contrast to the rules governing the culture of guilt, which was based on introspection, the inner voice, confession and remorse, the culture of shame was dominated by the need to keep one's dignity in public. In the brief comparative table in which the author formulates the salient rules of these two cultures,[13] he contrasts, among other things, the pangs of individual conscience with social fear, the aspiration to be at peace with oneself with the requirement to adopt socially expected behaviour, introspection with the primacy of the other's gaze. External signs, being immediately visible, became decisive.

In *Post-Expressionism: Magic Realism*,[14] the first ambitious text ever devoted to the New Objectivity, in 1925, the German art critic Franz Roh, considering the detachment and coldness of the verist works,[15] refused to judge them negatively. On the contrary, the rejection of the picturesque and the sweetened struck him as salutary, because by awakening consciences and destabilising the most indifferent, art was working to improve the world.

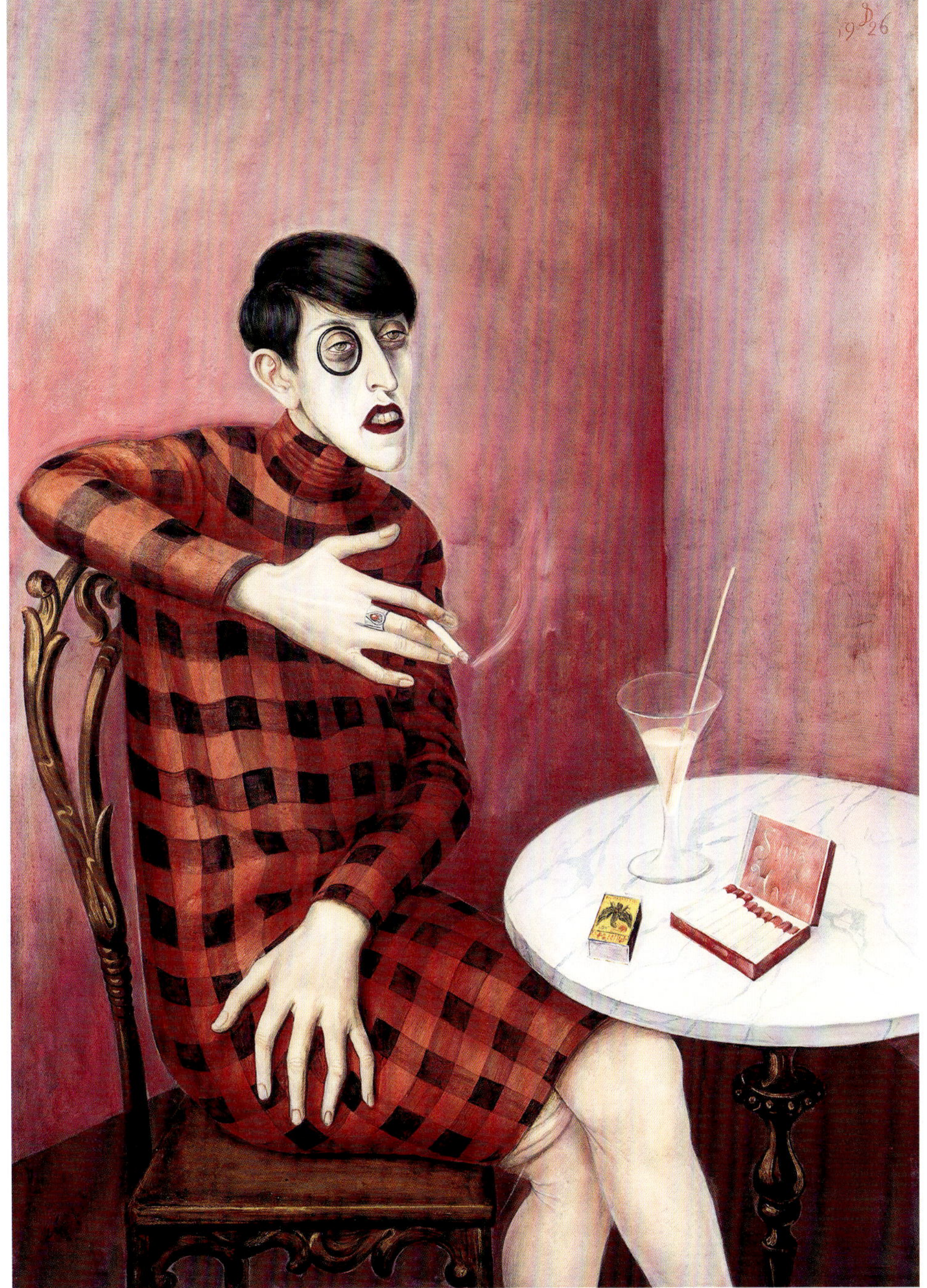

OTTO DIX *Bildnis der Journalistin Sylvia von Harden (Portrait of the Journalist Sylvia von Harden)*, 1926

all wounds that tend to close hastily,"[17] thereby preventing the infection from lasting and spreading. The surgical metaphor refers to a hardening that is seen as positive, and the image of the shiny, smooth skin of reptiles evokes the cold, new beauty of their representations. This is praise of shock treatment, of insensitivity and impassivity, of an ideal that drove artists to don an engineer's coat, as George Grosz did in the early 1920s, or, like Otto Dix, a surgeon's coat. Christian Schad's *Operation* (1929, p. 22) could be a metaphor for the art of this period. Dominated by white light and the glare of cold metal instruments, this appendectomy scene shows the specialists in close-up removing the inflammatory core. The composition is reminiscent of religious art, while the patient, sedated but awake, undegoes the operation in a state of impassiveness, without suffering. Art offers a model of being in the world and with others, based on restraint and treating pity and commiseration as symptoms of softening. It values productive detachment and sees radical disillusionment as a strength.

Most of the time, the persons represented in the paintings of the New Objectivity do not look at us. They do not try to transgress the limits of the canvas to the point of invading our space, as did the figures in the paintings of the Expressionist period, those of German Ludwig

No doubt the author had in mind directly political paintings, those that had chosen class struggle rather than compassion for the poor and exploited, thereby giving direct access to artistic representation to a social group that had not enjoyed it in the same way at the time of Expressionism. Finally, the author noted the beauty of clean forms, even in the midst of abjection, "when surfaces shine with the shimmering polish of wet reptile skins."[16] Further on, he welcomed the fact that artists worked with the same detachment as doctors, that they "bleed

Meidner for example. Even when the face-to-face becomes confrontational, a brick wall or some other two-dimensional background finally holds the force that wanted to escape on the surface. More often than not, the figures stand at a distance, in corners and nooks. In these finite and yet hardly measurable spaces, they seem simultaneously protected from a dangerous proximity to others, and cornered, trapped by the artist's gaze, which scrutinises them with no concern to spare them, let alone embellish them. When the eyes are turned towards viewers, they seem to pass through them, or stare at them, indifferent and impenetrable. Almost all of them seem to obey one of the precepts written by Walter Serner for aspiring con artists: "Trust no one, look at no one."[18]

To find out who you are looking at in portraits from this period, you can first read the titles of the paintings and look at the attributes of the models. To go further, there is the tool of physiognomy. The extraordinary favour it enjoyed in all fields in the Weimar period was not confined to the proponents of race theory.[19] Its appeal was fundamentally linked to the more or less explicit rejection of depth psychology, to a willingness to stick to the surface and to judge by appearances. By way of an example, we might consider German Ludwig Klages. A physicist, chemist, psychologist and philosopher, he set out to replace Freudian psychoanalysis with an analysis based on observation of the body, gesture and facial expression. In medicine, German Ernst Kretschmer's bio-typological theory posited the existence of direct links between body structures and psychic profiles. First published in 1922 by Julius Springer in Berlin, his book *Physique and Character*, which continued to be regularly reprinted in Germany until the 1950s, distinguishes three main types: the pycnic, of medium stature and rather corpulent; the athletic, with highly developed muscles; and finally, the narrow and slender leptosome. Each of these types is said to have a particular temperament. Clear and easy to read, Springer's book was read beyond the circle of specialists. As late as 1965, in an interview with Otto Dix, the journalist Maria Wetzel described the hands of one of his models from the 1920s as "pycnic".[20]

Art, certainly, did not escape this contemporary fascination, feeding on the ambient climate and nourishing it with the same enthusiasm. Wieland Herzfelde, friend and publisher of the cartoonist George Grosz, bore witness to this. Fascinated by the artist's ability to reveal bourgeois turpitudes, he wrote in 1921 that he expected paintings to show the beauty of the world and the ugliness of human relationships, that they would "teach you to read every wrinkle in your own face, and in that of your fellow man, to know whether you can trust him or yourself, or whether, on the contrary, you should be wary."[21] So it did not matter if one was facing oneself as one would another person, submitting to the scrutiny of an uncompromising gaze, or if one really was facing another person. Dix, the most prominent portraitist of the period, refers repeatedly to the importance of physiognomy for him. In 1955, at a time when

abstraction was dominant in Germany and the painter, far removed from the art scene, continued to defend the principles he had once espoused, he said of portraiture: "The essence of every human being is expressed in *their external appearance; the exterior* is the expression of *the interior*, i.e. the exterior and the interior are identical. This goes so far that even the folds of his clothes, his posture, his hands, his ears immediately enlighten the painter about the soul of his model; the ears often even more than the eyes and the mouth."[22]

In 1965, when the journalist asked him about his painting in the 1920s, Dix replied that the hand was not just a claw that the artist would paint without too much difficulty.[23] On the contrary, "its expression totally coincides with the character of the sitter,"[24] which it was his job to capture. Not on the basis of the systems constructed by specialists, but on the basis of his own sensitive intuition.

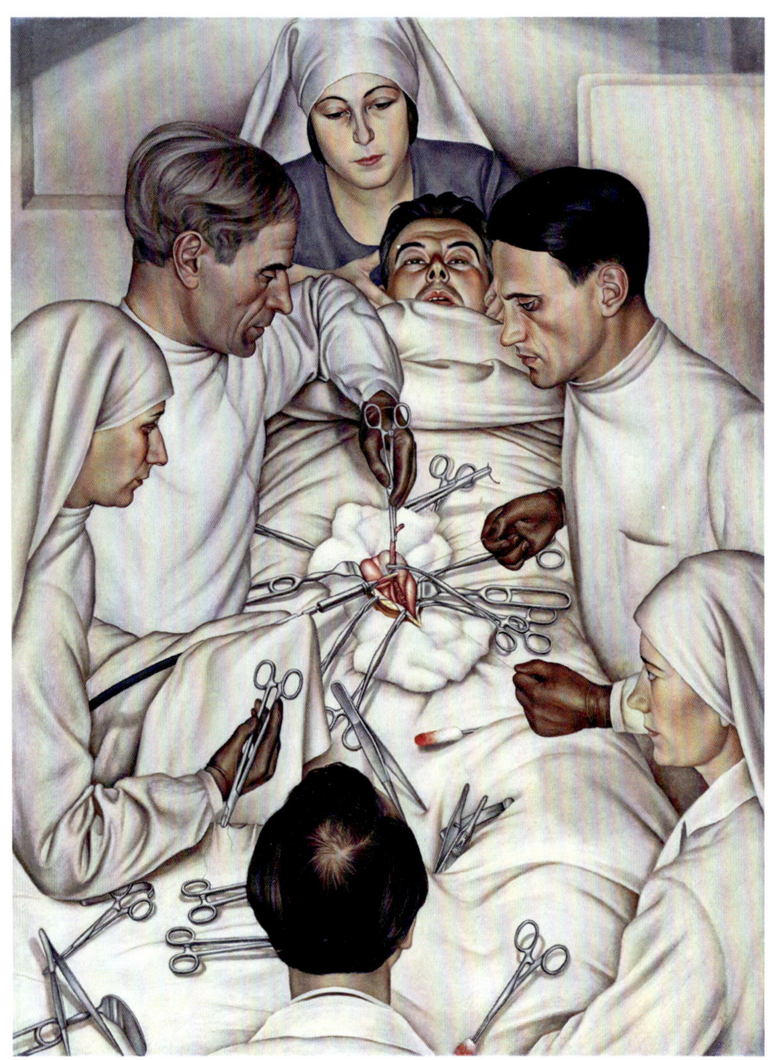

CHRISTIAN SCHAD *Operation*, 1929. Oil on canvas, 124 × 95 cm
Städtische Galerie im Lenbachhaus and Kunstbau Munich

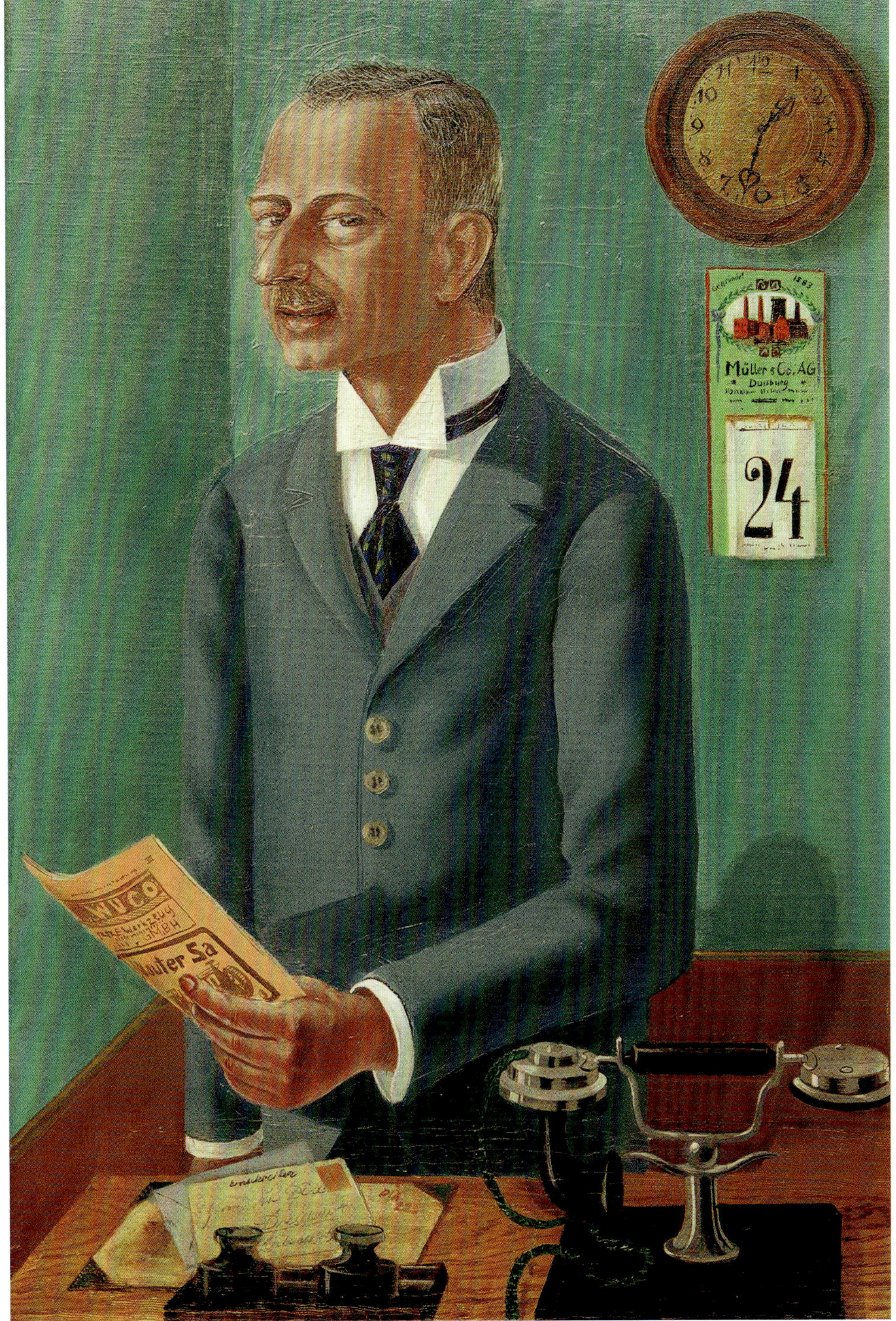

OTTO DIX *Der Kaufmann Max Roesberg, Dresden (The Businessman Max Roesberg, Dresden)*, 1922

importance of the details that he has chosen as significant. The meticulous pictorial technique that he imposed on himself did not aim to duplicate reality in an illusionist manner, but rather to render, with the greatest possible presence, this inner image constructed from perception. Hence the enigmatic plasticity of the motifs, caught in the painting as they would be in the mirror, the almost hallucinatory rendering of a model's hair, of the slightest of her wrinkles, of the details of her clothing, provided that the latter had held the artist's attention. Often, in Christian Schad's work, hyper-precision immediately rubs shoulders with areas that are closer to flatness than to volume, introducing into the canvas a discontinuity that is all the more disturbing because it was initially masked by a coherent surface.

Although Dix used terms identical to those of the specialists who are attentive to the physiognomy of beings, he also claimed to be radically different from them: "It is always imagined that the portrait painter is a great psychologist and physiognomist, able to read immediately in any face the hidden virtues and vices, and then represent them in the painting. This is a literary conception, because the painter does not judge, he looks. My motto is: 'trust your eyes.'"[26]

A look at the paintings he produced in the 1920s tempers these assertions somewhat. The portrait of the businessman Max Roesberg (1922), for example, gives the impression that Dix found this patron a little *flat* and painted him that way. In the bare, impersonal space of the office, it is rather the shiny new telephone that seems to have really caught the artist's eye. *Portrait of Sylvia von Harden* (1926, cover and p. 21) is even more illuminating. For it is clear that, regardless of the real person, Dix considers the claims of the model he has commissioned to be ridiculous because she

Drawing after a model was followed by the stage of painting *without* a model. This allowed him to fix on the canvas the first impression that he had tried to keep in memory. It protected him from the pitfalls of naturalism and the uncontrollable crowd of details that would overwhelm him and undermine the result he wanted to achieve. Dix speaks of "fantastic" realism,[25] of form in itself and of the

manifests all the contemporary signs of the "new woman" (*Neue Frau*), as those seeking to emancipate themselves from the constraints of their gender were then known. Dix's rendering is so parodic that it continues to inspire new parodies today. The learned and restrained pictorial technique is put to use in a caricatured treatment which, this time, does not simplify, but on the contrary exaggerates features and proportions, and echoes widely shared prejudices, prejudices from which women painters depicting emancipated women during this same period radically distanced themselves.

Traditionally a man's accessory, the monocle, then frequently adopted by the lesbians of Berlin[27] and applied here to the triangular face of the journalist, is part of the formal game that, everywhere in the painting, at once opposes and ensures the coexistence of angle and curve. But it seems that, for the artist, Sylvia von Harden was not at the same time angle and curve, male and female, but rather neither. He who usually depicted his models with the attributes of their work has stripped the journalist of hers, even though he defines her profession in the title given to his painting. This is his way of reducing her pretentions to a simple pose and a few accessories. The framing abruptly breaks off the circle of the table, symbolically representing the solitude of this woman, which he considers inevitable. Her arms and immense hands mask her breasts and hide the salience of her hip. Her whole body, with its volumes already erased by the checked pattern of the dress, seems to fold up, as if constrained by an invisible limit. Dix renders his object in detail, painstakingly painting in the space that he has ironically saturated with pink the wrinkled stockings, the nicotine stains on the fingers and teeth, the purplish bags under the eyes, the flesh that we can already guess has been corrupted beneath the skin. The artist's patient technique – a mixture of tempera and multiple glazes – produces a smooth and precious pictorial substance so fine that we can make out the cocktail straw that leant leftwards in the preparatory drawing. In comparison, the paint appears thick and imprecise on the mouth, becoming lipstick, as if the painter wanted to denounce the make-up, the faking. Even more than the subject's presence in the café, or her cigarettes, the monocle is a sign of power. It is the prerogative, first of all, of those who look, as opposed to those who are looked at. To adopt it is, beyond lesbian circles, to want to be the one doing the looking. But the glassy eyes given by the painter to this specimen of a new woman ruin this claim.

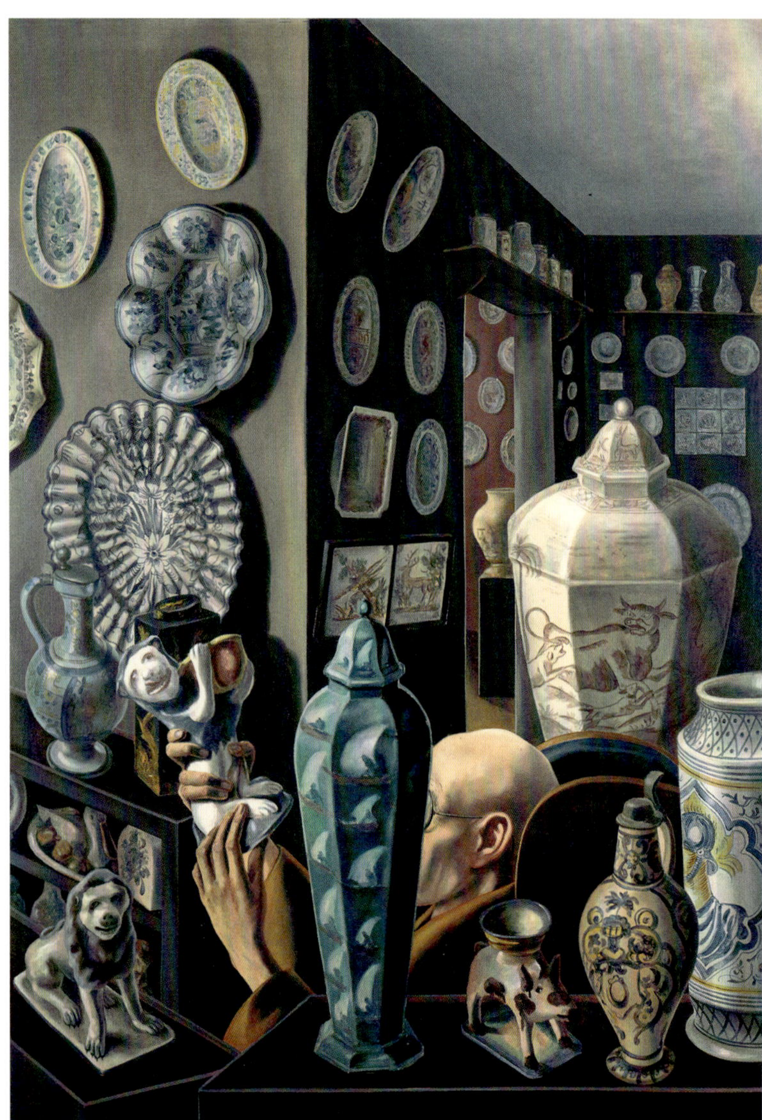

WALTER SCHULZ-MATAN *Der Fayencesammler* (The Faience Collector), 1927

If Dix portrayed the journalist Sylvia von Harden it was because of her extreme singularity as well as her proximity to the type of the new woman, and because of the artist's own views about this type. The period's taste for typology – which does not always manifest itself as dialectically as in this painter's work – is a symptom of the need to bring order and control to a social body and an environment that are both perceived as unreadable and shifting. The same desire for mastery is apparent in the choice of precise techniques, allowing for the hermetic enclosure of forms and motifs, the *ad libitum* detailing of any object, the rendering of every hair on an eyebrow for the viewer to contemplate at length, just as the painter has done. These ways of painting, marked out by obligatory stages that give them the value of rituals, and the tools they use, are expected to rule out chance as much as possible, to protect against accidents, such as the drips or overflows that many painters before them, or they themselves, before the war, had put to good use. Formerly traversed by multiple obliques, agitated in every possible way by impetuous currents, the now static compositions, dominated by energetic verticals even more than by horizontals, in which, more often than not, the diagonals cancel each other out, seem to struggle against the unstable, the inconstant. They give beings a singular stiffness, the air of wax models or dolls, and entire paintings a strangeness that also finds expression in spaces that are difficult to grasp with their compressed depths, a reminder of the Italian metaphysical paintings discovered in the pages of the magazine Valori plastici; their angles that are too sharp or, on the contrary, too blunt, giving the feeling that the ground is rising up, merging with the walls, as in a theatre set.

Efforts to flush out the other and render it harmless, to tame reality and the fear it inspires deep down, to stop time, to push aside the formless, can lead only to melancholy. Relegated to the very bottom of the canvas, Walter Schulz-Matan's *Der Fayencesammler* (The Faience Collector, 1927) appears to be almost completely buried under his collection, as much as protected by it, and therefore conveniently hidden from prying eyes. Vases, plates and other small objects, some of which come from distant continents, occupy the space, covering all the walls up to the ceiling, which looks like a false sky, inhabiting all the niches and filling all the shelves, while never or almost never touching. Each one has a particular physiognomy, more or less large, more or less stocky or flowing, they invade the adjacent rooms, driven by a vain quest for completeness. They represent motionless journeys, animals wild and domestic, flowers and plants of all kinds, stylised miniatures of the living cloistered under the brilliant enamel which guarantees the changelessness of the colours. The collector, whose skull has already become as smooth as his pots, seems not so much absorbed in the contemplation of his fragile trinket as to be engaging in a tête-à-tête with it. He lifts it up and looks underneath, just to know a little more about the latest object of his desire, which, turned towards the spectator, sends them a grimacing smile.

CATHERINE WERMESTER is a lecturer in contemporary art at Université Paris I Panthéon-Sorbonne in Paris. She has contributed to a number of art historical catalogues.

1. Robert Musil, "The German as Symptom," in *Robert Musil – Precision and Soul*, texts edited and translated by Burton Pike and David S. Luft, Chicago: University of Chicago 1990, p. 176.
2. Kurt Pinthus, "Männliche Literatur," *Das Tagebuch*, no. 10, 1929; reprinted in Thomas Rietzschel (ed.), *Kritik in der Zeit. Fortschrittliche deutsche Literaturkritik*, 1919-1933, Halle-Leipzig: Mitteldeutscherverlag, 1983, pp. 245-253.
3. Ibid., p. 247.
4. Ibid., p. 246-247.
5. Robert Musil, "The German as Symptom," op. cit., p. 177.
6. Béla Balázs, "Männlich oder kriegsblind?" (Manly or War Blind?), *Die Weltbühne*, 1929; reprinted in T. Rietzschel (ed.), *Kritik in der Zeit*, op. cit., pp. 254-257.
7. Ibid., p. 255.
8. Idem.
9. Robert Musil, "The German as Symptom," op. cit., p. 177.
10. Sigmund Freud, *Civilization and Its Discontents* (1930), Norton, 1989.
11. Helmut Lethen, *Cool Conduct: The Culture of Distance in Weimar Germany* (1994), Los Angeles: University of California Press, 2001.
12. Ibid;, see in particular "Fending off Shame," p. 12.
13. Ibid. , p. 33.
14. Translated into French as *Postexpressionnisme. Réalisme magique. Problèmes de la peinture européenne la plus récente*, Dijon: Les Presses du Réel, 2013.
15. The adjective was used at the time to describe works that were vectors of a critical left-wing discourse.
16. F. Roh, *Postexpressionisme...*, op. cit., p. 102.
17. *Ibid*.
18. Walter Serner, Last Loosening: *A Handbook for the Con Artist & Those Aspiring to Become One* (1927), translated from the German by Mark Kanak, Twisted Spoon Press, 2020, p. 89.
19. Michel Hau, Mitchell G. Ash, "Der normale Körper, seelisch erblickt," in Claudia Schmölders, Sander Gilman (eds.), *Gesichter der Weimarer Republik. Eine physiognomische Kulturgeschichte*, Cologne: DuMont, 2000, pp. 12-31.
20. "Ein Harter Mann dieser Maler. Gespräch mit Maria Wetzel," 1965, interview reproduced in Diether Schmidt, Otto Dix im Selbstbildnis, Berlin: Henschelverlag Kunst und Gesellschaft, 1981, p. 264.
21. Wieland Herzfelde, *Gesellschaft, Künstler und Kommunismus*, Berlin: Malik Verlag, 1921, reprinted in W. Herzfelde, Zur Sache, Berlin and Weimar: Aufbau-Verlag, 1976, pp. 54-91, p. 75 for this quotation.
22. Otto Dix, *Gedanken zum Portraitmalen*, 1955, reproduced in D. Schmidt, *Otto Dix im Selbstbildnis*, op. cit., p. 224.
23. "Ein Harter Mann dieser Maler. Gespräch mit Maria Wetzel," interview quoted pp. 264-271.
24. Ibid., p. 264.
25. Ibid., p. 266.
26. O. Dix, *Gedanken zum Portraitmalen*, op. cit., p. 224.
27. Ruth Margerete Roellig, *Lesbiennes de Berlin* (1928), translated from the German by Charles Adam, Lille, GayKitschCamp, 2001, p. 12. It should be noted that in the early 1930s, in Paris, Le Monocle was the name of a popular lesbian meeting place.

AUGUST SANDER (1876-1964) has been called the most important German portrait photographer of the 20th century. He was born in 1876, the son of a mine carpenter in Herdorf in Westerwald. A common strand running through all his photographic activity was his close links to the rural population. After some years of education and work in Linz in Austria, August Sander settled in Cologne. From there he went out in the weekends to the villages in Westerwald, where he worked as an itinerant photographer. A decade later his farmer portraits marked the beginning of his ambitious photographic project *Menschen des 20. Jahrhunderts* (People of the 20th Century), a typology of German society divided into seven groups: the farmers, the artisans, the women, the social classes, the artists, the city and 'the last people'. Altogether the photographs present a cross-section of society from the peasants and their manual power to the revolutionaries in the cities, the authorities and the marginalised. One of the approaches he used in the project was to portray everyone with the same dignity and the same strengh. This sociologically aware method means that the hierarchies and structures in society emerge clearly, and one senses the change that German society underwent with modernisation.

August Sander himself said of the project, which has later inspired younger generations of photographers such as Diane Arbus: "The original idea behind my photographic work *People of the 20th Century*, which I began in 1910, and which comprises 500-600 photographs, a selection of which was published in 1929 under the title *Antlitz der Zeit* (Face of Our Time), was nothing less than a commitment to the photograph as a world language and the attempt to create a contemporary physiognomy of German humanity."

Bäuerliche Braut (Rural Bride), 1920-1925

AUGUST SANDER

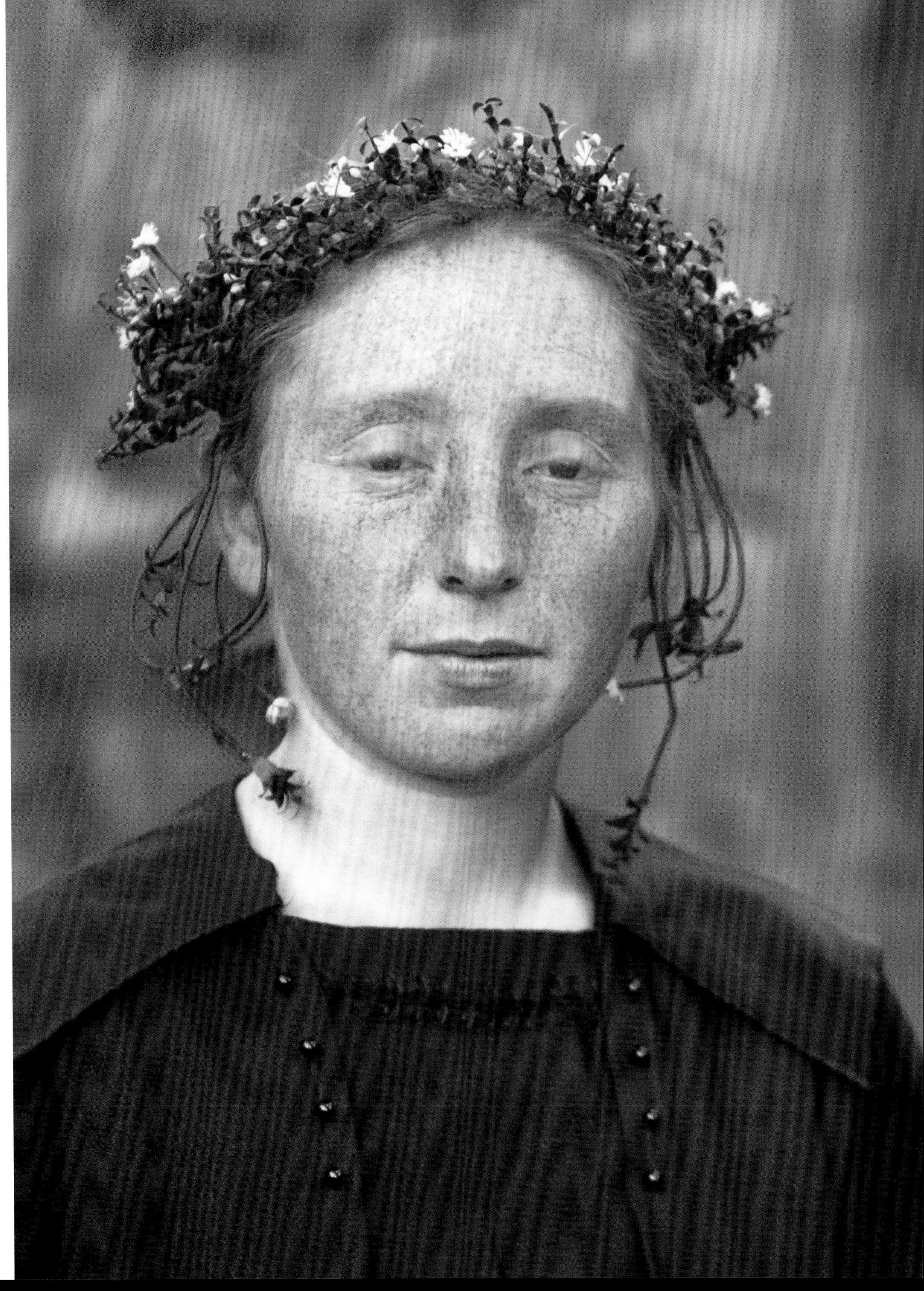

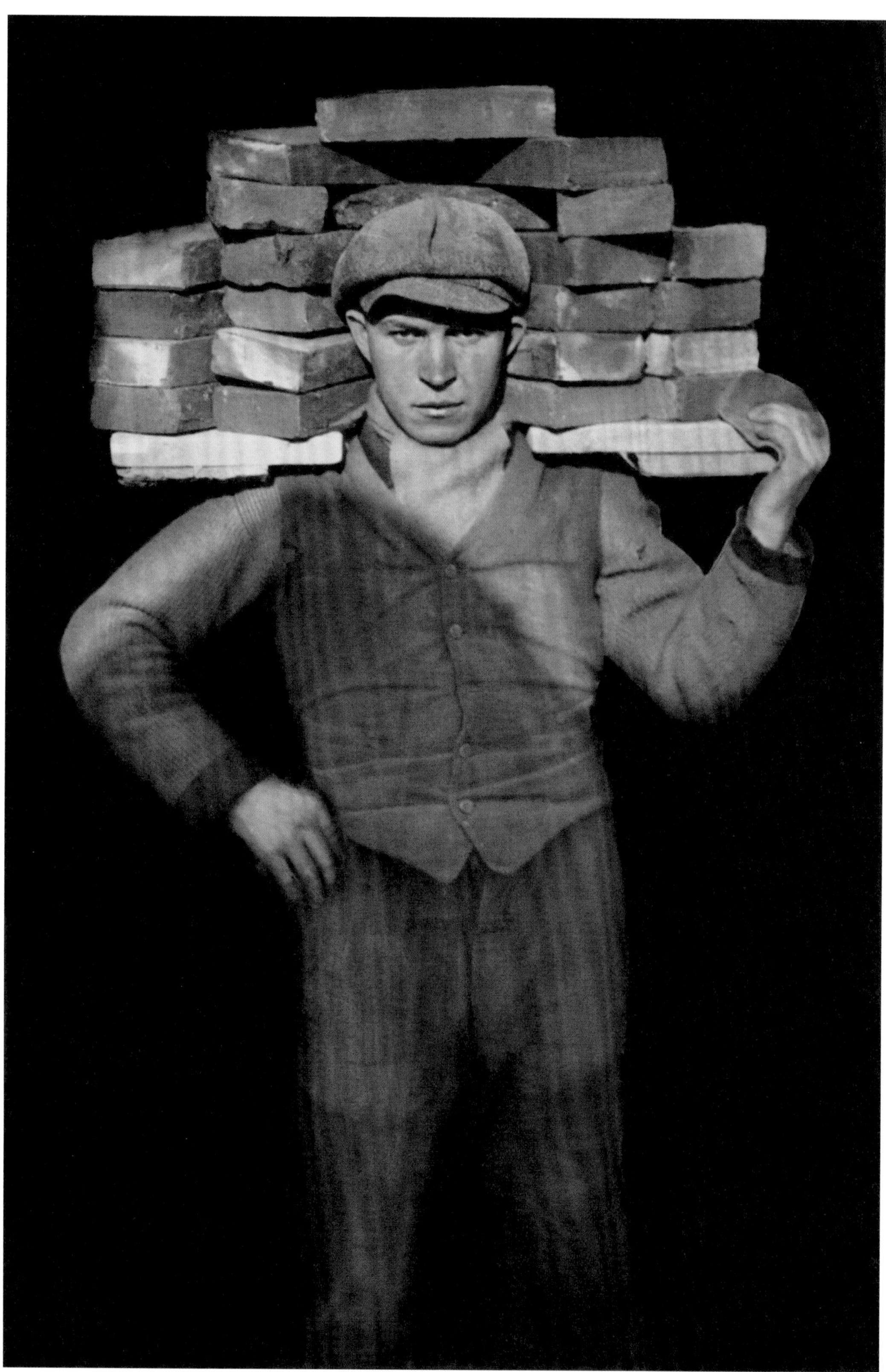

Handlanger (Bricklayer), 1928

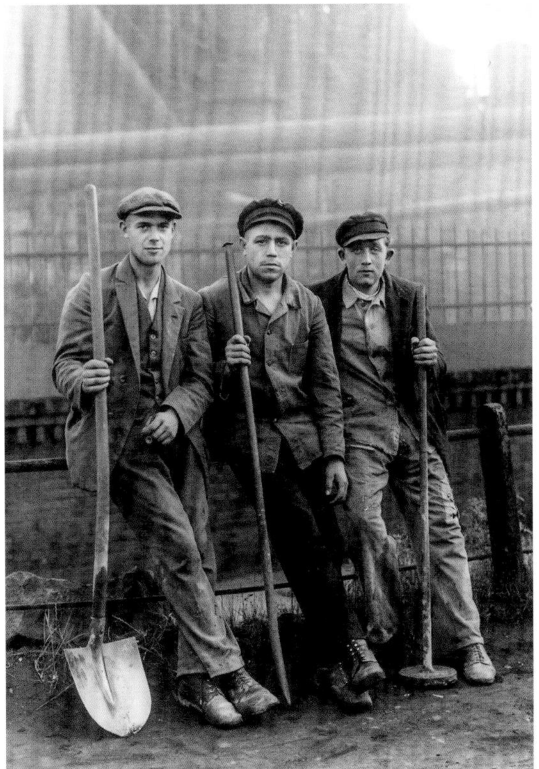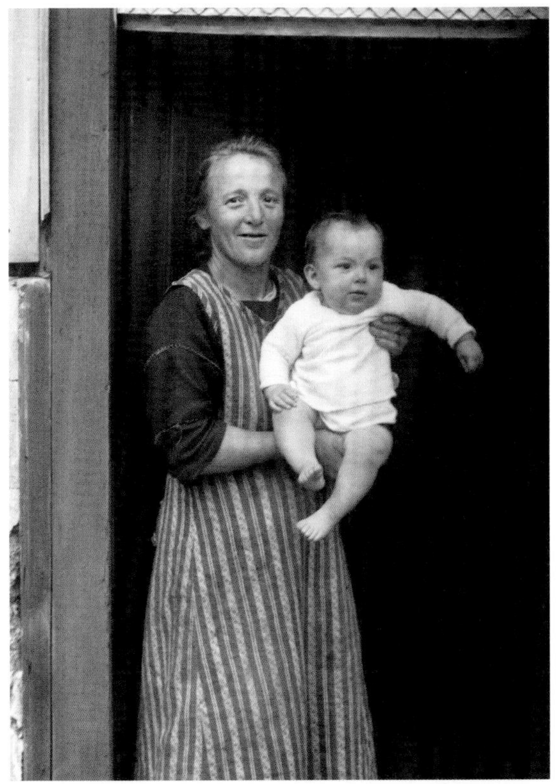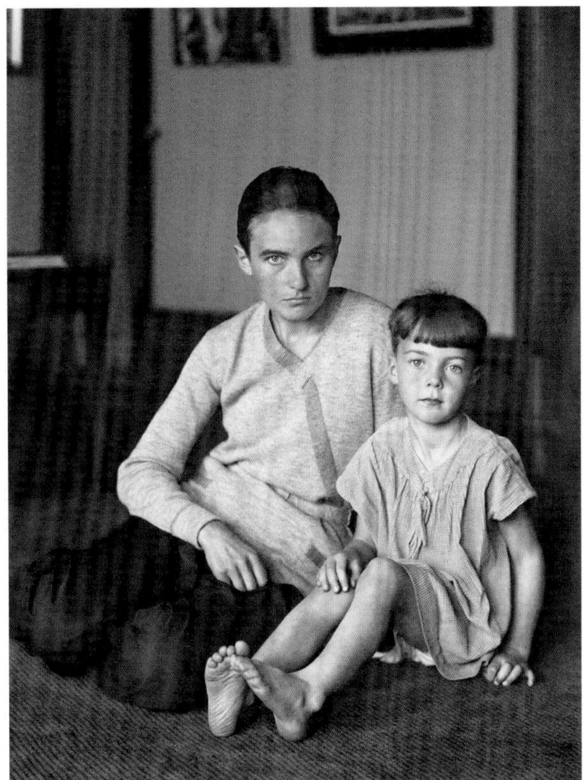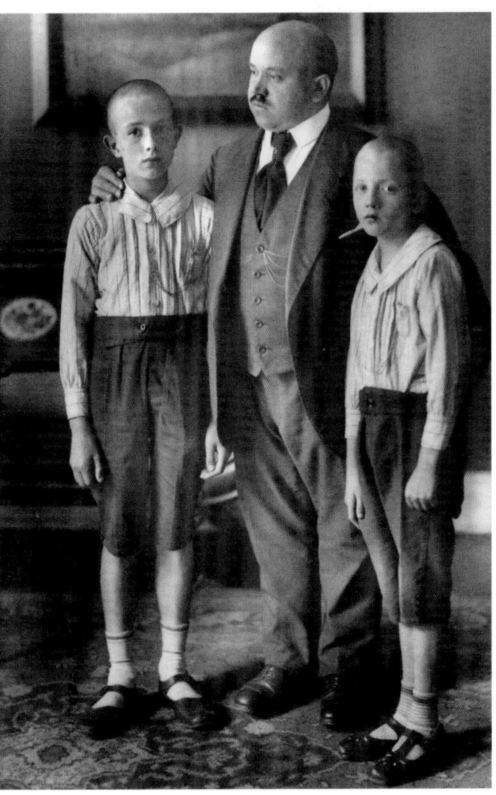

Straßenarbeiter im Ruhrgebiet (Workmen in the Ruhr Region), c. 1928
Proletariermutter (Working-class Mother), 1926
Mutter und Tochter [Helene Abelen mit Tochter Josepha] (Mother and Daughter [Helene Abelen with Daughter Josepha]), c. 1926
Witwer (Widower), 1914

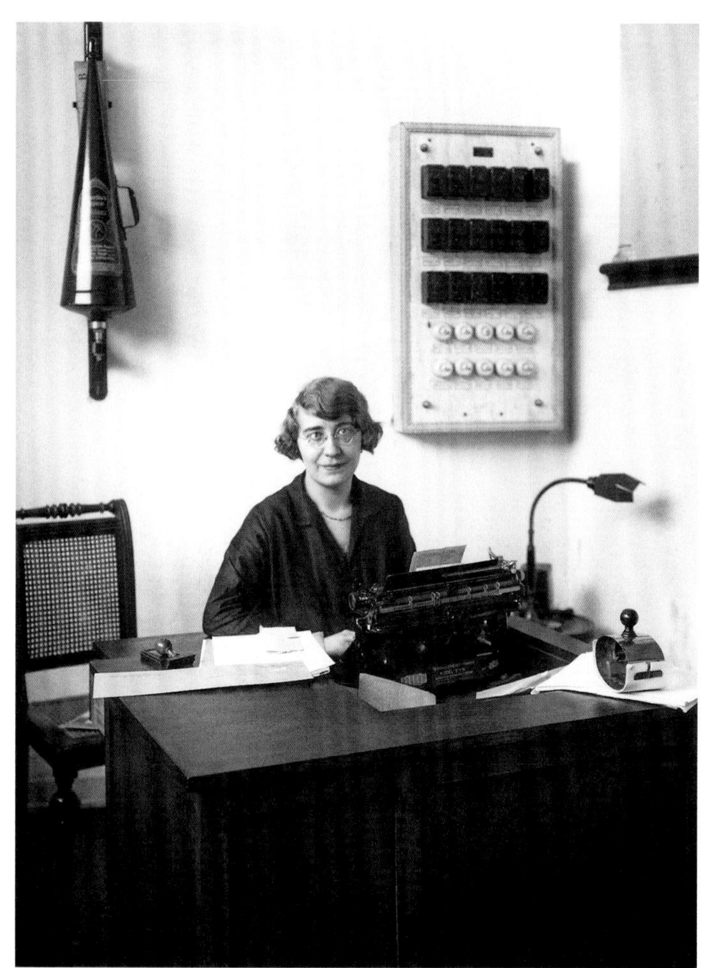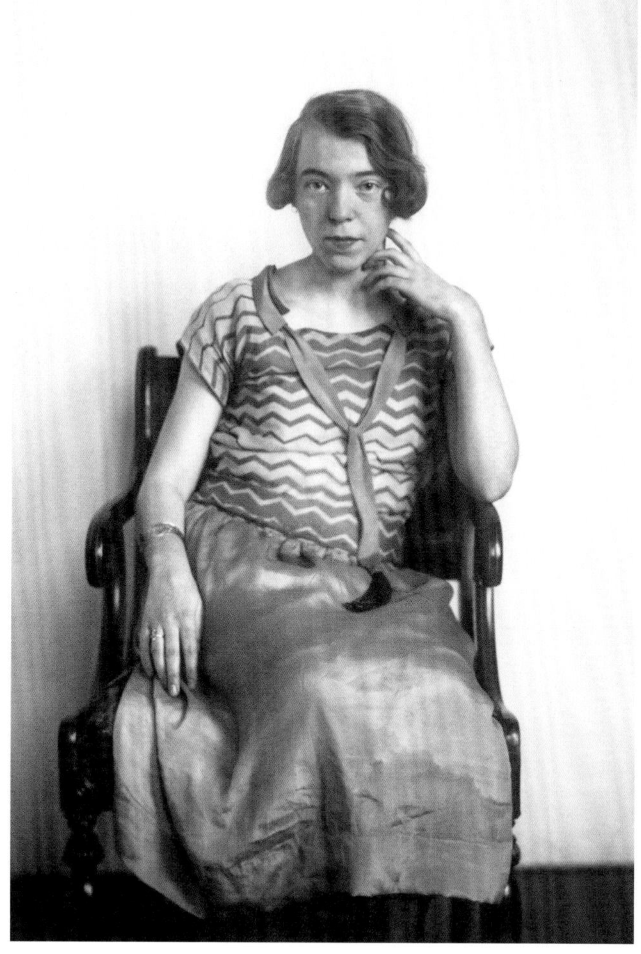

Kontoristin (Office Worker), c. 1928
Gymnastiklehrerin (Gymnastics Teacher), 1925

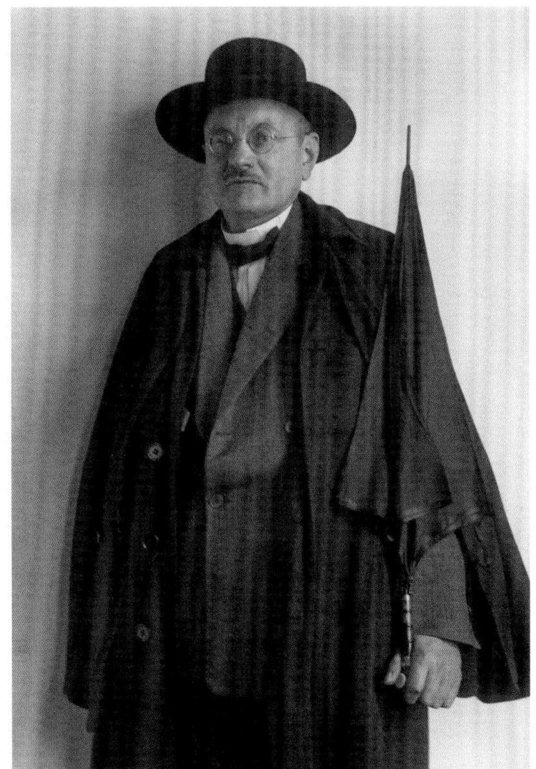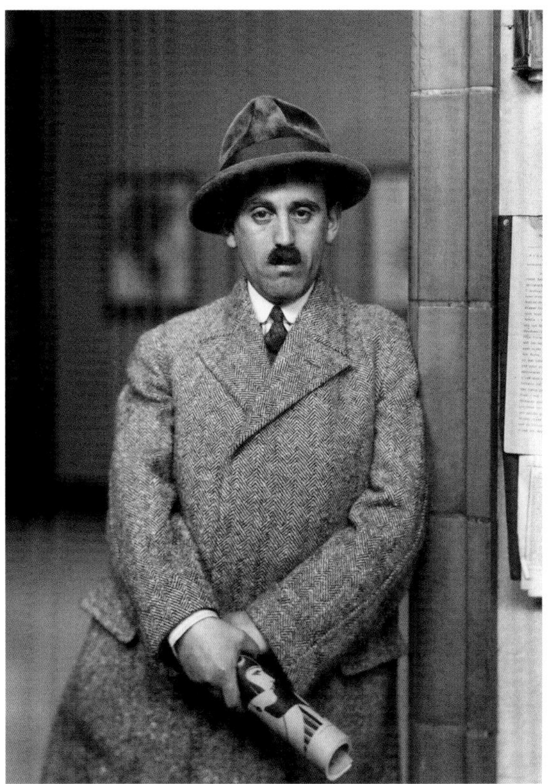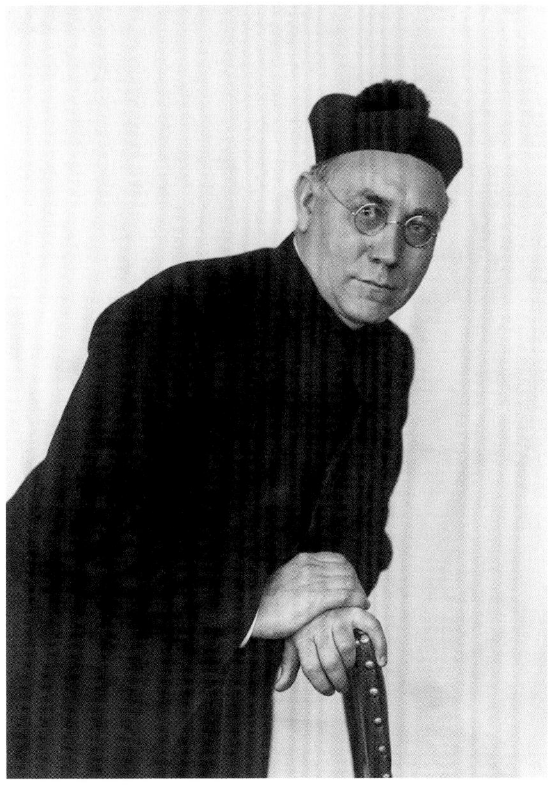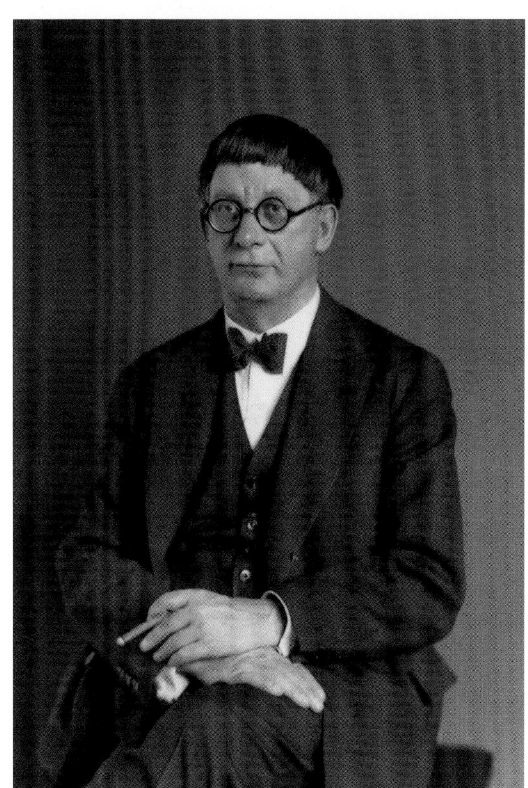

Abgeordneter (Demokrat) (Member of Parliament (Democrat)), 1927
Kunsthändler [Sam Salz] (Art Dealer [Sam Salz]), 1927
Katholischer Geistlicher (Catholic Priest), 1927
Der Architekt [Hans Poelzig] (The Architect [Hans Poelzig]), 1929

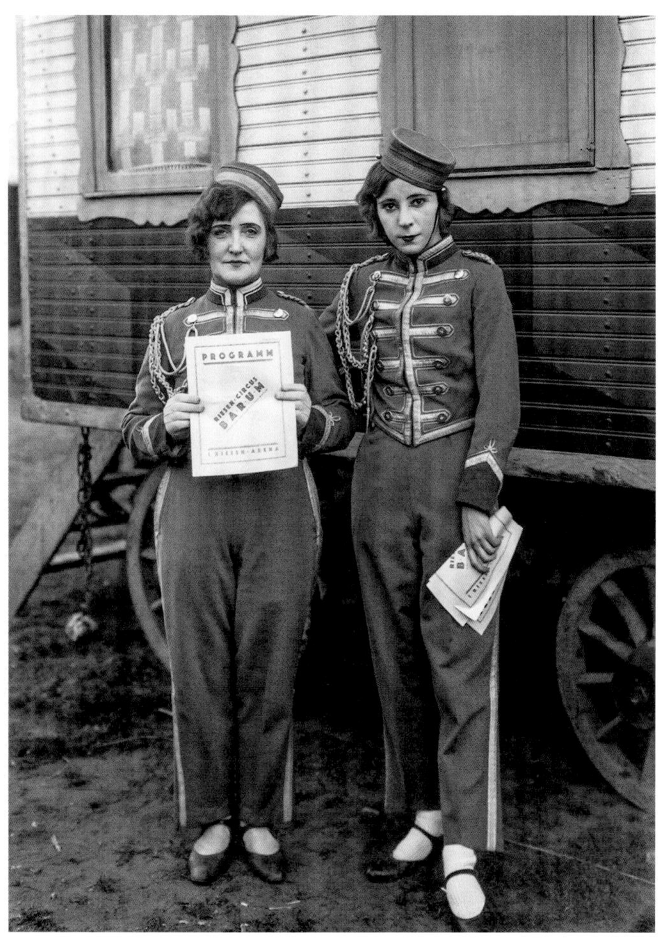
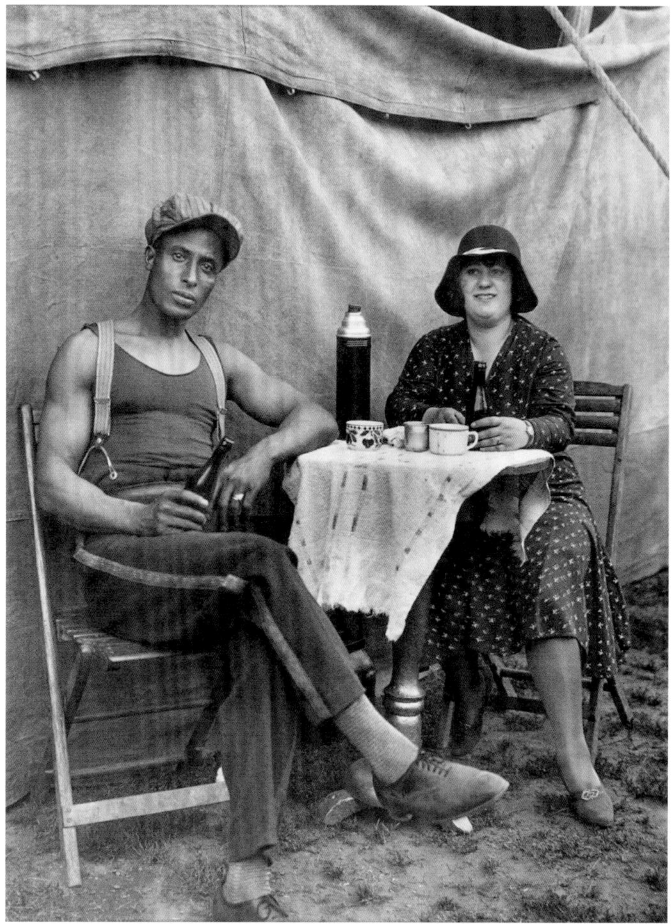

Platzanweiserinnen (Usherettes), 1926-1932
Zirkusarbeiter (Circus Workers), 1926-1932

Opposite page: *Mädchen im Kirmeswagen* (Girl in Fairground Caravan), 1926-1932

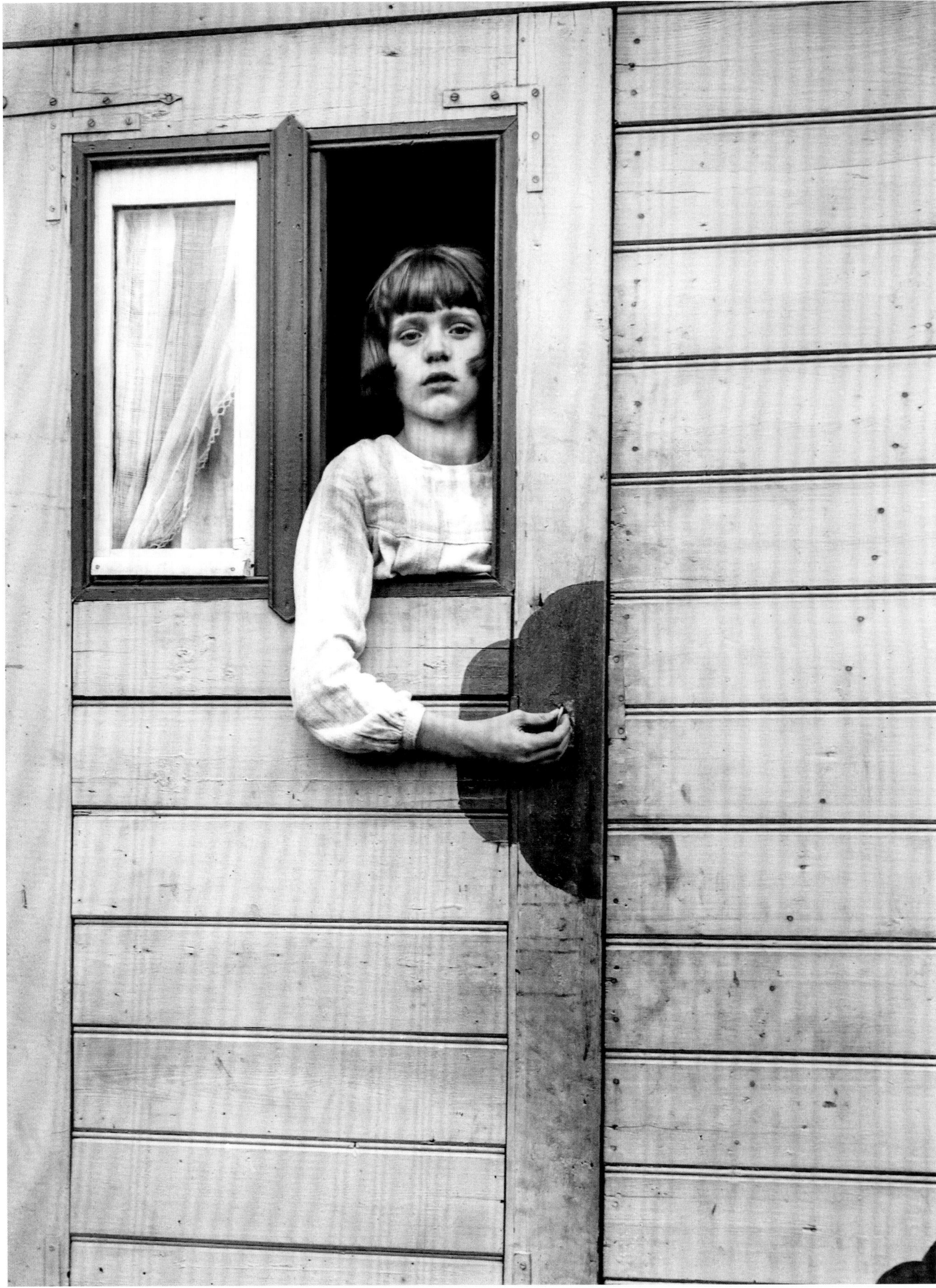

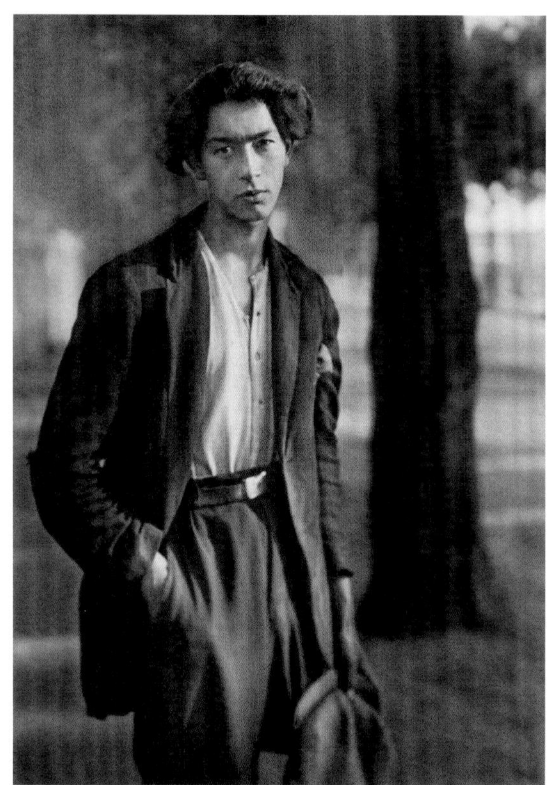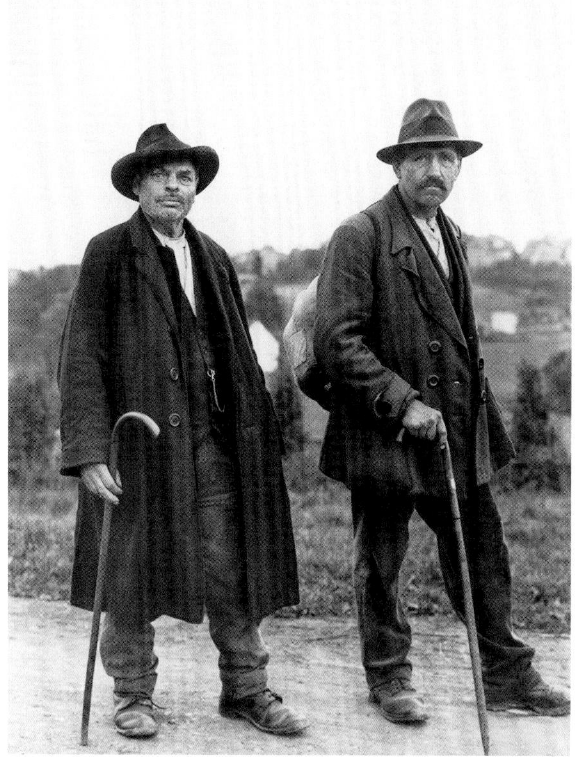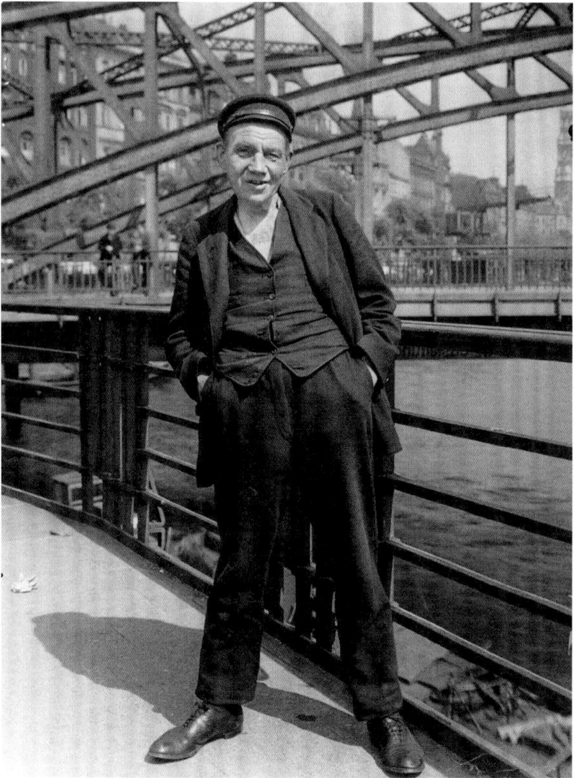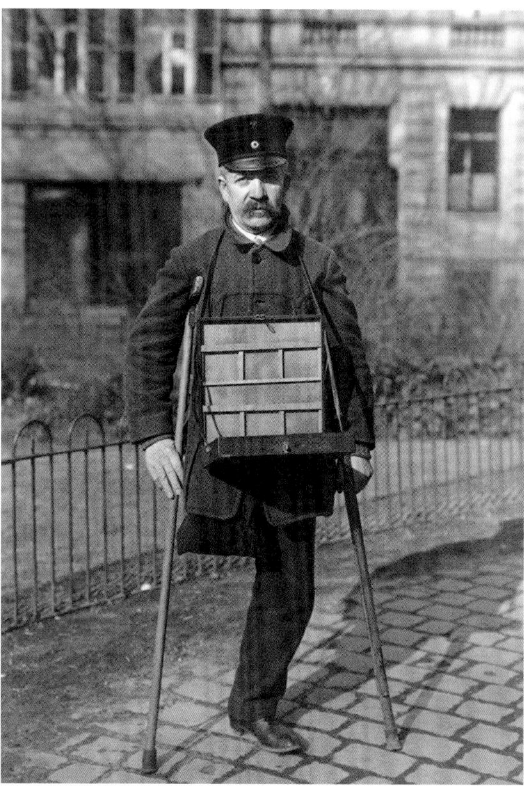

Zigeuner (Gypsy), c. 1930
Landstreicher (Vagrants), 1929
Abgebauter Seemann (Unemployed Sailor), 1929
Berginvalide (Disabled Miner), 1927-1928

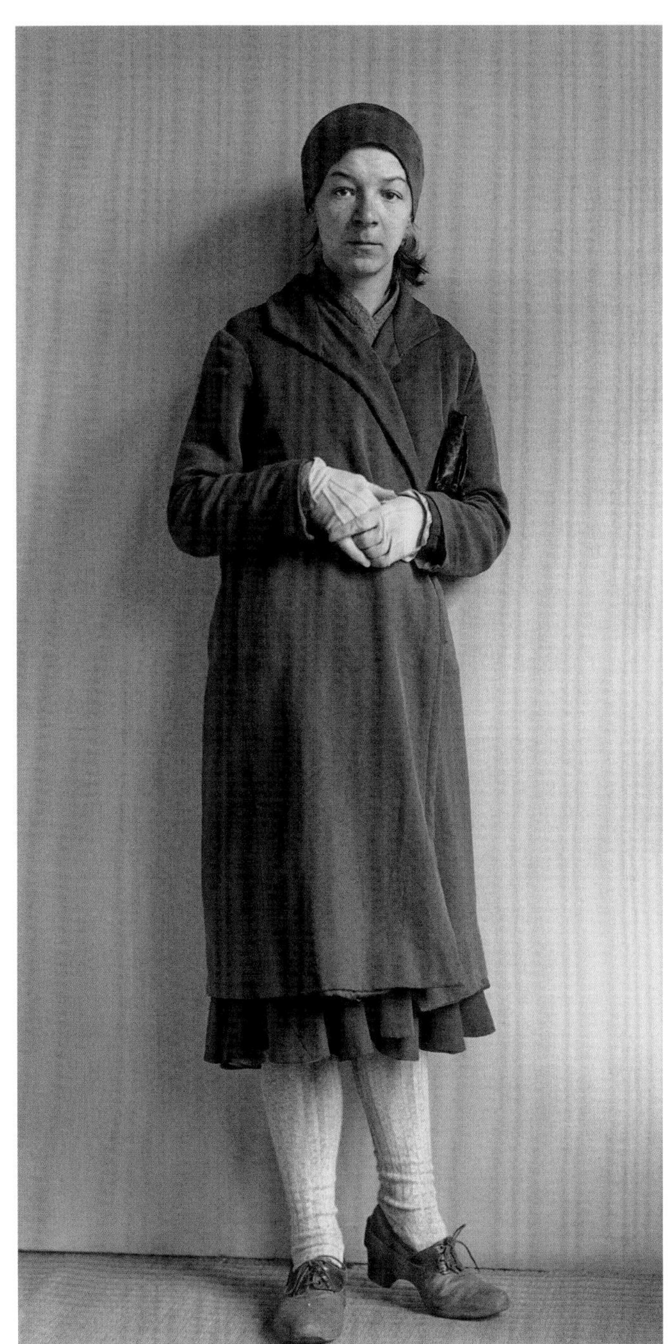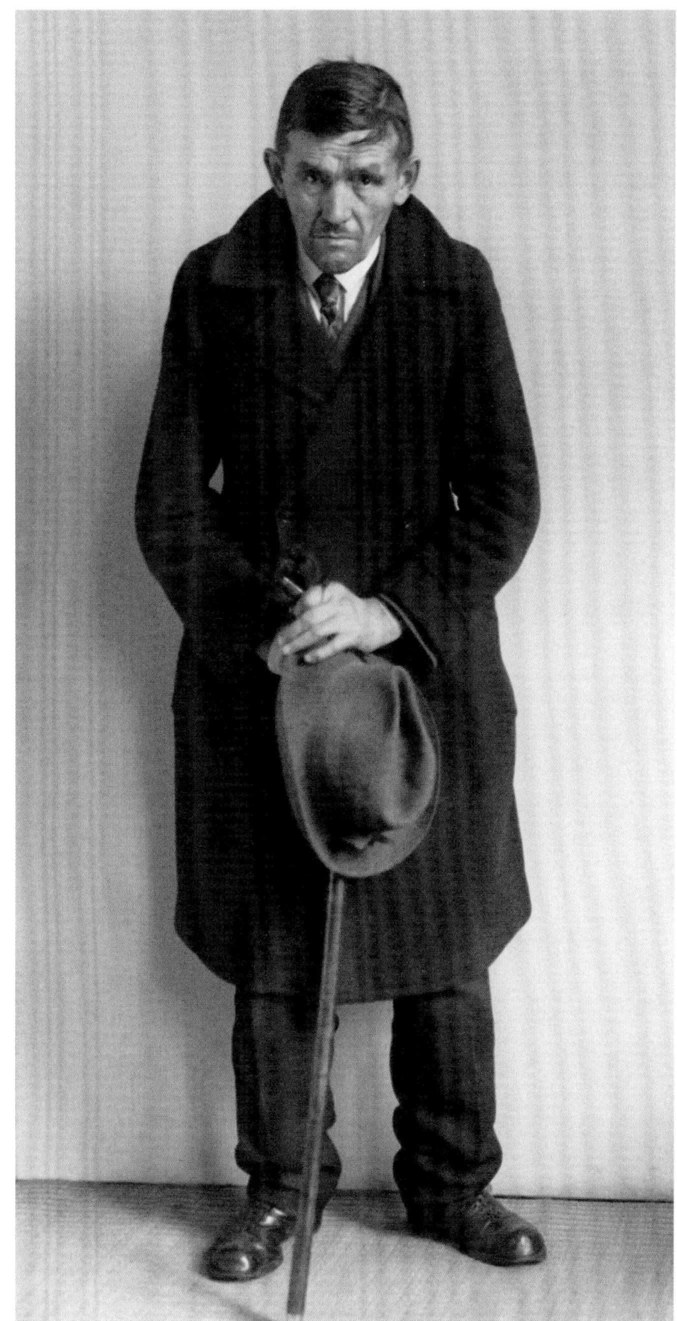

Bettlerin (Beggar), 1930
Almosenempfänger (Welfare Recipient), 1930

Faces In The Crowd.
August Sander's Germans

By Anthony Lane

How do you book your place in an August Sander photograph? Well, it helps to be German, and to have lived in the first half of the 20th century. You should be a farmer, perhaps, with a rutted face and a wrinkled coat, heading off to church along a dirt road in the Westerwald, the region outside Cologne, sometime around 1925. That is how Sander sees you, and that is how he wants you to remain: full length in the frame, from the hazy air above your top hat to the shine on your toe caps. He likes the way you cock your hand against your hip, like the handle of a cup; neither fey nor jaunty, but as though you were propping yourself up. After all, he has already noticed the fatigue in the grooves around your mouth and the skin that sags over the far corners of your eyes. As so often with Sander, there is next to nothing behind you – a grey blur of farm buildings, the track winding away, but little to distract us from the sense that all we need, in order to get the fullest measure of you, is you.

Sander was born in 1876 and lived until 1964. He came to photography in the early eighteen-nineties and stayed with it to his death. By any standards, the years in which he flourished were some of the most traumatic imaginable, and yet he remains among the least traumatized of modern artists. No blood is spilled in his pictures; none of the people would even dream of removing their clothes; no activity is so sudden or spasmodic that it threatens the sharpness of the image, which is recorded on a glass plate whose shortest side is at least a foot long. This is not to say that Sander was one of those molluscoid figures who crouch in their shells, refining their fantasies within; on the contrary, he never lost faith in what could be yielded by a close inspection of his countrymen, and the only person who escapes a full inquiry is Sander himself. There is a self-portrait from 1925 – entitled *Photographer*, nothing else – and he seems, with his wing collar, his receding hair, and his air of pointed kindness, to be a man whom you would like to know. He looks more like your bank manager, or your dentist, than the man who can grant you the immortality of art. But his character is hard to discern amid the vast, typically well-ordered archive of his work. He is a cipher, and he contains multitudes.

A fine selection from that throng can now be seen at Louisiana Museum of Modern Art, in Denmark. The exhibition consists of more than 250 photographs. Some will be recognized even by those who go blank at the name of Sander. His famous *Pastry Cook*, for instance, taken in 1928, has been widely reproduced, but it looks all the more edible in its original gelatin-silver print. Round as a bun, topped with a head like a shining cherry, the master of his craft stands firm and square on the tiles of his kitchen, one hand clasping the inch-thick handle of a spoon or whisk, the other curled around the handle of a large mixing bowl, whose curves are a perfect match for the swell of his paunch. There is not an ounce of mockery in the mixture, and the pastry-maker himself would consider the portrait fair, perhaps ennobling; yet the picture is lightly, irrefutably spiced with a pinch of the comic. In that balancing of the aesthetic scales, Sander has no equal.

The cook takes his place in a section of the exhibition entitled *The Skilled Tradesman*. You might say, without fear of condescension, that he knows his place, and that, thanks to the durability of his skills, he has few complaints about it. That may strike you as a reactionary view, but Sander was no reactionary; he was an exemplary realist who happened to find himself in a society

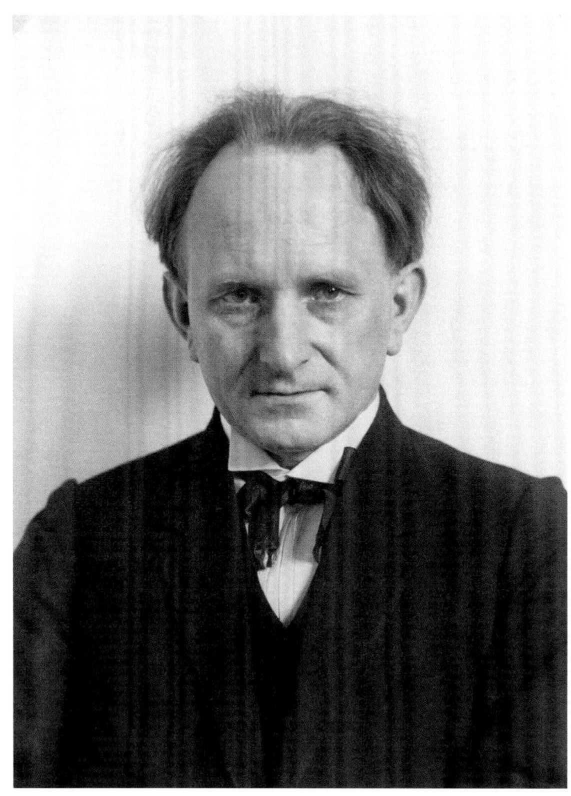

Photograph [August Sander] (Photographer [August Sander]), 1925

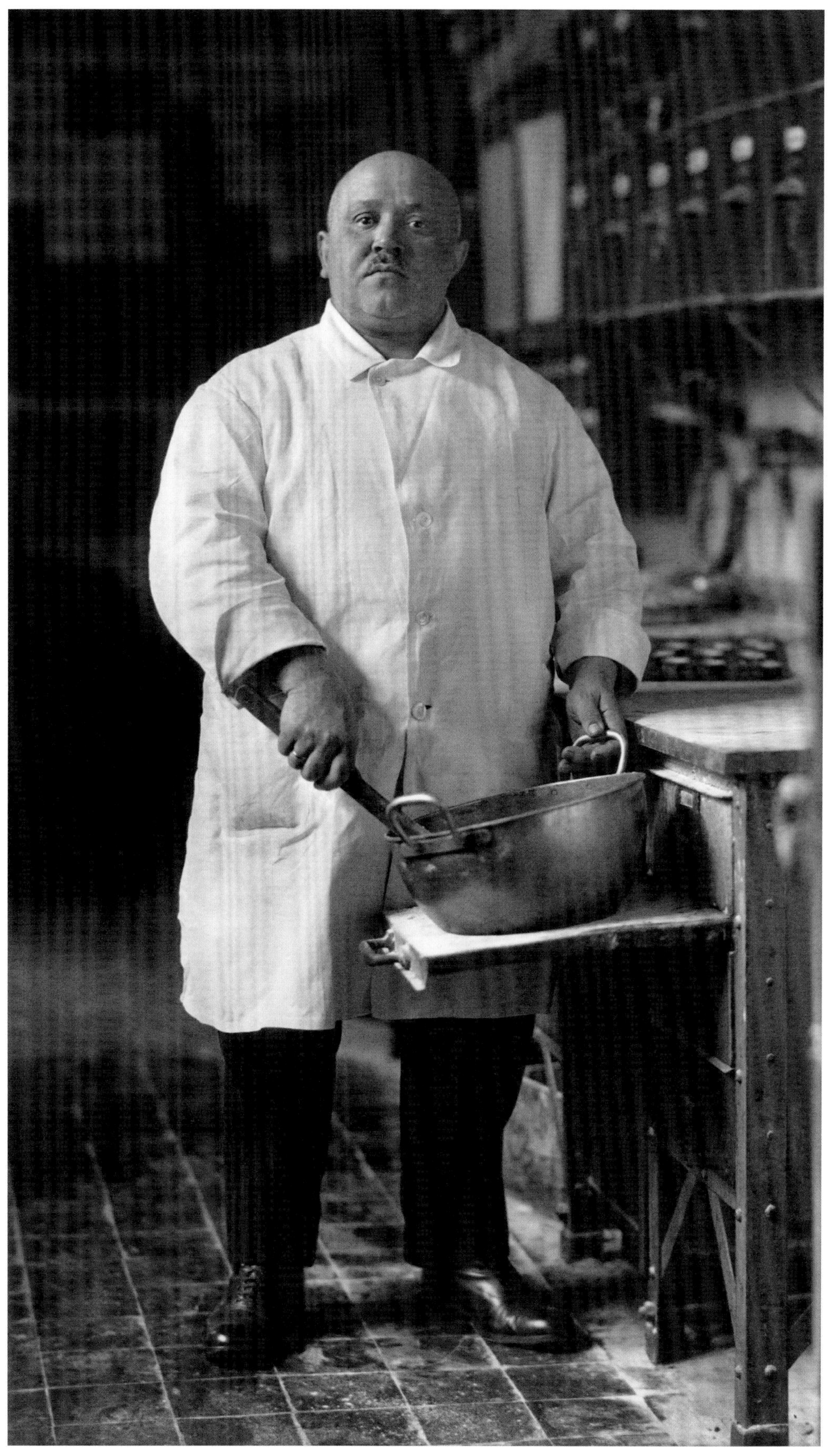

Konditor (Pastry Cook), 1928

whose deep-core conservatism – emotional, domestic, civic – survived all manner of political upheaval, and which survives to this day. "The Skilled Tradesman" is one of seven categories, as dry as hock, into which the show is divided. The others are, in order, "The Farmer," "The Woman," "Classes and Professions," "The Artists," "The City", and, by way of a mysterious finale, "The Last People".

These titles are neither arbitrary nor new. It was Sander himself who arranged forty-five portfolios of his work, each containing a dozen portraits, into seven groups, as if to rival the seven ages of man. Behind all these busy gatherings lay a grand plan, conceived in the mid of the 1920s, when Sander wrote his concept, whereby he also included earlier photographs from the time from 1910, in one case even from 1892, in his compendium. *People of the 20th Century* was the label that Sander gave to his project – an enterprise that few photographers have had the nerve, let alone the stamina, to attempt, and that was not confounded even by the loss of some thirty thousand negatives in a house fire in 1946. He called his magnum opus not a social history but a "physiognomic image of an age," founded on a desire to classify "all the characteristics of the universally human." This makes him sound like the loftiest of Victorian scientists, collecting men and women as if he were pinning butterflies to a board, and I recommend that you turn as soon as possible to the photographs themselves. Once you yield to the rhythm of their observational power, the slight chill of Sander's encyclopaedic scruples falls away, and you are left not with types but with *this* publisher, *that* coal carrier, the withered bouquets so unexpectedly held by those nurses, and the boundless moustaches of this unmistakable policeman, which unfurl outward like steam from the funnel of a train.

What was the physiognomy of Sander's age? He was born not long after Germany itself, which scarcely existed as a modern state until it was unified by Bismarck, in 1871, and, when one surveys the innumerable stances of its citizens, as caught by Sander, one senses, time and again, the half-thwarted urge toward cohesion. Even when he photographs vagrants, or avowed revolutionaries, he finds a stillness in their energy; where a romantic would rhapsodize, and where the satirist would see straight through, Sander grants dignity to the nomad and the anarchist alike – not just a social dignity, either, but the basic dignity that comes of cleaving to your purpose. That is why he doesn't like to trap his

fellow-Germans on the wing, or to creep up on them unnoticed, like a thief or a cat. He allows them to pose, head on to the camera, and thus to offer a considered rendition of themselves in their natural habitat – the smithy, the drawing room, the back yard, and the bare wall.

This sense of belonging, or, at least, of the need to belong, burns beneath the surface of the photographs, and it may account for the curious lack of bewilderment that his subjects betray in their moment of isolation before the lens. One thinks of the American historian William Sheridan Allen, who, for the purposes of his book *The Nazi Seizure of Power* (1965), studied a single Hanoverian town as it had been constituted in the 1930s, and discovered that in a population of fewer than 10,000 there were 161 clubs and societies – one for 60 people. It is just this kind of community that Sander sought to scrutinize, and the political implications were duly noted by Walter Benjamin in his *Short History of Photography* (1931). "You might come from the right or the left, but you will have to get used to being seen for where you come from, just as you will have to grow used to seeing others for their provenance," he wrote.

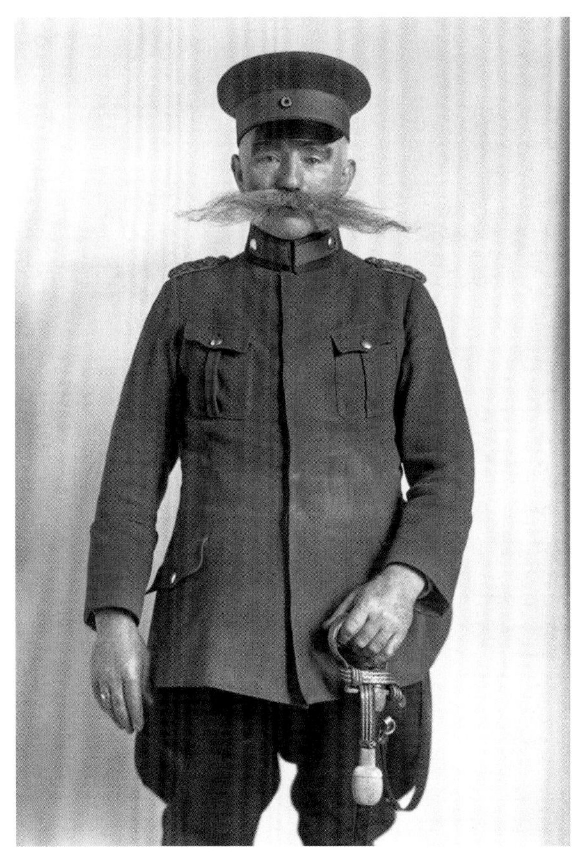

Polizeibeamter. Der Herr Wachtmeister (Police Officer), 1925

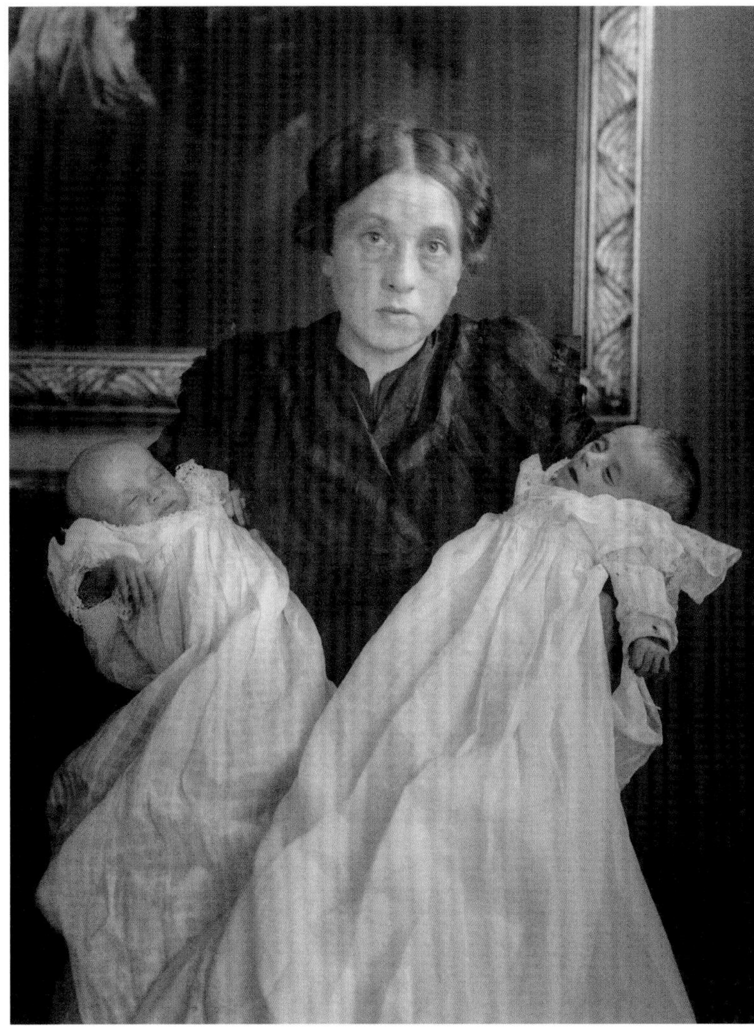

Meine Frau in Freud und Leid (My Wife in Joy and Sorrow), 1911

To take one example: just look at the teachers. They seem more substantial, in their way, than any of the men of God whom Sander so impartially inspects, or any of the industrialists, as plump and sleek as seals. And this, in turn, ties in with the exalted status that the teacher had enjoyed in the national reckoning since the middle of the nineteenth century. Gordon A. Craig, who distilled a lifetime's study into *The Germans* (1982), points out that, even during the student disturbances of the nineteen-sixties and seventies, the public sided heavily with the college authorities: "The German people have always had an inordinate respect for their professors – opinion polls in the fifties and sixties regularly showed them as being more admired than bishops, ministers of state, general directors of business concerns, military commanders, and other dignitaries." His list reads like an index to a volume of Sander, and it suggests that, in this matter at least, little had changed in half a century.

Thus it is that we get the languid, fine-boned gentleman in morning coat and striped trousers, who could easily be a British Parliamentarian on the make, but whom Sander identifies merely as *Teacher*. Another man stands on a woodland road with a hunting dog at his feet, a lit cigar between his fingers, and a nonchalant disdain in his eye. *Village Schoolteacher*, the title reads, and one instinctively fears for his cowering pupils. A third pedagogue is younger and stouter; his jacket strains at the buttons, yet in this case we get the impression that he himself is straining to appear more severe than he actually is. (The German Shepherd beside him is his choice of prop, one might say, rather than his tool of control). So many of Sander's characters are keen to tell us tales about themselves, and that very wish can be revealing.

Sander himself was socially mobile, more so than the majority of his sitters. He was the son of a mining carpenter from the Westerwald, but his career took him into other spheres – more artistic ones, though not necessarily more rarefied, for we are taught by his art not to rate one vocation higher than the next. He did two years of military service, starting in 1897, and was later conscripted into the territorial reserves for the First World War. In 1902, he married Anna Seitenmacher. They had two sons, Erich and Gunther, and then, in 1911, Anna gave birth to twins, Sigrid and Helmut. Sander took a photograph of her, entitled *My Wife in Joy and Sorrow*. She holds the twin babies, one cradled in each arm. A sleeping Sigrid looks healthy and primed for life; Helmut, swathed in the same lace, is skeletal and open-mouthed, like an ageing pauper. He died hours after the picture was taken, and you will not be able to look at it for long.

The image is unusual, because, although Sander never swerved from suffering, he preferred not to register it at first hand but to arrive much later and take a reading of the aftershocks. His portrait of a widower, from 1914, is the saddest photograph that I know. The tubby, balding stalwart of the bourgeoisie, whom in other circumstances we might describe as comfortable, seems utterly comfortless as he clutches his two sons and gazes off-camera – a rare instance of a Sander subject unable, in his quiet extremity of feeling, to meet the photographer's eye. The boys, deprived of their mother, are gaunt and stooping in their long shorts and striped shirts; their hair is cropped to the skull, and, in a terrible whisper of a million widowings to come, they remind you – there is no getting away from it – of the inmates of a labour camp.

But then Sander seemed to have an effortless understanding of children. Whether the death of Helmut left him with a rawness that he was unable to soothe we cannot tell. What is certain is that he got down to the level of the young and treated them seriously, knowing that there is nothing so serious as the rules by which children choose to govern their play. Of the pair shown here, holding hands, all we know for sure is that, as Sander tells us, they were *Bürgerkinder*, middle-class children. What else can one say?

*The little folk look like each other, with the strong undefined likeness of brother and sister [...] Not only is Snapper the sturdier and more compact, he appears consciously to emphasize his four-year-old masculinity in speech, manner, and carriage, lifting his shoulders and letting the little arms hang down quite like a young American athlete. [...] But all this masculinity is the result of effort rather than natively his. Born and brought up in these desolate, distracted times, he has *been endowed by them with an unstable and hypersensitive nervous system and suffers greatly under life's disharmonies. He is prone to sudden anger and outbursts of bitter tears, stamping his feet at every trifle; for this reason he is his mother's special nursling and care. His round, round eyes are chestnut brown and already inclined to squint, so that he will need glasses in the near future [...] Her eyes are now golden-brown, set far apart and with sweet gleams in them – such a clear and lovely look! [...] When she laughs, dimples come in her cheeks and she shows her teeth like loosely strung pearls. So far she has lost but one tooth, which her father gently twisted out with his handkerchief after it had grown very wobbly. During this small operation she paled and trembled very much.*

The words come from "Disorder and Early Sorrow," a short story by Thomas Mann. Like Sander's photograph, it dates from 1925. What is uncanny is not just the physical detail that is common to image and text but, so to speak, the pitch of extrasensory perception. Both Sander and Mann have the spectral gift of looking at a face and seeing a secret history: the anxieties that lie behind (the pulling of that tooth), and the landscape of fretfulness and waste that may stretch ahead. You worry, instantly, for these children, and it is not sentimental to gain consolation from the tight lock of their hands. To look at a Sander is not merely to consult a social record of his times, however thorough that may be, still less to be charmed or amused. The experience is more like entering into a novel.

With the *Bürgerkinder*, the apprehension deepens because, to some extent, we know how the story goes. When we stare at the boy, especially, we cannot restrain ourselves from asking: where he will be in twenty years? Heaven or Hell? And, if the latter, will it be the hell of the living or of the dead? Or will he somehow escape the horrors, become a village schoolteacher, and sit out the wrecking of his homeland? In short, Sander is as central to our grasp of the Weimar Republic, and hence of the Nazis' climb to power, as any of its more notorious documentarians. As his friend Alfred Döblin – the author of *Berlin Alexanderplatz*, the great pessimistic novel of the era – wrote of Sander's work in 1929, "The tensions of our time become clear when we compare the photograph of the working students with that of the professor and his so peaceful family, nestling contentedly and still unsuspecting." That last phrase is like ice.

Sander was a friend of the painter Otto Dix, and the category of "Artists" in *People of the 20th Century*, with its portraits of Hindemith, Furtwängler, Strauss, and lesser luminaries, contains more than one image of Dix, both alone and with his wife. Dix might not have painted the portly Dr. Mayer-Hermann (1926) if Sander had not led

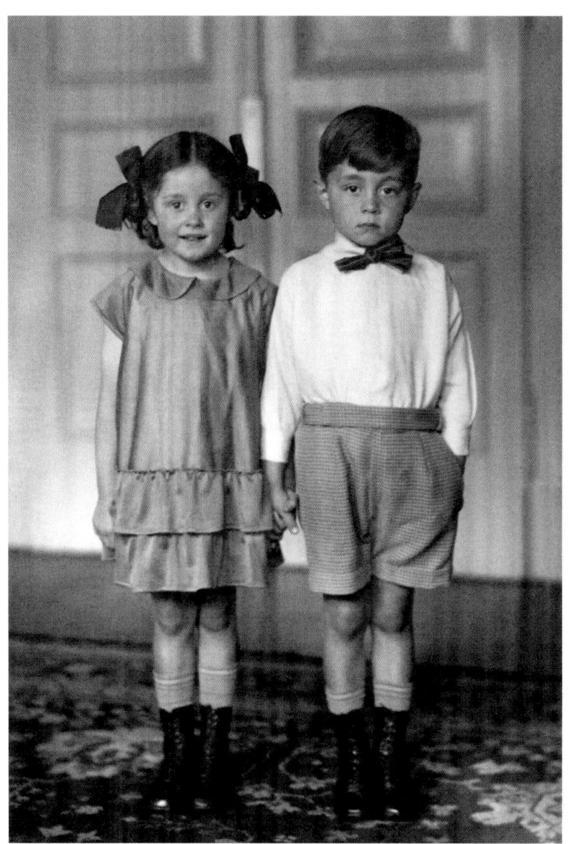

Bürgerkinder (Middle-class Children), 1925

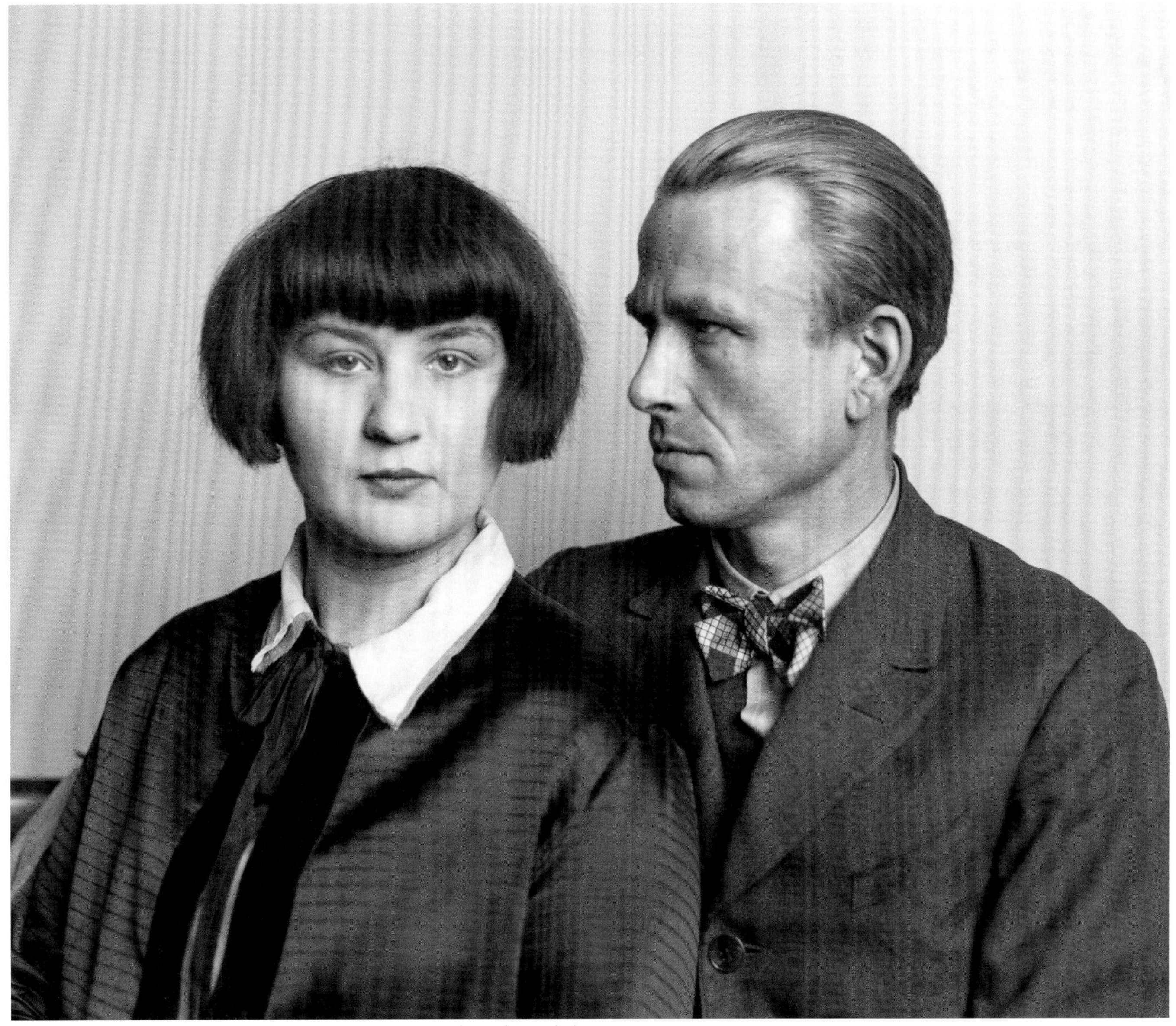

Malerehepaar [Martha und Otto Dix] (The Painter Otto Dix and his Wife Martha), 1925

the way with his own gallery of rotund professionals, and Sander's *Secretary at West German Radio in Cologne* (1931, p. 18) – she looks a bit fast for polite society, but also too fearful to cut it as a good-time girl – casts an appreciative backward glance at Dix's eel-like Sylvia von Harden (1926, front cover and p. 21), the original social X-ray, coiled up with her Martini and monocle. Sander took evident pleasure in the corpulent and the skinny alike, in all the everyday formations and deformations of the body. What he never insisted on was a corresponding deformation of the soul. Take his *Commercial Traveller*, of 1930, big and bearish, trussed up in a double-breasted coat. He is as pathetic as he is proud; he is a fat man, but he is not a fat bastard. If he were painted by

Dix, however, or, more scabrously still, by George Grosz, he would unequivocally be tagged as one of the damned. The full-bellied merchant is a stock figure in Grosz's bestiary; what Sander offers is, as it were, the basic, untreated material that Grosz will then inflate and pollute for the purposes of sulfurous lampoon. Confronted with both, I increasingly feel that Sander's art is not only more temperate than Grosz's but morally more difficult to sustain. Anybody can hate, but only a handful can clearly see.

This genius for calm, the refusal to cast judgement even when the stones are being thrown around your head, reached its peak in Sander's work of the nineteen-thirties and forties. He was part of a determined movement – *Neue*

Sachlichkeit, or New Objectivity, which held its first exhibition in Mannheim in 1925. Dix and Grosz were both members, and the stated aim was to outgrow, or wipe away, the indulgences of Expressionism, and to restore a figurative clarity to the art of the day. After all, political conditions were now so volatile and livid that simply to get them down on paper or canvas would be expressive enough. Looking back, one could claim that the ideals of New Objectivity were no more than a reforging, under pressure, of the Old Objectivity: the rage for representation that had driven so much German art, particularly graphic art, since the time of Dürer. Early draftsmanship brought its own moral commitment – Dürer, in his 1524 engraving of Frederick the Wise, Elector of Saxony, spies not just wisdom but a bullish determination in the puff of the Elector's cheeks and the stormy curls of his beard – and for Sander, four centuries later, the camera imposes an equal burden of justice. Admittedly, he could do nothing with the young Aryan from Hitler's S.S. bodyguard whom he photographed around 1940, and who gazes mistily offstage like a Wagnerian baritone posing for a publicity still. He, however, is Sander's only monster. The rest of his kind are all too human.

This is not to defuse or deny the strength of Sander's private opinions. In 1929, he published a selection of 60 photographs under the title *Face of Our Time*. In 1936, the National Socialists seized the book and destroyed the photographic plates. They could not countenance a man whose art lavished such care on Gypsies, black circus performers, and the mentally disabled. The state was gearing up to kill such people, and this man Sander was daring to give them fresh imaginative life. Worse still, he had a troublesome son. In 1934, Erich Sander, a student member of the Socialist Workers' Party, had been arrested, charged with anti-Nazi activities, and jailed for 10 years. He died in prison in March, 1944, before the end of his sentence. Yet the extraordinary fact remains that, throughout that decade of separation, his father continued to photograph individual members of the organization that had inflicted such a lasting wound on his family. From our perspective, that may sound tasteless or indifferent, but, as Sander wrote to friends in the New Year of 1940, "Have the courage to think for yourself".

With that courage in mind, look at his parade of Nazis. Look at all the variations on the bored, the quizzical, the puny, and the porcine, sometimes coexisting within a single frame. Look at the seated *National Socialist* in this exhibition: is he not hoping to hint – with his round spectacles, his decorously folded hands, and even his ghost of a smile – that he might not be quite as cruel as his confrères? Alternatively, consider the risible sample of Hitler Youth, standing in the long grass of his garden. He loves his jackboots, but he can't be bothered to iron the collar of his shirt. His hair could have been combed by his mother for school. He knows what to do with his right arm, when the occasion demands, but when a photographer comes he doesn't have a clue what to do with his left. And where, exactly, is his chin? The whole photograph adds up to a riveting depiction of human weakness: a meagre spirit, scarcely believing its luck, clutching at its unexpected chance to play the part of the strong, and knowing that for once it will not be found out, for all the other hopefuls will be sharing the stage.

The final volume of *People of the 20th Century* marks an exquisite coda to Sander's achievement. Here he photographs the blind, and those ravaged by worse misfortunes. He photographs those whom he calls midgets, which is not what we would call them, but the outcome is infinitely sober and respectful. Diane Arbus is often cited as an inheritor of Sander's legacy, but by his standards she seems too eager to seek people out

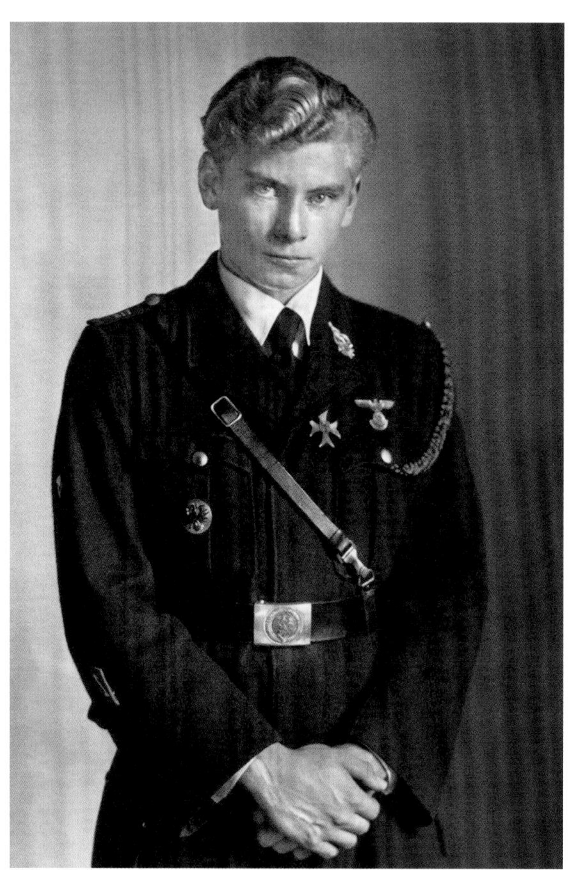

Junger Nationalsozialist (Young National Socialist), 1941

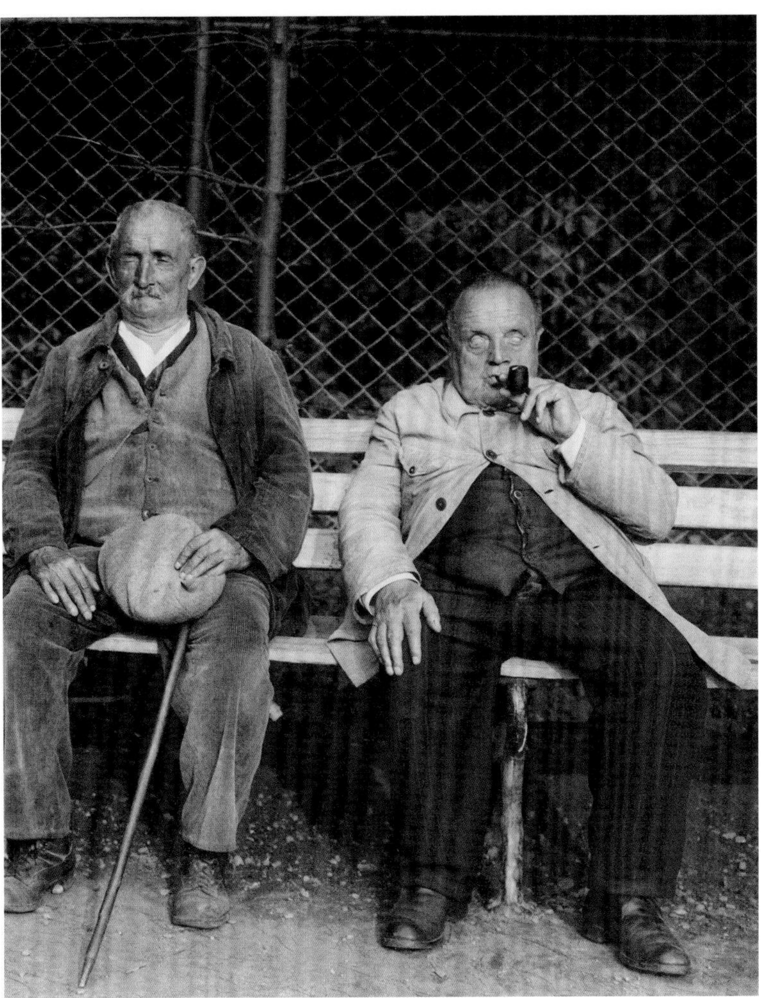

Blinder Bergmann und Blinder Soldat (Blind Miner and Blind Soldier), 1921-1930

but *Geist* will endure and be remembered, in fascination, fear, or love. For photographers, August Sander's tender but exacting work is about as good as it gets. He happened to be born in Germany, but one feels that he could have mapped any number of civilizations. If only he could have lugged his camera, bellows and all, back to the courts of Caligula or Louis XIV, or, with rather less fuss, set up shop at Plymouth Rock and photographed the new arrivals. In fact, we could use him now.

ANTHONY LANE has been a film critic for The New Yorker since 1993. He is the author of *Nobody's Perfect*. A version of this essay appeared in the magazine in 2003.

for their oddity, whereas that is the one thing that Sander does not care about and, indeed, barely appears to notice.

Lastly, he photographs the dead: a death mask of his son Erich, and then, unforgettably, two elderly Germans at peace. We see a bearded man, and a woman in a neat lace cap, and then we see the title of both pictures: *Matter*. I missed a beat when I first read that, thinking: Is that all? Is Sander so rigorous in his disillusion as to suggest that, when our trade is finished, when we have ceased to be pastry-makers, bricklayers, barons, mothers, S.S. officers, high-school girls, and cellists, we dwindle to nothing more than matter, as chimney sweepers come to dust? On reflection, the opposite is true. If Sander devoted himself to the collating of human variety, and to the minute annotation of quirks, it is because of his faith in Geist, in the animating force of spirit and thought. That is what allows us to distinguish not just the pastry-maker from the Nazi but one Nazi from the next. Matter will fade, like a photograph,

THE NOTION OF *GEBRAUCH* (utility) appeared in 1920s Germany in the fields of theatre, music and literature. This new concept favoured the emergence of works useful to society. They were supposed to be anchored in their time and immediately understandable for a wide audience.

Like the famous German-Czech reporter Egon Erwin Kisch (1885-1948), the modern writer now adopted a neutral style, consisting of simple, concise sentences, and favoured the recounting of facts over the exploration of feelings. In *Gebrauchslyrik* (utilitarian poetry), prose takes precedence over lyricism. German writer Erich Kästner (1899-1974) assigned poetry an educational purpose and wrote in simple, understandable language, devoid of psychology.

New musical styles imported from the United States now appeared in Germany and became very popular, especially jazz and dance music such as the foxtrot. The composers Ernst Křenek (1900-1991), Kurt Weill (1900-1950) and Paul Hindemith (1895-1963) were inspired to create a new musical genre, the *Zeitoper* (opera of the time), whose plots take place in the contemporary world and whose settings incorporate modern technology and machines such as trains, cars and telephones. The opera turned its back on the romantic tradition and addressed a wide audience, drawing its references from popular culture.

Director Erwin Piscator (1893-1966) and playwright Bertolt Brecht (1898-1956) developed what they called epic theatre. In their plays they subverted fiction by introducing new elements and thereby contributing to the political awakening of the spectators. The introduction of narrators or the breaking of the unity of the action are all elements that create a distance conducive to reflection. The sets designed by Traugott Müller (1895-1974) and George Grosz (1893-1959) further aided this anti-illusionist ambition. While remaining an entertainment, theatre thus became a place of education and a medium of information.

FRANZ ALOÏS FLACHSLANDER Poster for the staging of the opera *Jonny spielt auf* (Jonny Strikes Up) by Ernst Křenek at Städtische Oper in Berlin, 1927

THEATRE, LITERATURE AND MUSIC

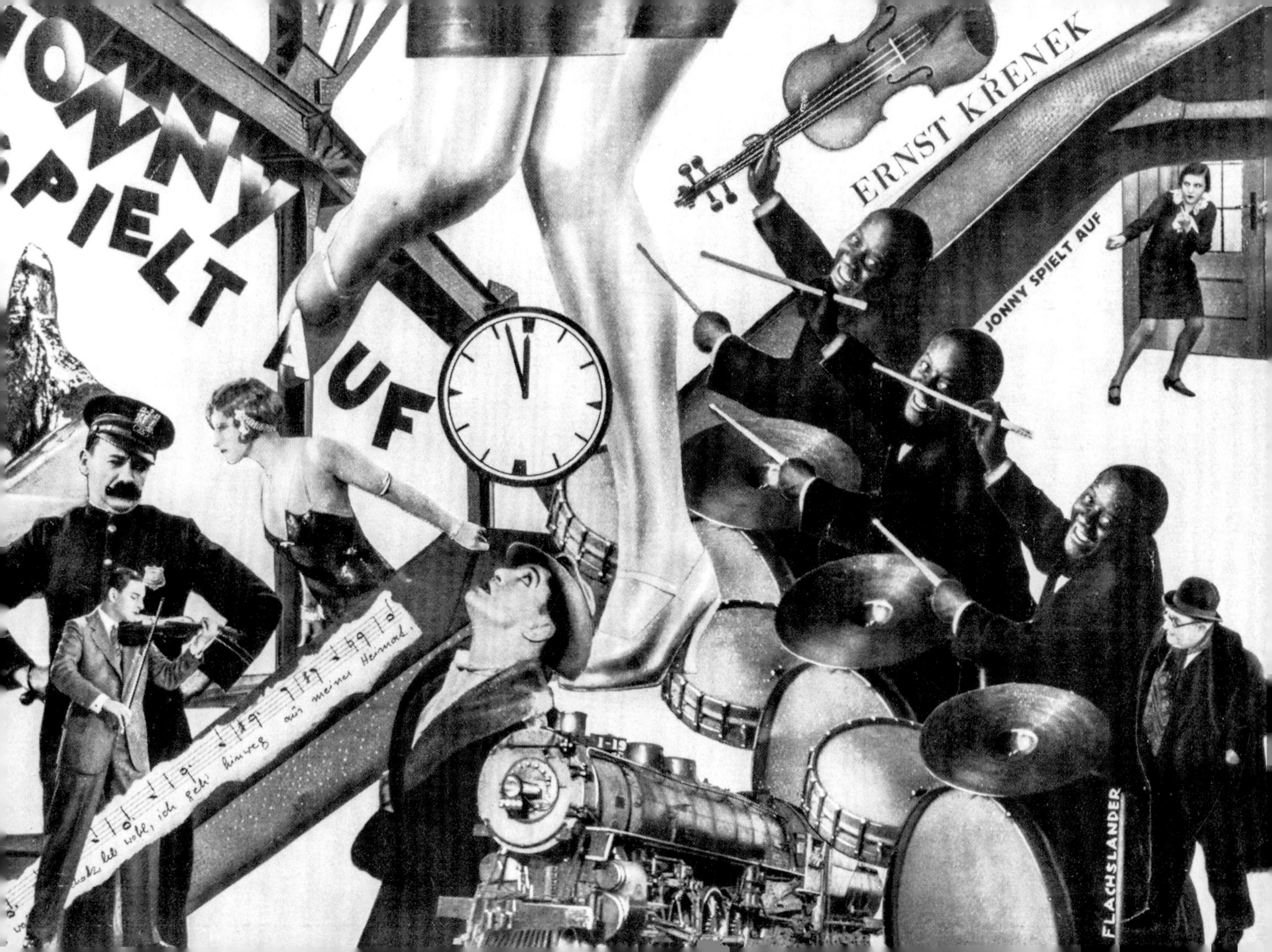

JONNY SPIELT AUF
ERNST KŘENEK
JONNY SPIELT AUF
willst du wohl, ich geh hinweg aus meiner Heimat.
FLACHSLANDER

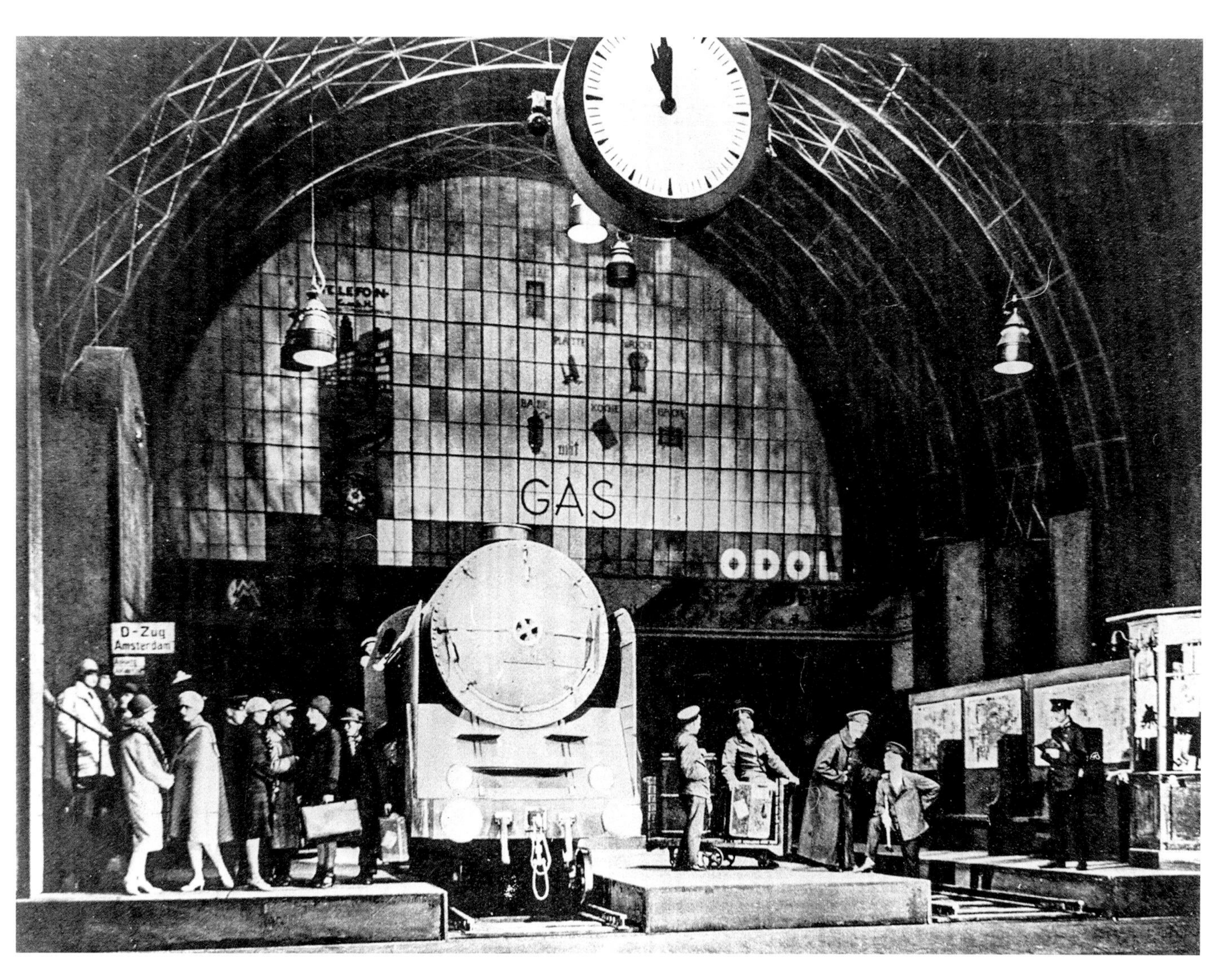

ERNST KŘENEK *Jonny spielt auf* (Jonny Strikes Up), Städtische Oper, Berlin, 1927
Stage photo from the opera

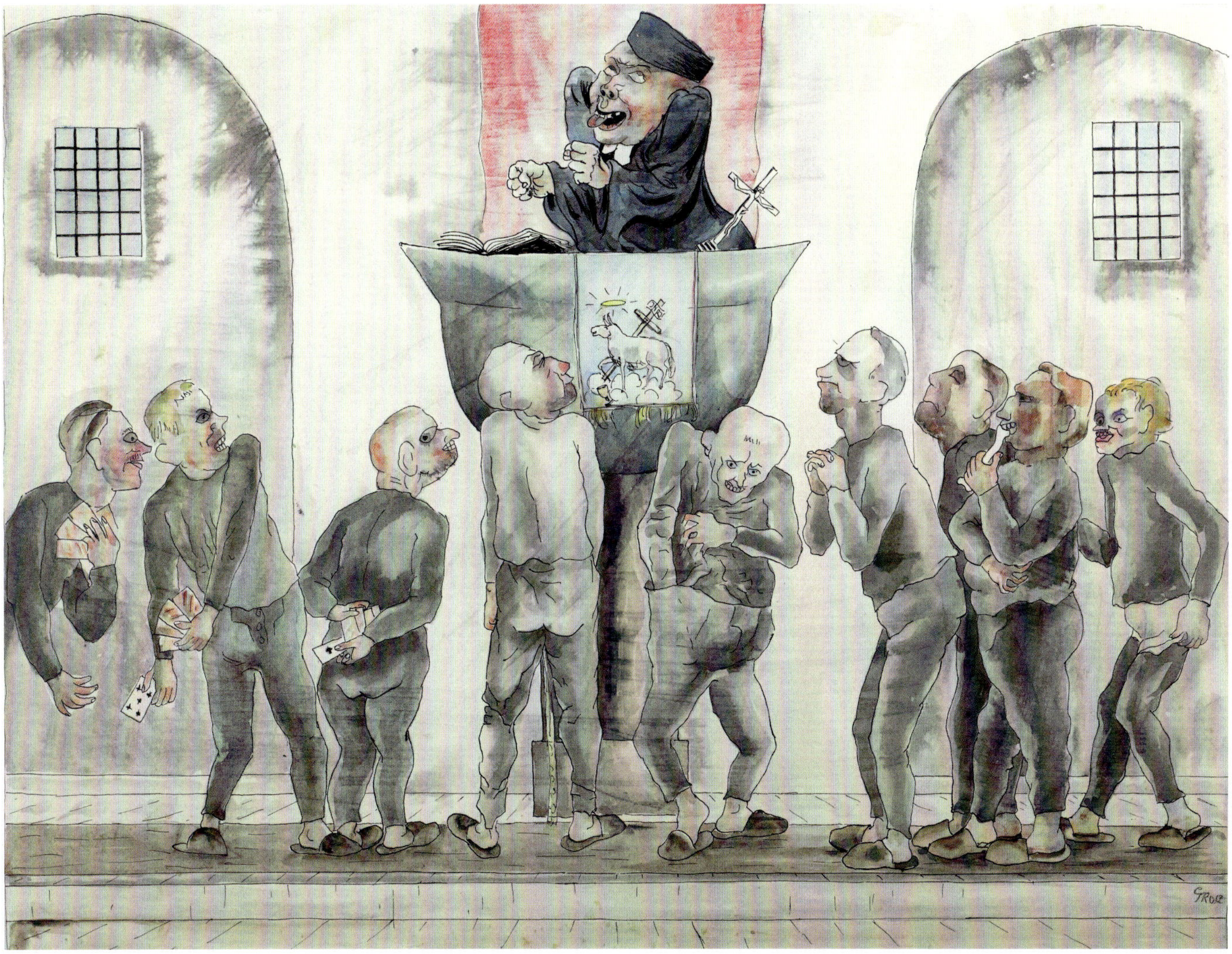

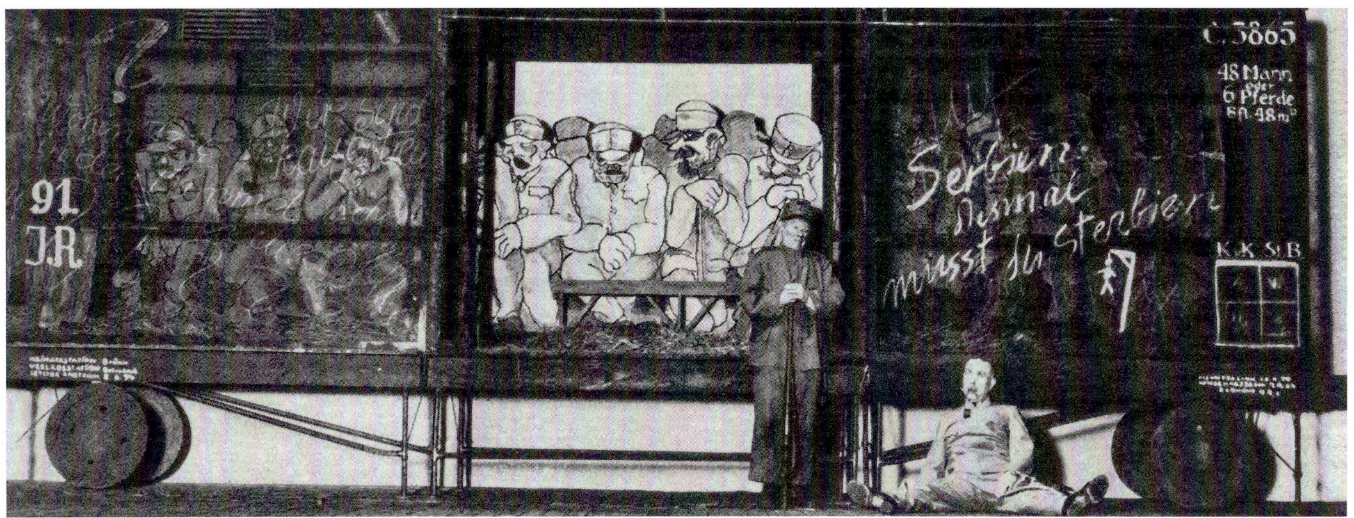

GEORGE GROSZ *Gefängniskapelle* (Prison Chapel), 1928
Set drawing for *Die Abenteuer des braven Soldaten Schwejk* (The Good Soldier Švejk) by Erwin Piscator

ERWIN PISCATOR *Die Abenteuer des braven Soldaten Schwejk* (The Good Soldier Švejk), Piscator-Bühne, Theater am Nollendorfplatz, Berlin, 1928
Stage photo with silhouettes drawn by George Grosz, on a stage equipped with a treadmill

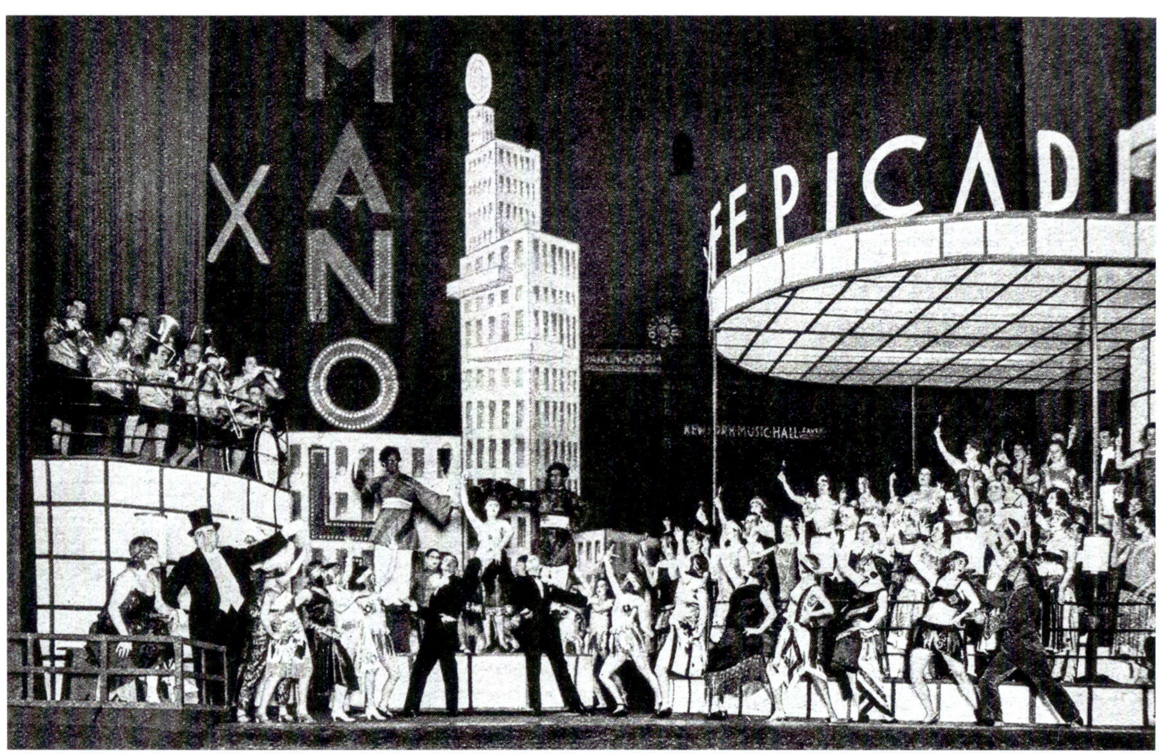

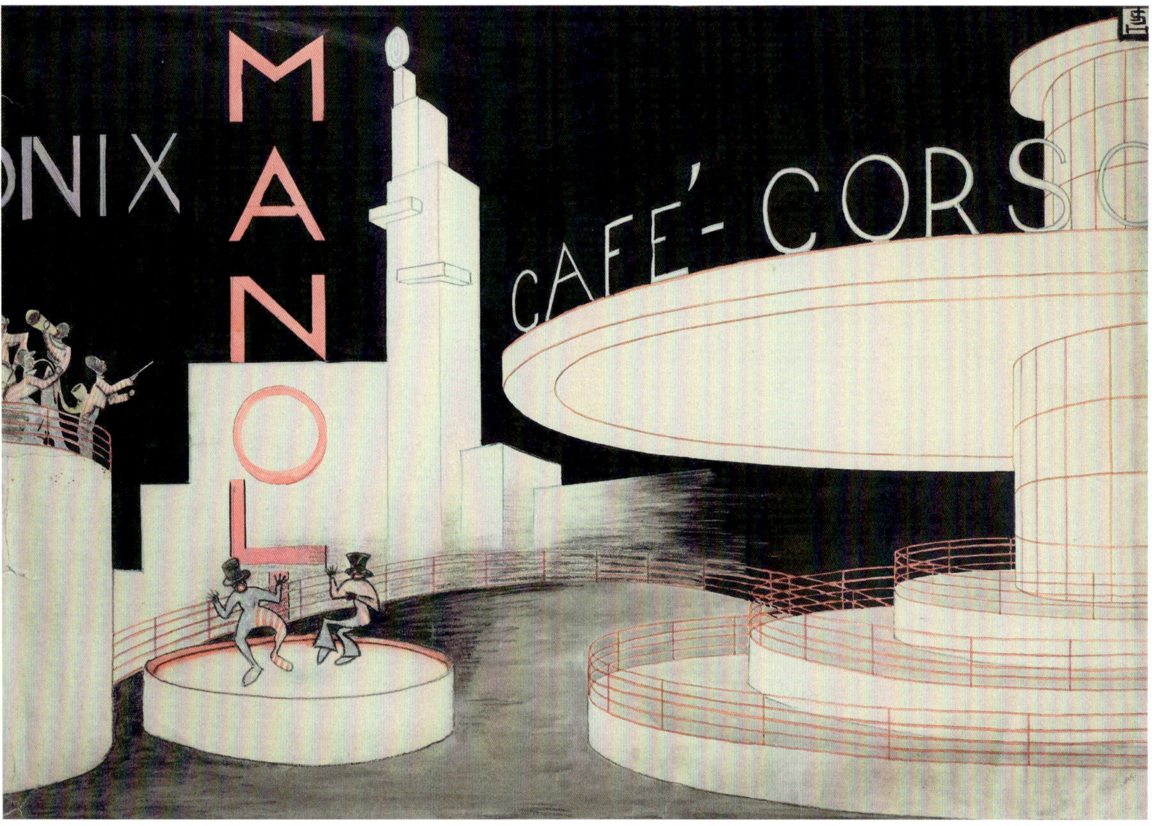

MAX BRAND *Maschinist Hopkins* (Machinist Hopkins), Vereinigte Stadttheater, Duisburg, 1929
Stage photo from the premiere of the opera

JOHANNES SCHRÖDER Set design for the opera *Maschinist Hopkins* (Machinist Hopkins) by Max Brand,
Vereinigte Stadttheater, Duisburg, c. 1929

Alfred Döblin:

Berlin Alexanderplatz (1929)

Boom boom goes the steam pile-driver outside Aschinger's on the Alex. It's as big as a house, and it drives the piles into the ground like nobody's business.

Glacial air. February. People in coats. Whoever owns a mink wears it, whoever doesn't, doesn't. The women wear thin stockings and are freezing, but it looks nice. The tramps have melted away. When it warms up, they'll stick their noses out. In the meantime they're on double rations of canned heat, but you wouldn't want to be the corpse pickling in that stuff.

Boom boom goes the steam pile-driver on the Alexanderplatz.

Lots of people take the time to watch the pile-driver at work. A man at the top keeps pulling on a chain, and bam! the pile gets one on the lid. Men and women stand there and boys especially and take pleasure in the easy motion: bam! the pile gets one on the lid. By the end it's no bigger than the tip of your finger, but it still gets another bam!, there's no getting around it. Finally, it's gone altogether. Crumbs, they got rid of that all right, and people move off satisfied.

Everything is boarded up. Berolina used to stand outside Tietz's, one hand out, a colossal wench, they've dragged her away. Maybe they'll melt her down to make medals out of.

They're everywhere, like a swarm of bees. Building and fiddling around the livelong day and night.

Boggler boggler go the trams, yellow ones with extra carriages, over the boarded-up Alexanderplatz. Do not dismount while vehicle is moving. The station is cut off, one-way street to Königstrasse, past Wertheim. If you're looking to go east, you need to follow Klosterstrasse round the back of the police headquarters. The trains boggle from the station to Jannowitz Bridge, the locomotives let off steam, it's slap bang on top of the Prälaten, Schlossbräu, entrance next block.

Across the road, they are knocking everything down, whole buildings along the S-Bahn are being demolished, where do they get the money from, Berlin is a rich city, and we pay our taxes.

Loeser & Wolff with the mosaic sign outside has been torn down and rebuilt twenty yards away, and there's another branch outside the station. Loeser & Wolff, Berlin-Elbing, first-class products in all types, Brazil, Havana, Mexico, Little Comfort, Liliput, No. 8s, 25 pfennigs apiece, Winter Ballad, packs of 25, 20 pfennigs, cigarillos No. 10, unsorted, Sumatra leaf, a special at the price, in boxes of a hundred, 10 pfennigs. I beat all comers, you beat all comers, he beats all comers with boxes of 50 and packs of 10, despatched to anywhere in the world, Boyero 25 pfennigs, this new product has made many converts, I beat all comers, you beat flat.

There is space next to the Prälaten, that's where the carts are with the bananas. Give your kids bananas. The banana is the most sanitary of fruits, its peel protects it from insects, worms and germs. (Except such insects, worms and germs as penetrate the peel.) Dr Czerny advises that even the very youngest infants may. I smash everything, you smash everything, he/she/it smashes everything.

The Alex is always windy, on the corner in front of Tietz's there's a howling gale. The wind blows in between the buildings onto the digs. You feel like taking shelter in a bar, but who can afford to do that, the wind blows the cash out of your pockets instead, you notice there's something going on here, no faffing about, you need to be up for it in this weather. Early in the morning the workers roll in from Reinickendorf, Neukölln, Weissensee. Cold or not cold, wind or no wind, coffee can out, pack me lunch, we gotta work, the parasites sit up at the top, they sleep in their featherbeds and leech us dry.

[...]

He tumbled into bed, grunted, groaned. She scratched her throat: 'You do make me laugh. You can lie still a moment. I'm not bothered.' She laughed, extended her plump arms, pushed her stockinged feet out of the bed. 'It's not my fault.'

Out on the street! Air! It's still raining. What can the matter be? I better find myself another one. Have a good sleep. Franz, my boy, what's wrong with you?

Sexual potency in the male is produced by the following, working in concert: 1. the glandular system, 2. the nervous system and 3. the sexual organs. The glands involved are: the pituitary, the thyroid, the suprarenal, the prostate, the seminal vesicle and the epididymis. The lead role is taken by the sperm gland, the entire sexual apparatus from cerebral cortex to genitals is activated by its secretions. The erotic trigger releases the erotic tension of the cerebral cortex, the charge moves in the form of sexual excitement from the cerebral cortex to the switch centre in the interbrain. This charge then funnels down the spine. Not unimpeded, because before it quits the brain, it needs to pass the inhibitors, mainly intellectual inhibitors, moral scruples, lack of self-confidence, fear of humiliation, fear of infection and pregnancy, etc. etc. play a great part.

Then dawdled down Elsasser Strasse at night. Don't hang about, mate, don't pretend to be tired. 'How much you asking?' The dark-haired one is good, the hips on her like a pretzel. If a girl's got a guy she likes. 'You're in a good mood, darling. You must have come into some money.' 'Sure I have. I'm good for a thaler.' 'Why not.' But he's still nervous.

And then up in her room, flowers behind the curtains, tidy little room, sweet little room, she's even got a gramophone, she sings for him, in Bemberg's artificial silk stockings, blouse off, eyes blacker than kohl: 'You know, I'm a shantoose. Guess where? Anywhere that takes my fancy. I'm just between engagements now. I go to bars I like, and then I enquire. And then: my song. I've got a song. Hey, stop tickling me.' 'Come on, cut it out.' 'No, hands off, that's bad for business. My song, be nice, sweetie, I conduct a proper auction in the bar, no passing round a hat. Anyone who can afford it gets to kiss me. Wild, eh. In the public bar. None under fifty pfennigs. I get it every time. Here on my shoulder. You can, too.' She puts on a gentleman's top hat, cackles in his face, waggles her hips, arms akimbo: 'Theodor whatever did you have in mind when you eyed me up last night? Theodor what have you gone and done, you rotter when you trett me to champagne and trotters.'

The way she perches on his lap, sticks a cigarette in her bill that she's sneaked out of his weskit, looks meltingly in his eye, rubs her earlobes softly against his, tootles: 'Do you know what homesickness is? Homesickness that breaks your heart? Everything around feels so cold and empty.' She trills, stretches out on the chaise. She smokes, strokes his hair, trills, laughs.

ALFRED DÖBLIN *Berlin Alexanderplatz*. Translated after *Berlin Alexanderplatz. Die Geschichte vom Franz Biberkopf* by Michael Hofmann. Penguin 2018, pp. 169 & 29.

Alfred Döblin's (1878-1957) New Objectivity masterwork tracks convicted murderer Franz Biberkopf through a pulsating, chaotic Berlin. Mirroring the New Objectivity's realistic portrayal of life, Döblin mixes cabaret songs, dive-bar dinner specials, textbook writing and statistics with advertising slogans and newspaper headlines. The novel portrays the hard lives of day labourers, the unemployed, prostitutes and criminals in a style that has been likened to James Joyce's *Ulysses* (1922).

Irmgard Keun:

Gilgi, One of Us (1931)

Gilgi is sitting in the streetcar. Actually she wanted to walk, but she's run out of time. Next to her, in front of her, the line-up of office workers. Tired faces, discouraged faces. Each one resembles the next. Their daily routines are the same, their emotions are the same, they look mass-produced. Any new passengers – anyone else without a ticket? None of them like doing what they do. None of them like being what they are. Little pale girl with the nice legs, wouldn't you rather stay in bed and have a proper sleep? Suntanned girl with the hiking shoes, looks like it'll be a nice day today – wouldn't you rather take a long walk in the city forest and feed the tame deer with the chestnuts you collected in the fall?

Anyone else without a ticket – anyone else without a ticket? They're riding to work. Day after day, to work. Each day resembles the next. Dingadingding – they get off, they get on. They ride the streetcar. Ride and ride. Eight-hour day, typewriter, steno pad, salary cut, end of the month – always the same thing, always the same thing. Yesterday, today, tomorrow — and in ten years.

You young ones, the ones under thirty, is this dispirited early-morning face all you've got too? It's Sunday tomorrow. Won't little images of your desires light up your eyes this afternoon?

I mean, young man, you don't buy yourself such a beautiful, lustrous yellow necktie if you don't secretly believe that one day you'll be the boss, with your own car and a foreign bank account, do you? I mean, nice girl from a good family, you wouldn't put on that pretty necklace if you weren't hoping that a man would come and say that it suits you perfectly, would you? Little redhead, would you have spent twenty marks on that perm if you weren't dreaming of a beauty pageant and a film contract? Greta Garbo was a salesclerk once too. The ride to work. Day after day. Will something come to break the monotony of the days? What? Mr. Douglas Fairbanks, a lottery win, a film contract, the dreamed-of promotion, the shower of gold from heaven? Will that come? No. Is there no prospect of a change or a break? Yes, there is. What is it? Illness, rationalization, unemployment. But you're still riding to work. Yes, still. That's good.

Gilgi looks out the window. The hopeless people in the streetcar — no, she has nothing in common with them, she doesn't belong with them, she doesn't want to belong with them. They're gray and tired and lifeless. And if they're not lifeless, they're waiting for a miracle. Gilgi isn't lifeless, and she doesn't believe in miracles. She only believes in what she creates and what she earns. She isn't satisfied, but she's pleased. She's earning money.

You people in the streetcar, aren't you happy?
We're so tired.
But you're earning money, aren't you?
It's so little.
You could turn that little into more.
That's so hard.
That's what makes it fun.
It's not fun.
Times are tough. No-one likes being what they are. No-one likes doing what they do.

IRMGARD KEUN *Gilgi, One of Us*. Translated after *Gilgi, Eine von uns* by Geoff Wilkes. Penguin 2019, p. 7.

Irmgard Keun's (1905-1982) debut novel follows young, ambitious Gilgi, a secretary by day and language student by night, when she's not going to cafés and meeting male suitors. Gilgi represents the new generation of women challenging gender roles and family patterns. Branded "asphalt literature" by the National Socialists, Keun's novel was denounced as decadent big-city literature, anti-German and disloyal to traditional German values.

Christopher Isherwood:

Goodbye to Berlin (1939)

Autum 1930

From my window, the deep solemn massive street. Cellar-shops where the lamps burn all day, under the shadow of top-heavy balconied façades, dirty plaster frontages embossed with scroll-work and heraldic devices. The whole district is like this: street leading into street of houses like shabby monumental safes crammed with the tarnished valuables and secondhand furniture of a bankrupt middle class.

I am a camera with its shutter open, quite passive, recording, not thinking. Recording the man shaving at the window opposite and the woman in the kimono washing her hair. Some day, all this will have to be developed, carefully printed, fixed.

CHRISTOPHER ISHERWOOD *Goodbye to Berlin*. Vintage Classics 1969, p. 7.

The British writer Christopher Isherwood (1904-1987) lived in Berlin from 1929 to 1933, finding a haven as a gay man in the city's creative, flamboyant nightlife. Set in the last years of the Weimar Republic before the onset of the Nazi regime, this partly autobiographical novel portrays a rapidly changing society on the verge of collapse. Hailed as one of the greatest Berlin classics, the novel is the source of the musical *Cabaret*, later adapted into the 1972 film starring Liza Minnelli as cabaret singer Sally Bowles.

Bertolt Brecht:

"700 intellectuals worship an oil tank" (1928)

Uninvited
We have come
700 (and many more still on their way)
From wherever there is no wind of change
From the mills that grind slowly and where
No sleeper awakes.

And suddenly overnight
We behold you
Oil tank.

Yesterday you were not there
But today
There is only you.

Hasten hither all you
Who are sawing off the branch you are sitting on
Workers!
God has come again
In the form of an oil tank.

Ugly one
You are the loveliest!
Do us violence
Lord of the facts!
Extinguish the ego
Make us collective.
For not as we will
But as you will.

You are not made of ivory
And ebony but of
Iron.
Gory! Glory! Glory!
Unprepossessing as you are.

You are not invisible
Nor without end
But seven metres high.
There is no mystery in you
There is oil.
And you deal with us
Not at your own discretion nor inscrutably
But by calculation.

What is grass to you?
You sit on it.
Where formerly there was grass
There you sit now, oil tank
And in your presence a feeling
Is nothing.

Hear us therefore
And deliver us from the evil of the spirit
In the name of electrification and statistics
Forwards with Ford!

BERTOLT BRECHT Translated after "700 Intellektuelle beten einen Öltank an" by David Constantine in Tom Kuhn, David Constantine & Charlotte Ryland (ed.): *The Collected Poems of Bertolt Brecht*. Liveright Publishing Corporation 2019, p. 330.

Poet, director and playwright Bertolt Brecht (1898-1956) was one of the most influential and controversial writers in Germany. Producing radio shows, Brecht, a Marxist, saw the new mass medium as a vehicle for raising public awareness. But, as in this satirical poem, he also exposed the uncritical fascination with technology as harmful mass hysteria. Brecht presents a clear-cut example of the ambivalence that Americanization and mass industry fostered in 1920s Germany.

Marieluise Fleißer:

An Adornment for the Club:

A Novel on Smoking, Exercising, Loving and Selling (1931/1972)

To the side, the meadow slopes downwards. Across it, the year's first crocuses are
blooming, and now the flowering succession of colors will not stop changing until autumn.
The city gardener puts a lot of work into this open meadow.

From time to time, something can be heard falling into the water, followed by
angry splashing.

"It's the rats", says Gustl.

His fingers, stubby and coarse and smelling of tobacco, seem more delicate when he reaches
for her hand. His expression becomes increasingly romantic. He even throws away his half-smoked
cigarette. In a minute he'll be walking on air.

Frieda doesn't look like she'll be walking on air. What's wrong with Frieda today?

When she sits down, her coat opens slightly, and a cold draft chills her legs, Frieda stands
up again and wraps the long coat closely around her calves. She can't move.

Is this it for Gustl's love life in February?

"You have to understand me", says Frieda.

Gustl understands everything about her. It is no small thing to sit outdoors for hours at this
time of year just so she can be in his esteemed company.

Gustl has toughened up. It's different with him. In March, he'll be chopping up the ice so that
he can put on a show in the winter water, this lunatic. He doesn't charge admission. He darts around
in the wetness like a fish while the other shore inhabitants gasp for air in the cold. Red as a lobster,
he climbs out before their astonished eyes, jeering into their faces with his naked skin.

He hasn't been pampered like the young kids. Sheer will has steeled his body against feeling.
He can't be so rough with Frieda, he knows this.

"Do you have on sturdy shoes?", he asks, concerned.

Frieda: "The long ones."

Gustl: "Who knows why you bought them for yourself. They're men's shoes."

"You just don't get it again. They're in now. In the city, people are wearing them already."

"Yes", Gustl says, "But don't they look like you have to get up and dance the
Shimmy in them?"

MARIELUISE FLEIßER Translated after *Eine Zierde für den Verein. Roman vom Rauchen, Sporteln, Lieben und Verkaufen*
by Elizabeth Volk, 2022.

The only novel by Marieluise Fleißer (1901-1974) is set in her hometown, the small city of Ingolstadt. Gustl, a local
swimming champion, and Frieda, a car-driving flour saleswoman, make an odd couple. In a cool, quirky style, Fleißer
portrays Frieda as a liberated *Neue Frau*, a New Woman, who dresses in a man's coat and shoes, wears her hair short and
runs her own business. In 1924, Fleißer, mainly a travel writer and playwright, met Bertolt Brecht, who became an important
figure in her life and career. Brecht directed her play *Pioneers in Ingolstadt* (1929), whose overtly sexual theme caused one
of the biggest theatrical scandals of the Weimar Republic. Brecht left Fleißer to deal with the press storm, which reportedly
ended their friendship. A few years before her death, Fleißer published a revised edition of *Ein Zierde für den Verein*
(An Adornment to the Club), in which she called places and persons by their real names. This excerpt is from that edition.

Erich Kästner:

"Matter-of-Fact Romance" (1928)

Once they had gotten to know one another
(and after eight years, one might say: quite well)
abruptly their love went missing one day.
Like some people lose a hat or a cane.

They cheated with joy, united in grief
tried kissing as if the end wasn't nigh,
and looked at each other in sheer disbelief.
She started crying. And he stood nearby.

Out of the window to ships you could wave
He pointed out it was quarter past four
and about time to have coffee someplace.
Someone was playing the piano next door.

They went into town, the smallest café
stirring around in their cup with a spoon.
They sat there until the end of the day
Sitting together with nothing to say
And simply couldn't believe it was true.

ERICH KÄSTNER Translated after "Sachliche Romanze".

Erich Kästner's (1899-1974) 1928 poem, with its simple, easy-to-understand language, is typical for poetry of the New Objectivity period. Practically didactic, it is devoid of psychology and romance. Beyond poetry, Kästner is known for the novel *Fabian*, whose titular protagonist is a moralist, melancholic and pacifist. The novel portrays Germany's rampant inflation, unemployment and abject poverty, yet its tone is joyful and sometimes absurd. Even the tragicomic ending, where Fabian, having finally decided to make a difference, drowns trying to rescue a small boy (who, it turns out, actually knows how to swim), is written in an unsentimental, ironic style that is typical of Kästner's work and the New Objectivity writers.

Vicki Baum:

Grand Hotel (1929)

Odd creatures, women, thought Gaigern behind the curtain. Strange animals. What can she see in the glass to make such a frightful face over?

He himself saw her as a beautiful woman, undeniably beautiful, even though the makeup on her cheeks was beginning to run. Her neck, above all, reflected twice over in the side mirrors, was incomparably delicate and flexible. Grusinskaya fixed her eyes on her face as though on the face of an enemy. With horror she saw the telltale years, the wrinkles, the flabbiness, the fatigue, the withering; her temples were smooth no longer, the corners of her mouth were disfigured, her eyelids, under the blue makeup, were as creased as crumpled tissue paper. Another fit of shuddering, more violent than the previous one in the street, came over her while she looked at herself. She tried to control her lips but could not. She hurried across the room and hastily turned out the uncompromising light suspended from the ceiling and turned on the table lamp, but even this did not lend any warmth. With a few impatient movements she tore off her costume and went naked, but for the tights that covered her as far as her hips, to the radiator and leaned her breast against the gray-colored pipes. She scarcely thought at all as she did so. She only desired warmth. Enough, she thought, enough. Never again. Finished. Enough. She whispered her irrevocable decision in every language, her teeth chattering all the while. She went into the bathroom and undressed completely. She held her hands under the hot tap and let the warmth flow over her arteries till it began to hurt. She took a friction brush and rubbed her shoulders with it. Then, suddenly, she left off in a fit of disgust and came back naked and shivering and went straight across the room to the telephone. She had to put her lips twice to the telephone before she could speak.

"Tea," she said. "A lot of tea and a lot of sugar."

"Then, still naked, she went to the mirror and looked in it with gloomy intensity. Her body, however, was of unique and faultless beauty. It was the body of a sixteen-year-old ballet pupil, which the severe and disciplined work of a lifetime had preserved unaltered. Suddenly the hatred she felt for herself changed into tenderness. She clasped her shoulders and stroked their smooth sheen. She kissed the hollow of her right arm and cupped her hands like shells to receive her small and perfect breasts. She stroked the delicate upward curve of her stomach and her slender shadowed hips. She bent her head down and kissed her poor slim sinewy knees as though they were sick children whom she loved. *"Bjednaiaia, malenkaia,"* she murmured to them. It was an endearment from her early days. You poor one, you little one, it meant.

Unconsciously Gaigern, between the curtains, showed pity and admiration in his face. He was embarrassed by what he saw. He knew many women, but he had never seen one whose body was so delicately and perfectly formed. Yet this was really a secondary consideration. It was the helplessness, the lost and tremulous despair of this pitiful Grusinskaya as she stood before the mirror that impressed him most. It inspired a sweet and painful sympathy and made him flush to his ears. Though he was a crook, ready to carry off stolen pearls worth five hundred thousand marks in his pocket, Gaigern was far from being inhuman. He let go of the pearls and took his hands out of his pockets. He felt in his hands and in his arms a compelling desire to support this poor lonely woman, to take her away and console and warm her – to do anything to put a stop to that terrible shuddering and almost crazed, despairing whispering.

The room-service waiter knocked at the outer door. Grusinskaya put on her dressing gown – the same one that had startled Gaigern in the darkness – and went to the door in her worn slippers. The tea was discreetly handed in and Grusinskaya locked the door behind the retreating waiter. It had come to this, she thought. She poured out a cup of tea and took a vial of Veronal from the bedside table. She swallowed a tablet, drank some tea, and then took a second. She got up and began to walk rapidly back and forth across the room, four paces this way, four paces that.

"What is the use of it all? she thought. What is the use of living? What is there to wait for? Why endure the torture? Oh, I am tired. You don't know, any of you, how tired I am. I promised myself to stop when the time came. Tiens, the time has come. Am I to wait till I am hissed off the stage? It is time, *malenkaia* – poor little one. Gru is not going to go to Vienna tomorrow. Gru gives up. Gru is going to sleep. You don't know how cold it is to be famous. Not a soul to care for me, not one. They all live off me. Nobody lives for me. Nobody. Not one."

VICKI BAUM *Grand Hotel*. Translated after *Menschen im Hotel* by Basil Creighton. New York Review Books 2016, EPub.

This novel, set in Berlin's exclusive Grand Hotel, gave the Austrian writer Vicki Baum (1888-1960) her big international breakthrough, boosted by the 1932 Oscar-winning adaptation starring Greta Garbo. Echoing the cool detachment of New Objectivity, Baum, in this excerpt from the novel, describes an ageing, world-famous ballerina, Gruzinskaya, being watched by Gaigern, a dashing, young thief. Breaking into her hotel room to steal her pearls, he is caught by surprise when she returns home early from that night's performance, having left before the final curtain – perhaps to end her life by swallowing a double dose of sleeping pills with her evening tea.

Hans Fallada:

Little Man – What Now? (1932)

He was one of millions. Ministers made speeches to him, enjoined him to tighten his belt, to make sacrifices, to feel German, to put his money in the savings-bank and to vote for the constitutional party.

Sometimes he did, sometimes he didn't, according to the circumstances, but he didn't believe what they said. Not in the least. His innermost conviction was: they all want something from me, but not for me. It's all the same to them whether I live or die. They couldn't care less whether I can afford to go to the cinema or not, whether Lammchen can get proper food or has too much excitement, whether the Shrimp is happy or miserable. Nobody gives a damn.

And all these people standing round in the Little Tiergarten, and a real zoo it was, full of proletarian animals rendered harmless by lack of food and lack of hope, they shared the same fate. Three months' unemployment and – goodbye, reddish-brown overcoat! Goodbye to any prospects for the future! Jachmann and Lehmann could have a quarrel on Wednesday evening, and suddenly I'll be worthless again. Goodbye.

These are my only comrades, these men here, though to them I'm stuck up, a proletarian in a suit with a starched white collar. But that's temporary. Only I know how little it means. Today, yes, today, I can earn a few bob, tomorrow, tomorrow, I'll be out of a Job ...

Perhaps he was still too new to living with Lammchen, but standing here looking at these people, he scarcely thought about her. And he wouldn't be able to tell her any of this. She wouldn't understand. However gentle she was, she was much tougher than him. She wouldn't stand here. She'd been in the Socialist Party, and the Anti-Fascist League but only because her father was in them, she actually belonged in the Communist Party. She had a few simple ideas: that most people are only bad because they have been made bad, that you shouldn't judge anybody because you never know what you would do yourself, that the rich and the powerful think ordinary people don't have the same feelings as they do – that's what Lammchen instinctively believed, though she hadn't thought it out. Lammchen's heart was with the Communists.

And that is why he couldn't tell her. Now he had to go to her and announce that he has a job, and they have reason to be happy. And he really is happy. But behind that happiness lies the fear: will it last?

No, of course it won't last. So, how long will it last?"

HANS FALLADA Translated after *Kleiner Mann – was nun?* by Susan Bennett, 1996. Melville House Publishing 2009, p. 148.

Hans Fallada's (1893-1947) protagonist, Johannes Pinneberg, is "one in a million" among the "white-collar proletariat", as Fallada sarcastically calls the type of functionary who, dressed in his nice shirt, feels superior to the proletariat. Like so many other Germans in the interwar years, Pinneberg and his beloved "Lämmchen" are weighed down by job insecurity and money troubles. Typical for the New Objectivity period, Fallada's novel has been referred to as gritty realism.

Es liegt in der Luft

Früher, das war'n einmal Zeiten!
Der Satz ist nicht zu bestreiten!
Man bestand von früh bis spät
Nur noch aus Nervosität
Starb ein Vögelchen im Bauer
Trug gleich die Familie Trauer
Heut' ist eine andere Zeit
Triffst zum Beispiel du Herrn Koch
Fragst du ihn voll Sachlichkeit:
„Was Herr Koch, sie leben noch?"

Es liegt in der Luft eine Sachlichkeit
Es liegt in der Luft eine Stachlichkeit
Es liegt in der Luft, es liegt in der Luft, in der Luft
Es liegt in der Luft was Idiotisches
Es liegt in der Luft was Hypnotisches
Es liegt in der Luft, es liegt in der Luft
Es geht nicht mehr raus aus der Luft!

Was ist heute in der Luft los?
Was liegt heute in der Luft bloß?
Durch die Lüfte sausen schon
Bilder, Radio, Telefon
Durch die Luft geht alles drahtlos
Und die Luft wird schon ganz ratlos
Flugzeug, Luftschiff, alles schon
Hört, wie's in den Lüften schwillt
Ferngespräch und Wagnerton
Und dazwischen saust ein Bild

Es liegt in der Luft eine Sachlichkeit [...]

Fort mit Schnörkel, Stuck und Schaden
Glatt baut man die Hausfassaden
Nächstens baut man Häuser bloß
Ganz und gar fassadenlos
Krempel sind wir überdrüssig
Viel zu viel ist überflüssig
Fort die Möbel aus der Wohnung
Fort, mit was nicht hingehört
Ich behaupte ohne Schonung:
„Jeder Mensch, der da ist, stört!"

It's in the Air

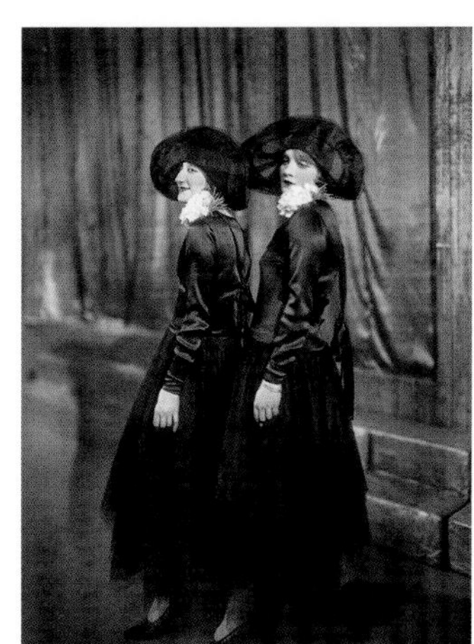

Things were so different back in the day!
Cast all your doubts on that fact far away!
Everyone I know from morning till night
Was nothing but a big bundle of fright
If in its cage a bird were to die
For days on end, the whole family would cry
But nowadays, in this new generation
If past Mr. Koch you were to drive
This'd be your objective interrogation:
"What, Mr. Koch, you're still alive?"

There's an objectivity floating in the air
There's a thorniness floating in the air
It's in the air, it's in the air, in the air
There's something silly floating in the air
There's something hypnotic floating in the air
It's in the air, it's in the air
It's in the air and not going anywhere!

What ever happened to the air today?
What did they put in the air today?
Zipping through the air and the walls
Images, radios, telephone calls
Flying through the air without a wire
The air feels like it's been set on fire
Aeroplanes, airships floating around
Hear their sound growing, it's getting loud
Long distance calls and Wagner sound
Look at that image zip through the clouds

There's an objectivity floating in the air [...]

Away with the flourish, the stucco, the blemished
All the façades are now sleek and polished
Before you know it, heed my calls
Façades will be nothing but vertical walls
All these trinkets make us weary
So many things we find unnecessary
Throw out the furniture, out on the streets
Empty the house, down to its core
Hear my opinion, I won't lie anymore:
"Even the humans trouble the peace!"

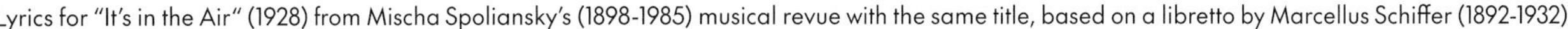

Lyrics for "It's in the Air" (1928) from Mischa Spoliansky's (1898-1985) musical revue with the same title, based on a libretto by Marcellus Schiffer (1892-1932)

MISCHA SPOLIANSKY (composer) and **MARCELLUS SCHIFFER** (librettist) *Es liegt in der Luft*
(It's in the Air), Komödie am Kurfürstendamm, Berlin, 1928
Stage photo with Margo Lion and Marlene Dietrich

THE NEW OBJECTIVITY ARTISTS were particularly interested in the still life genre. Inspired by the hyper-realistic fidelity of photography, painters seized upon the visual language of the camera, and an intense dialogue was established between the two media. None of them, however, presented objects according to a purely mimetic logic; rather, they often placed them in strange spaces, which seem both empty and under tension, in compositions with incoherent perspectives.

Cacti and rubber plants were very popular in Germany in the 1920s, where they were seen as the vegetal equivalent of crystalline stone: architectural, geometric, and abstract. Xaver Fuhr (1898-1973) and Alexander Kanoldt (1881-1939) painted ficus plants with great meticulousness in pure compositions that reveal their clear structure. Georg Scholz (1890-1945) emphasises the stiffness of the cactus, in keeping with the rigid pictorial style of New Objectivity. The enigmatic aspect of these plants is often heightened by placing them in deliberately empty surroundings. In *Urformen der Kunst* (Art Forms in Nature, 1928), Karl Blossfeldt (1865-1932) photographed plants in close-up against a neutral background, making them appear inanimate, strangely inert.

This reified nature is part of a broader fascination with the world of objects. In his album *Die Welt ist schön* (The World is Beautiful, 1928), Albert Renger-Patzsch (1897-1966) captures standardised, mass-produced industrial products. Photographers and painters were also interested in glass objects, light bulbs and crockery. This fascination with transparency, also evident in Ella Bergmann-Michel's (1896-1972) films on modern architecture, reflects a desire to depict objects unfiltered, with objectivity.

GEORG SCHOLZ *Kakteen und Semaphore* (Cactuses and Signal Masts), 1923

STILL LIFE

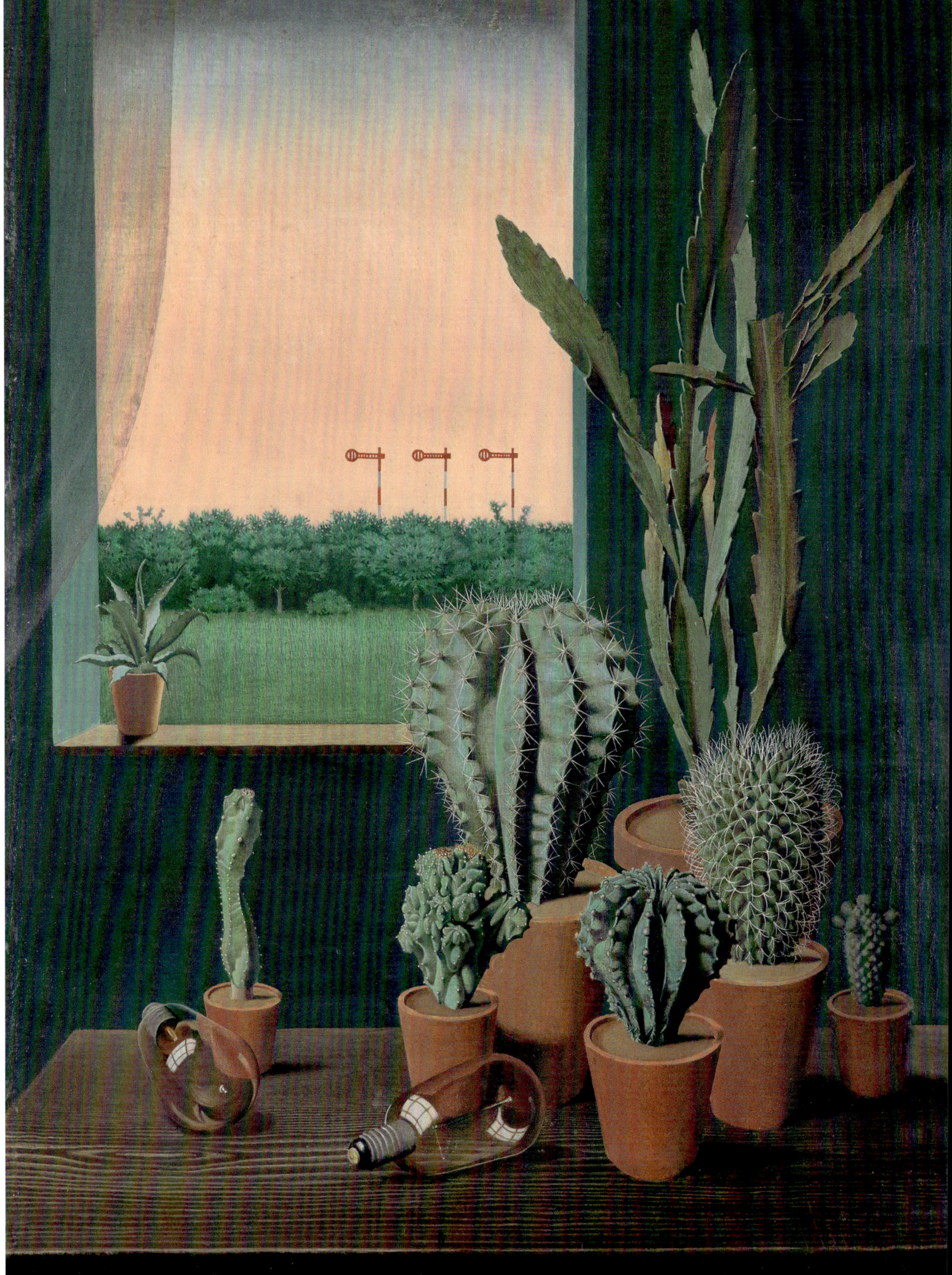

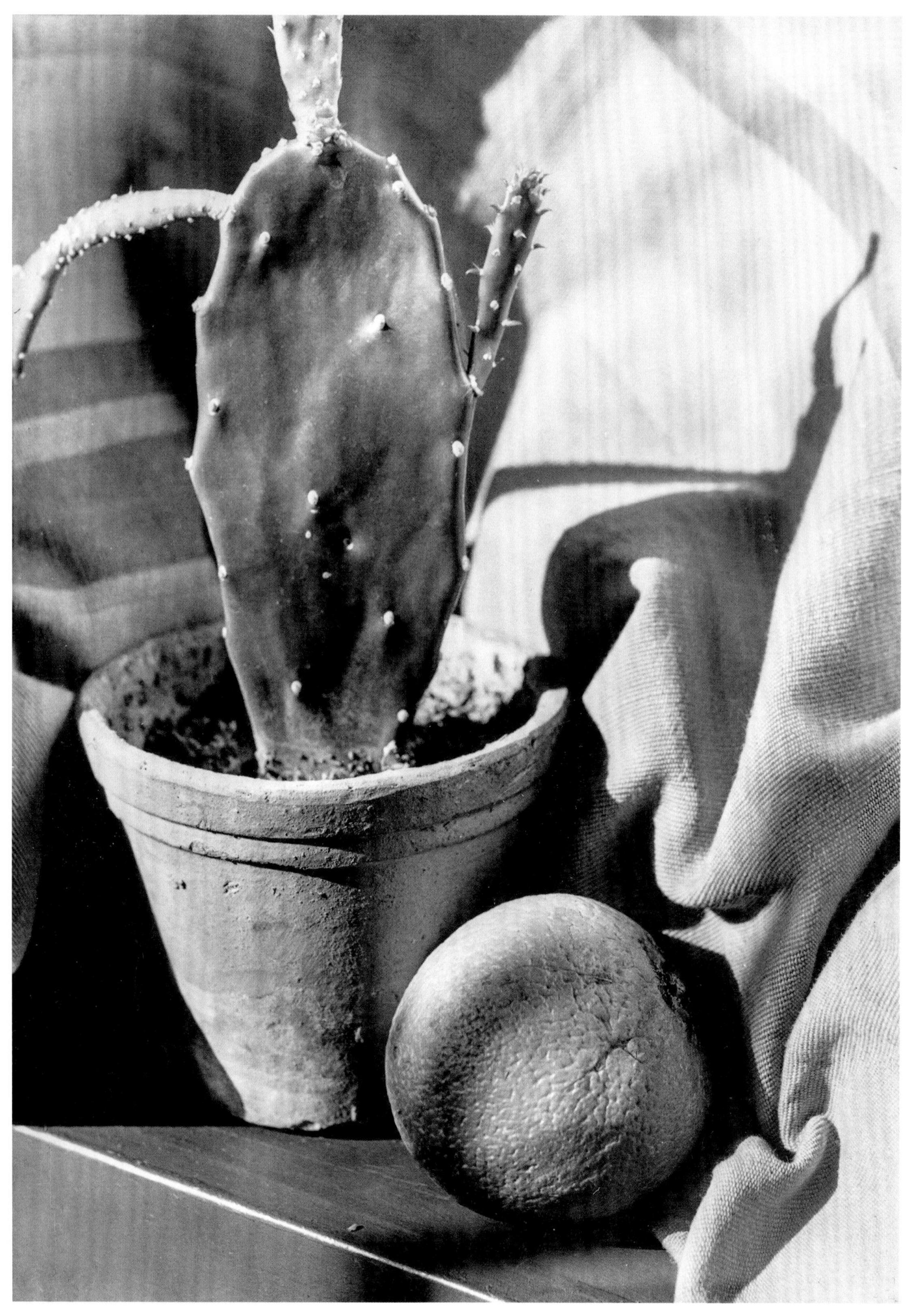

WILLY ZIELKE *Stillleben (Kaktus und Orange) (Still Life (Cactus and Orange))*, c. 1930
Gelatin silver print, 11.9 × 8.9 cm. Galerie Berinson, Berlin

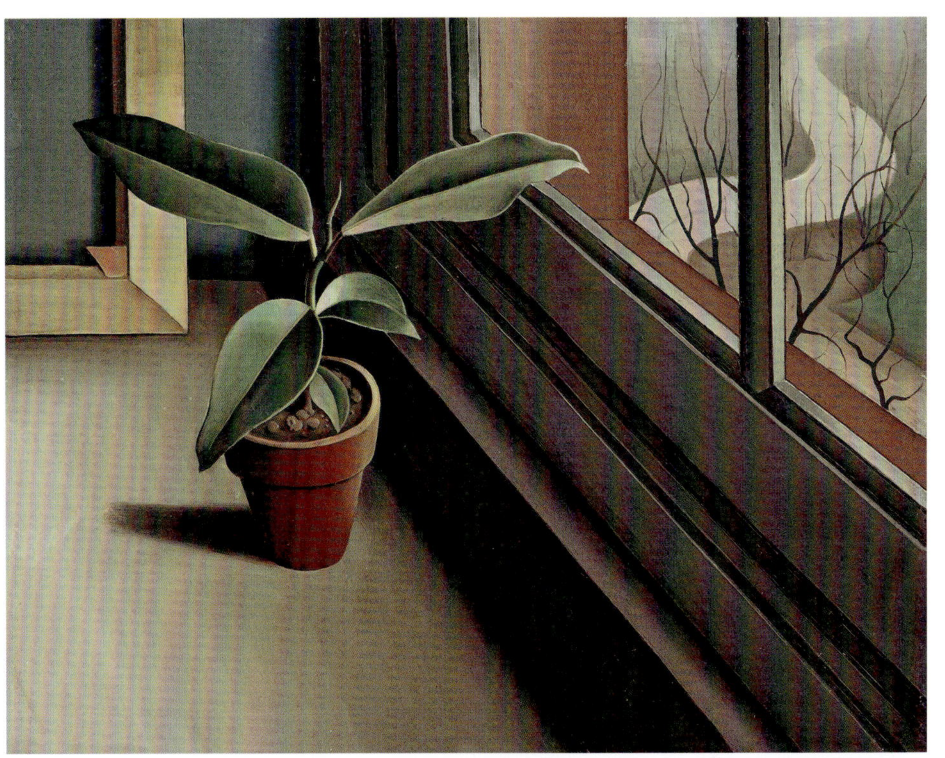

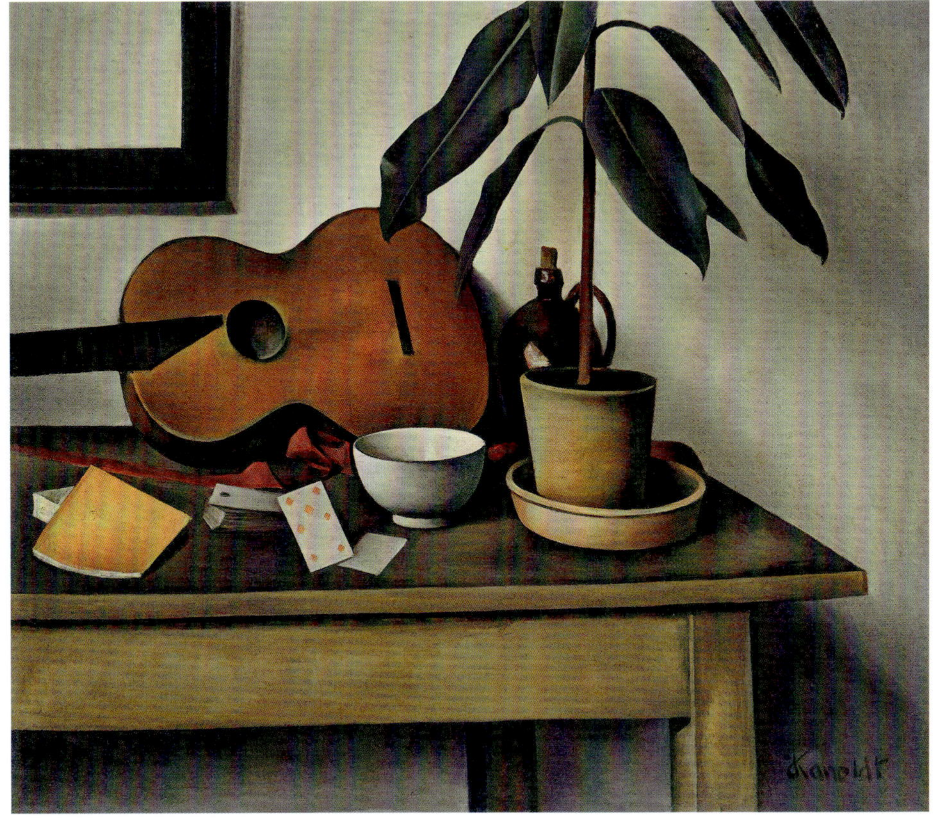

FRANZ XAVER FUHR *Stillleben (Gummibaum) (Still Life (Rubberplant))*, c. 1925
ALEXANDER KANOLDT *Stillleben mit Gitarre (Still Life with Guitar)*, 1926

61

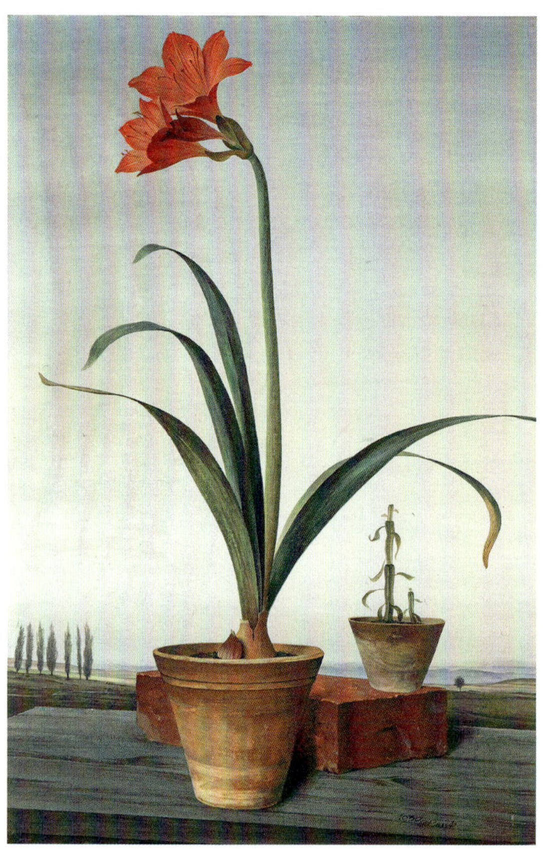

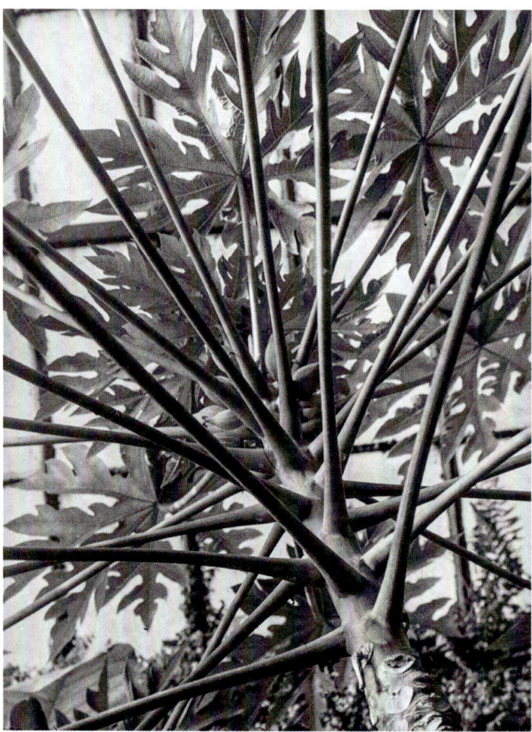

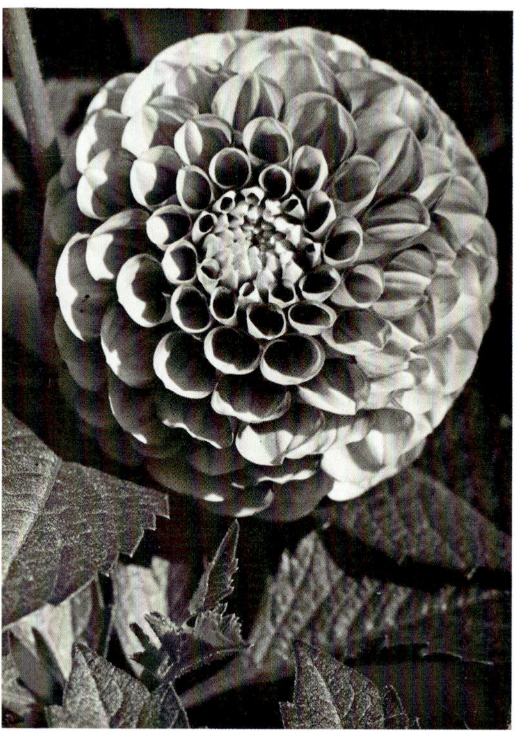

FRANZ LENK *Amaryllis,* 1930
ALBERT RENGER-PATZSCH *Brasilianischer Melonenbaum von unten gesehen* (Brazilian Melon Tree Seen from Below), 1923
Gelatin silver print, 22.2 × 17.1 cm. Galerie Berinson, Berlin
Dahlia variabilis. Asteraceae, 1923
Gelatin silver print, 23.2 × 17 cm. Galerie Berinson, Berlin

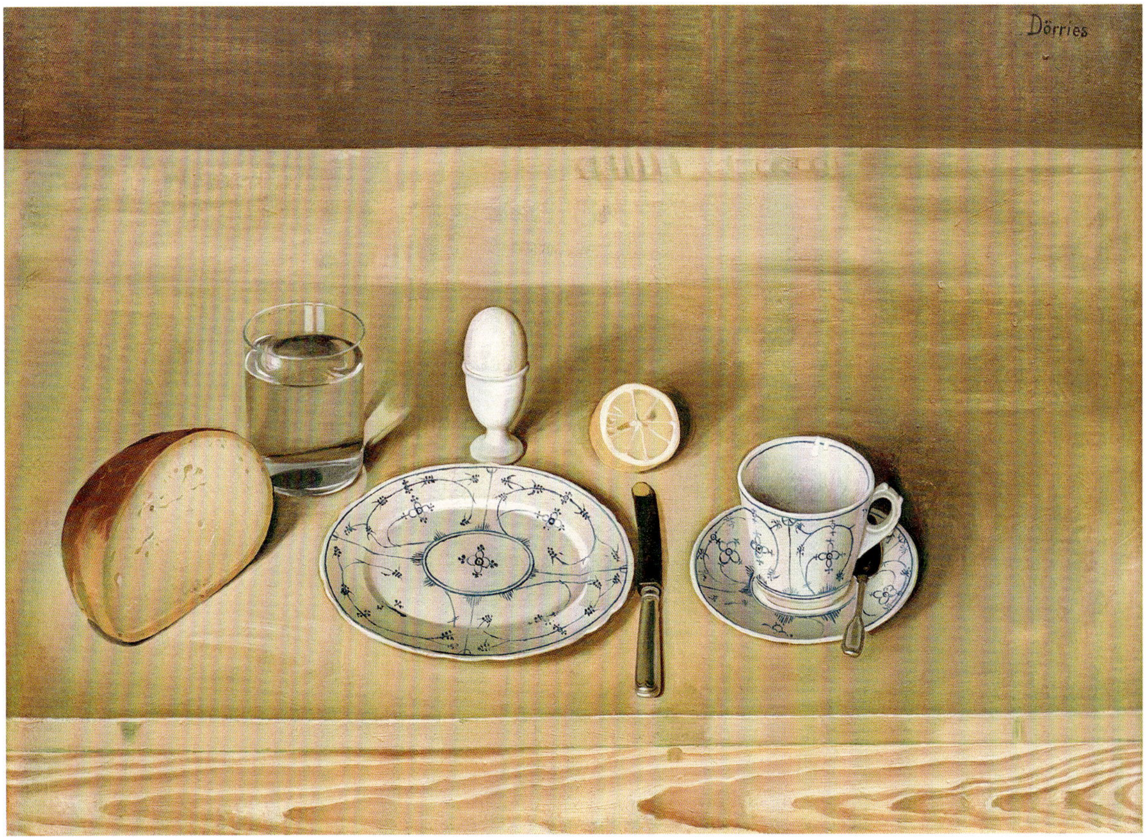

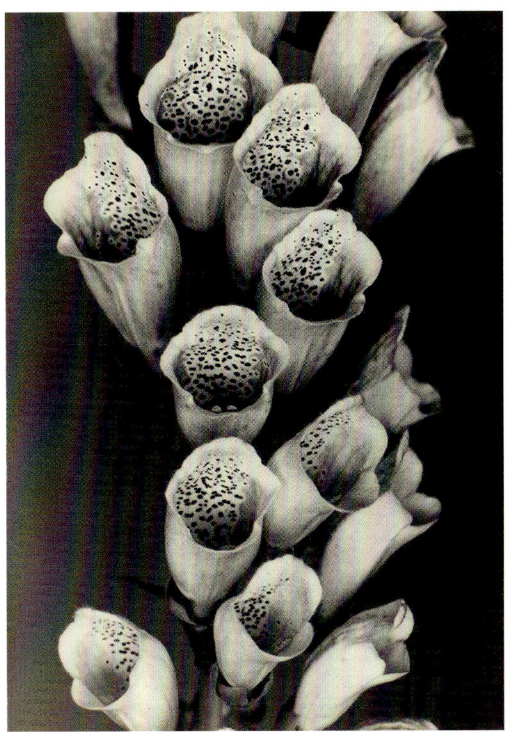

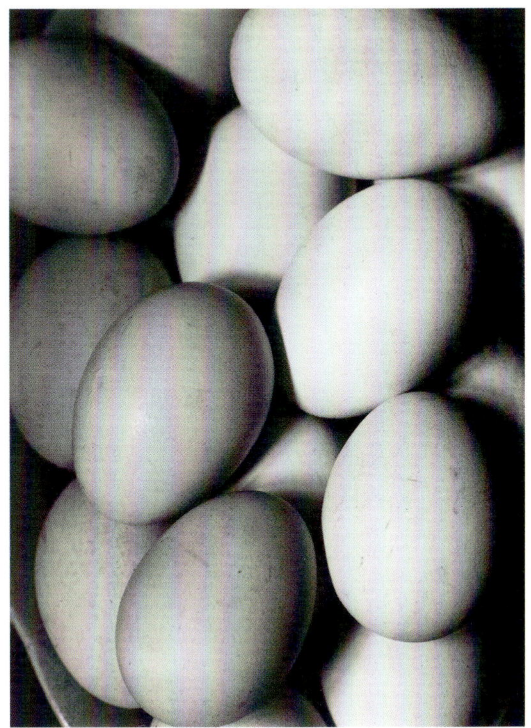

BERNHARD DÖRRIES *Frühstücksstillleben* (Breakfast, still life), 1927
ALBERT RENGER-PATZSCH *Fingerhut* (Foxglove), 1928
WERNER MANTZ *Titelblatt programmheft des WDR* (Front page, WDR's programme), 1928

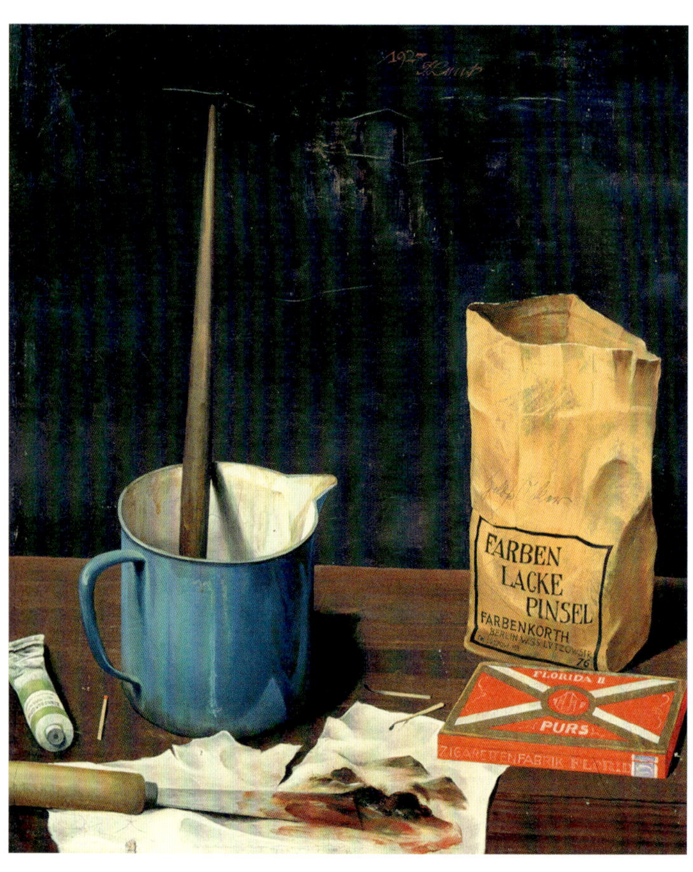
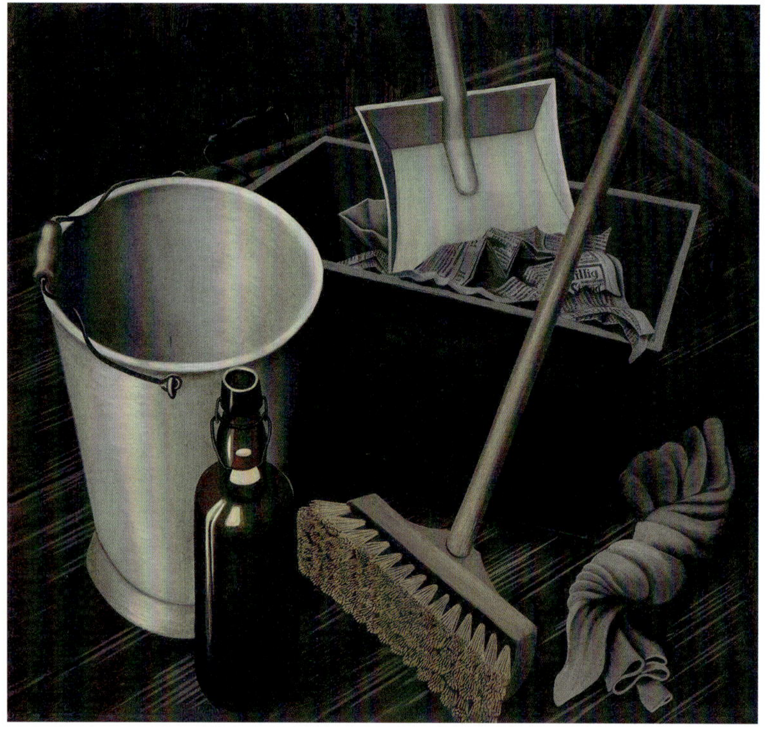

FRANZ LENK *Stillleben mit gelber Tüte* (Still Life with Yellow Bag), 1927
HANS MERTENS *Stillleben mit Hausgeräten* (Still Life with Kitchen Utensils), 1928

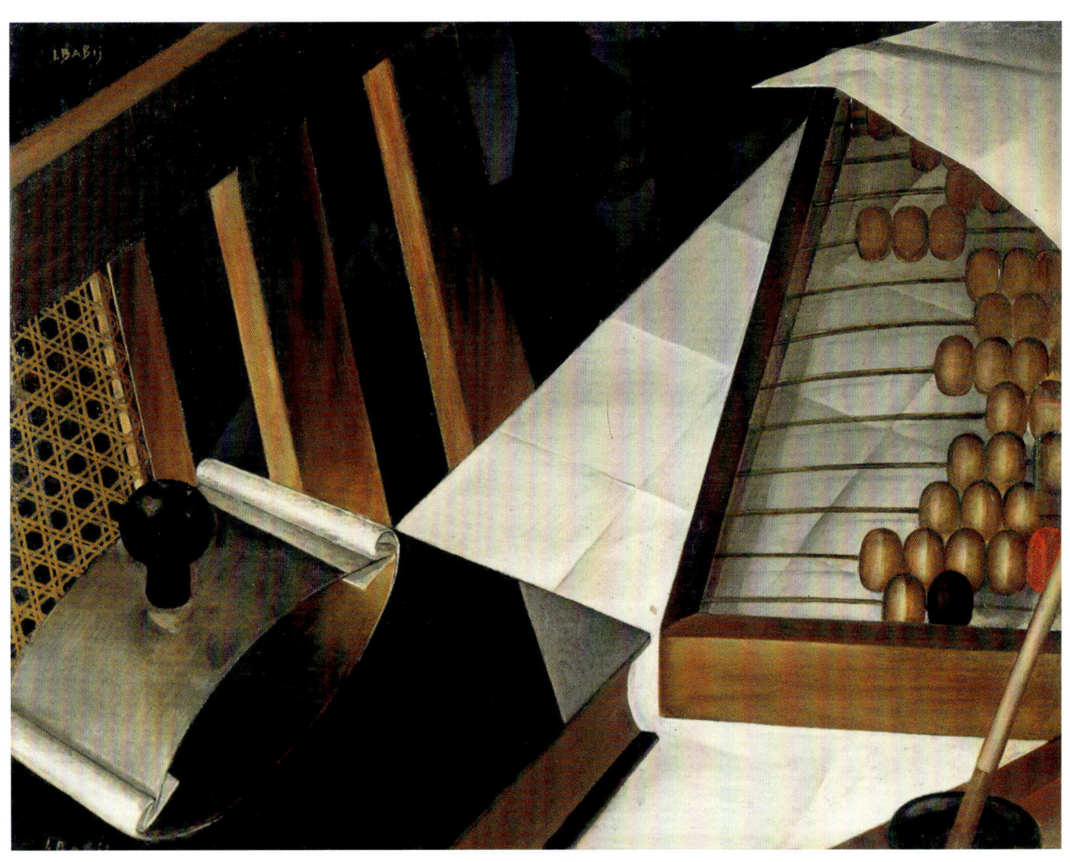

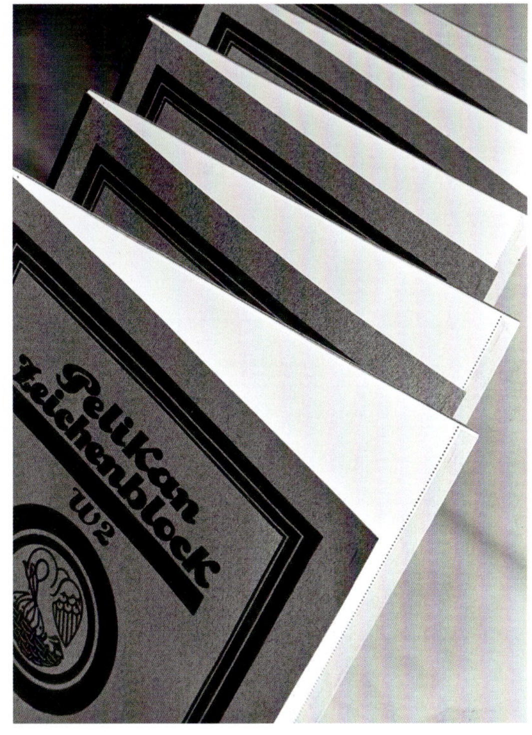

IVAN BABIJ *Rechenstilleben* (Still Life with Abacus), 1924
HEIN GORNY *Pelikan Zeichenblöcke* (Pelikan drawing pads), c. 1930
Gelatin silver print, 23.2 × 17.5 cm. Galerie Berinson, Berlin

IN THE 1920S, the exaltation of the individual that characterised Expressionist aesthetics was replaced by an ideal of standardisation: singularities were erased in favour of recourse to models, standardised types, simple forms reproduced in series. In painting, Anton Räderscheidt (1892-1970) and others depicted faceless human figures, in strangely empty and impersonal urban settings. The impasto and vivid colours of Expressionism disappeared in a smoother, muted colour scheme.

Rather than physical characteristics, artists now focused their attention on the individual's social background. In Cologne, the artists Gerd Arntz (1900-1988), Heinrich Hoerle (1895-1936) and Franz Wilhelm Seiwert (1894-1933) formed the Cologne Progressives group. Inspired by socialist utopias, they produced compositions in which exploiters and exploited are depicted. In *Zwölf Häuser der Zeit* (Twelve Houses of Our Time, 1927), a series of woodcuts, Gerd Arntz represented social classes using a set of easily identifiable codes. This recourse to schematisation was intended to raise the proletariat's awareness by revealing the reality of its oppression by means of simple forms. Arntz later worked with the philosopher and economist Otto Neurath (1882-1945) on developing a universal visual language called Isotype (International System of Typographic Picture Education). These pictograms with simple colours, readable by all, served to classify and render comprehensible complex political or economic data.

In urban planning, the unprecedented shortage of housing after the First World War led to the construction of vast estates. As part of the *Neue Frankfurt* (New Frankfurt) programme, architect Ernst May (1886-1970) headed a project that was to build almost 10,000 dwellings in five years. These were grouped together in uniform estates comprised of simple, identical forms, designed from standard prefabricated elements. Architect and furniture designer Marcel Breuer's (1902-1981) company, Standardmöbel, designed furniture made in pure forms using tubular steel, which was easy to reproduce on an industrial scale.

ANTON RÄDERSCHEIDT *Haus Nr 9* (House No. 9), 1921

STANDARDISATION

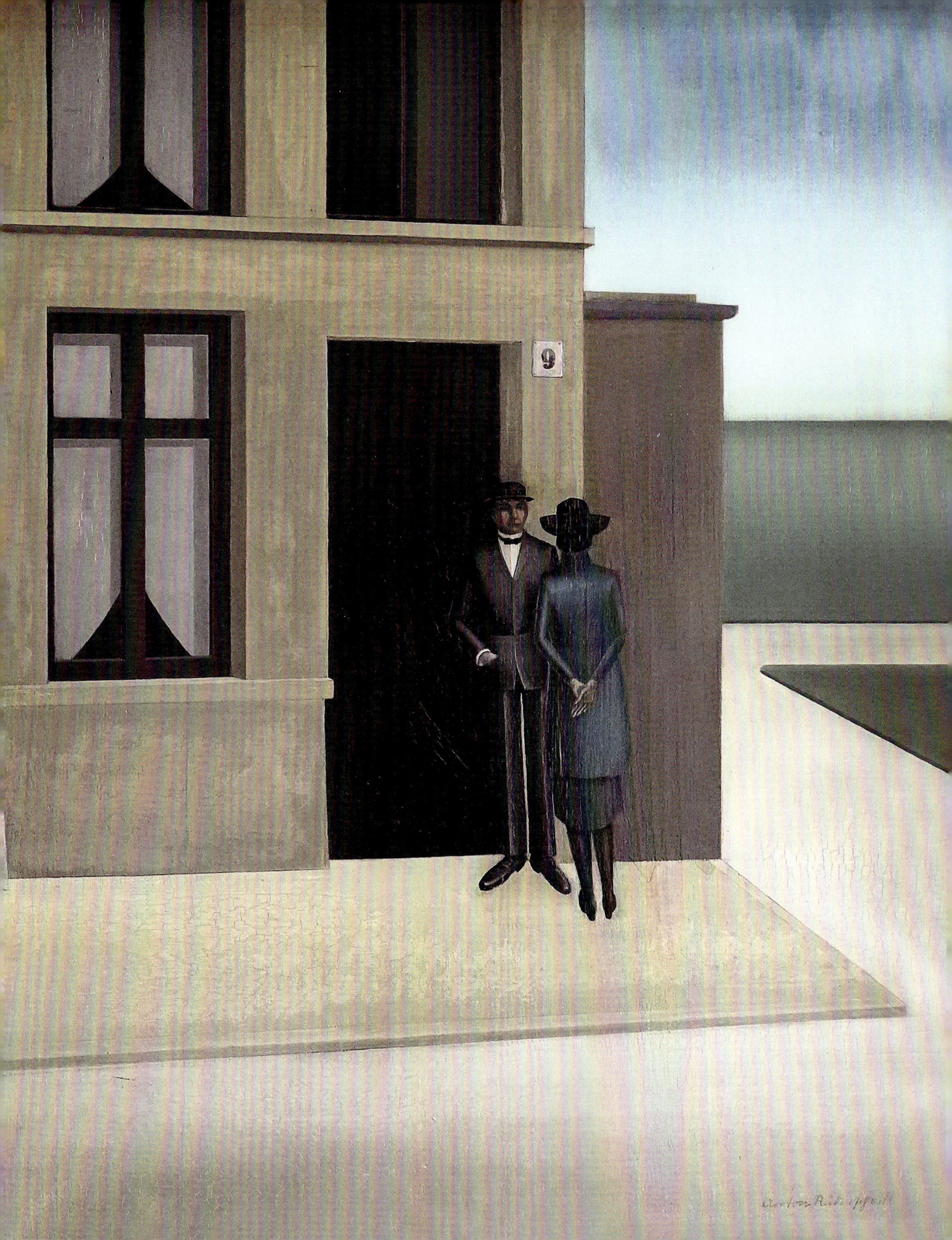

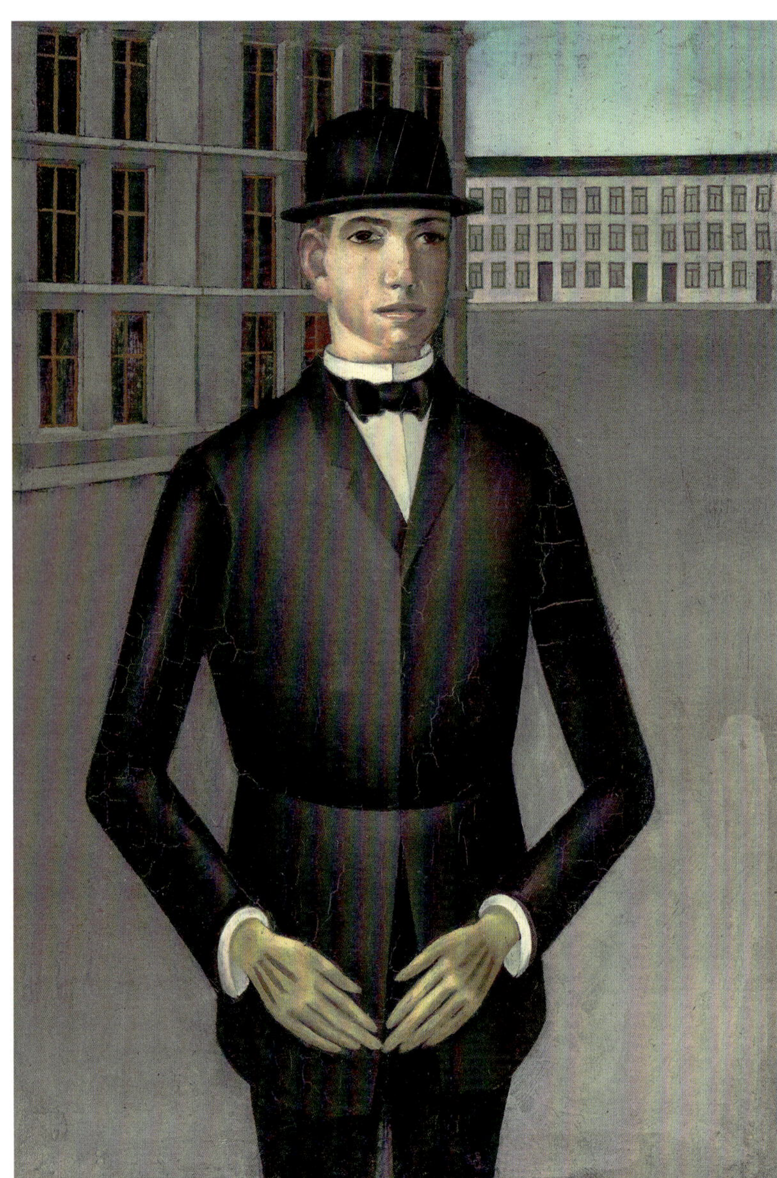

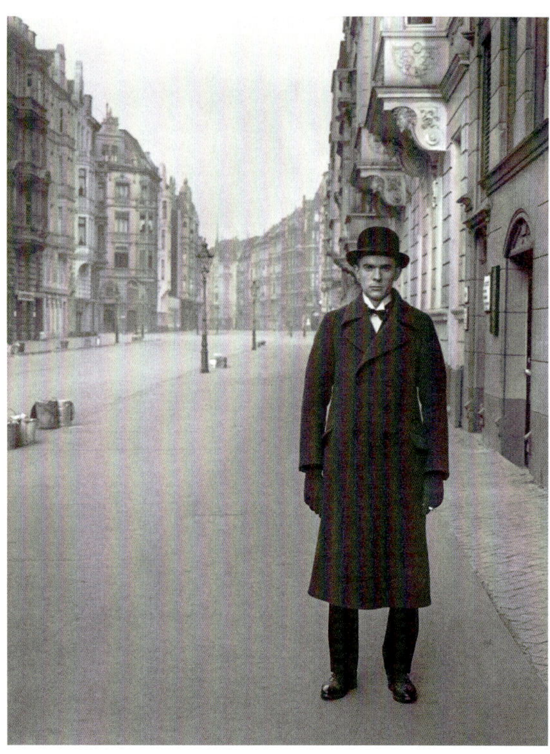

ANTON RÄDERSCHEIDT *Junger Mann mit gelben Handschuhen (Young Man with Yellow Gloves)*, 1921
Oil on wood, 27 × 18.5 cm. Galerie Berinson, Berlin
AUGUST SANDER *Maler [Anton Räderscheidt] (Painter [Anton Räderscheidt])*, 1926

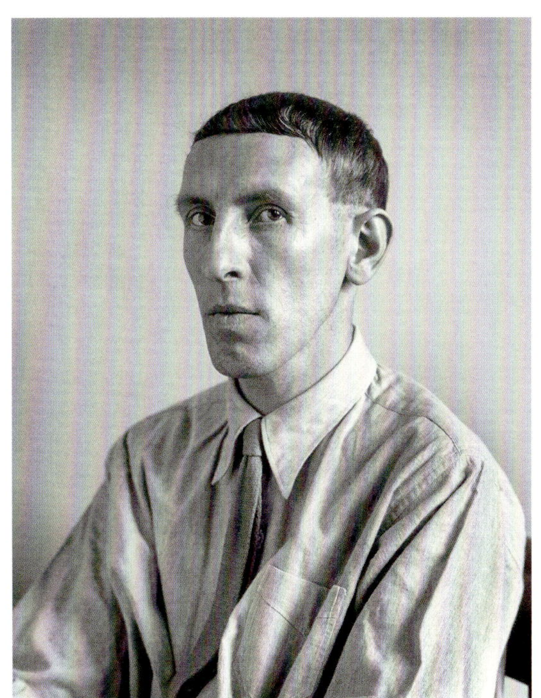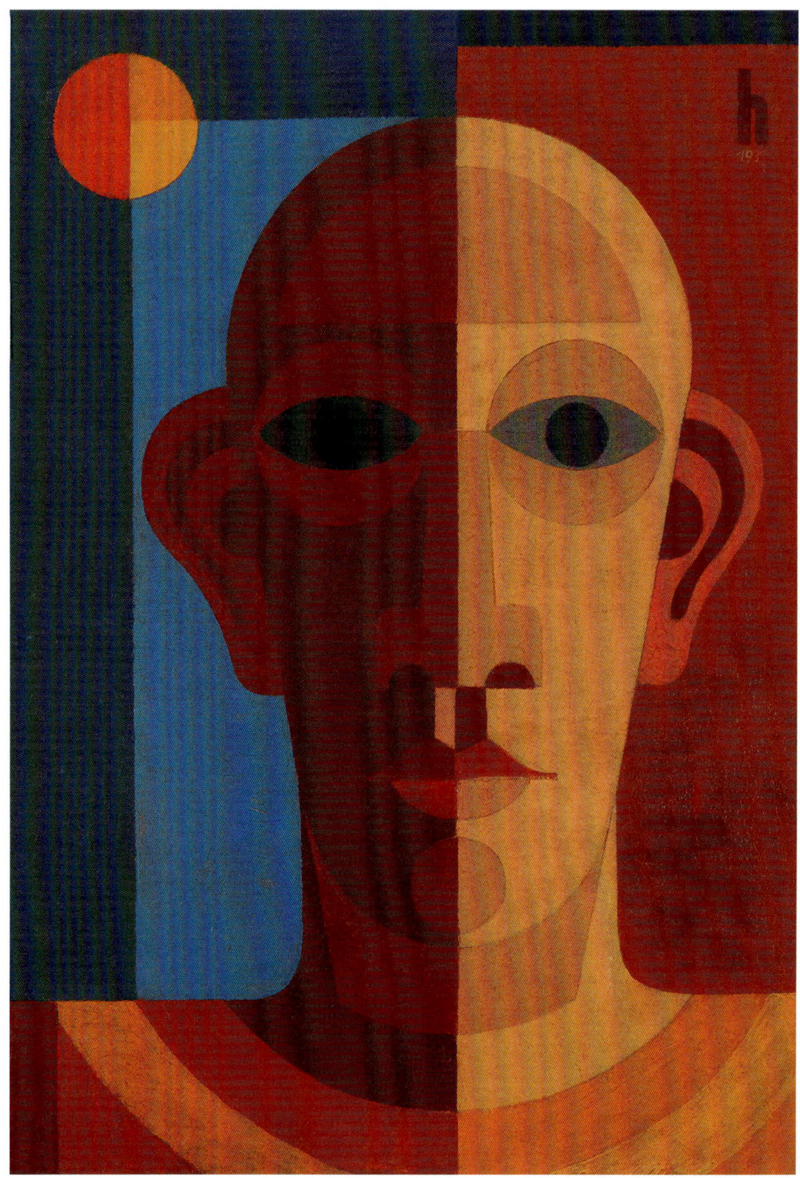

AUGUST SANDER *Maler [Heinrich Hoerle]* (Painter [Heinrich Hoerle]), 1928-1932
HEINRICH HOERLE *Selbstbildnis* (Self-Portrait), c. 1931

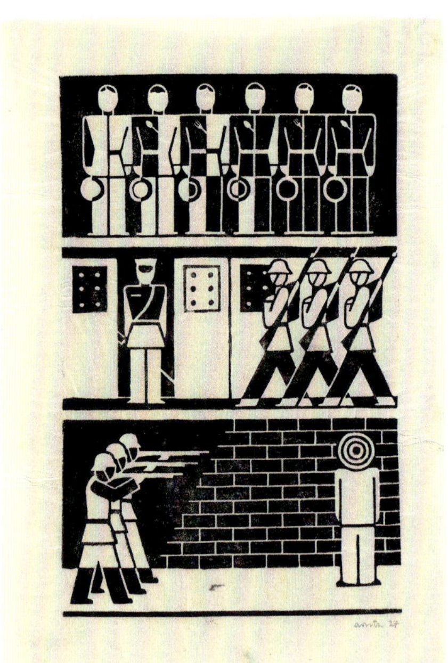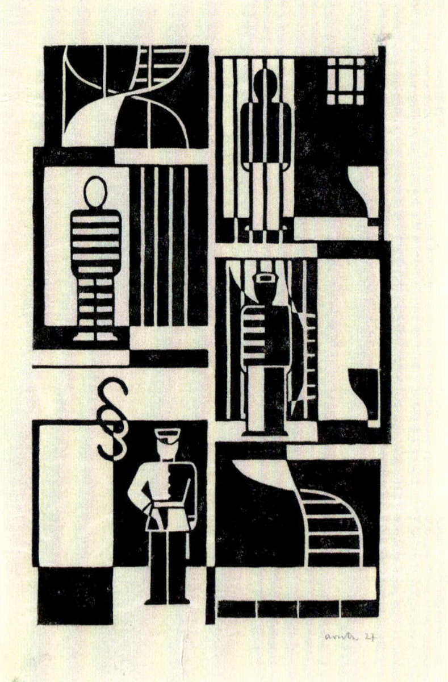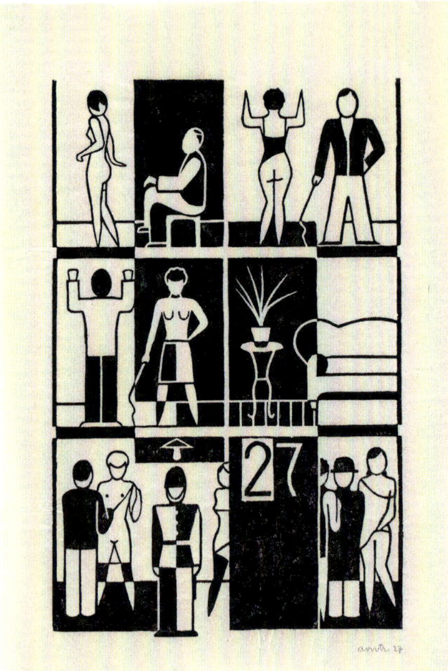
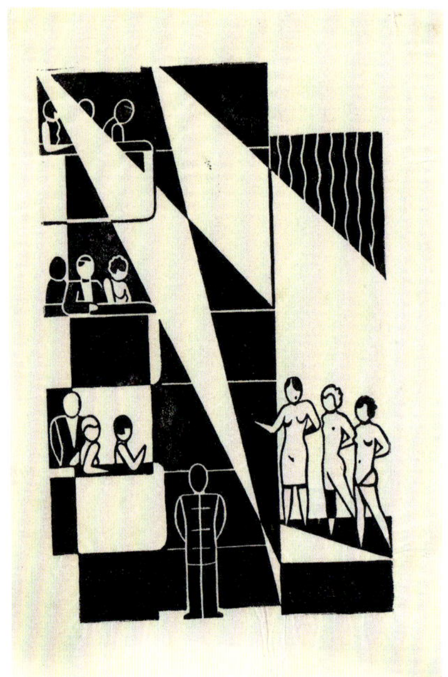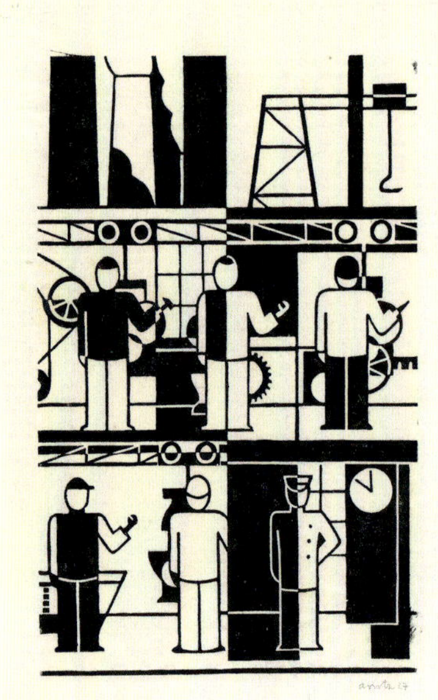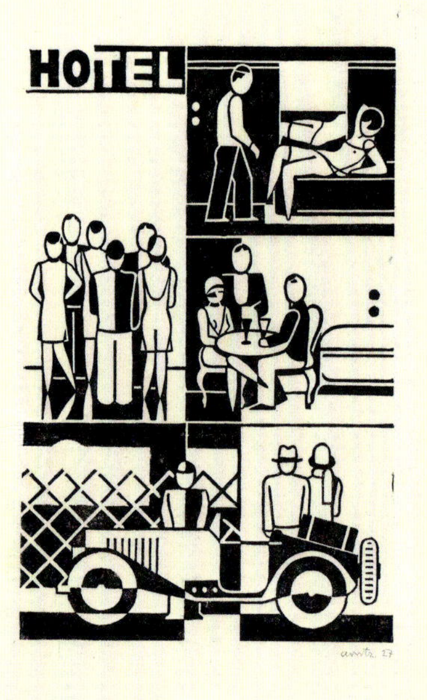

GERD ARNTZ *Zwölf Häuser der Zeit (Twelve Houses of Our Time)*, 1927
Kaserne (Barracks), *Gefängnis* (Prison), *Bordell* (Brothel),
Theater (Theatre), *Fabrik* (Factory), *Hotel*

ISOTYPE

is de internationale taal die beelden inplaats van woorden gebruikt. Het is reeds meer dan tien jaar geleden, dat de eerste tentoonstelling werd geopend, waar de moderne beeldstatistiek en het beeldonderricht konsekwent werden doorgevoerd. De staf van eminente medewerkers, die voor deze beeldentaal internationale bekendheid heeft verworven, werkt voort onder leiding van haren directeur, Dr. Otto Neurath, teneinde deze methode in toepassing te brengen op steeds weer nieuwe gebieden. De centrale van het Isotypewerk is in Den Haag gevestigd. De Internationale Stichting voor Beeldpaedagogie, gevestigd te 's-Gravenhage en New York, heeft ten doel deze beeldentaal in de geheele wereld te verbreiden; het Mundaneum Instituut in Den Haag verricht het wetenschappelijke en grafische werk. Van het Bestuur dezer beide instellingen maken onder anderen de volgende personen deel uit: Mary L. Fleddérus, Director International Industrial Relations Institute, Den Haag; Dr. Josef Frank, Architect, Stockholm; Professor Dr. Philipp Frank, Praag; Dr. Mr. P. J. de Kanter, Advocaat en Procureur, Den Haag; Mary van Kleeck, Director Department of Industrial Studies, Russell Sage Foundation, New York; C. H. van der Leeuw, firmant van de Erven de Wed. J. van Nelle, Rotterdam.

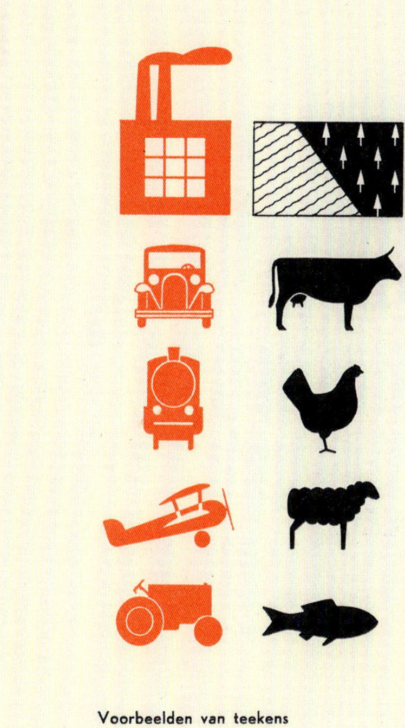

Voorbeelden van teekens

Zooals men uit de beeldstatistieken van dit prospectus kan zien, wordt een grootere hoeveelheid van een bepaalde zaak door een grooter aantal van dezelfde teekens aangegeven. Het ISOTYPE-lexikon bevat reeds 2000 zorgvuldig uitgewerkte teekens; het wordt steeds verder uitgebreid. De moeilijkste taak is, met deze duidelijke teekens sprekende grafische voorstellingen te vormen. De jarenlange ervaring der aan het instituut verbonden medewerkers garandeert het goede resultaat hetwelk berust op de konsekwentie en helderheid van de methode die als grondgedachte heeft:

Het is beter vereenvoudigde beelden te onthouden dan nauwkeurige getallen te vergeten.

Men wende zich voor nadere inlichtingen tot:

INTERNATIONALE STICHTING VOOR BEELDPAEDAGOGIE

MUNDANEUM INSTITUUT TE 'S-GRAVENHAGE

N.V. ISOTYPE i. o.

Den Haag, Obrechtstraat 267 Telefoon 33 57 32

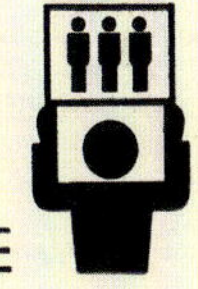

Isotype Brochure (Front and back pages), c. 1935

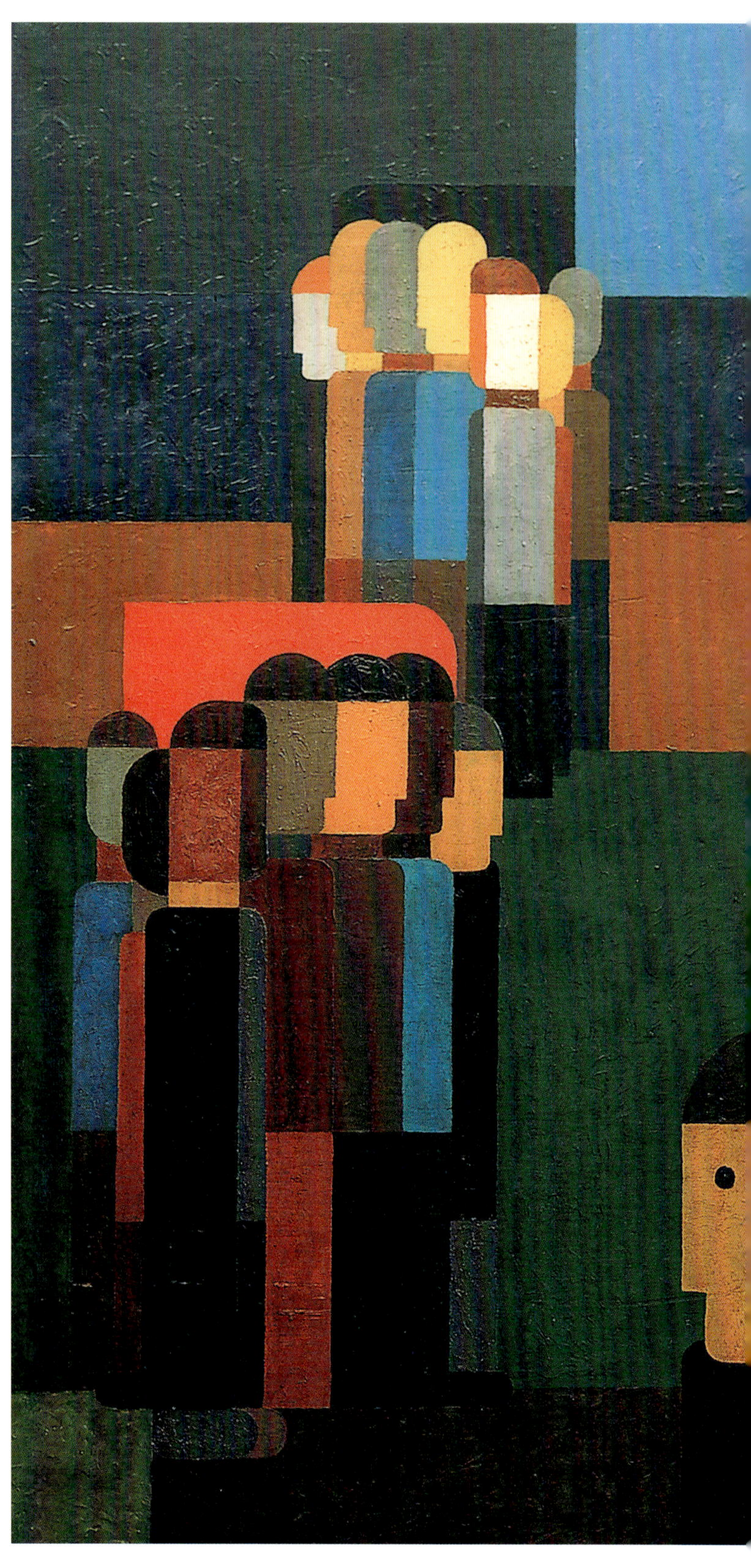

FRANZ WILHELM SEIWERT *Der deutsche Bauernkrieg* (The German Peasants' War), 1932

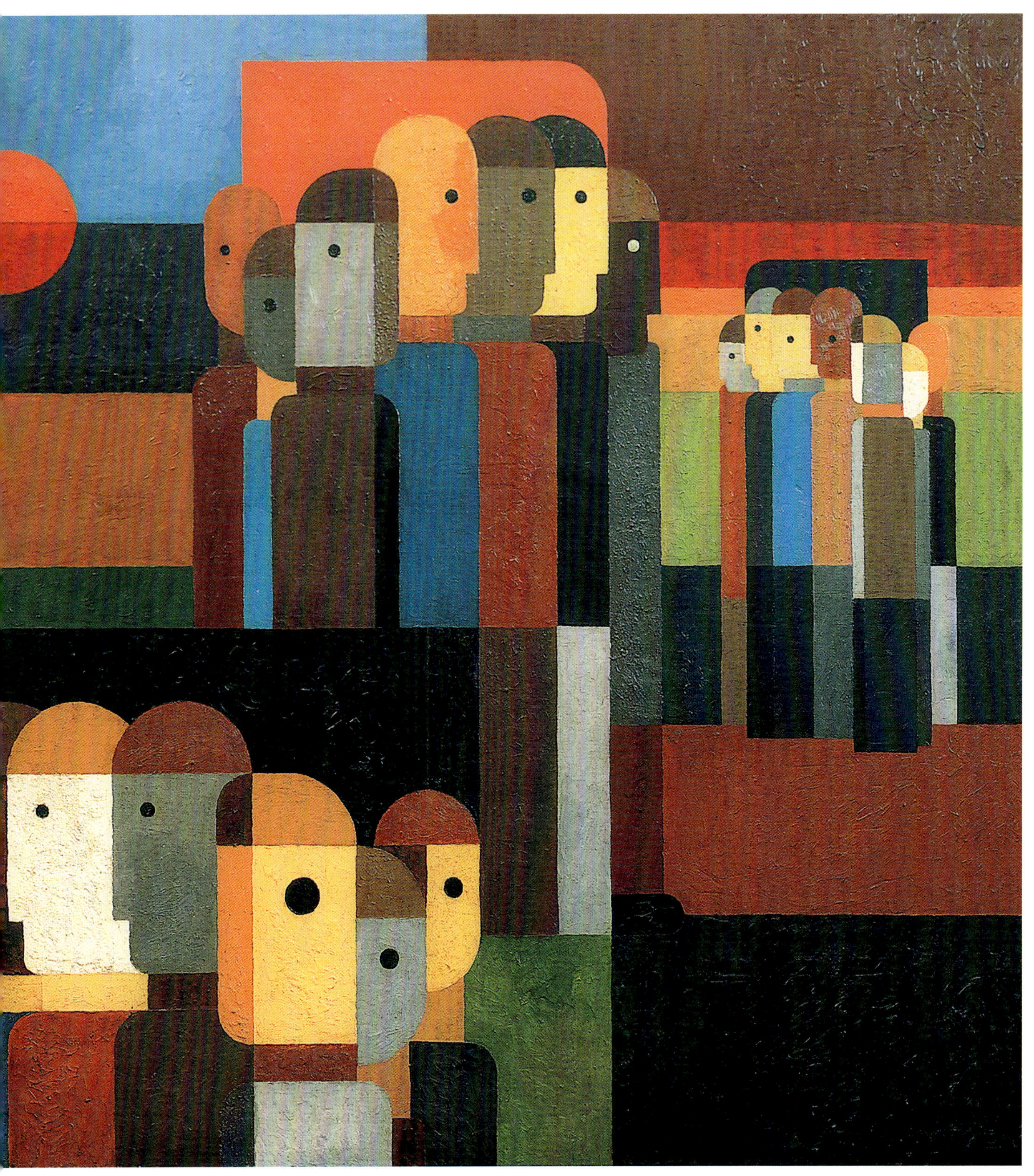

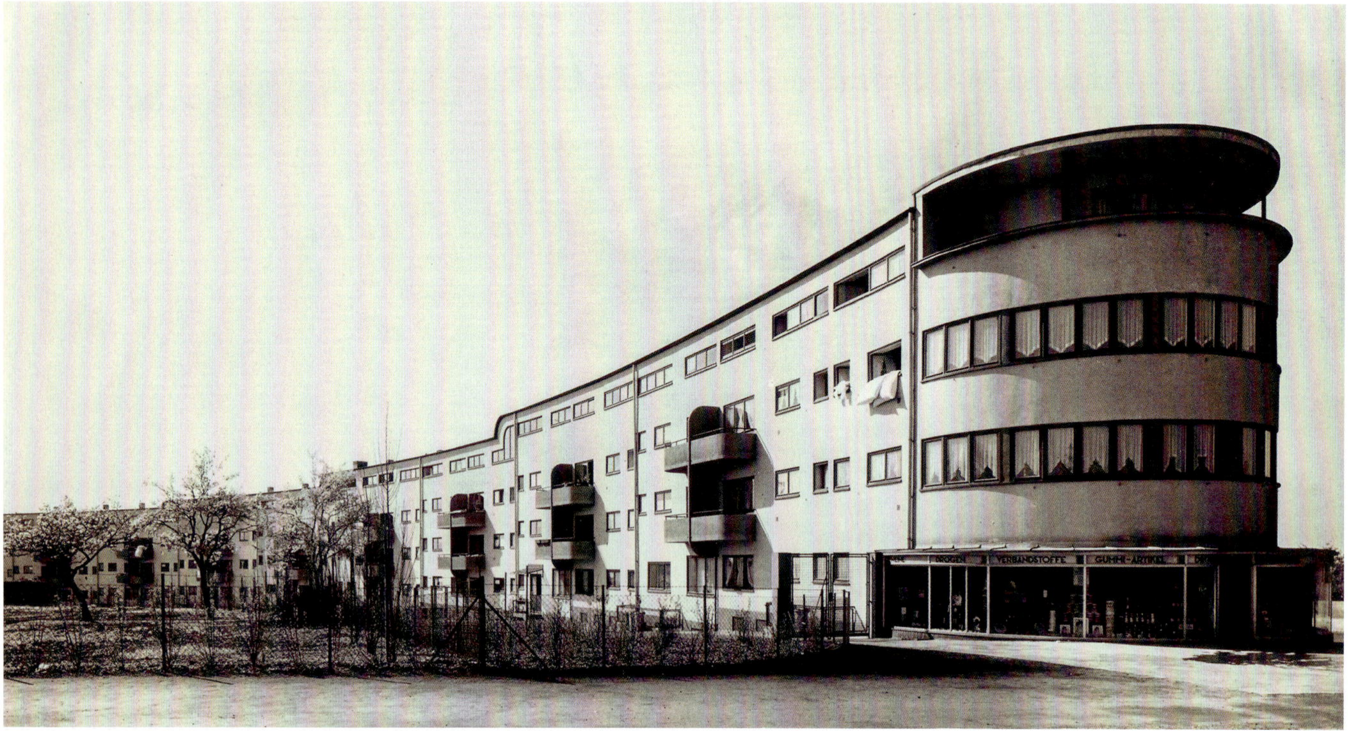

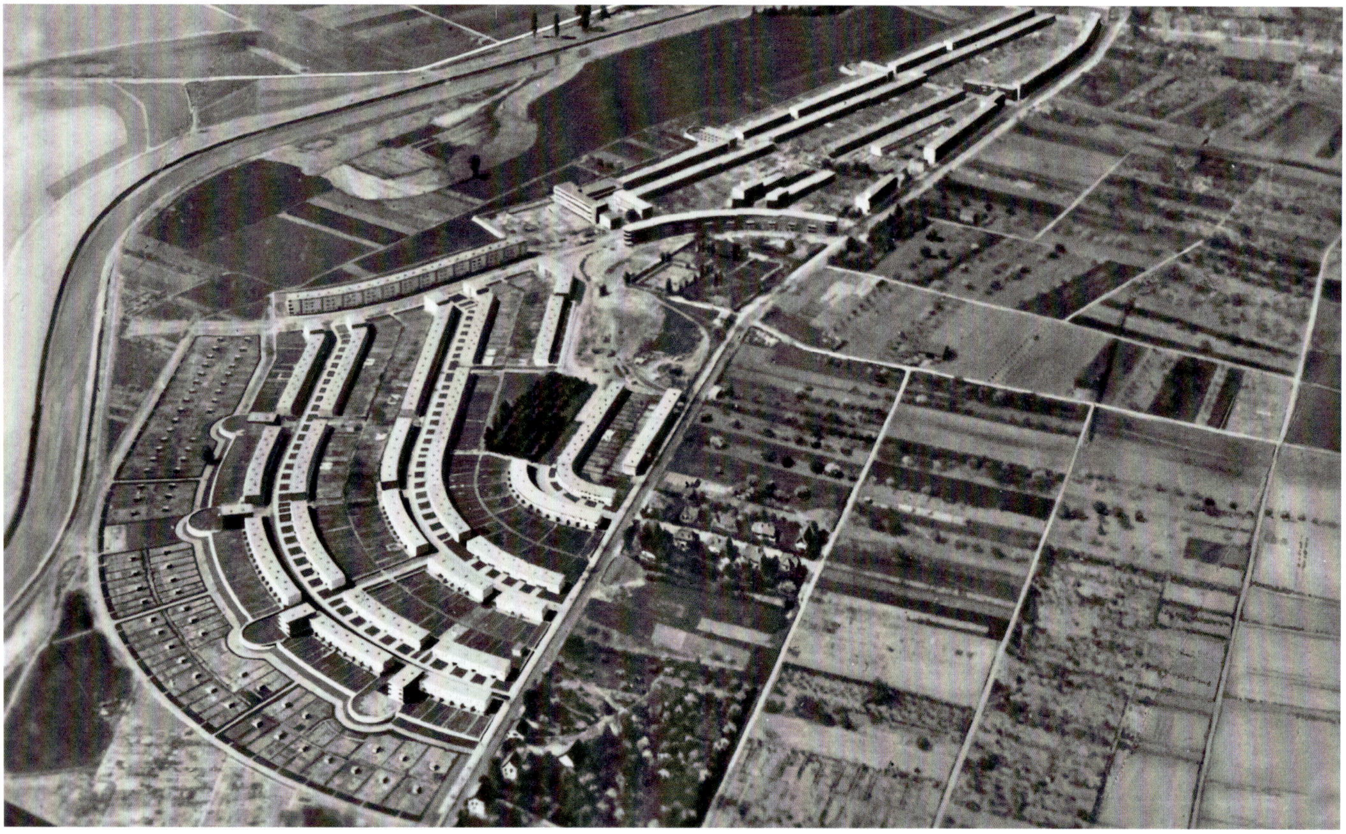

CARL-HERMANN RUDLOFF and **ERNST MAY** *Römerstadt, Frankfurt am Main*, Hadrianstrasse, block of flats with street level shops, c. 1929
Römerstadt, Frankfurt am Main, aerial photo, c. 1930

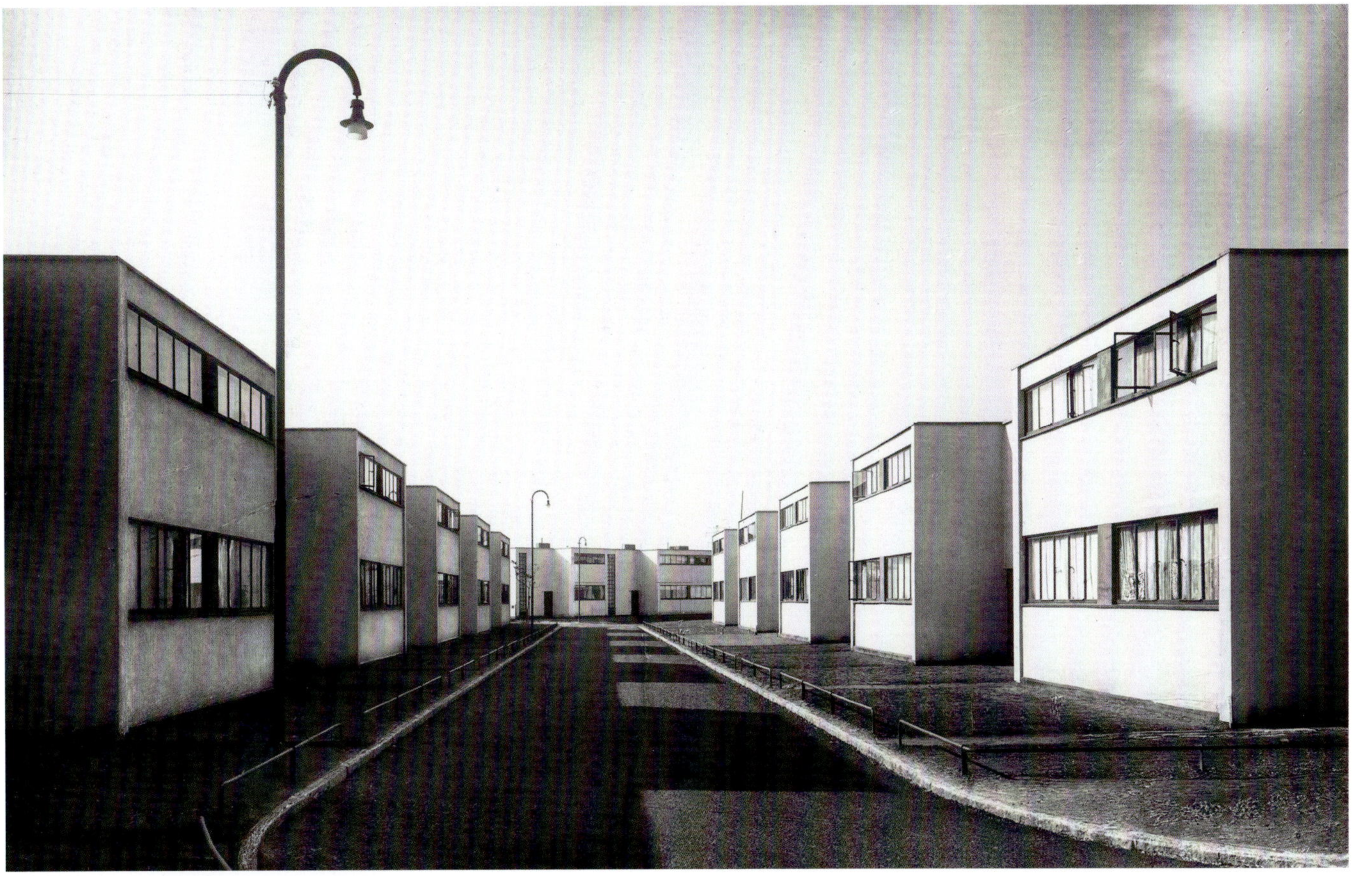

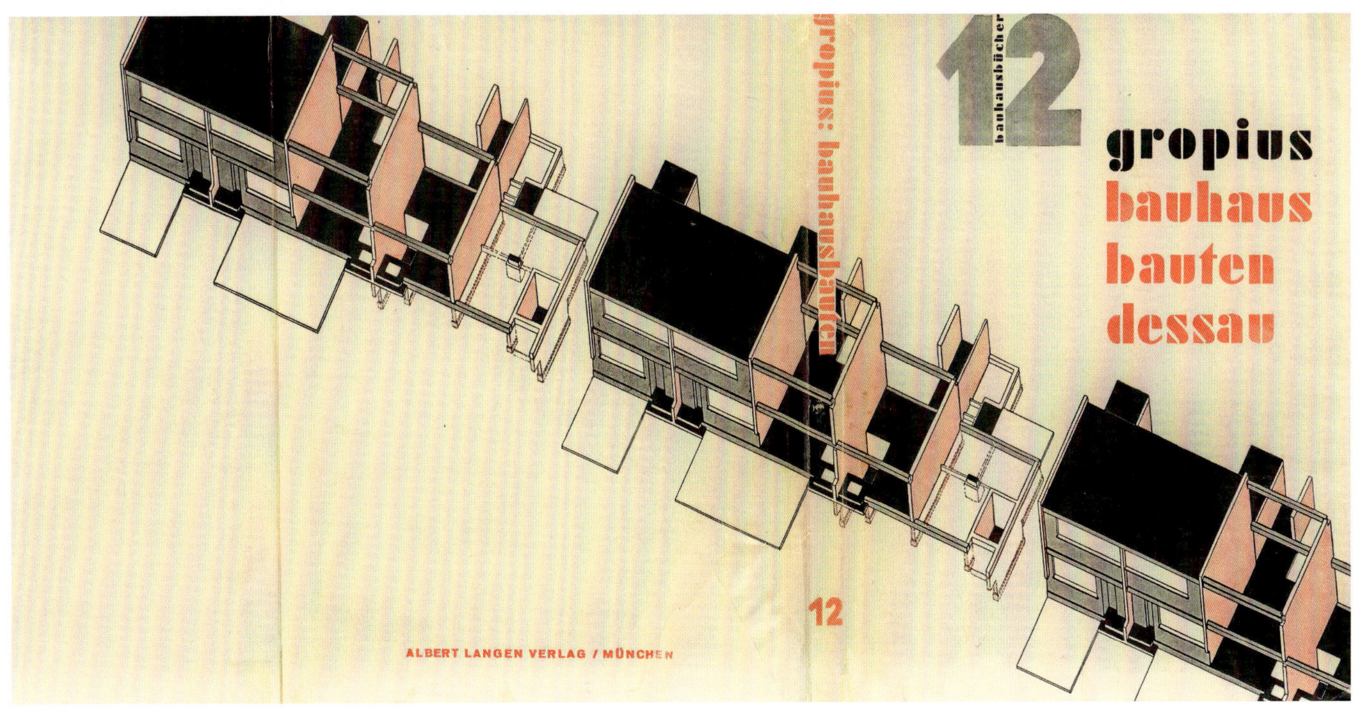

WALTER GROPIUS Residential area Dessau-Törten, street view, houses from the improved 1927 model, built 1928
Book cover of *Bauhausbauten Dessau* (Bauhaus Buildings, Dessau), 1930

New Furniture for the New Home. Marcel Breuer's Standardmöbel

By Werner Möller

Along with type classification and the establishment of norms, the essence of the industrial age was the standardization of its products. In this, the no-frills, systematized pre-production of uniform, primary parts for simple further processing constituted the key to the economic success of industrially-manufactured mass goods. In broad circles of the modern age's avant-garde, standardization had become the profession of faith in a new world where technical, social, and design progress jointly contributed to the well-being of all. One symbol of the avant-garde showing just how standardization can change an entire living environment was the Ford Model T automobile that first came off the production line in 1908. This set benchmark standards in all aspects, from production to price, all the way up to simple operation and servicing – even in terms of its factual aesthetics that were all but self-generated on the basis of rational and technical considerations. For the first time, because of standardization, the Ford Model T cast off the automobile's status as a symbol of affluence to become a vehicle for everyman. It was not until 1972 that the sales figures of the Ford Model T were supassed, by those of the VW Beetle.

The step to establish these modern achievements in the area of private living needs as well turned out to be much more difficult. Living conditions as the creation of a safe haven and an expression of individuality and personal representation epitomized the exact opposite of any anonymous, technology-based standardization. Not least because, besides being a blessing of progress, it was also synonymous with the inhuman, exploitative misery of industrial mass production – and thus not exactly associated with domestic coziness, comfort or protection. For a profound change in thinking to be brought about so that the future of the individual worlds for living and dwelling might lie in a new, objective and technical design, not only did the consumers have to be brought around, but producers and dealers had to be convinced as well.

The Deutscher Werkbund, founded in 1907, was also tackling this topic at roughly the same time the Ford Model T was being introduced. Legendary examples for this Werkbund alliance consisting of leading designers, industrialists and politicians were the model exhibitions such as at Stuttgart-Weißenhof, as well as the AEG design office of Peter Behrens and the Deutsche Werkstätten at Hellerau.

Nevertheless, it was to take another 20 years before the tubular steel furniture, omnipresent today as New Objectivity insignia, achieved its market readiness in the special segment of living accessories. And this despite the fact that comparable tubular metal furniture had been widespread in everyday life much earlier, for example, in the health sector.

The breakthrough came in 1927 with the Werkbund exhibition at Stuttgart-Weißenhof. Prior to this, already from 1925 on, Marcel Breuer had been consistently and systematically research-

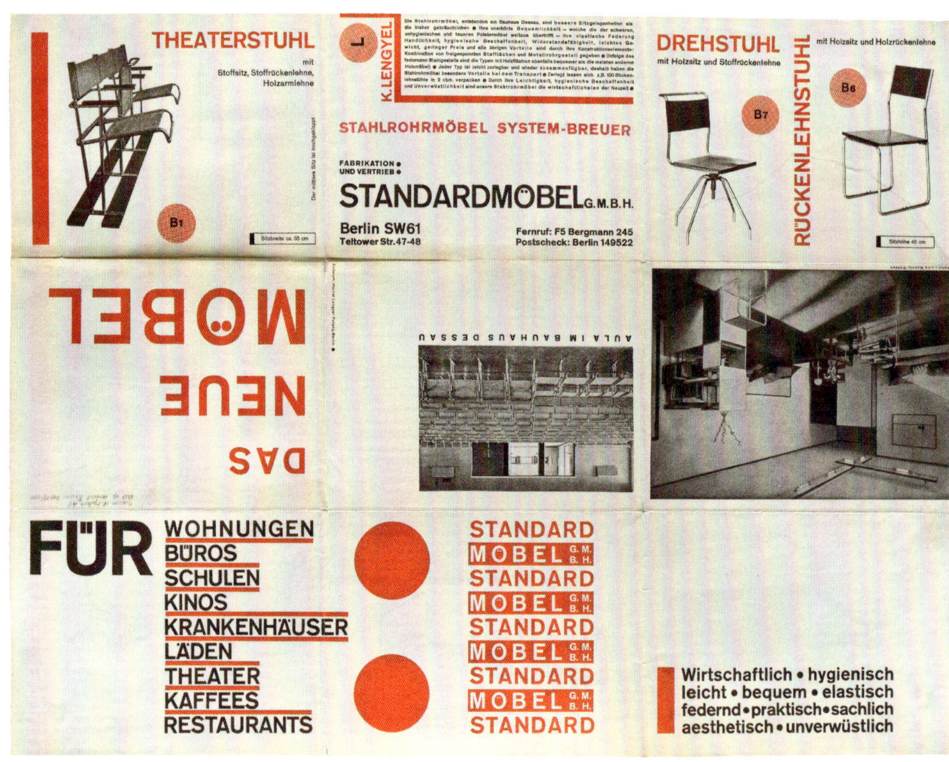

HAJNAL LENGYEL-PATAKY Leaflet for the company Standardmöbel showcasing furniture designed by Marcel Breuer, 1928

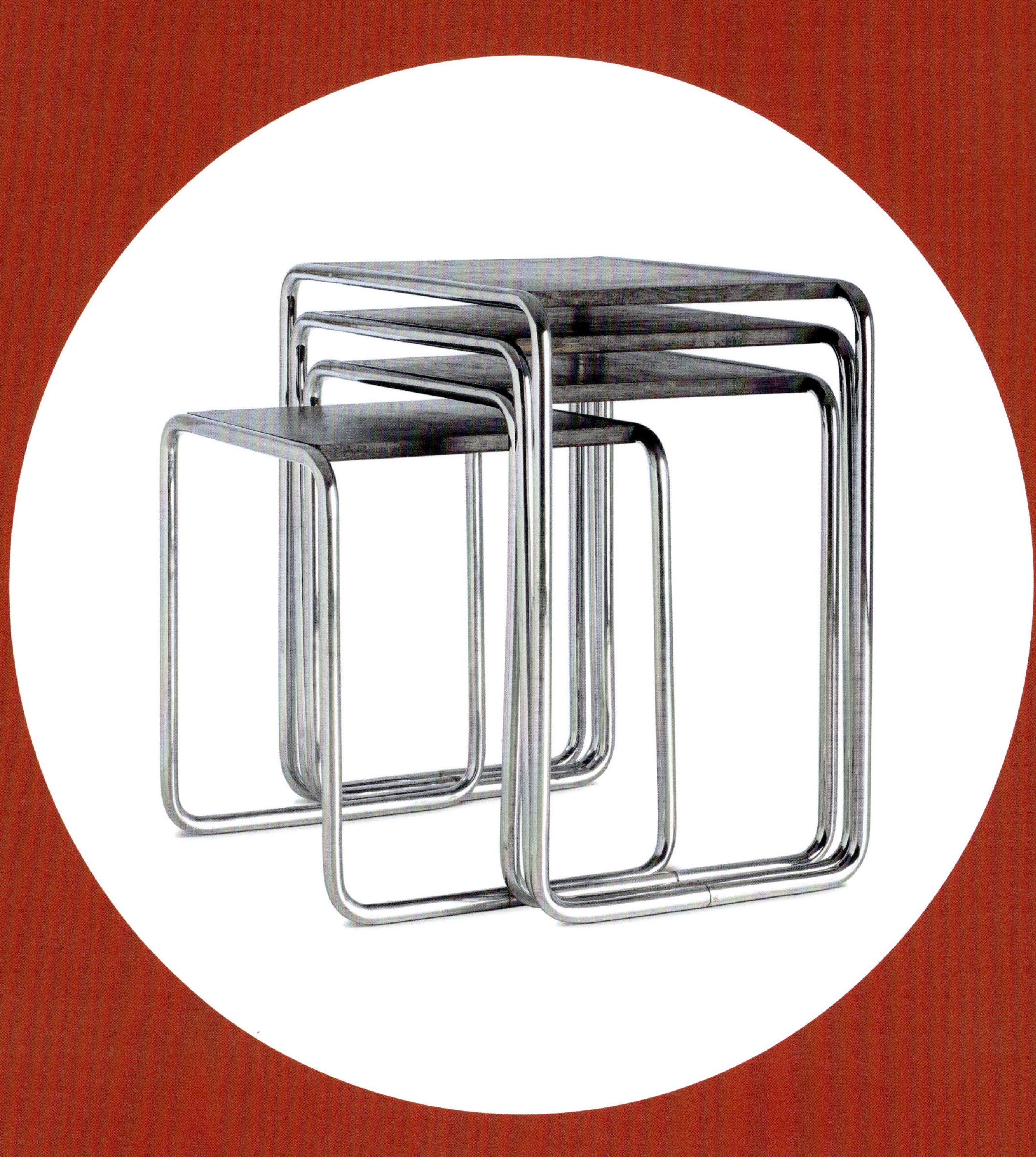

MARCEL BREUER *B 9-9c, 1925*

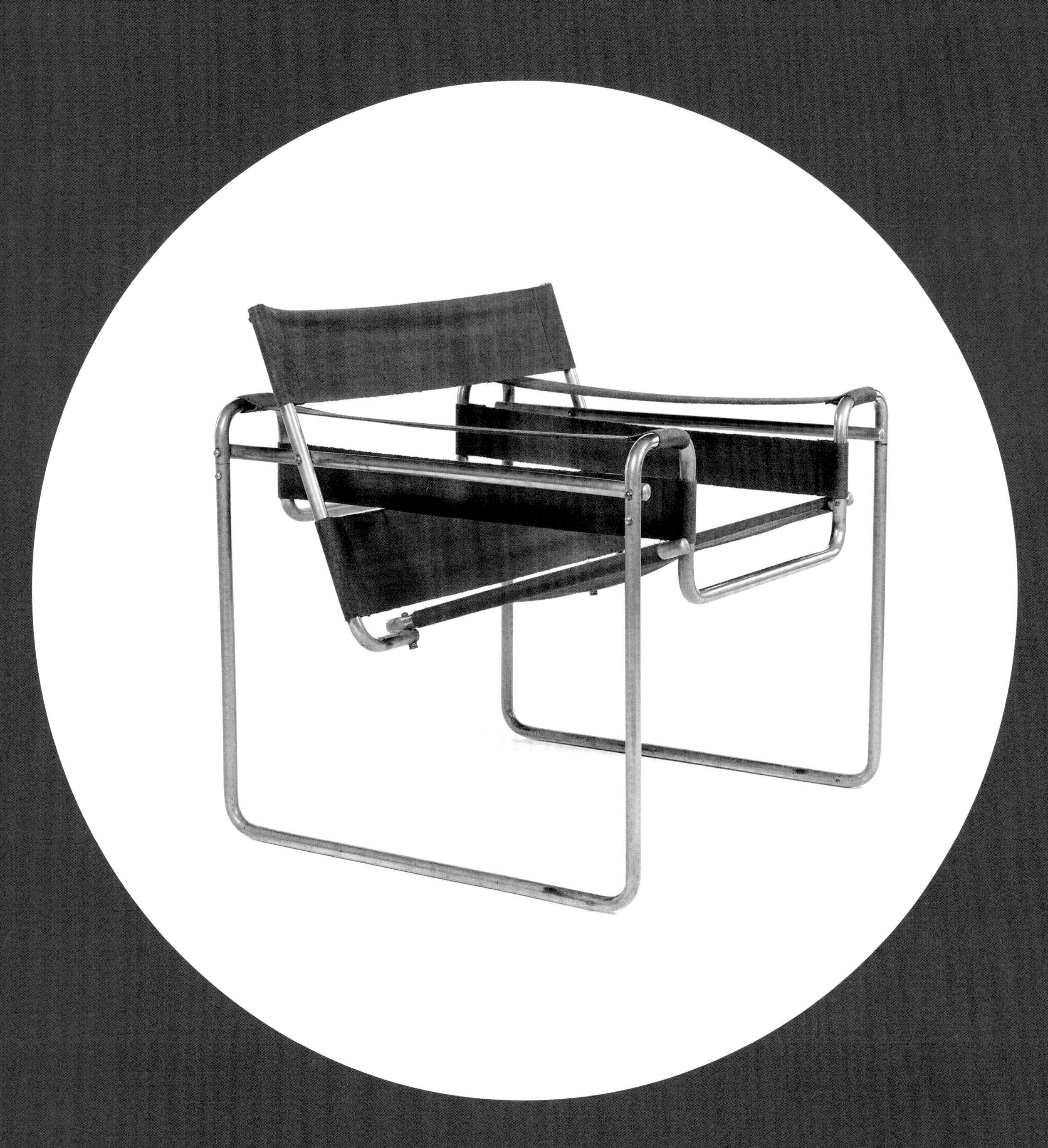

ing the use of steel tubing for furniture design at the Bauhaus in Dessau. He developed new, ascetic and reduced prototypes for chairs, stools, armchairs and tables that would become the basic standards for all subsequent designs – with the exception of the cantilever chair.

Because no interest was shown by the furniture manufacturers in these innovative products, in Berlin at the turn of the year 1926/27, Marcel Breuer founded his own company together with Kálmán Lengyel with the programmatic name of Standardmöbel (Standard Furniture). But because of a lack of business acumen, the undertaking was doomed from the outset. Only in 1929, when Thonet took over the production and marketing, did this furniture attain the market success that remains unsurpassed today.

The most outstanding piece of furniture was the *Club Armchair* (model B 3). Here, Breuer exemplarily dissected not only the reduction of customary furniture types to their standardized basic elements of material, construction and technical manufacture. He also emphasized in particular how the tube, seating, and chairback elements as individual, standardized parts are connected with the frame. All in all, it seems more appropriate to refer to this as the design for a constructivist spatial sculpture rather than a simple armchair.

Marcel Breuer pursued a different path when creating the stools and table sets *B 9* and *B 9a-B 9c* (p. 77). For their design, the emphasis was less on the additive quality of the elements than it was on how the steel tubing could be used to bend an endless line in three levels that, in connection with the seating or table surfaces, would describe a transparent cubic space in a minimalistic way.

Breuer himself considered the club chair design as his most mechanical.[1] To his amazement, the criticism he had been expecting for transforming this type of furniture that itself stands for comfort into a technical object of modern living needs never came. This furniture had already found its clientele in a new type of bourgeois middle class and intellectuals who had increasingly been developing into the leading class since the end of the 19th century as a result of the changed work and production worlds of industrialization and a new metropolitan culture.

These New Objectivity developments in society and design were accompanied by and commented on with critiques such as those voiced in Bertolt Brecht's "North Sea Crabs" or in humorous caricatures of New Objectivity living styles and their somewhat strange inhabitants.

WERNER MÖLLER is the Head of Collections at Stiftung Bauhaus Dessau in Germany. His work focuses on architecture and design of the modernism. He has among other things co-curated the exhibition *Simultanität der Moderne – die Van-Nelle-Fabrik in Rotterdam und das Bauhaus in Dessau* in 2016.

1. Marcel Breuer, "Metallmöbel", in Werner Graeff (ed.), *Innenräume*, Stuttgart, 1928, p. 134.

Additional literature / sources:
Bertolt Brecht, *Nordseekrabben oder Die moderne Bauhaus-Wohnung*, 1926. First published in the Münchner Neuesten Nachrichten, 9 January 1927.
Marcel Breuer, "Metallmöbel", in Werner Graeff (ed.), *Innenräume*, Stuttgart, 1928.
Sigfried Giedion, *Mechanization Takes Command, A Contribution to Anonymous History*, Oxford University Press, 1948.
Karin Kirsch, *Die Weißenhofsiedlung, Werkbund Exhibition "Die Wohnung" – Stuttgart 1927*, DVA, Stuttgart, 1987.
Robin Krause, "Die frühen Stahlrohrmöbel von Marcel Breuer", in, Stiftung Bauhaus Dessau, Kentgens-Craig, Margret (ed.), *Das Bauhausgebäude in Dessau 1926 – 1999*, Birkhäuser Verlag, Basel, Berlin, Boston, 1999.
Werner Möller and Otakar Mácel, *Ein Stuhl macht Geschichte*, Prestel Verlag, Munich, 1992.
Stiftung Bauhaus Dessau, Bittner, Regina (ed.), *Bauhausstil, Zwischen International Style and Lifestyle*, Edition Bauhaus, vol. 11, Jovis Verlag, Berlin, 2003.
Alexander von Vegesack, Mathias Remmele (ed.), *Marcel Breuer. Design und Architektur*, Vitra Design Museum, Weil am Rhein, 2003.

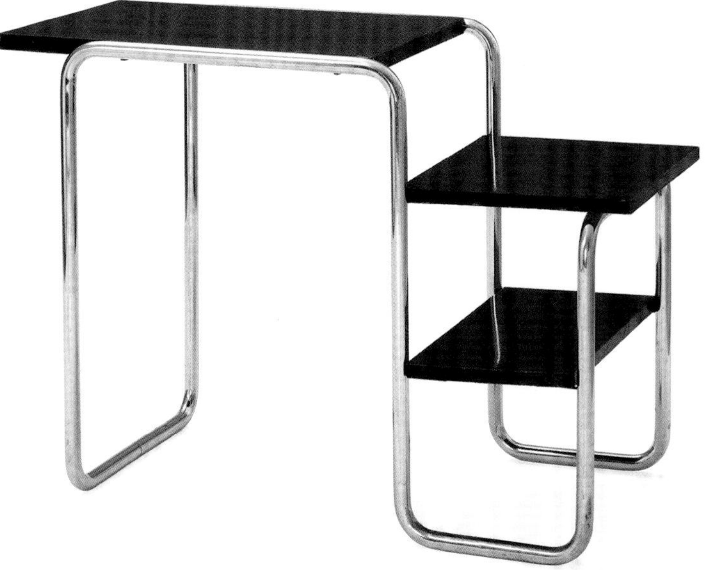

MARCEL BREUER
Opposite page: *Klubsessel B 3* (Club Armchair B 3), 1925
B 21 Bauhaus Schreibtisch (B 21 Bauhaus Typewriter Desk), 1928

THE POST-WAR ECONOMIC CRISIS and spectacular inflation were followed by a period of relative stabilisation and growth, encouraged in particular by the American-led Dawes Plan, which among other things reorganized the Reichsbank. Germans began to develop a fascination for America and its social model. The rationalisation of work developed by the American engineer F.W. Taylor (1856-1915) was imported into German companies, leading to rapid industrialisation and the mechanisation of tasks.

The principle of rationalisation and the aestheticization of machines soon became a new norm that structured social and cultural life: The Tiller Girls, a troupe of dancers who performed synchronised choreographies in a mechanical rhythm, were the visual expression of assembly-line work. Albert Renger-Patzsch's (1897-1966) photographs and Carl Grossberg's (1894-1940) paintings show sparklingly clean industrial sites in pared-down, meticulously detailed compositions. The graphic designer Paul Renner (1878-1956) created the Futura typeface (which is used in a redesigned version in this catalogue), based on elementary geometric shapes. The architect Margarete Schütte-Lihotzky (1897-2000) designed a modern and functional kitchen, organised as a work space to limit the housewife's movements back and forth.

ANONYM Female workers at the production line, 1932

RATIONALITY

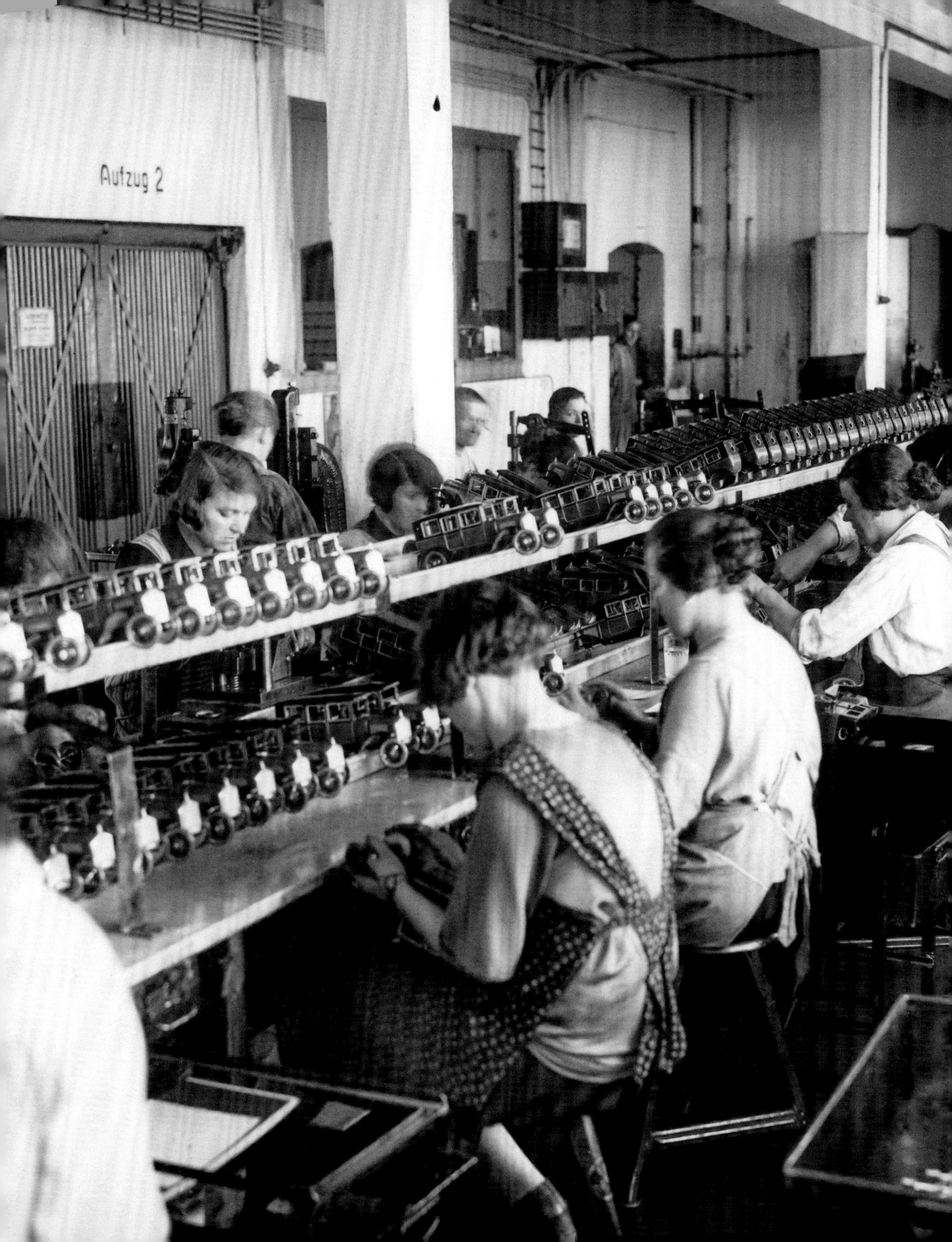

Aufzug 2

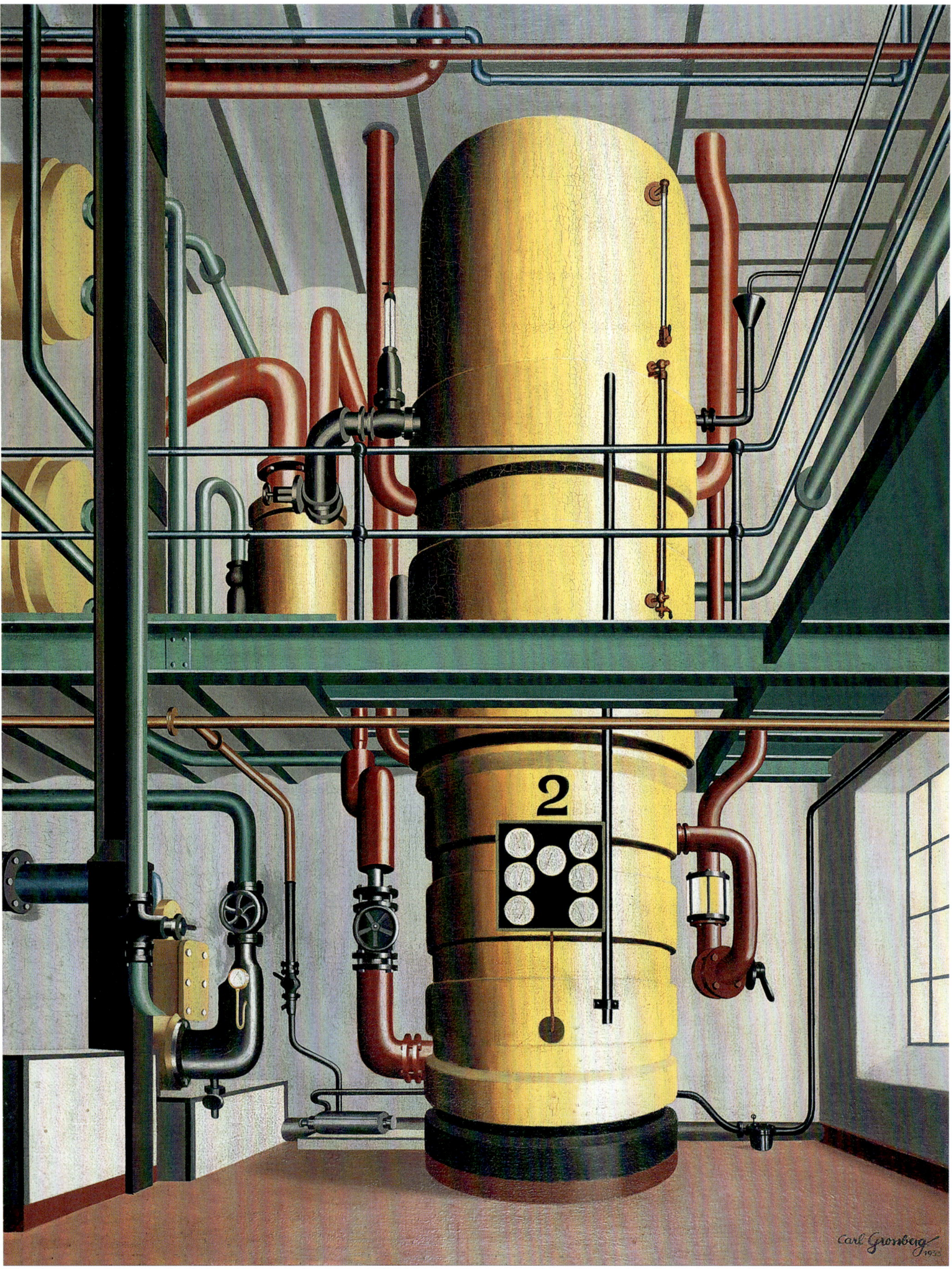
2
Carl Grossberg
1932

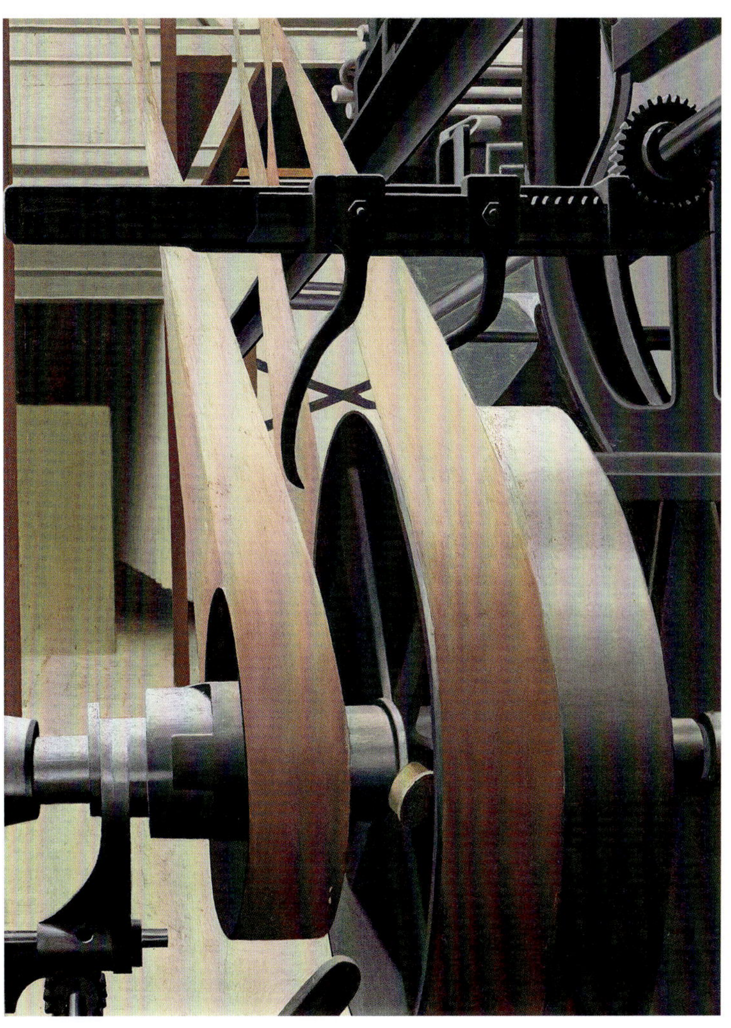

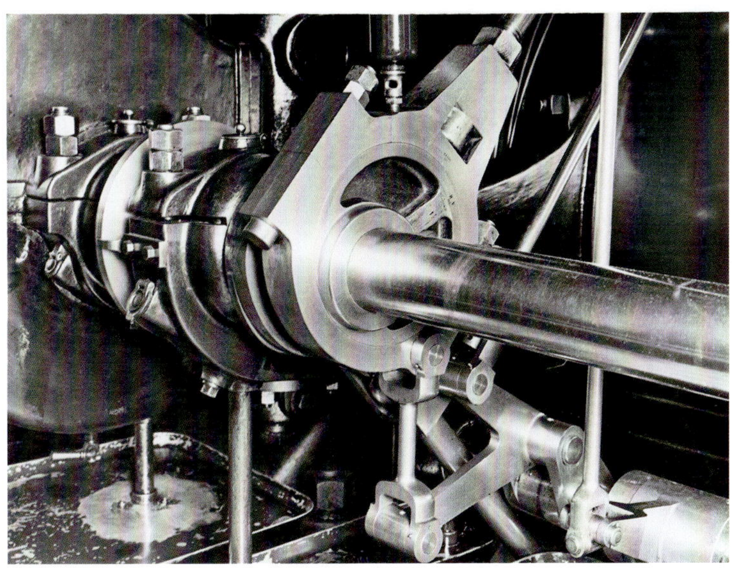

Opposite page: **CARL GROSSBERG** *Der gelbe Kessel* (The Yellow Boiler), 1933

CARL GROSSBERG *Schwungrad mit Treibriemen* (Flywheel with Driving Belt), 1934
ALBERT RENGER-PATZSCH *Nockenwelle einer Dampfmaschine* (Camshaft of a Steam Engine), 1927
Gelatin silver print, 17.3 × 23.1 cm. Galerie Berinson, Berlin

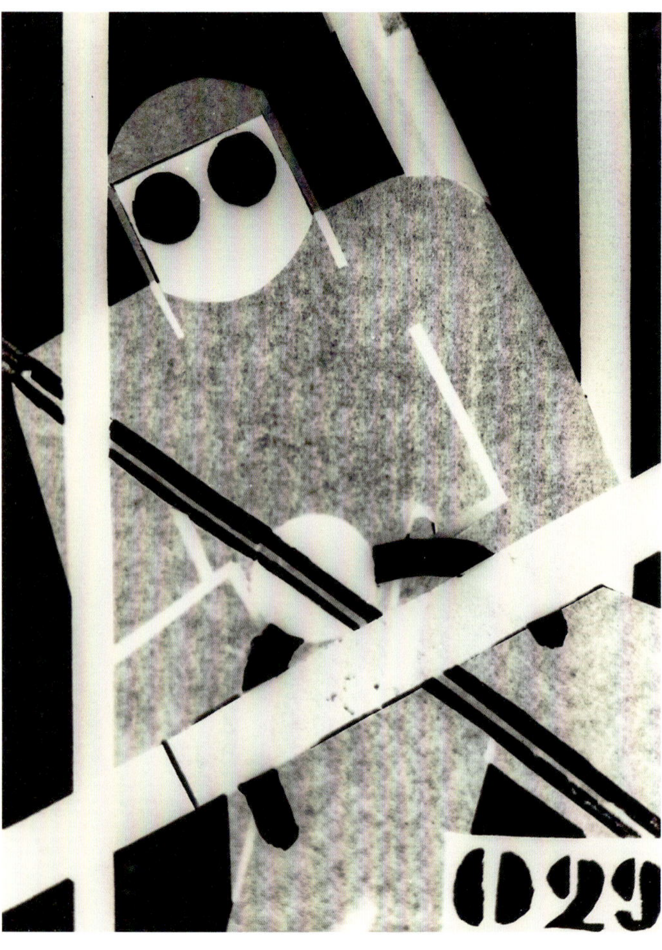

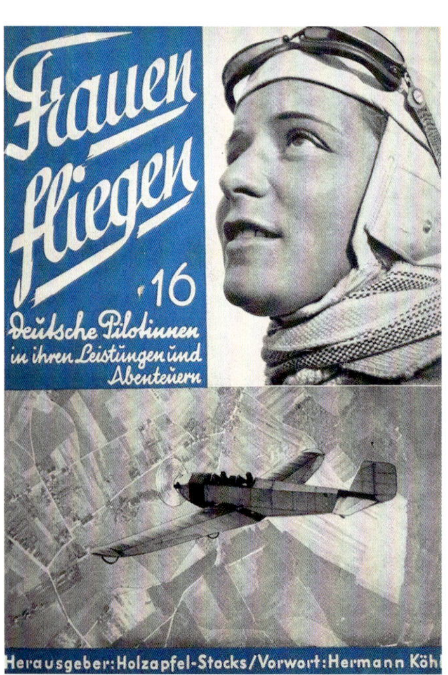

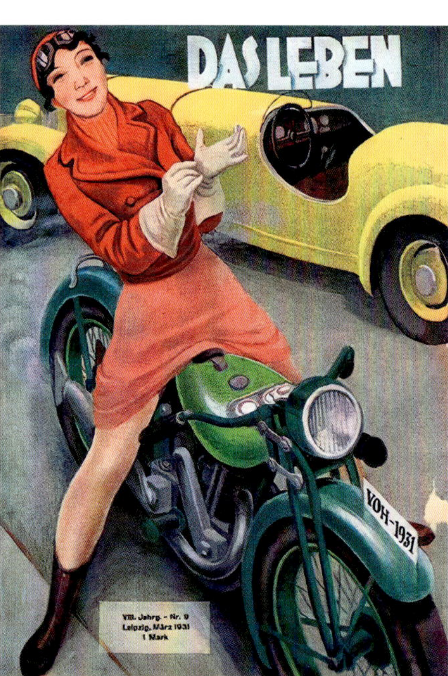

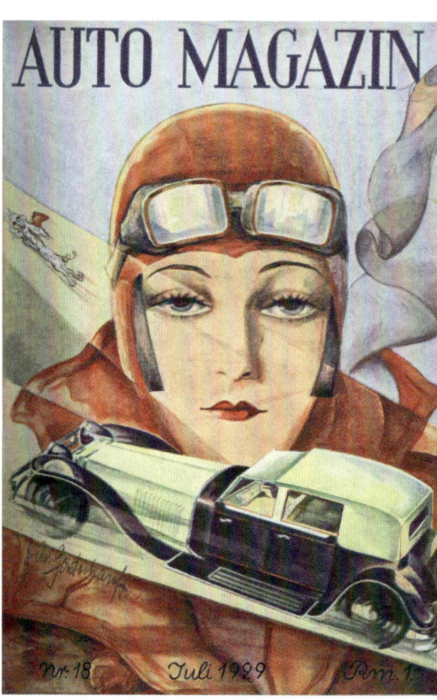

ALICE LEX-NERLINGER *Der Flieger* (The Pilot), c. 1930. Photogram, 23.9 × 17.9 cm. Galerie Berinson, Berlin
CARL MARIA HOLZAPFEL, KÄTE STOCKS and RUDOLF STOCKS *Frauen fliegen. 16 deutsche Pilotinnen in ihren Leistungen und Abenteuern*
(Women Fly. 16 Pilots, Their Achievements and Adventures), book, 1931
OSWALD VOH *Das Leben* (Journal), Vol. 8, No. 9, March 1931
ANONYM *Auto-Magazin* (Journal), No. 18, July 1929

Opposite page: **MAX RADLER** *Der Radiohörer* (The Radio Listener), 1930

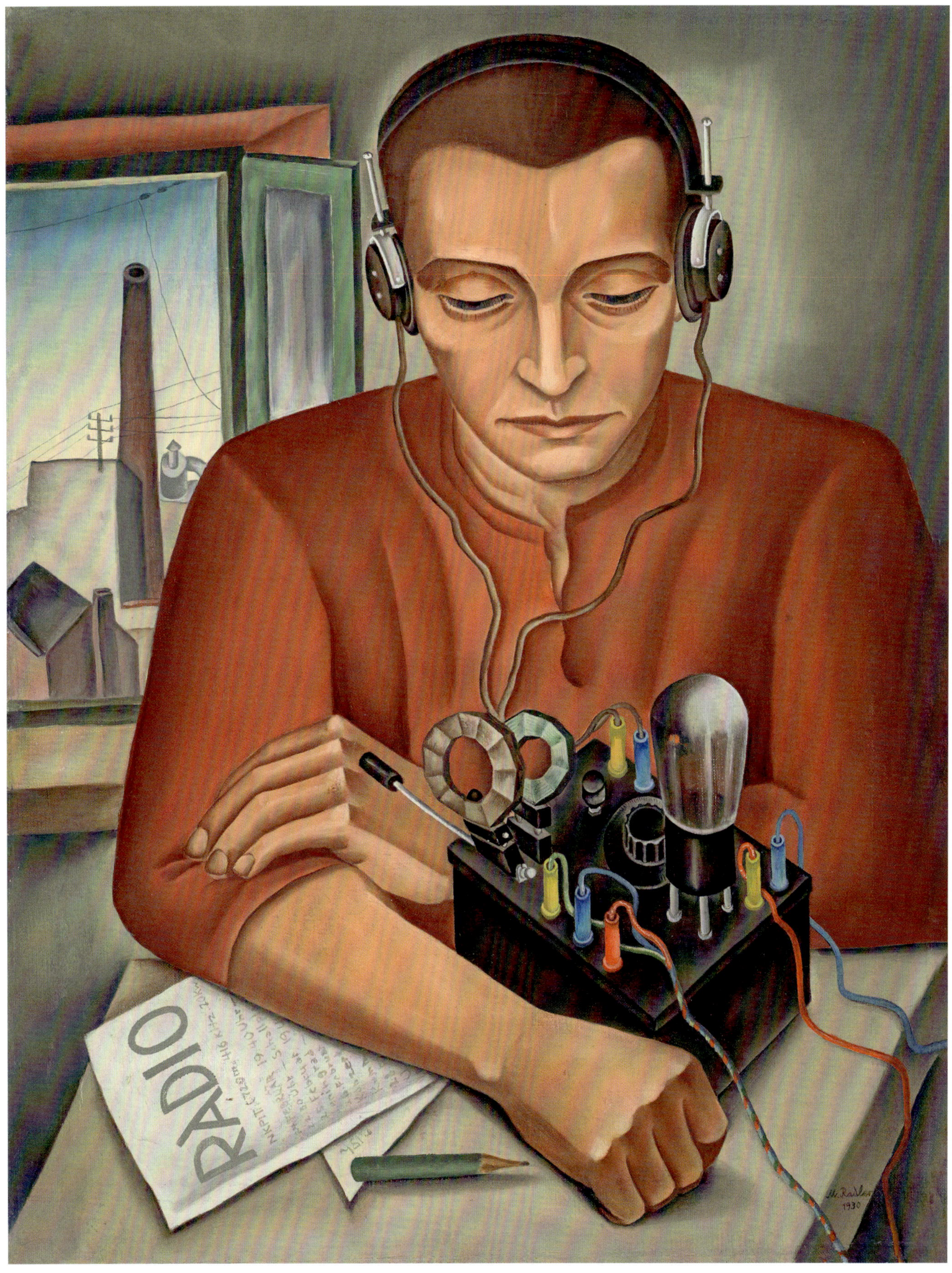

RADIO.

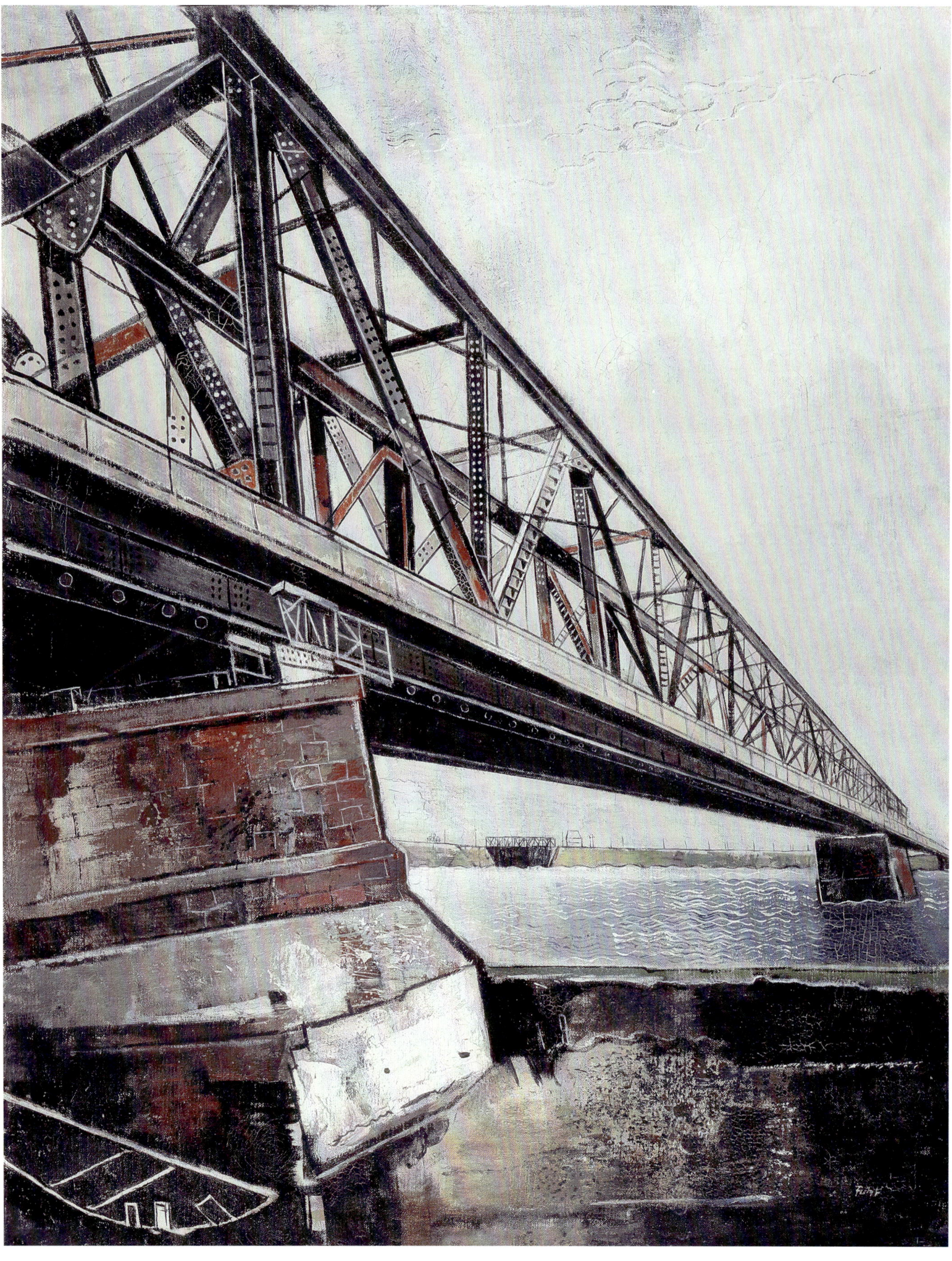

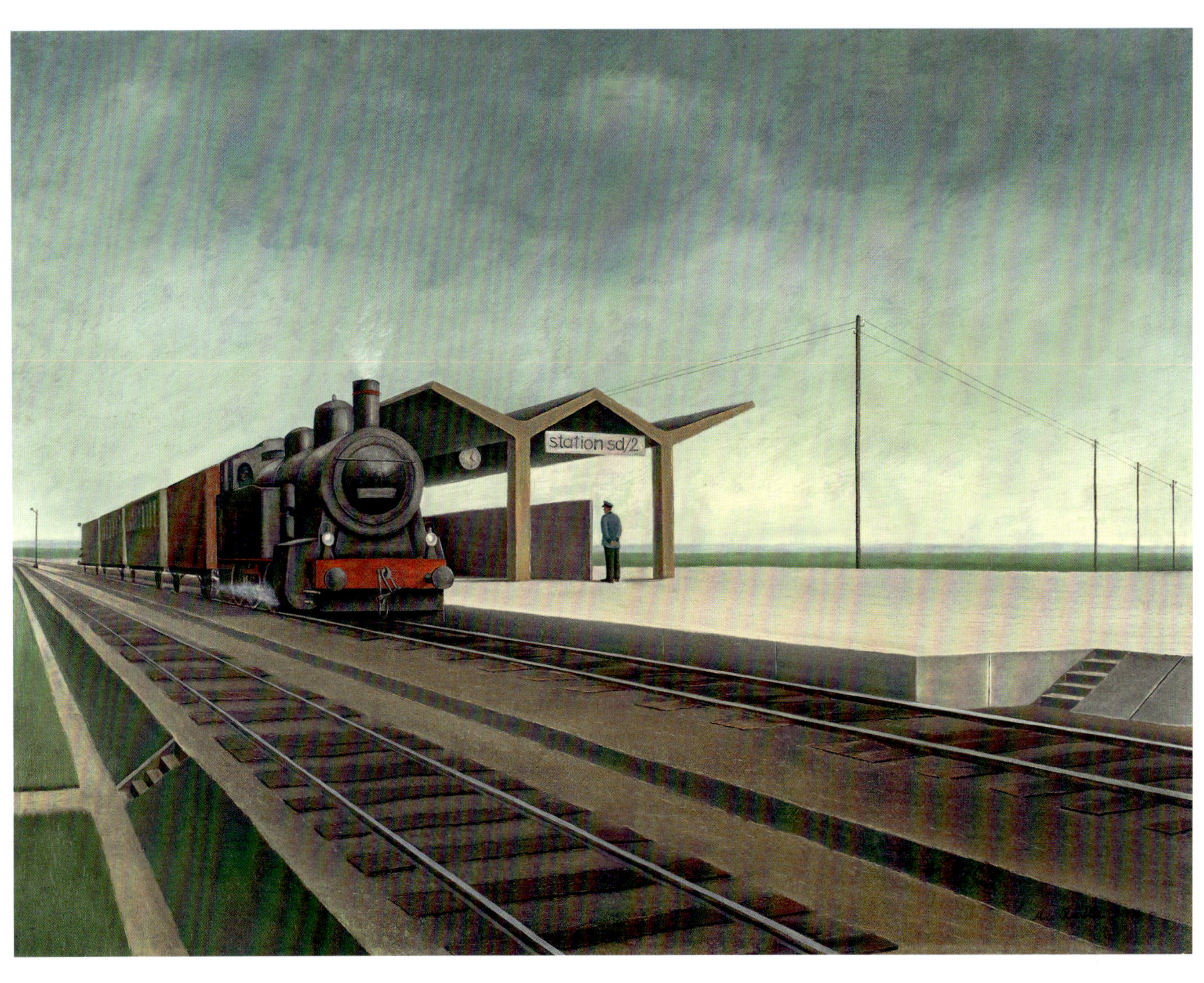

Opposite page: **FRANZ XAVER FUHR** *Eisenbrücke* (Iron Bridge), 1928

MAX RADLER *Station SD/2*, 1933
Oil on panel, 64 × 84 cm. Galerie Berinson, Berlin

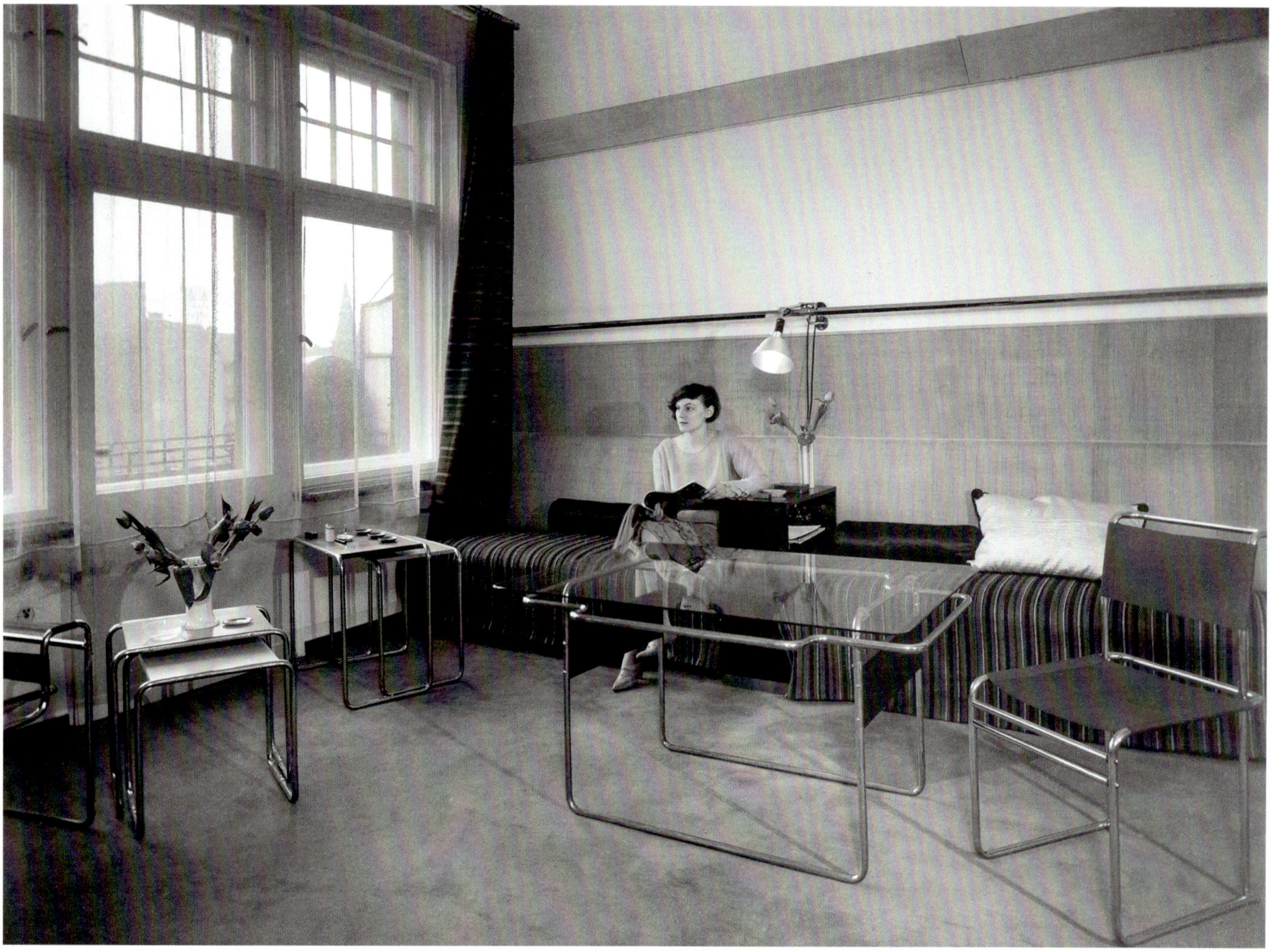

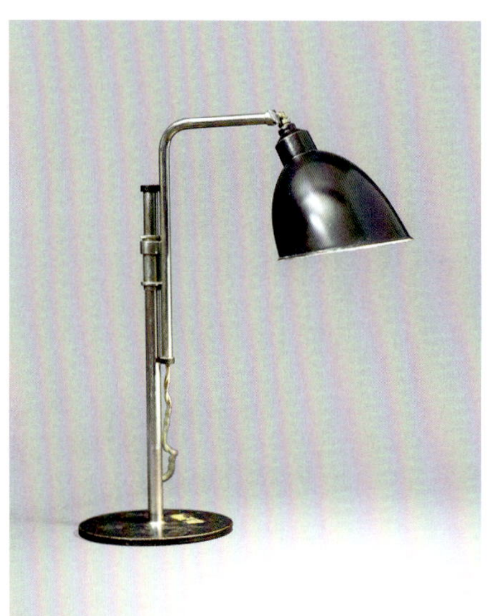

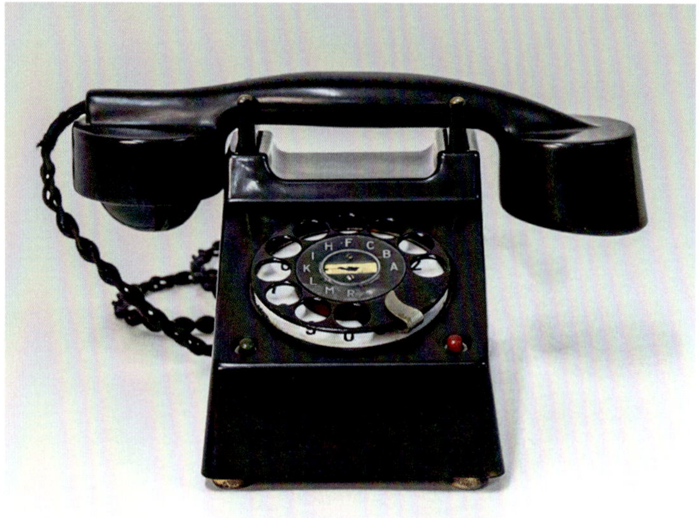

LOTTE JOHANNA JACOBI *Frau Piscator im Wohnzimmer (Mrs. Piscator in the Living Room)*, 1927
CHRISTIAN DELL *Rondella-Polo Lamp*, 1929
RICHARD SCHADWELL and **MARCEL BREUER** Telephone, the Frankfurt Model, with handset, 1929

Opposite page: **MARGARETE SCHÜTTE-LIHOTZKY** *Die Frankfurter Kücke (The Frankfurt Kitchen)*, 1927
Reconstruction of the kitchen in the exhibition *Die neue Wohnung und ihr Innenausbau mit Sonderschau des Frankfurter Hausfrauenvereins*

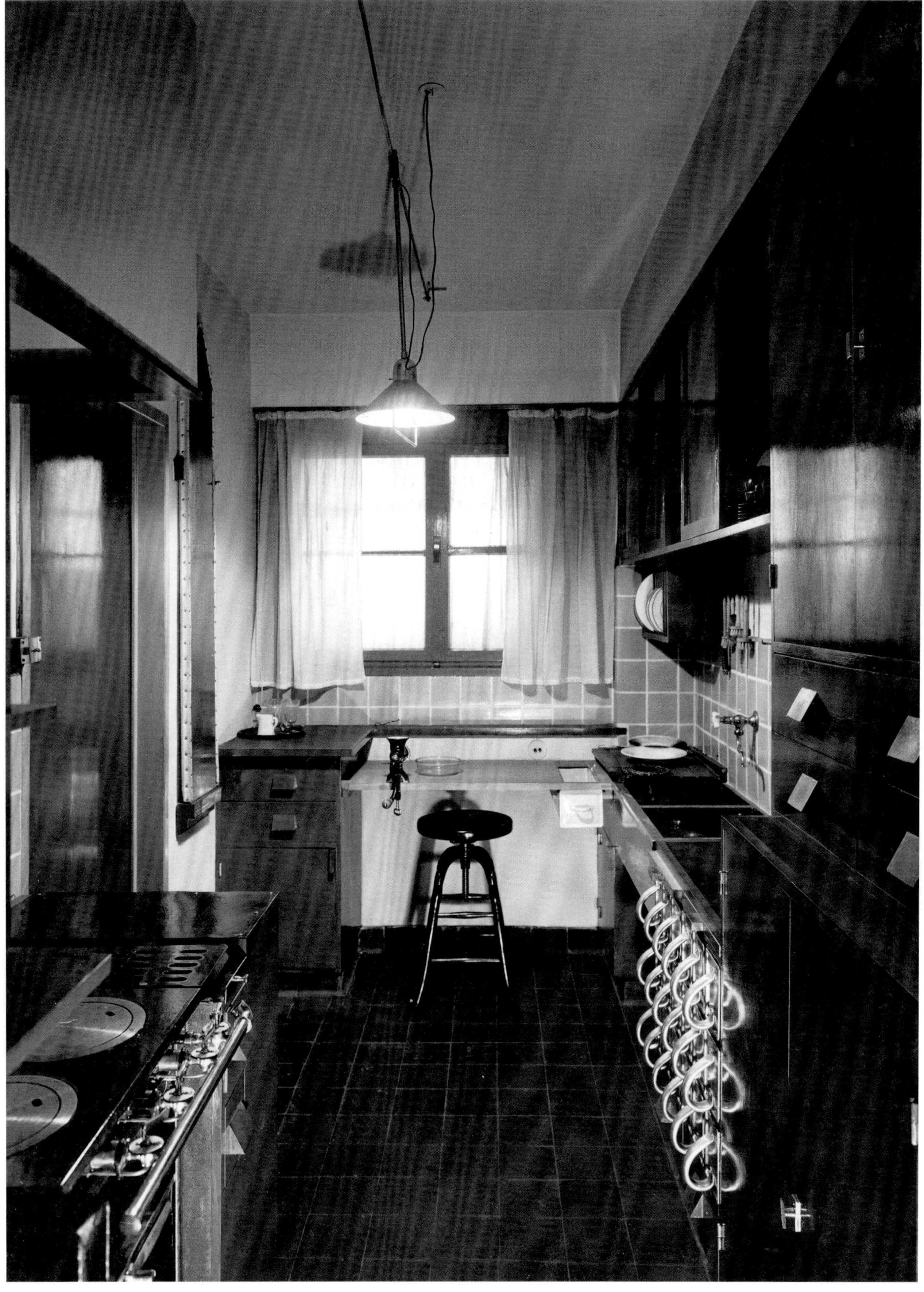

Americanism as World View, Ideology and Creed.
On the Technology Cult in Photography during the Weimar Republic

By Herbert Molderings

Following the four years of a self-destructive world war and a further four years of revolutionary turmoil, civil war-like conditions and devastating inflation, people in mid-1920s Germany found themselves confronted with the fact that, with America, a new political and economic world power had entered the stage of history. Suddenly it became clear to what extent production systems in the USA had been revolutionized during the past decade. There, since around 1910, a new scientific method had gained acceptance for rationalizing work processes. Known by the name of Taylorism, it had led to an unprecedented increase in work productivity. With the founding of the Reich Committee for Labor Studies (REFA) in 1924, the Taylor system was established in Germany as the recognized model for business organization in German capitalism. In certain economic sectors, where up to that point craftsmanship manufacturing had prevailed (for example, in the construction industry), full-scale industrialization was now being pressed forward. In addition, an intensive rationalization took place in industries that already existed. American production methods and ways of life were imported on a grand scale. At the time, just about everything was "Americanized", ranging from revue theater and music life to film production, office business to newspaper layout, sports culture to love, cashless payment transactions to drinks. "The Americanization of Adventure" was the title of a satiric article written by Richard Huelsenbeck in the Literarische Welt in 1926, in which he introduced a new type of traveler seeking to experience foreign cultures at production-line speed. This phenomenon of enthusiastically espousing American inventions, lifestyle and philosophy formed the concrete empirical basis of what became known as "Americanism", a strong intellectual movement during the Weimar Republic, which saw in present-day America the model for the future of a new and democratic Germany. At times, this enthusiasm for America took on ecstatic features, such as those found on the perspective-crashing photographs and in the breathless, staccato commentaries published by Erich Mendelsohn at the turn of the year 1925/26 in his photography *Amerika. 82 Photographs*. Here, using revolutionary new photographs, a sensory view was provided for those who loved the idea of America, but who had never seen the country with their own eyes.[1] The geographical center of this new world view was Berlin, which for a short time, had overtaken Paris as the liveliest and most modern European metropolis. In September 1927, Walter Ruttmann's experimental documentary film *Berlin: Symphony of a Great City* premiered there. An edition of the Illustrierter Film-Kurier served as an advertising brochure for the film, its full-page formats filled with photo collages of the modern Berlin.[2] These were studded all over with skyscrapers soaring up into the sky, though in reality, they were not in Berlin – at this point in time there was not a single high-rise building there yet – but in New York, Chicago and Detroit.[3] The photographs of the skyscrapers that formed the architectural background of the Berlin collages had nearly all been cut out from the picture pages of Mendelsohn's America book. The most famous of these "sticker pictures" was Umbo's photo collage of *The Racing Reporter* dating from the end of 1926.[4] It shows the legendary reporter Egon Erwin Kisch striding like a metallic giant across a landscape of mountaintops, sky-

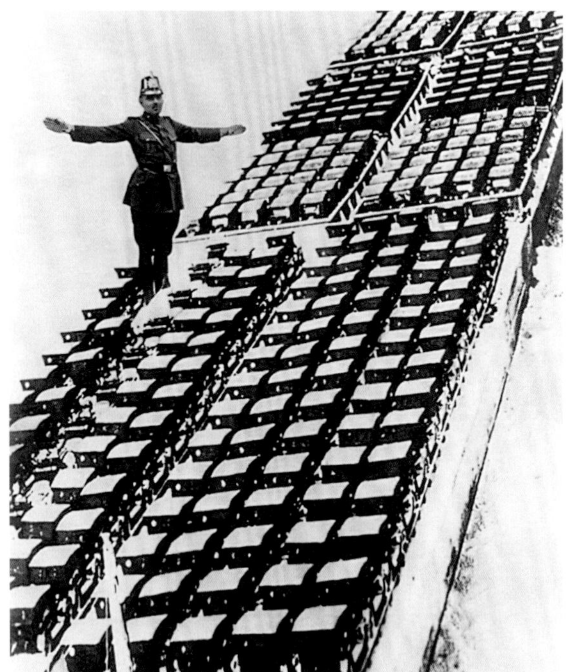

FOX EUROPA PRODUKTION Photo collage advertising the film *Berlin: Die Sinfonie der Großstadt* (Berlin: Symphony of a Great City) by Walter Ruttmann, 1927
Opposite page: **UMBO** *Der Rasende Reporter* (The Racing Reporter) (Egon Erwin Kisch), 1926

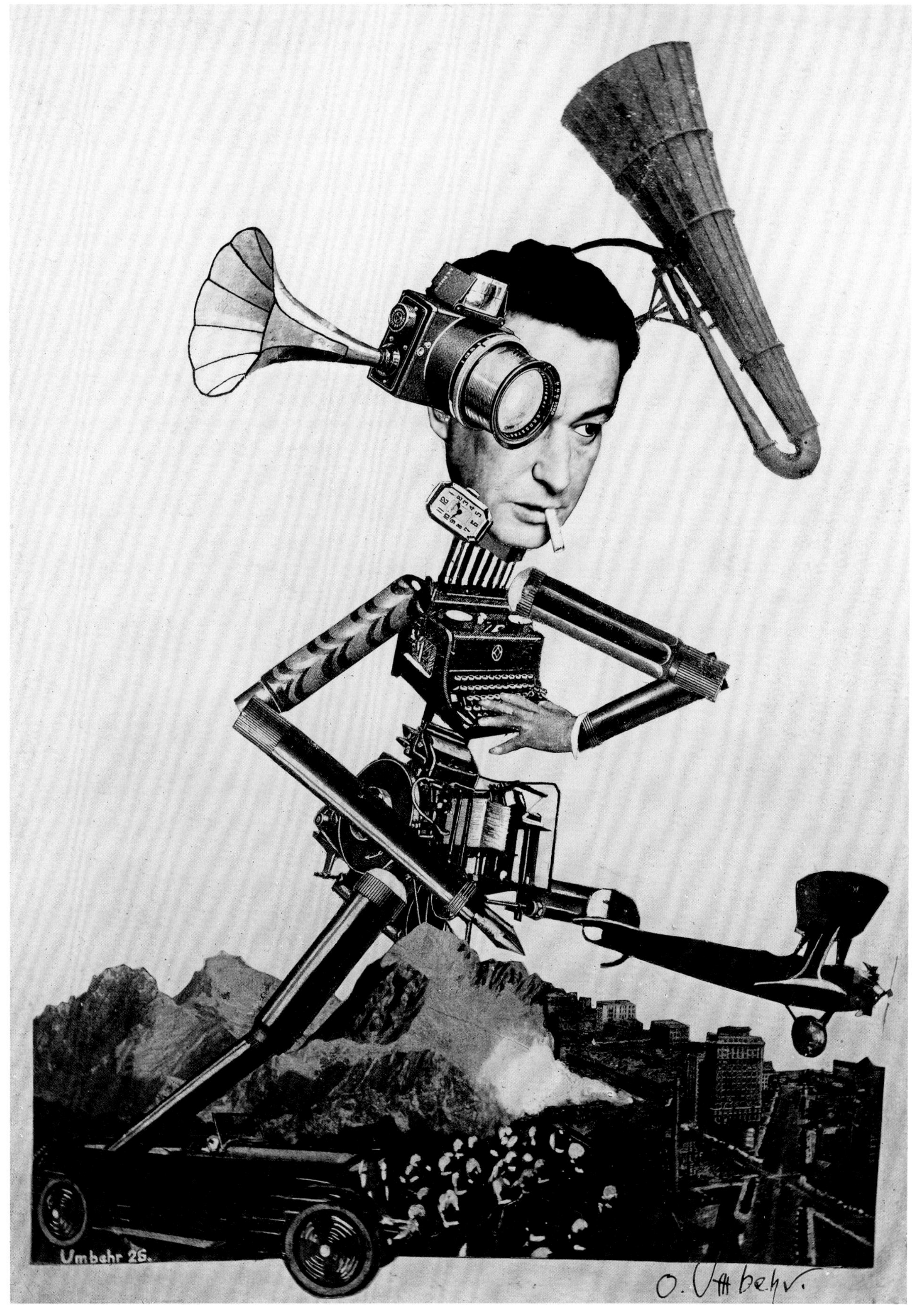

Umbehr 26.
O. Umbehr.

scrapers and a crowd of people. The automobile and airplane raise him above the constraints of time and space, the typewriter and printing press command his inner life, with the gramophone and camera constituting his ear and eye. Nothing of the natural organism of the actual person is left but the outer skin of his physiognomy. All of his sensual organs have been replaced with equipment, and he is left with only one hand free and one eye open to operate it all. Kisch embodied a new literary type. In 1925, he had published a collection of factual accounts called "The Racing Reporter", which had made such reporting socially acceptable as a literary form.[5] The Racing Reporter, this was the "speedy American correspondent",[6] the journalist in the age of the assembly line, Taylorism and wireless communication.

Whereas the skyscraper and assembly line constituted the external symbols of Americanism, its intellectual core was shaped by the notion that in the USA, a society of technology experts had come about who were in a position to solve in an objective and rational way the social problems that had torn apart the European nations. It was the industrialist Henry Ford, whom the republican and left-wing liberal German intelligentsia regarded as embodying those ideals, that had excited them about America. His autobiography *My Life and Work*, published in German translation in 1923, became a 1920s bestseller.[7] It bore the promise "to make the industrial desert bloom like the rose".[8] Characteristic of Ford's companies were the introduction of the "moving assembly line", the rationalization of all planning and production processes, as well as the transfer of the production of components from the sub-contractors and suppliers to his own factory. For the SPD (Social Democratic Party of Germany) and the social-democratically-oriented union leaders, Ford's maxim that "well-paid workers do not go in for merely destructive revolution"[9] bore promise of allaying the constant threat of social revolution that had been present since 1918. The influential economist Friedrich von Gottl-Ottlilienfeld recognized in Ford's organization methods the chance for a "white socialism with a pure and energetic mind".[10] He writes in his 1924 book on Fordism that Ford had proven that a peaceful coexistence between capital and work is possible, if only the classes fighting each other perceived themselves as partners and subordinated themselves to an "enthusiastic service to the community".[11]

While Ford dismissed the health dangers of extreme rationalization for the workers on his assembly lines as the fixed notions of "sa-

Ion experts" and "professional agitators"[12], after visiting the plants in Detroit, German economic experts, engineers and writers attested to him that the workers in the assembly halls did not look like proletarians, but like gentlemen executing their monotonous manual labor with a sports-like attitude. This is how the famous travel writer Heinrich Hauser, who illustrated his books with his own photographs beginning in 1928, described it in his work of 1931, *Dirt Tracks to Chicago*.[13] Even as he denounces the inhumanity of life in the large American cities, he is full of praise for Ford's River-Rouge Factory in Dearborn, Michigan. "One works, but does not sweat at Ford", he writes about the working conditions at the foundry and Martin blast furnace.[14] "The conveyor belts often run at surprising speed. The workers walk along with them as they work, often turned backwards. An almost sportive impression came about,

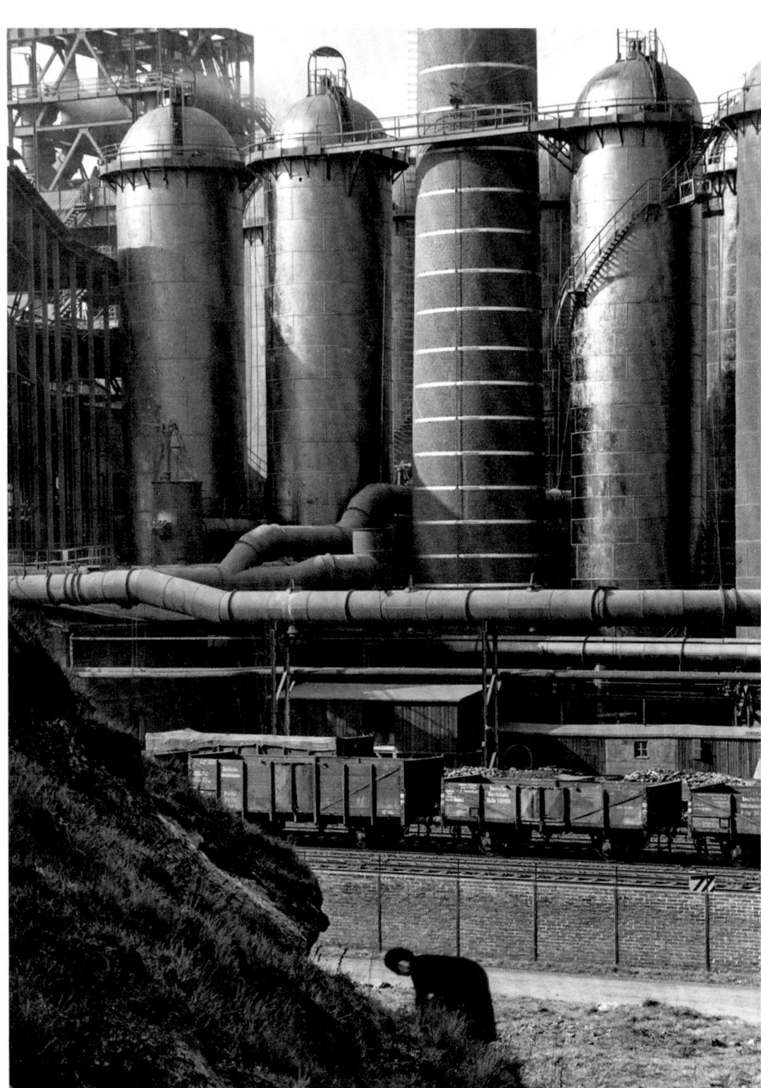

ALBERT RENGER-PATZSCH *Gute Hoffnungshütte* (The Steel Mill of Good hope), 1934
Gelatin silver print, 22.5 × 16.5 cm. Galerie Berinson, Berlin

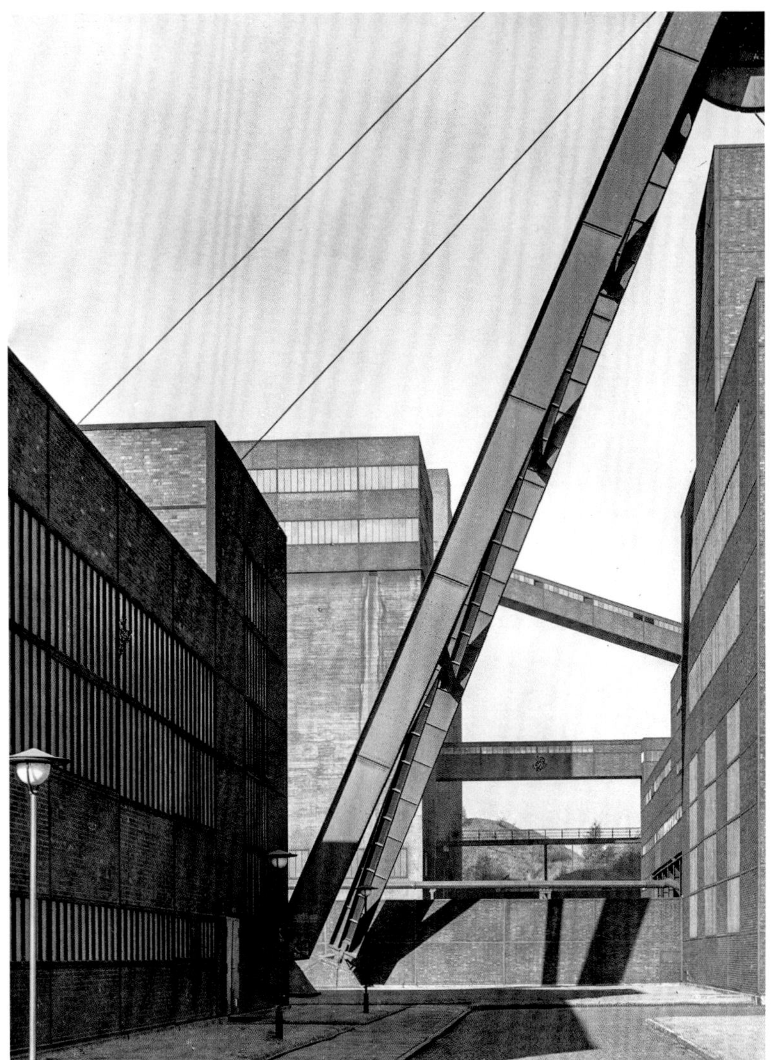

until now, but the way is open, and with diligence and spirit, someday all of mankind can follow those children of good fortune", declared the political philosopher and founder of the Paneuropean-Union, Count Coudenhove-Kalergi, in his book of 1925 *Practical Idealism*.[17] As an alternative to the specter of socialist revolution in the East, he propagated the "world revolution of technology". "We, too, stand at a turning point in world affairs. Mankind today expects from the socialist era the dawn of the Golden Age. The turning point hoped for will come perhaps: though it will not come through politics – it will come through technology; not from a revolutionary, but from an inventor."[18] The technology cult, New Objectivity and Americanism are different facets of the same socio-cultural process: rationalization driven forward in all areas of work and life. As early as 1927, one could read in the German newspaper BZ am Mittag that the rallying cry of New Objectivity in art and literature ultimately centered around purely economic considerations. "The New Objectivity came from the modern office, from factory operations", the article stated. "Today there are societies that have thought through their office operations down to the last detail – of course, putting commercial interests first – in order to achieve swift work results and ensure the most efficient use of manpower in the office. [...] Factory? For many decades, the Taylor system has been tantamount to New Objectivity."[19] The realization that it was even possible to organize offices patterned after machine models sparked enthusiasm in the feuilleton pages of the newspapers more than any other phenomenon of the rapidly advancing Americanization of Berlin. In 1926, the popular magazine UHU, published each Monday by Ullstein Verlag, featured an 8-page photo reportage by Fritz Zielesch and Sasha Stone called "The Hundred-Horsepower Office – No Utopia".[20] It demonstrated just how much efficiency concepts taken over from industry, such as the introduction of scheduling time values for work processes and new forms of organization systems, made office work more and more similar to piece-work in factories.

"Technology" as a goddess of a substitute religion, the dreams of fully-automated businesses in the way they were depicted in the new objective literature, found its pendant-piece images in the photographs of manufacturing halls emptied of workers, which Albert Renger-Patzsch created for the Werkbund-book *Iron and Steel*, 1931.[21] Only rarely does a person happen to appear on the production premises in the 97 photographs reproduced here. In gazing at the pictures, the impression arises

something like 'footwork' in boxing."[15] Describing lunchbreak, it would appear that memories of a city stroll through Paris get mixed in: "Brilliant food in the canteen: a French chef, 'high-priced'. A strange smell in the factory: almost scented – hot iron often smells like flowers."[16]

In order to lower production costs and become more competitive on the global market, German companies began an intensive rationalization process in the 1920s following the American model. By taking over the American production methods, politicians, union leaders and intellectuals in both leftist and rightist camps believed they would soon be able to overcome the misery of the postwar years and attain the legendary standard of living American society had. In this situation, technology became the magic formula. "Technology has burst open the gates of Paradise; through this narrow entrance only few (the dollar millionaires) have tread

as if the flywheels, cranes and automatic milling machines were producing steel sheets, crankshafts, motorcycles, cash registers, etc. all on their own, and all that was left for the people to do was to make use of them. In connection with a maximum of rationalizing all production methods, type classification and norming had become basic issues of aesthetics in the 1920s and were applied to the art of building as well as to typography, the areas of product design and the realm of photography. In this case also, it had been Albert Renger-Patzsch, who found a new aesthetic form for experiencing the type-classified, industrial world of things. He had understood that the industrial mass product only unfolds its intrinsic aesthetics in the comparative form of repetition, i.e. at the moment when in the picture the serial principle is immediately visualized as a basic feature of industrial production. The rhythm of standardized things, the ornamental accumulation of what is always the same counts among the typical characteristics of the new kind of photographs of aluminum pots and shoe lasts, which Renger-Patzsch had presented in 1928 in his pioneering photography book *The World is Beautiful*.[22] Its paradigmatic images, subsequently repeated en masse in New Objectivity photographs, aestheticized Taylorism. In June of 1927, at about the same time Renger-Patzsch was working out this new aestheticism in connection with commissions he had received from the Faguswerk factory in Alfeld and the Schocken department store in Zwickau, Siegfried Kracauer published an essay in the Frankfurter Zeitung that would later become famous, "The Mass Ornament". Here, he used the example of the Tiller Girls to demonstrate that the principles of the Taylor System: Rationalization, type classification and norming not only controlled the sphere of production, they also proved equally effective as new aesthetic principles in the newly emerging entertainment industry. "These products of the American distraction factories", he wrote about the new American dance groups, who had been performing regularly in revue theaters in Berlin and Munich since 1924, "are no longer individual girls, but indissoluble girl clusters whose movements are demonstrations of mathematics".[23] Like the girl working on the assembly line, each in her movements carries out "a partial function without grasping the totality".[24] As an isolated particle of the mass, she participates in the production of the abstract, ornamental movements of the dance group as a whole. Kracauer understood the dance performance of the Tiller Girls imitating the rhythm of the machine as "the mass ornament", which he defined as a "rational and empty form"[25] of the

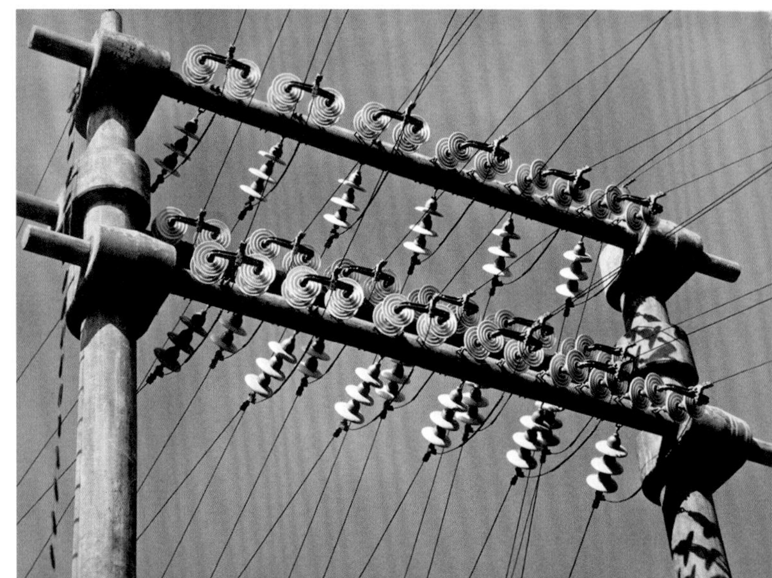

ALBERT RENGER-PATZSCH *Isolatorenkette* (Insulator Chain), 1925
Gelatin silver print, 27.3 × 37.5 cm. Galerie Berinson, Berlin

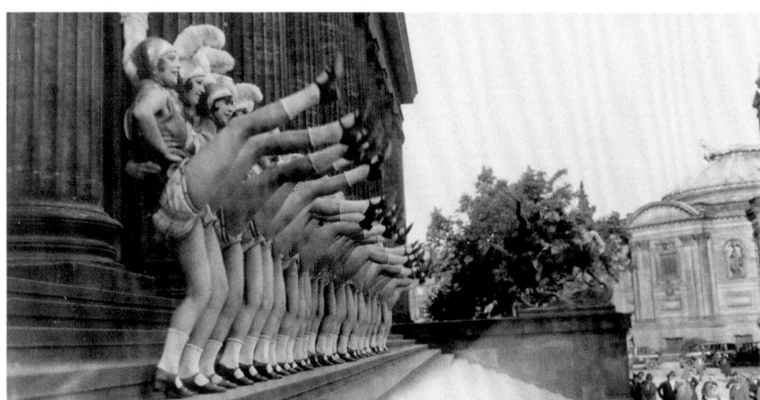

ATLANTIC PHOTO GMBH *Die Alfred-Jackson-Girls. Ein Tausendfüssler*
(The Alfred Jackson Girls. A Millipede), 1928

anonymous, physical and cultural organization of the mass in the offices and factories: "The mass ornament is the aesthetic reflex of the rationality to which the prevailing economic system aspires".[26] An iconic photograph of such a mass ornament is the 1928 snapshot of the Alfred Jackson Girls reclining on the lawn in Berlin, reproduced as a paradigm of the new "Woman of 1930"[27] in the photography book *20 Years of World History in 700 Pictures*.

Fordism and Taylorism were essential components of Americanism, though they were not completely synonymous with the latter concept. It was the political and liberal, pacifistic and libertarian ideas that fit with the enthusiasm for America and dominated in the cultural sphere of the Weimar Republic. Unlike the Fordism that excited Nazi politicians and economists as well as the pacifist politician Coudenhove-Kalergi, these ideas went contrary to the views of right-wing conservative thinkers. In the eyes of conservative cultural criticism, the increasing Americanization of life was "poison and plague, a lack of character, the repudiation of our most sacred attitudes towards life and historical tradition".[28] In his book of 1927 on Americanism, the political journalist and later Nazi editor of the Hamburger Fremdenblatt, Adolf Halfeld described the United States as a country "of machine people, which derives from a single basic principle of success a world order of most insulting paltriness, robbing life of its eternal secrets. [...] America has destroyed Eros to make possible the emergence of the machine person."[29] This life of the American people, purportedly stripped of all its mysteries, is something he portrays in all shades of complete disdain. "Even the common man can, with some effort, outfit himself with the typical accoutrements of the chic citizen, including a radio, gramophone, electronic piano, vacuum cleaner, automatic stove and the like. In accordance with unwritten law, on a certain day of the year, he can cast off his felt hat to don a straw one, and then, together with all the millions of other New Yorkers, take his girl out for a drive as a dapper gentleman."[30] Halfeld contrasts this genre image of petit-bourgeois material happiness against the image of the youth in Germany after the First World War, one deeply influenced by the death on the battlefield, deprivation and need: "Instead, I praise the spiritual needs of a youth battered by war and revolution which, for all its despair, is strong enough to glimpse the man of tomorrow. Frictions produce fresh sparks". The horror the German nationalist cultural critic had of the New York masses goes hand-in-hand here with his emphatically distorted picture of the First World War as a kind of spiritual adventure: "Frictions create fresh sparks."[31] Before the backdrop of this cynically-reactionary apologia, "Americanism" was understood as espousing pacifism and social reform. "We insisted on making the present honest; and sympathized with the future," wrote the literary critic and author of radio plays, Hans A. Joachim in 1930 in an omnibus review of "Novels from America" in the Neue Rundschau. "We followed America. America was a good idea; it was the country of the future. It was at home in its own decade. We were too young to know it; meanwhile, we loved it. For us here, it was long enough that the glorious discipline of technology had only appeared in the form of tank, mine, and the Blue Cross[32] and only for the purpose of destroying human lives. In America, technology was used in the service of human lives. The sympathy expressed for the lift, the radio tower, and jazz was demonstrative. It was a creed. It proffered a way to reforge the flamethrower into a vacuum cleaner and the ploughshare into a steam plough. Technology demonstrated that the time had come to make civilization a matter for civilians. The way we stood to America showed where we stood."[33]

HERBERT MOLDERINGS is an art historian and professor emeritus at Ruhr-Universität Bochum in Germany. He has curated exhibitions in Europe and contributed to several publications.

1.   Berlin: R. Mosse, 1926, 2nd expanded version 1928. (Edition in English: Erich Mendelsohn's "Amerika": 82 Photographs, Mineola, New York, Dover Publications, 1993).
2.   See Herbert Molderings, Umbo. Otto Umbehr 1902-1980, Düsseldorf: Richter, 1995, pp. 89-93. (Edition in English: Herbert Molderings, Umbo. Otto Umbehr 1902-1980, Düsseldorf, Richter & Fey, first edition, 1 Jan. 1996).
3.   See here as well the advertising brochure Symphonie d'une grande ville published in 1928 by the Société des films artistiques (SOFAR) to go along with the film in France.
4.   See Molderings, Umbo (as in footnote 3), pp. 92-94.
5.   Berlin: Erich Reiss Verlag Publishers.
6.   Quoted from a new edition by Sieben-Stäbe-Verlag Publishers, Berlin 1930, p. 10. Quote translation: ev
7.   Henry Ford, My Life and Work. https://freeditorial.com/en/books/filter-author/henry-ford, accessed 21 June, 2022.
8.   Ibid., p. 224.
9.   Henry Ford, Today and Tomorrow, New York: Doubleday, Page and Company, 1926, p. 259.
10.   Friedrich von Gottl-Ottlilienfeld, Fordismus. Über Industrie und technische Vernunft, Jena: G. Fischer, 1924. Quoted here from the 3rd expanded version of 1926, p. 40. Quote translation: ev
11.   Ibid., p. 38. Quote translation: ev
12.   Quoted from Helmut Lethen, Neue Sachlichkeit 1924–1932. Studien zur Literatur des »Weißen Sozialismus«, Stuttgart: Metzler, 1970, p. 21. Quote translation: ev
13.   Heinrich Hauser, Feldwege nach Chicago, Berlin: S. Fischer Publishers, 1931. Quote translation: ev
14.   Ibid., p. 230.
15.   Ibid., p. 231.
16.   Ibid., p. 233.
17.   Richard Nikolaus von Coudenhove-Kalergi, Praktischer Idealismus. Adel – Technik – Pazifismus, Wien, Leipzig 1925, p. 113. Quote translation: ev
18.   Ibid., p. 105.
19.   Christian Buchholtz, "Die neue Parole Sachlichkeit", in: BZ am Mittag, Berlin, 13 April 1927. Quote translation: ev
20.   In: UHU, II, 7, Berlin, April 1926, pp. 52–59. Quote translation: ev
21.   Albert Renger-Patzsch, Eisen und Stahl, Berlin: Reckendorf Publishers, 1931. Quote translation: ev
22.   Albert Renger-Patzsch, Die Welt ist schön, Munich: Kurt Wolff, 1928. p. 50, p. 55.
23.   Siegfried Kracauer, "Das Ornament der Masse" [1927], in Kracauer, Das Ornament der Masse, Frankfurt am Main: Suhrkamp Publishers, 1977, p. 50. Edition in English: Siegfried Kracauer, The Mass Ornament (Das Ornament der Masse): Weimar Essays, Cambridge, Harvard University Press, 1995, p. 76.
24.   Ibid., p. 78.
25.   Ibid., p. 84.
26.   Ibid., p. 79.
27.   1910-1930 Zwanzig Jahre Weltgeschichte in 700 Bildern. Introduction by Friedrich Sieburg, Berlin: Transmare Publishers, 1931, p. 234.
28.   In: Die Tat, year 20, vol. 1, 1928/29, p. 60. Quoted from Lethen (as in footnote 13), p. 25.
29.   Adolf Halfeld, Amerika und der Amerikanismus. Kritische Betrachtungen eines Deutschen und Europäer, Jena: E. Diederichs, 1927, p. 37, 277.
30.   Ibid., p. 42.
31.   Ibid., p. 43.
32.   This term referred to the poisonous gases used in the first world war.
33.   Hans A. Joachim, "Romane aus Amerika", in: Die Neue Rundschau, XXXXI, 9, Berlin/Leipzig, 1930, p. 398.

Futura That Conquered the World

By Patrick Rössler

Fonts rarely attract the attention of the art world. It seems as if they are 'just there', a minor factor except perhaps in graphic design. Paul Renner's Futura, however, not only tells a different story – it tells a story at all, the "type of today and tomorrow", as it was touted in an early 1928 prospectus. With its geometric structure, slender lines and clear organization of semantic information, Futura stands for rationality as the goal of modern typography like no other typeface. And indeed, it has witnessed all sorts of applications over the past almost 100 years, many of them related to technical and social progress.[1] Left-wing protest against the Hitler regime? Dada artist John Heartfield favored Futura for the captions of his photomontages. Introduction of the television set on the occasion of the Olympic Games in Berlin? The official brochure from 1936 displays its contents in four languages, printed in Futura. A need for signage for the territories occupied by Germany during the Second World War? The official Nazi training course for typography recommends Futura among other fonts – in 1940. And guess what font NASA used for the plaque the astronauts left on the moon in July 1969 to commemorate the first human landing? You know the answer.[2]

The number of examples seems endless, and Paul Renner, a leading typeface designer of the interwar period, must himself have been surprised at the success of his invention which, as he put it when it was introduced in 1927, struck a chord with the zeitgeist: "exact, precise, and impersonal", a legible characters produced by a typesetting machine rather than a typeface in the sense of a kind of handwriting, he wrote in an article for the magazine of the German Werkbund, Die Form.[3] Although Renner's concept of constructing a font from simple geometric figures was also pursued at other institutions such as the Bauhaus, his Futura became accepted as the standard sans serif typeface within the global avant-garde.[4] Bauer'sche Gießerei, one of the world's leading type foundries and part of the "New Frankfurt" movement, highlighted this image in marketing Futura.

Two quarto-sized leaflets from 1929, inserted in the bilingual trade magazine Gebrauchsgraphik (International Advertising Art), reached all the relevant figures in the printing industry and

conveyed precisely this image: using the example of photomontage, Futura is identified as the perfect counterpart to contemporary visual design, thus addressing the iconic turn of the period, when more and more photographers and picture agencies were flooding the editorial offices with press images. The second leaflet emphasizes type as the "soul of all advertising" – while celebrating "the purity of the simple line" represented by Futura. Tellingly, it is claimed, in an all-lowercase writing

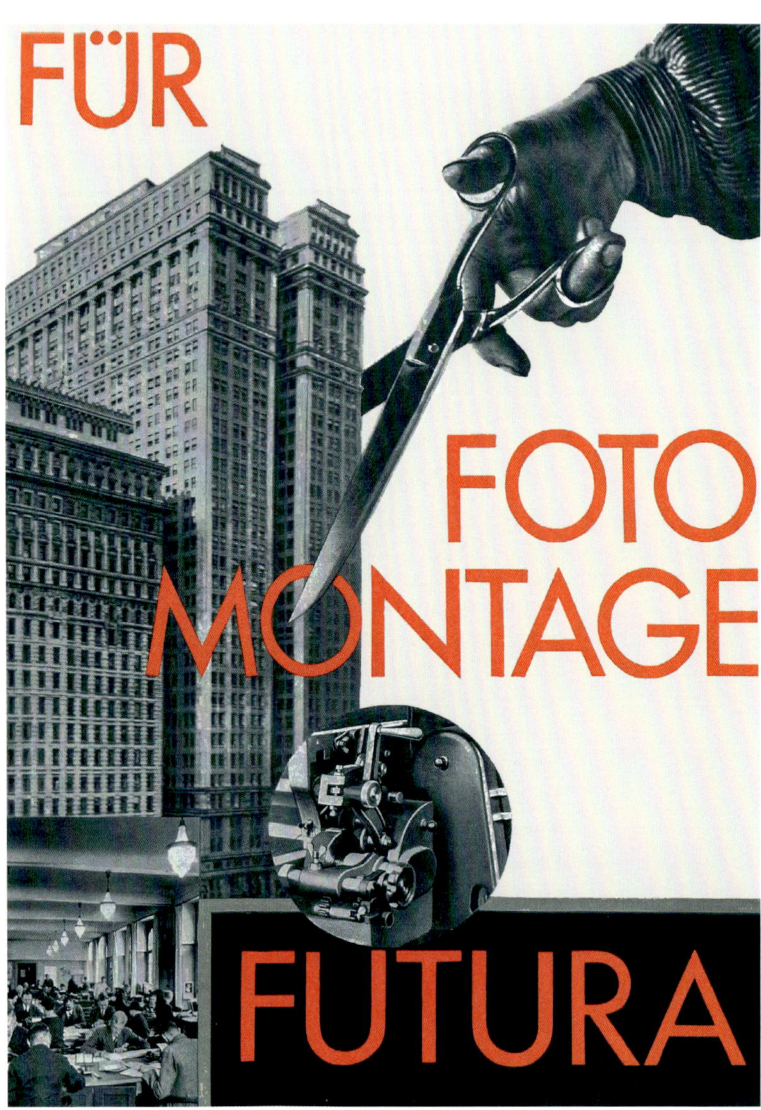

HEINRICH JOST *Für Fotomontage Futura* (For Photomontage Futura) Promotion in the journal *Gebrauchsgraphik*, Vol. 6, No. 3, March 1929

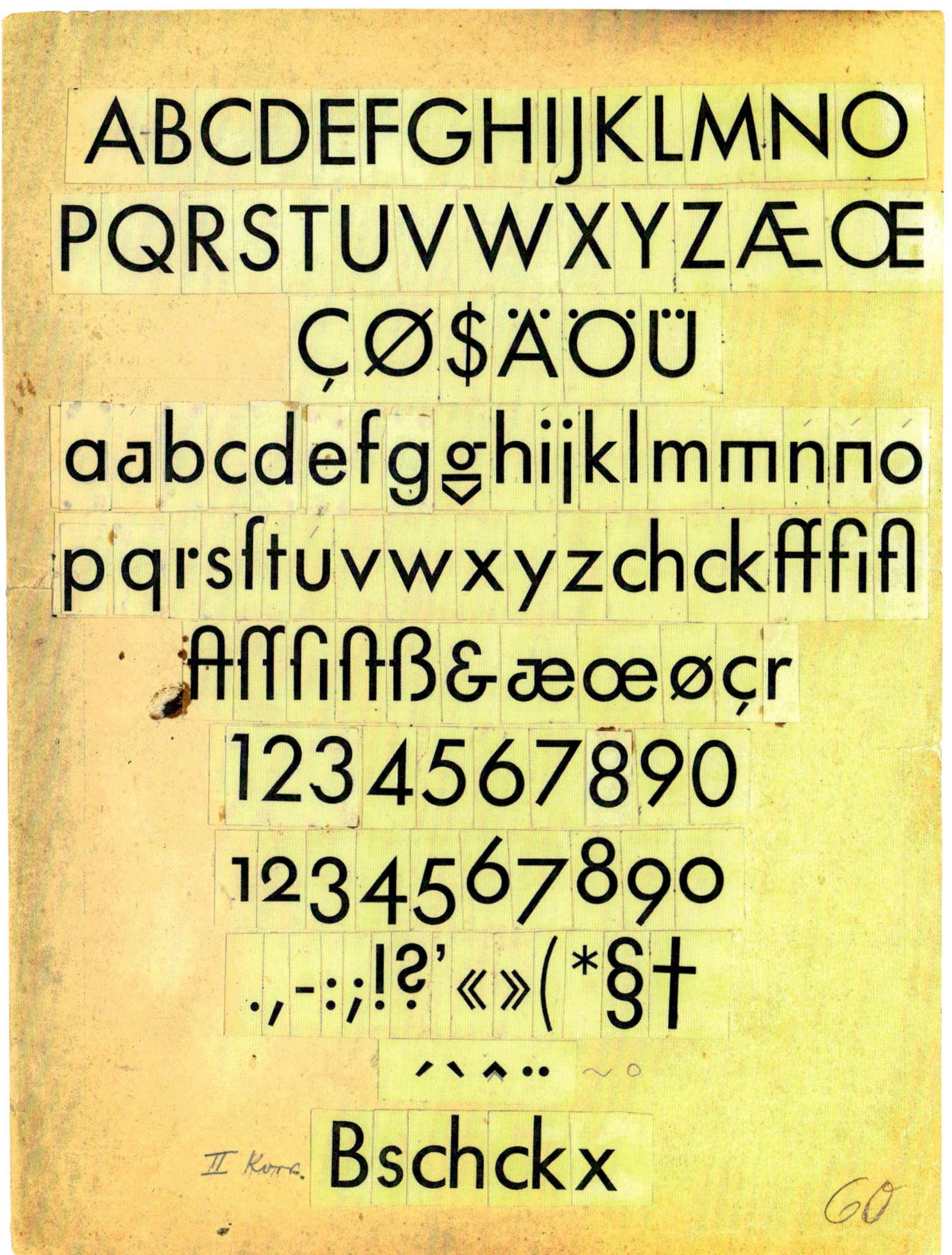

PAUL RENNER *Futura, Die Schrift unserer Zeit (Futura, the Font of our Time), trial proof of Futura semibold, 1926-1927*

their publications, as in Czecho-slovakia (e.g. Telehor), Spain (A.C.) and Italy (Casabella). The same was true for France (Arts et métiers graphiques), where, however, it was marketed by Deberny & Peignot under the title Europe to avoid anti-German hostility. In addition, thanks in part to the numerous émigrés, Futura became a must have for the U.S. design scene around Paul Rand, and the popular lifestyle magazine Vanity Fair contributed significantly to its distribution. Later Futura competed with Helvetica, which was based on Akzidenz Grotesk from the Berthold type foundry, and proved to be a preferred choice for the Swiss style of the mid-century. Thus it seems safe to say that what we now call visual socialization, at least in the Western hemisphere, was largely shaped by the fact that Renner's simple but elegant letters were omnipresent in public spaces.

PATRICK RÖSSLER is professor in communication at University of Erfurt in Germany. He is also the author of books on Germany in the 1920s, including *Bauhausmädels. A Tribute to Pioneering Women Artists* from 2019.

of course (which was promoted by the Bauhaus faculty, among others), that "the typographer now has a typeface on a par with the best art of our time."[5] From today's perspective it seems puzzling how confidently the foundry claimed a recognition normally reserved for works of fine art.

The importance of Renner's creation for the perception of the New Objectivity can hardly be overestimated. Most importantly, Futura as a "cultural phenomenon", as it was described by later observers,[6] did not remain limited to its country of origin, Germany. In the early 1930s, avant-garde movements gladly embraced the typeface for

1. Petra Eisele, Annette Ludwig & Isabel Naegele, *Futura. Die Schrift*, Mainz, Verlag Hermann Schmidt, 2016.
2. See Douglas Thomas, *Never use Futura*, New York, Princetion Architectural Press, 2017.
3. Paul Renner, "Die Schrift unserer Zeit", in *Die Form*, vol. 2, 1927, No. 4, p. 109–110.
4. Christopher Burke, *Paul Renner. The Art of Typography*, London, Hyphen Press, 1998.
5. For a reproduction see Patrick Rössler, *New Typographies. Bauhaus & Beyond: 100 Years of Functional Graphic Design in Germany*, Göttingen, Wallstein, 2018, p. 101.
6. Here and in the following see Alexandre Dumas de Rauly & Michel Wlassikoff, *Futura. Une gloire typographique*, Paris, Éditions Norma, 2011.

IN GERMANY, TRADITIONAL GENDER ROLES were redefined after the First World War. Women were now established on the labour market and obtained the right to vote in 1918. Artists were also interested in changing gender norms – one of August Sander's sections in *Menschen des 20. Jahrhunderts* (People of the 20th Century), for example, was titled 'The Woman.' With an almost sociological eye, the artists constructed a typology of the emancipated *neue Frau* (New Woman): short haircuts, cigarettes, shirts, flat chests and even ties became recurrent attributes in female portraits of the time. This new androgynous appearance incorporating the codes of masculinity is shown in Kate Diehn-Bitt's (1900-1978) *Selbstbildnis als Malerin* (Self-portrait as Painter, 1935).

In Berlin, in the famous Eldorado cabaret, an important subculture emerges, developed amongst homosexuals and transgendered, which is tolerated by the police. Artist Jeanne Mammen (1890-1976) depicted the daily life of lesbian meeting places, representing relationships between women with a certain tenderness, as also evidenced in the artist Christian Schad's (1894-1982) drawing of two young boys in love.

Transgressions of heterosexuality and the decompartmentalization of genders generated an anxiety in certain male artists that was reflected in their works in which the norm is violently avenged. Rudolf Schlichter (1890-1955), Karl Hubbuch (1891-1979) and Otto Dix (1891-1969) all produced fantasies of *Lustmorde*, sexual crimes in which women are stabbed to death or have been hanged. For some, female emancipation, especially sexual emancipation, was perceived as a threat that these representations indirectly warded off.

KATE DIEHN-BITT *Selbstbildnis als Malerin* (Self-Portrait as Painter), 1935

TRANSGRESSIONS

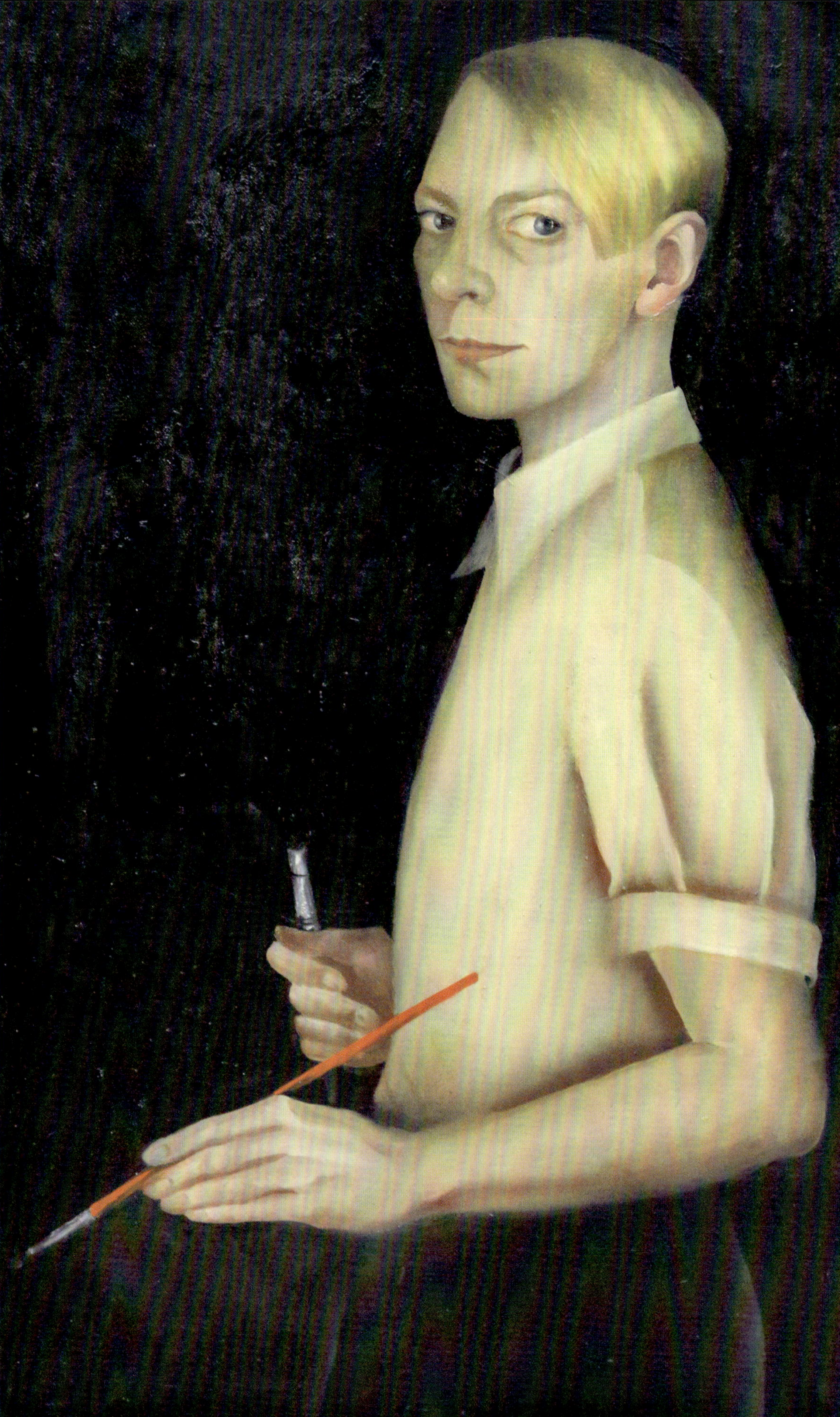

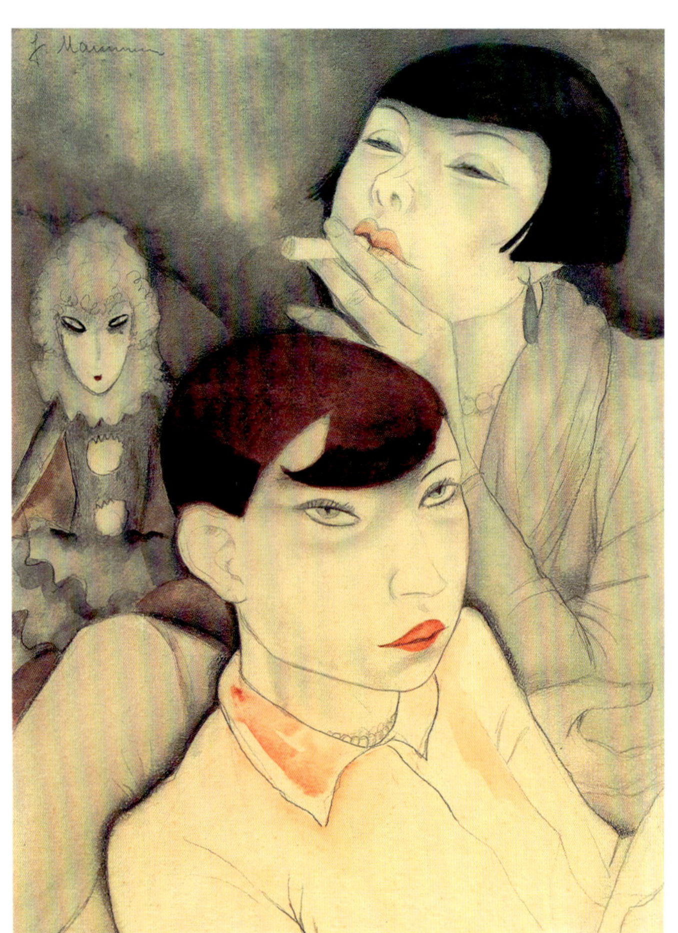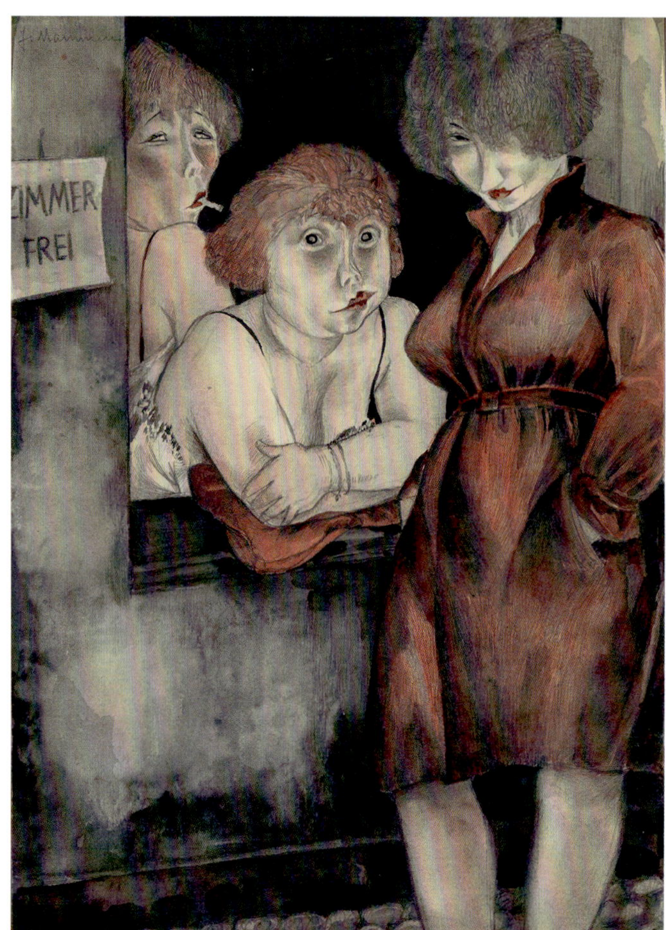

JEANNE MAMMEN *Langweilige Puppen (Boring Dolls)*, 1929
Brüderstrasse (Zimmer frei) (Brüderstrasse (Free Rooms)), 1930

100

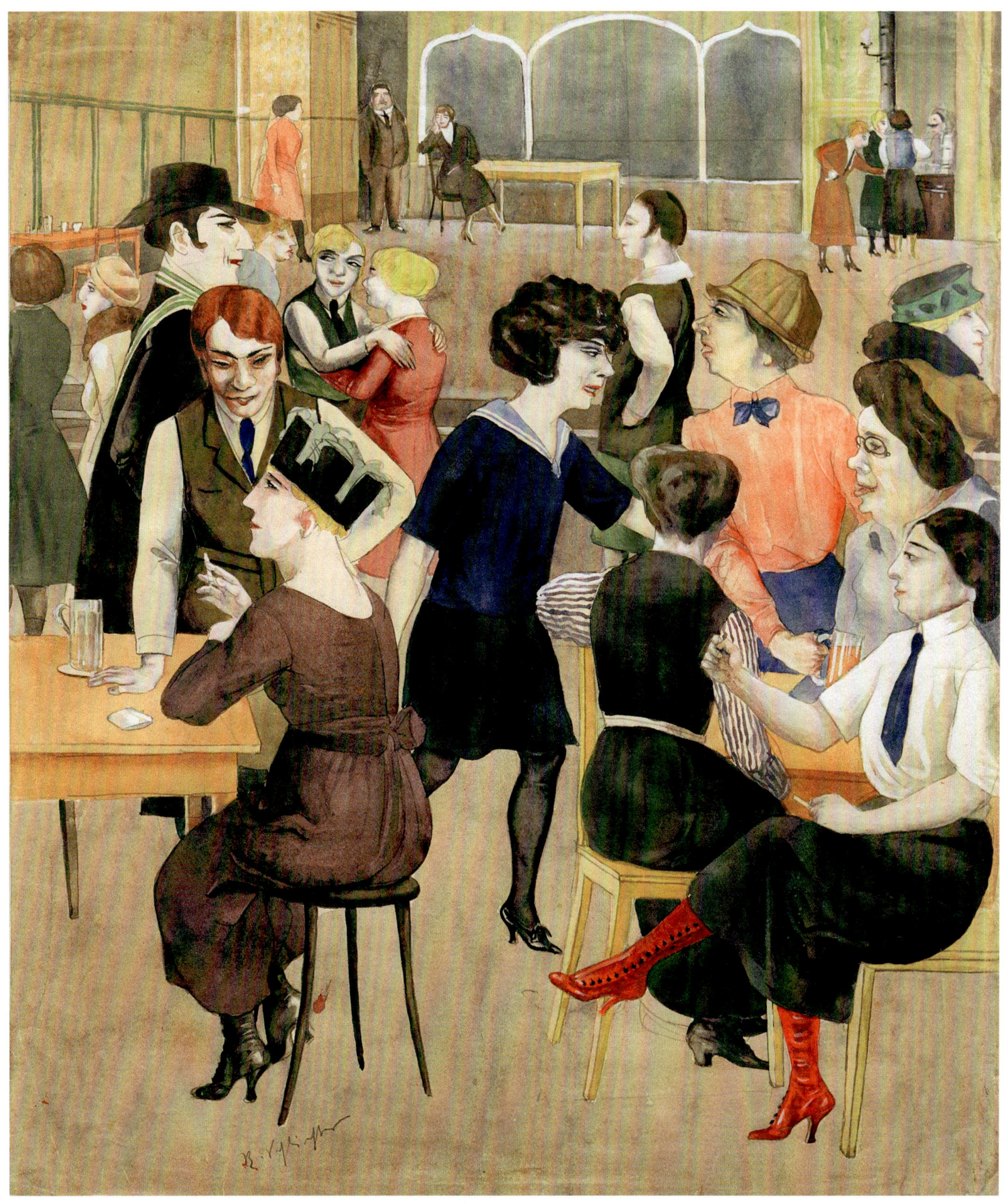

RUDOLF SCHLICHTER *Damenkneipe* (Ladies' Pub), c. 1925

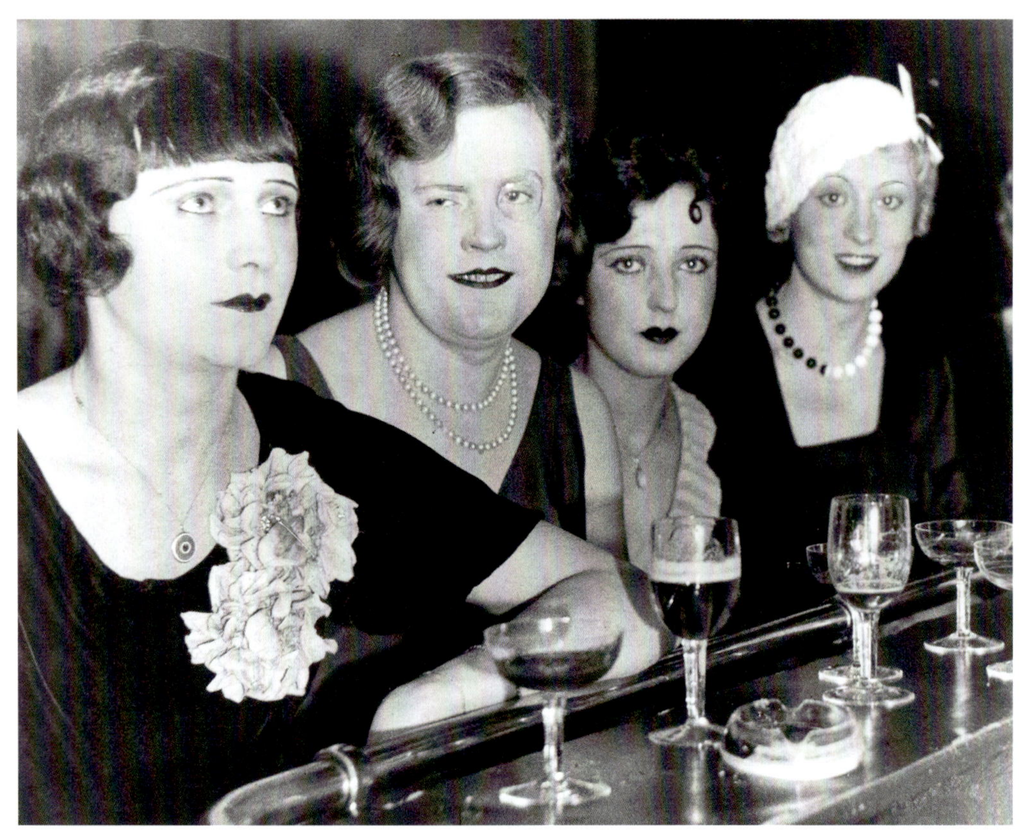

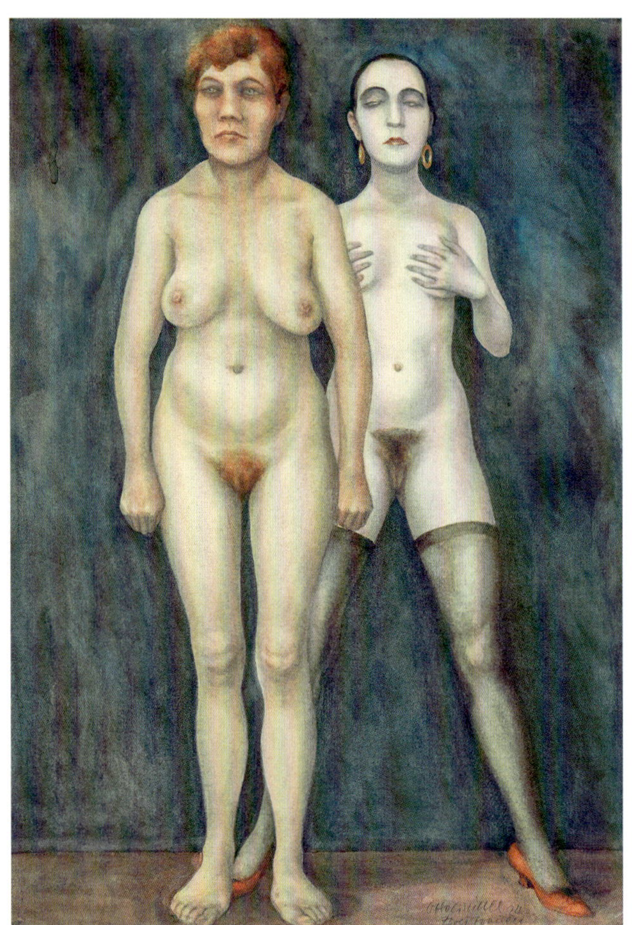

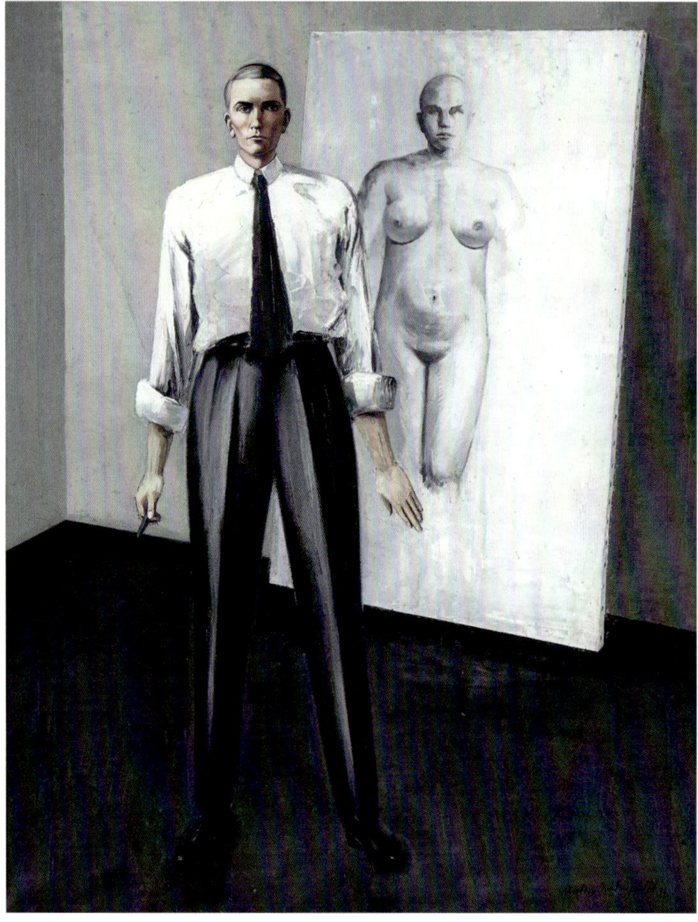

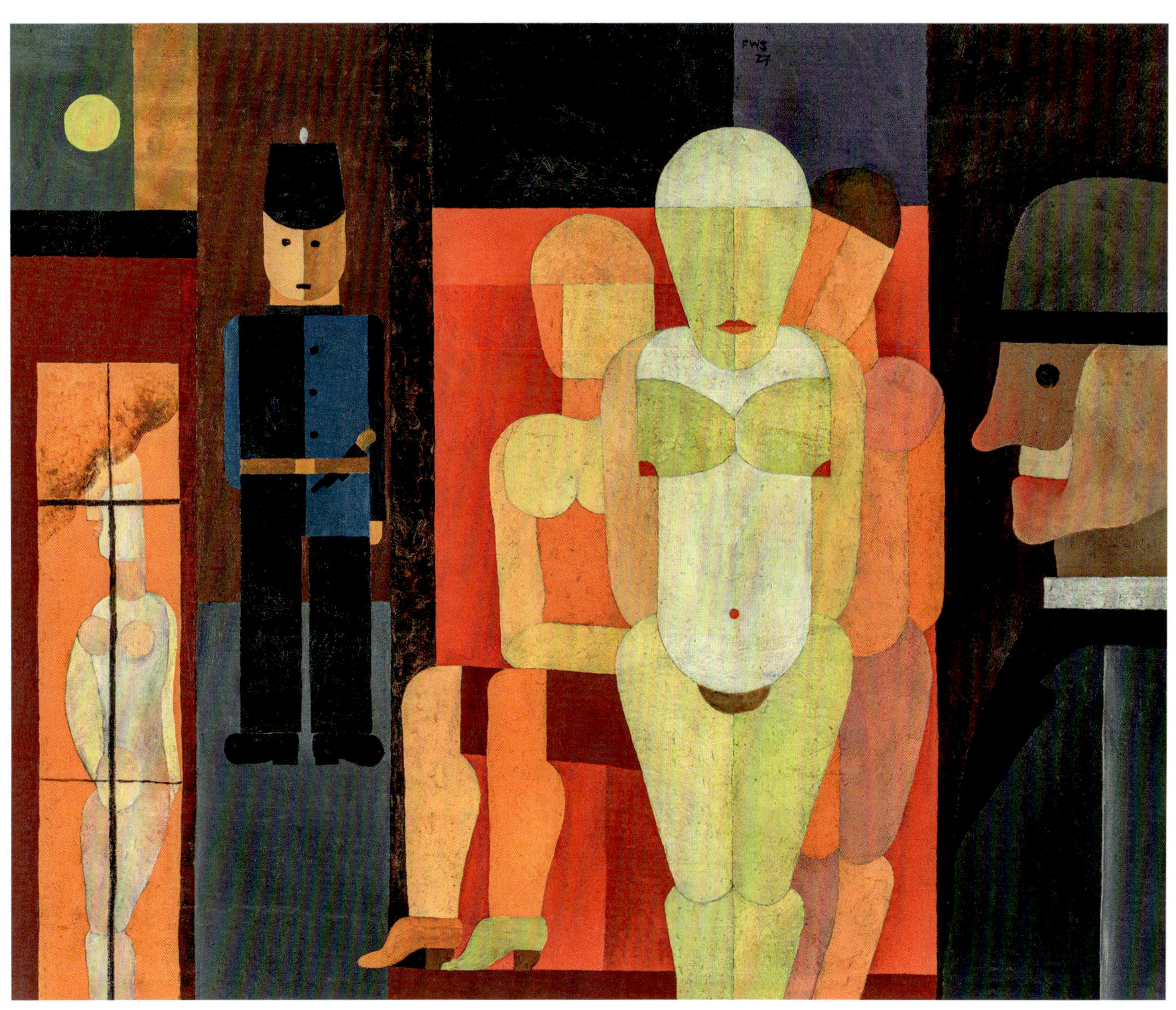

Opposite page: **HERBERT HOFFMANN** *Transvestiten im Eldorado* (Transvestites in Eldorado), Berlin, 1928-1933
OTTO GRIEBEL *Zwei Frauen* (Two Women), 1924
ANTON RÄDERSCHEIDT *Selbstbildnis* (Self-Portrait), 1928

FRANZ WILHELM SEIWERT *Freudlose Gasse* (Joyless Street), 1927
Oil on canvas, 65.5 × 80 cm. Galerie Berinson, Berlin

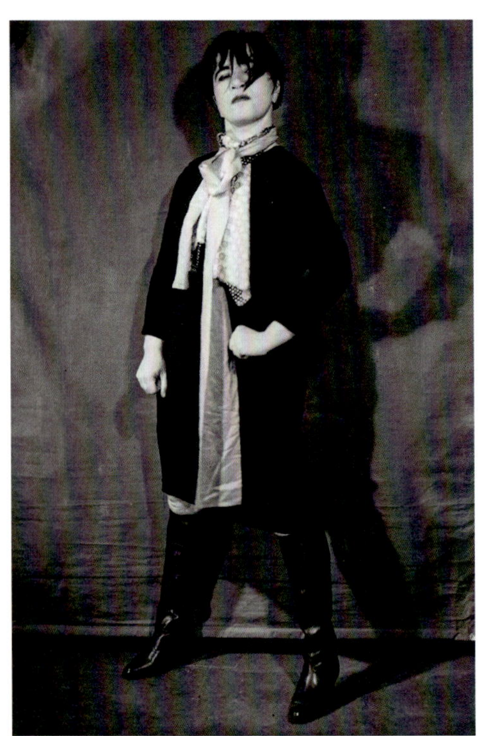
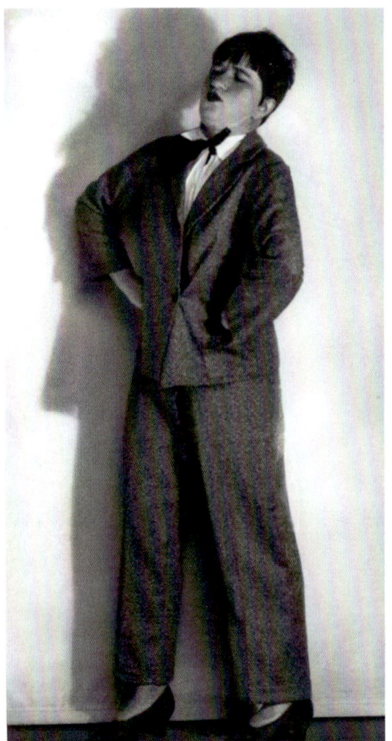
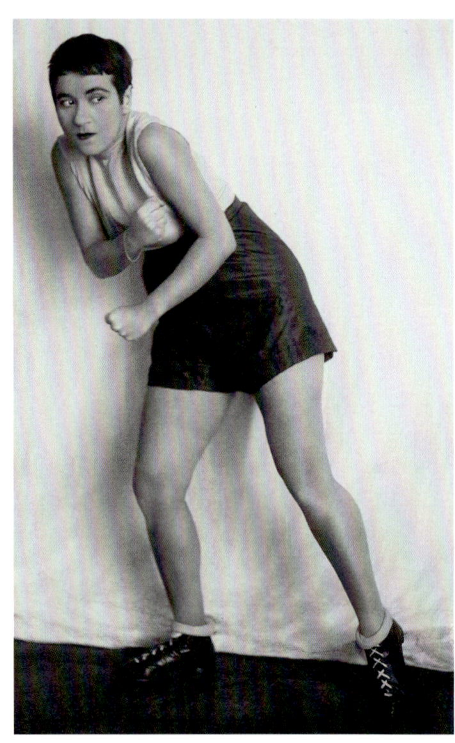
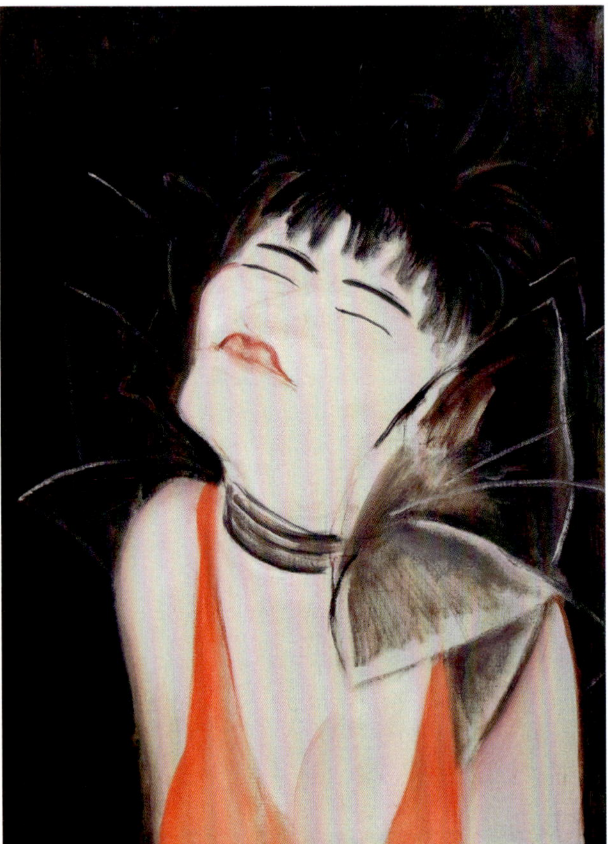

WILLIAM DAVIS *Valeska Gert, "Berlin Unterwelt" (Valeska Gert, "Berlin Underworld"), 1934*
ELLI MARCUS *Versammlung (Reunion), 1934*
LOTTE JOHANNA JACOBI *Valeska Gert, "Boxen" (Valeska Gert, "Boxing"), 1927*
JEANNE MAMMEN *Valeska Gert, 1928-1929*

Opposite page: **GERT WOLLHEIM** *Ohne Titel (Paar) (Untitled (Couple)), 1926*

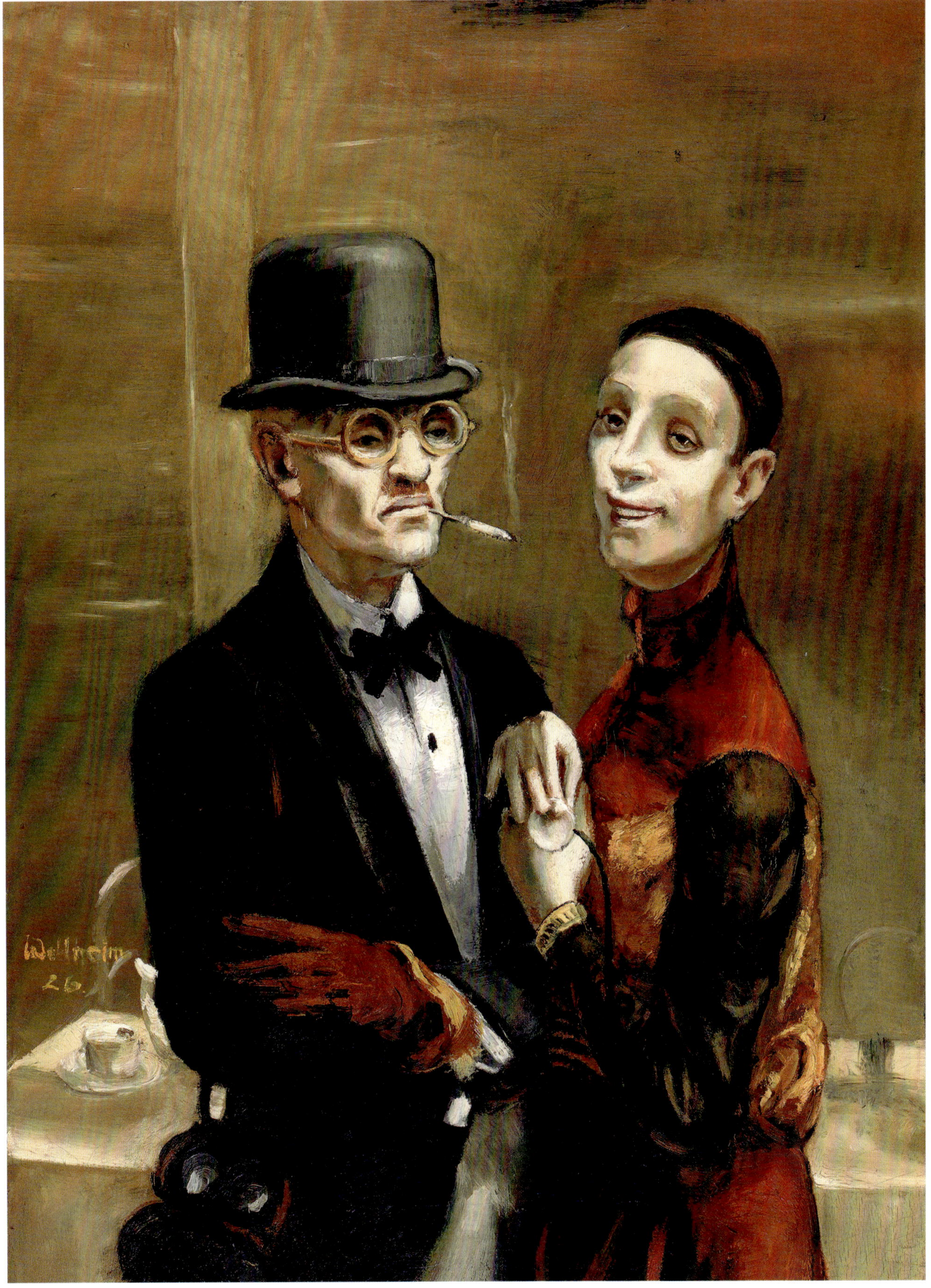

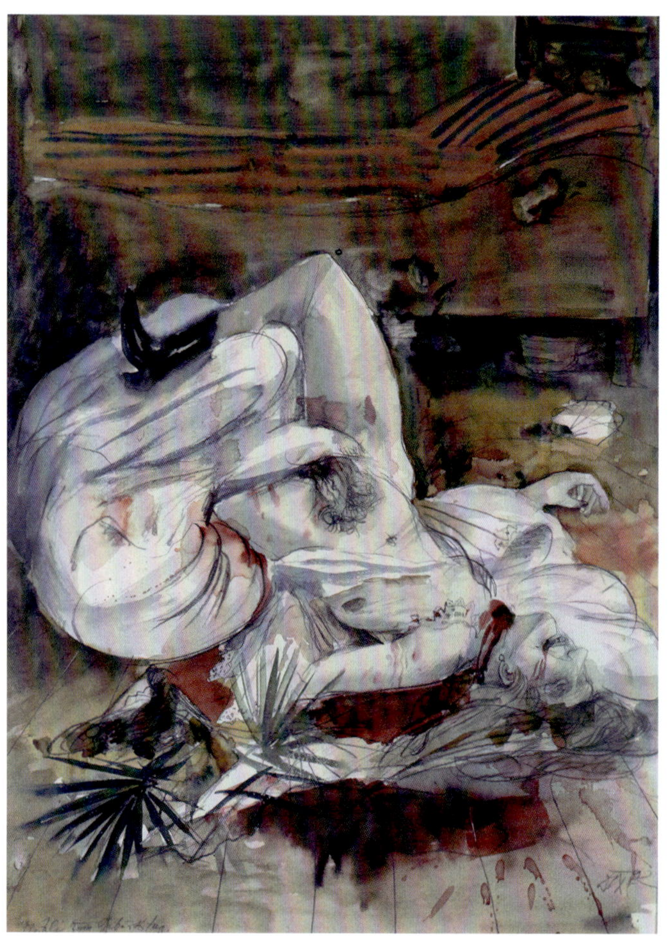

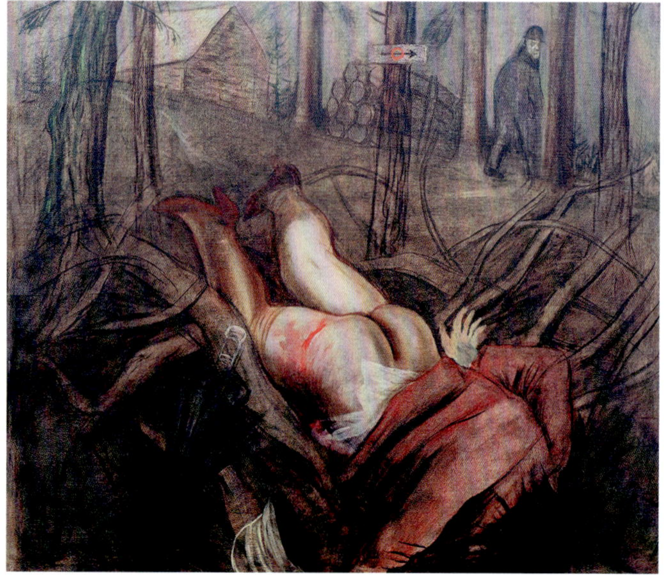

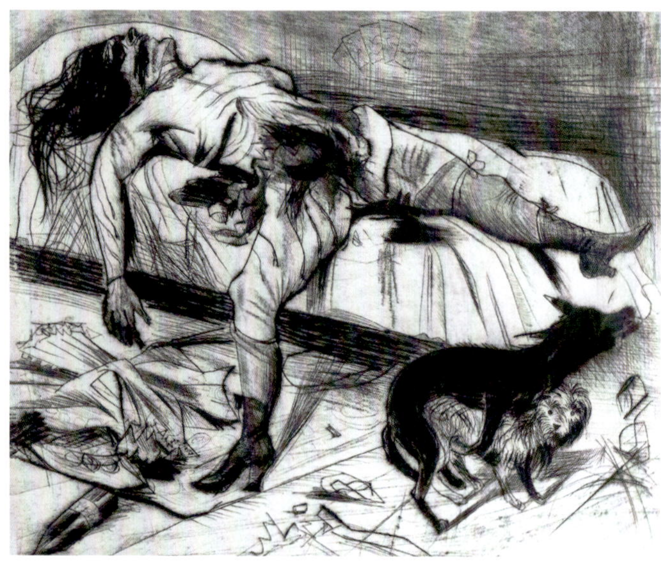

OTTO DIX *Szene II (Mord) (Scene II (Murder))*, 1922
KARL HUBBUCH *Der Lustmord* (The Sex Murder), 1930
OTTO DIX *Lustmord* (Sex Murder), 1922

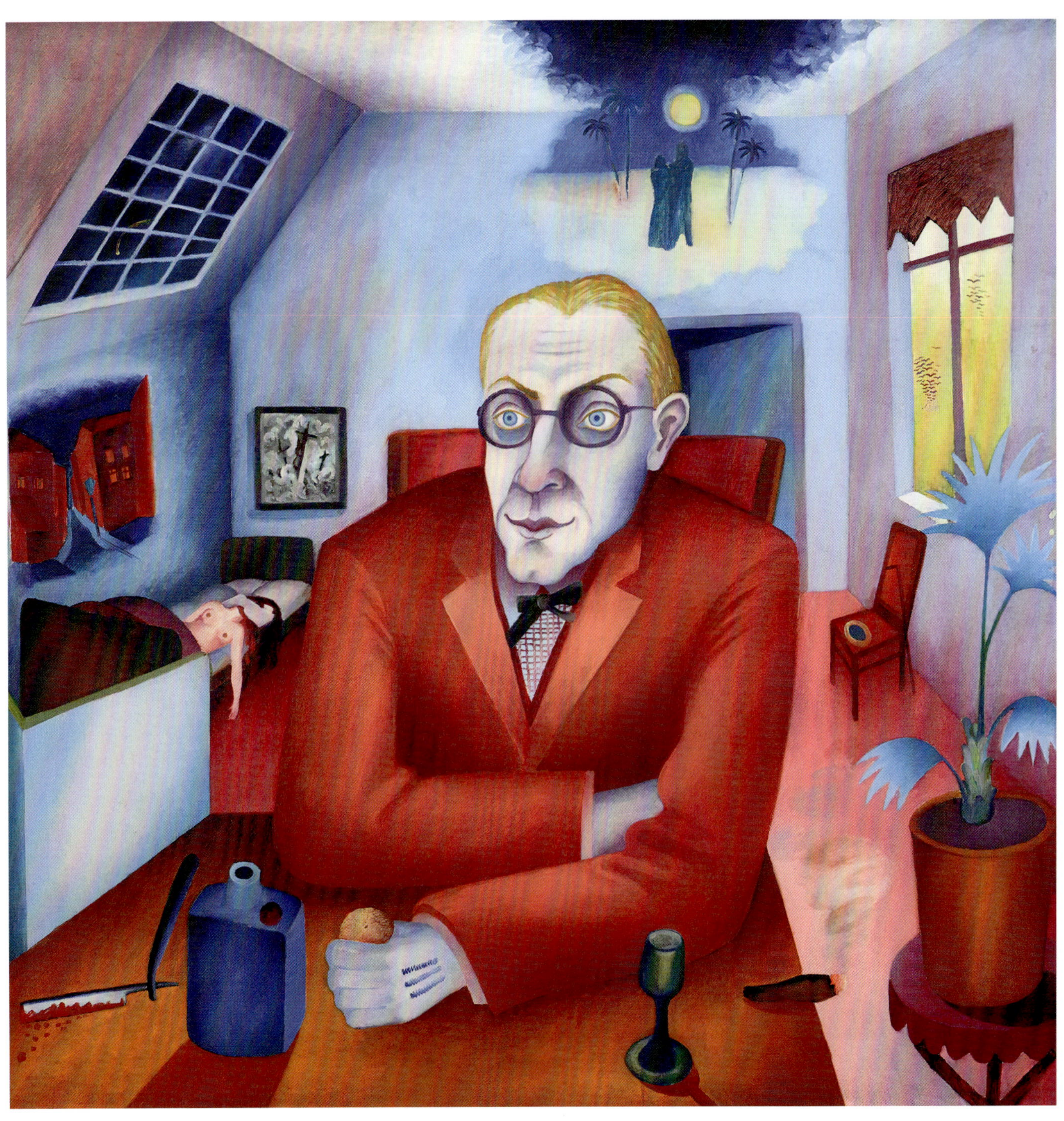

HEINRICH MARIA DAVRINGHAUSEN *Der Träumer* (The Dreamer), 1919

FASCINATION WITH INDUSTRY and machines clashed with the harsh reality of everyday life for the most modest populations. Driven by a desire to represent the downside of triumphant capitalism, some New Objectivity artists turned their gaze towards those "invisible people" whom technical progress excludes or affects. Although they claimed to represent the social world objectively, they refused to be politically neutral, as most of them were involved with the Communist Party.

The appearance of a richly illustrated workers' press such as the Arbeiter Illustrierte Zeitung (AIZ), helped to publicise the daily lives of workers. Documentary films also denounced their cramped and unhealthy housing. In Berlin, the journalist Siegfried Kracauer (1889-1966) published *Die Angestellten* (The Employees, 1930), a vast survey of this social group subjected to the same mechanisation of work as the proletarians, from whom they nevertheless felt distant.

This development of documentary, reportage and investigative work fed into the practice of photographers and painters, who adopted the same analytical and distanced approach. The artists Karl Völker (1889-1962) and Oskar Nerlinger (1893-1969) produced portraits of anonymous crowds of workers in the oppressive environment of industrial architecture, where the exploitation of these working masses benefits the better-off.

In a detached style, artists depicted the precarious populations living on the edge of the large modern urban centres, the showcases of German capitalism. In *Menschen des 20. Jahrhunderts* (People of the 20th Century), August Sander depicted the marginal populations of the city: travellers and Romani people leading a life of homelessness, but also the unemployed, beggars and the destitute. Far from the busy boulevards and their illuminated signs, Hans Baluschek (1870-1935) and Hans Grundig (1901-1958) painted the outcasts of urban entertainment, poor families living in the wastelands on the outskirts of the city.

HEINZ HAMISCH *Arbeitsloser Hafenarbeiter (Max Barthel)* (Unemployed Docker (Max Barthel)), 1932

THE DOWNSIDE

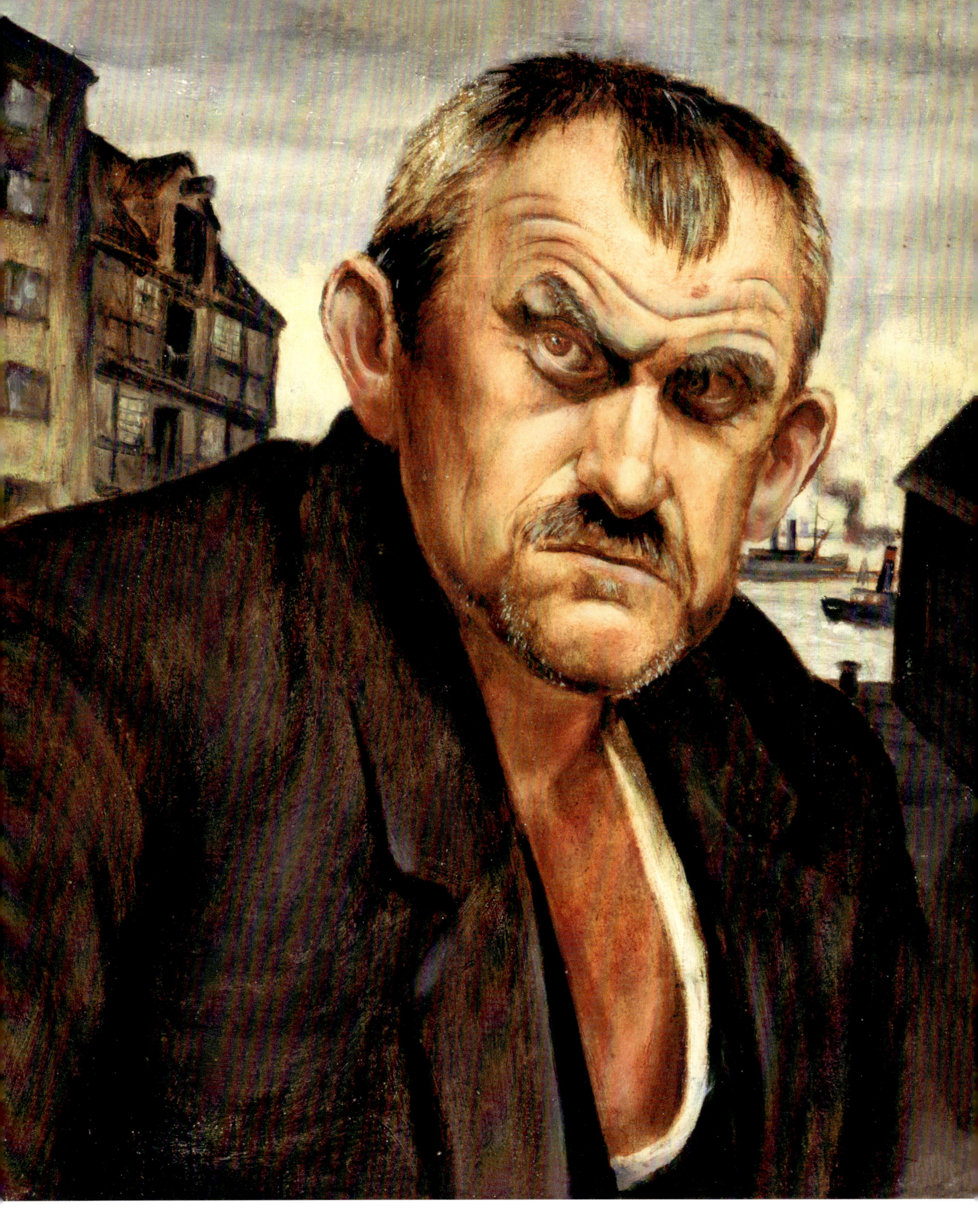

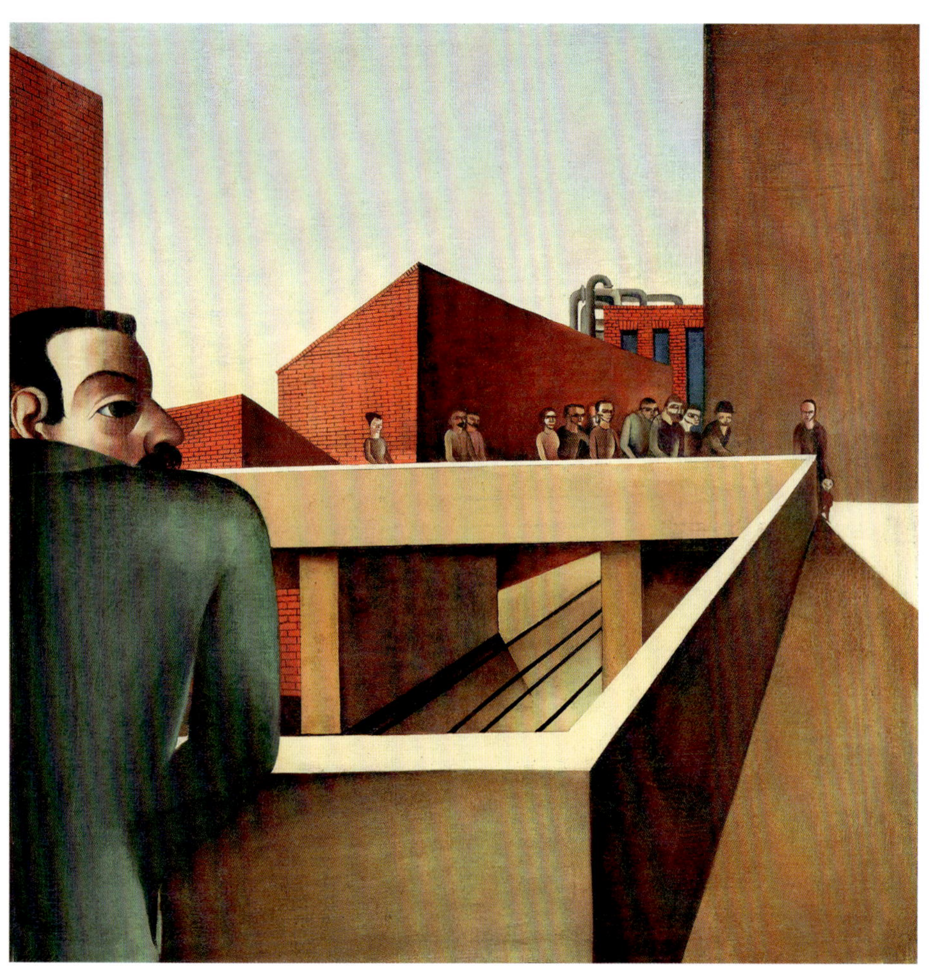

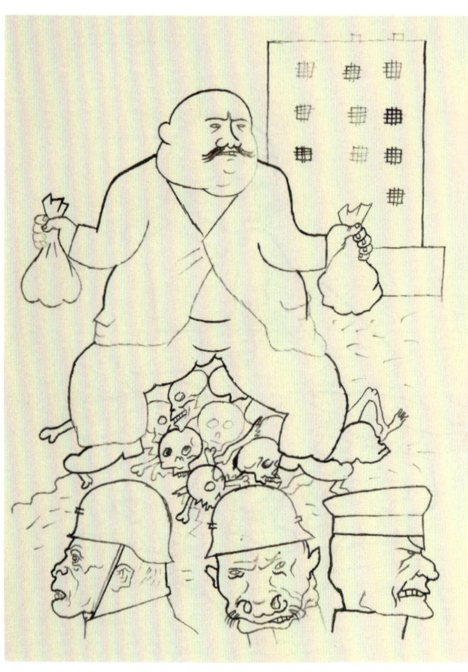

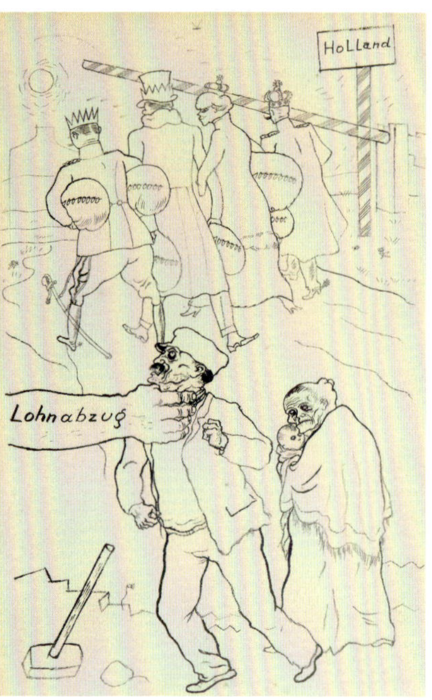

KARL VÖLKER *Industriebild* (Image of a Factory), c. 1924
GEORGE GROSZ *Ausbeuter* (Exploiter), 1919
Lohnabzug (Wage Reduction), 1918

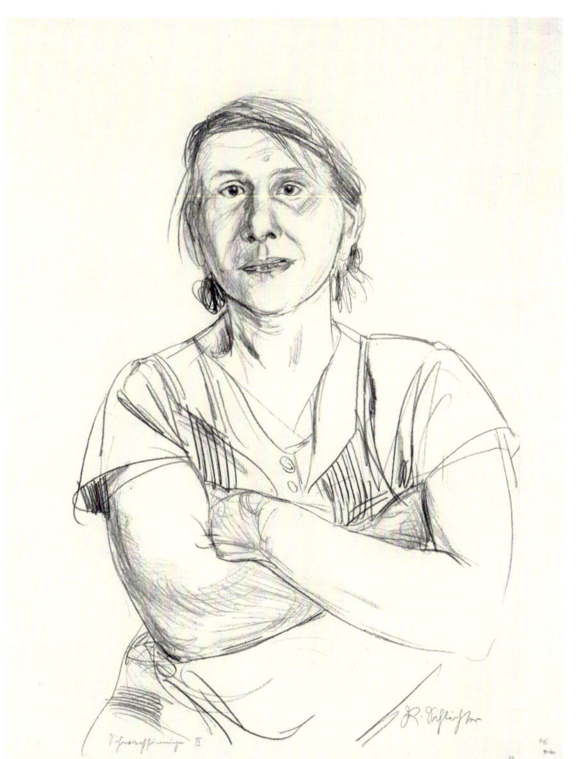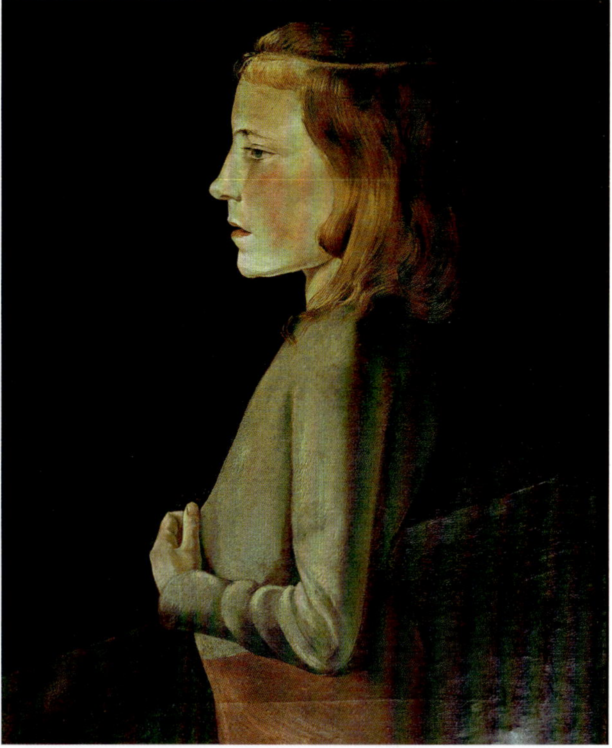

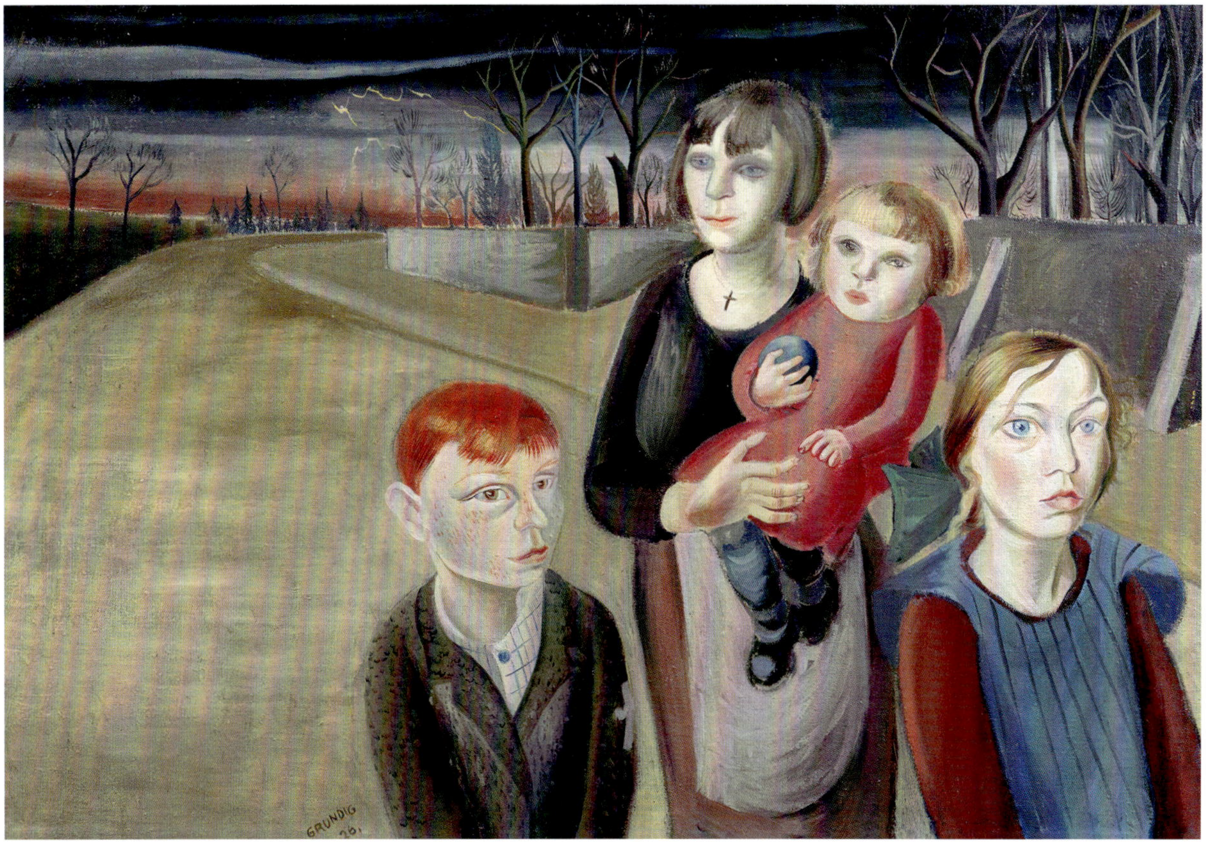

RUDOLF SCHLICHTER *Schwachsinnige II (Mentally Impaired II)*, 1923-1924
WILHELM LACHNIT *Schwangeres Proletariermädchen (Pregnant Working-class Girl)*, 1924/26
HANS GRUNDIG *Am Stadtrand (On the Outskirts of the City)*, 1926

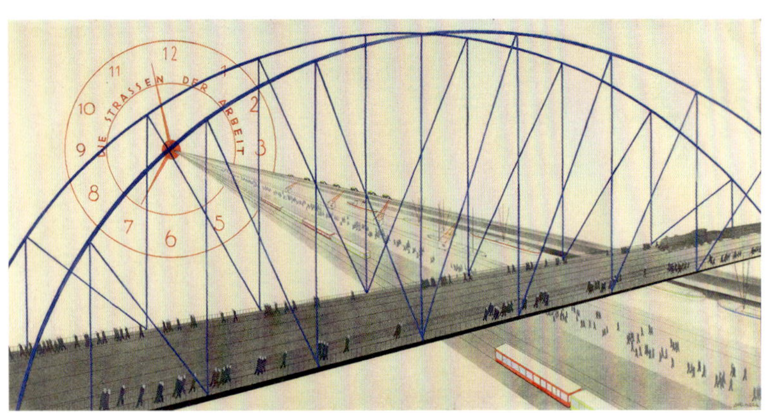

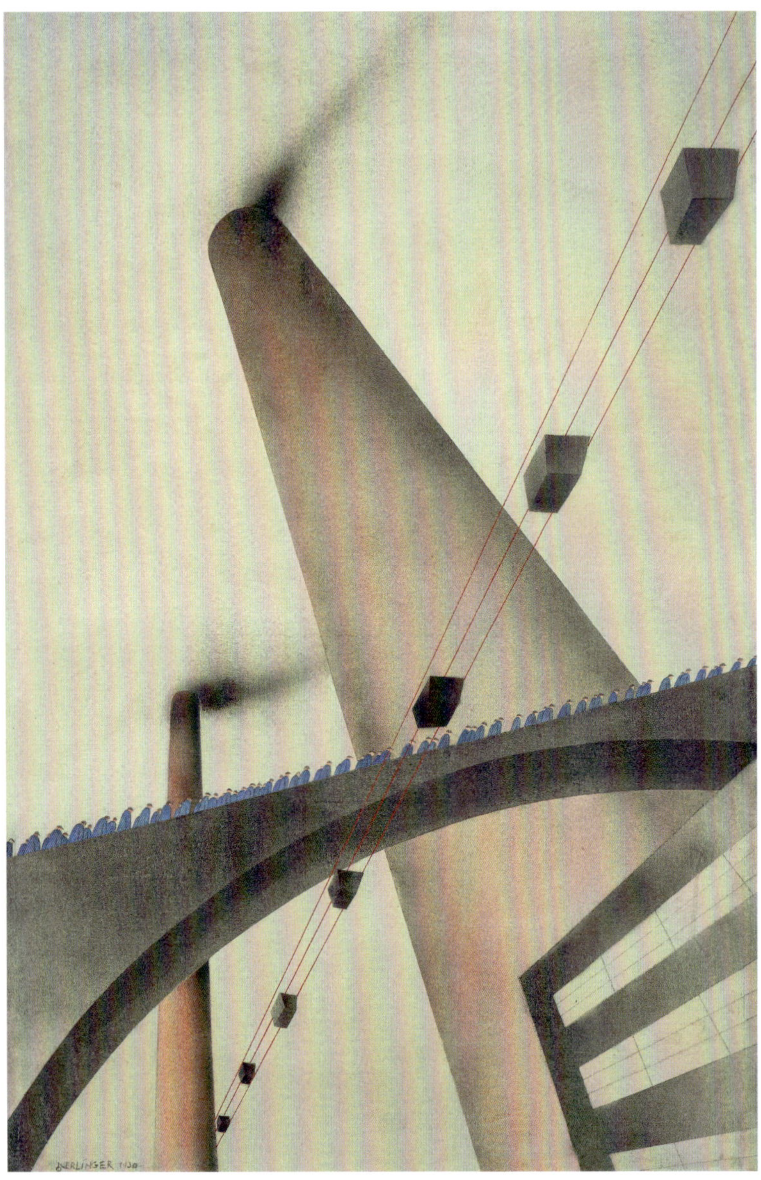

OSKAR NERLINGER *An die Arbeit* (To Work), 1930
Straßen der Arbeit (Work Roads), 1930

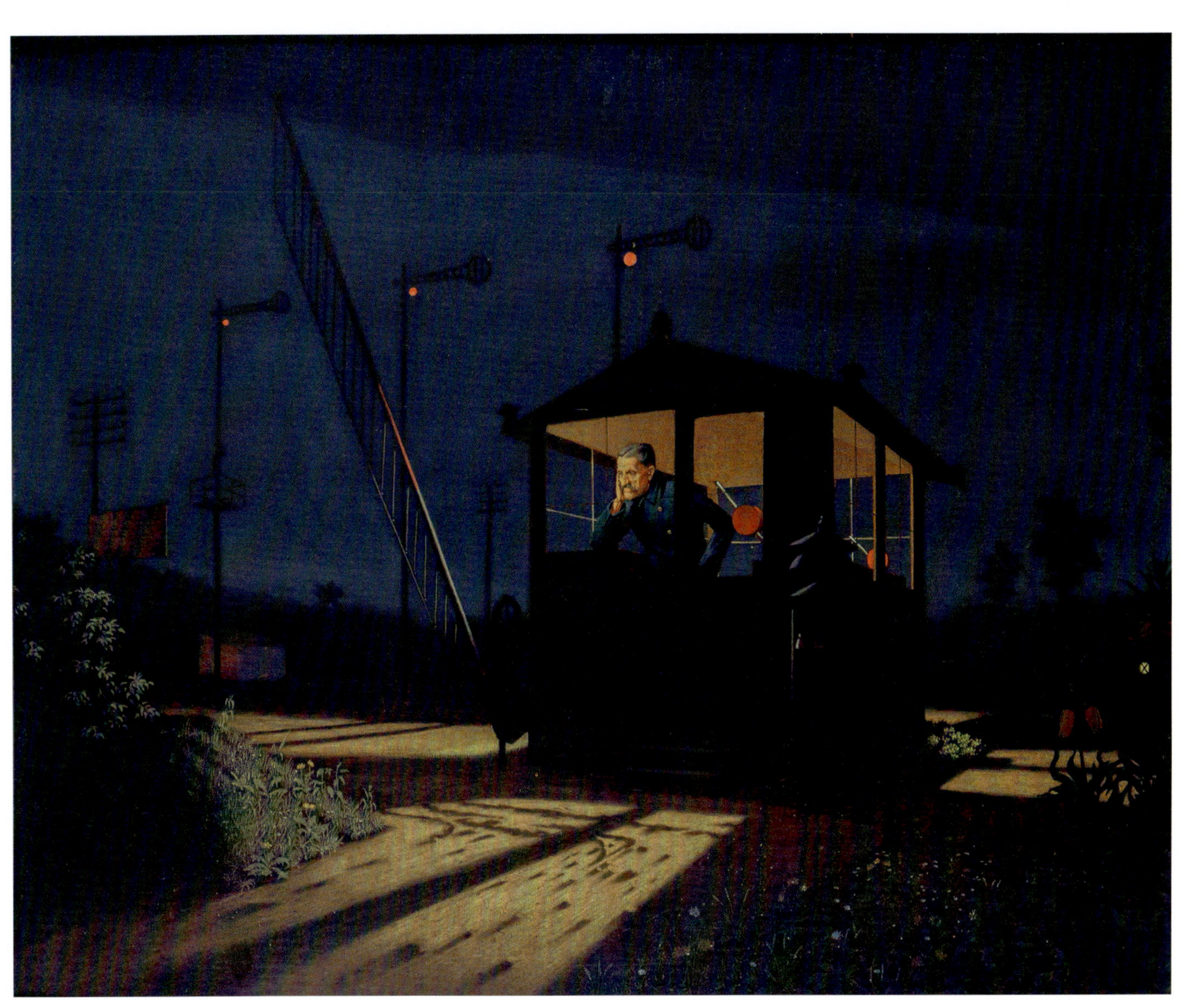

GEORG SCHOLZ *Bahnwärterhäuschen* (Signalman's Cabin), 1920

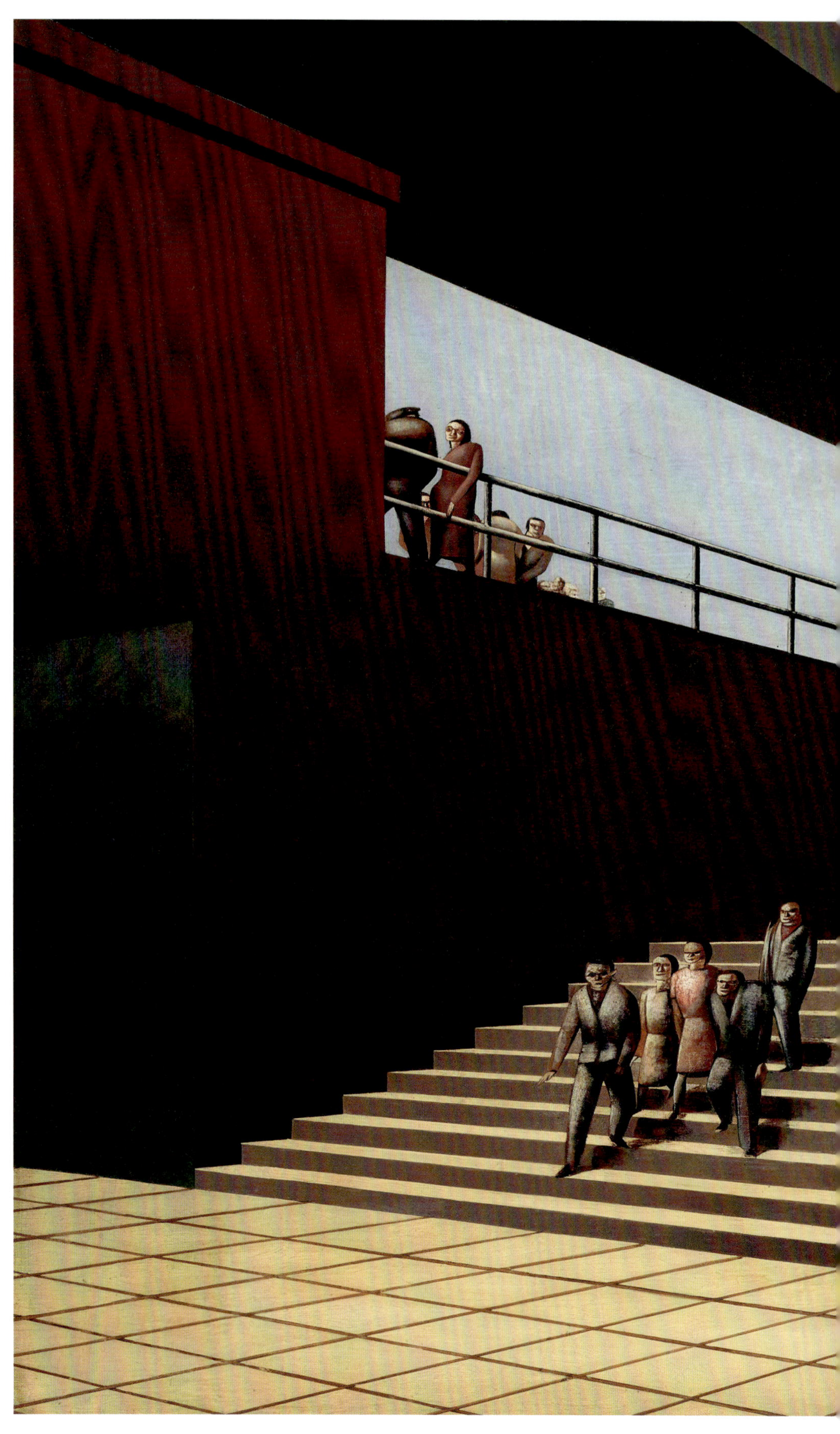

KARL VÖLKER
Bahnhof (Railway Station), 1924-1926

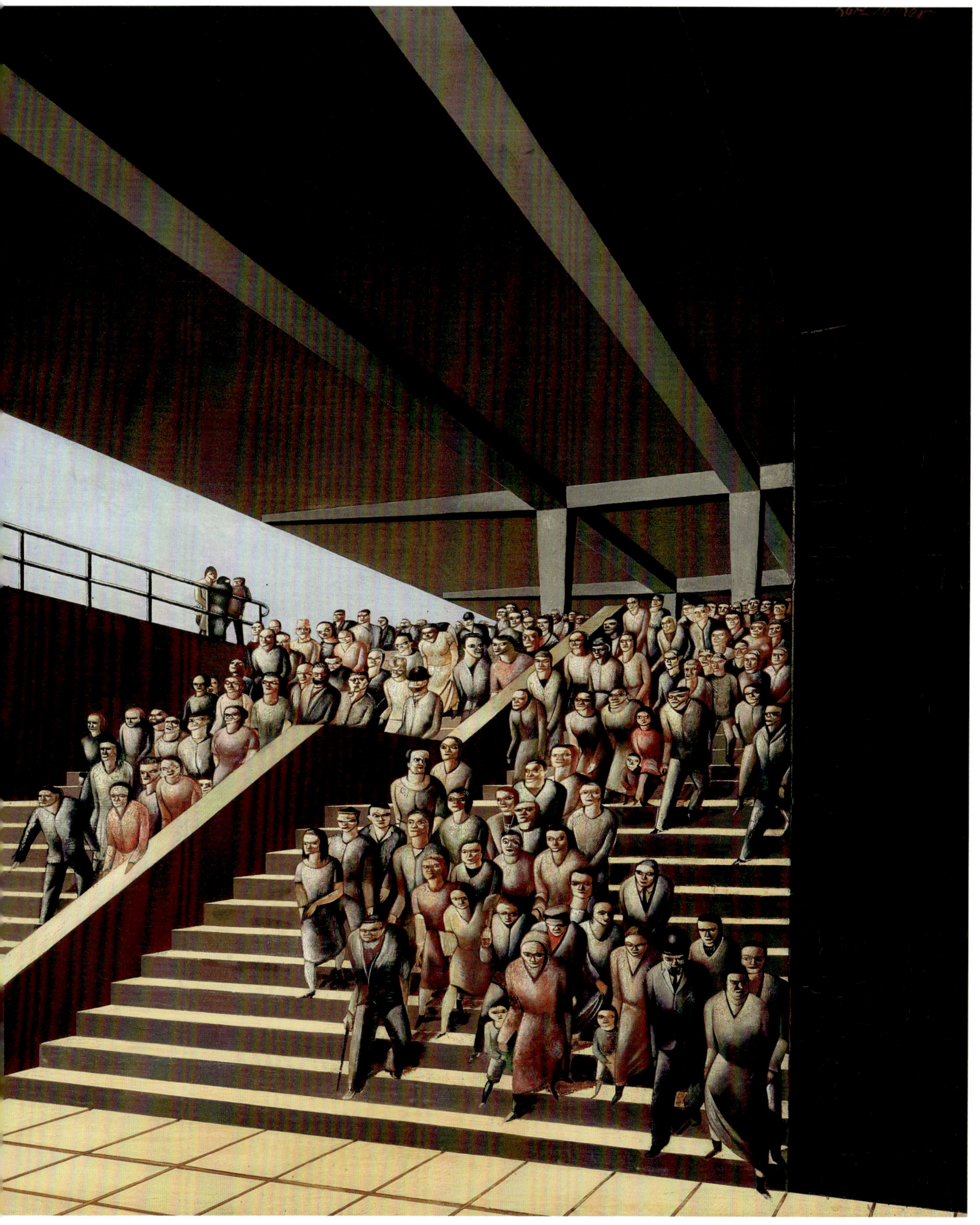

The Cold Order

By Angela Lampe

"We have gained reality and lost dream."

Robert Musil:
Der Mann ohne Eigenschaften
(The Man without Qualities, 1930)[1]

As soon as it appeared, the German term *Neue Sachlichkeit* disconcerted international commentators. In France, André Warnod introduced it in the Bulletin de la vie artistique, and distorted it into "Neue Sarlichkeit." "Expressionism," he wrote, "which was essentially cerebral, was bound to lead to a reaction and so *Neue Sarlichkeit* was born, which can be translated as New Objectivity." Warnod went on to describe this new orientation as "a return to direct, exact, precise art" and concluded: "the idea is to take care to reproduce objects faithfully, and to that end any method is acceptable."[2] Now that the translation "New Objectivity" has come into use, it is possible to regret the alternatives proposed at the time to characterise this new tendency in Germany, in particular the one that the Germanist Félix Bertaux introduced in 1928 in his *Panorama de la littérature allemande contemporaine*. He described the successor to Expressionism not in terms of objectivity, a term he dismissed, but as "a return to the cold order." "It is the transition from ecstasy to knowledge that has been called '*die neue Sachlichkeit*,'" he wrote. After "a high temperature phenomenon" – the term used by the author to refer to Expressionism – it was the sovereign attitude of a cold and detached observation, with "open eyes,"[3] which, for Bertaux, would henceforth characterise the art from the other side of the Rhine.

In using the epithet "cold" to describe the Post-Expressionist period, the French critic chose a metaphor that was then in vogue among German writers, from Ernst Jünger to Bertolt Brecht, before it became a cliché, particularly in relation to vision.[4] Already in 1922, in his essay "Those Who Wait", Siegfried Kracauer called for "a certain coldness,"[5] which he perceived as a redeeming attitude in a world torn apart. The notion proposed by Bertaux, although welcomed by the great writer Joseph Roth,[6] did not go anywhere. It was not until much later, in 1994, that the literary historian Helmut Lethen seemed to return to it with his seminal work *Verhaltenslehren der Kälte* (Behavioural Lessons from the Cold),[7] a brilliant analysis of the different social types that prevailed between the two wars in Germany, a country that sought to hide its shame and malaise behind a cold, smooth and distant façade. With its definition of three fictitious figures, emblematic of New Objectivity: *kalte persona* (cold persona), *Radar-Typ* (radar type) and *Kreatur* (creature),[8] the study itself appears to be an attempt to put things in order in the spirit of the Weimaraner era, which was so rich in schemes, categorisations and taxonomies. From Gustav Hartlaub's division of neo-objective artists into left and right wings for his seminal exhibition in 1925, to August Sander's ambitious project to classify an entire society into social categories and groups, *Menschen des 20. Jahrhunderts* (People of the 20th Century, pp. 26-43), the art world seemed to be in the grip of what might be called an "*Ordnungswollen*," a desire to order and objectify individuality, a common desire to distance people and things. Oskar Schlemmer wrote in his diary in April 1926: "If today's arts love the machine, technology and organisation, if they aspire to precision and reject anything vague and dreamy, this implies an instinctive repudiation of chaos and a longing to find the form appropriate to our times."[9] The recourse to a *cold order* was thus presented as both a means and an end, as a way out of a destabilising era and as the mirage of a new society.

It soon became clear, however, that this new orientation was not without its problems. The impact of this *Sachlichkeit* [objectivity] "in the air" was the theme of Mischa Spoliansky's musical revue *Es liegt in der Luft* (It's in the air), which was a great popular success in 1928. This modern comedy, set behind the scenes in a department store, appealed to the public with its ability to deride the spirit of the age. The title song (p. 57) praises the fetishes of the new age such as electricity, radio, telephone, aeroplane, airship, while mocking the values of the past, such as love and sensibility, since these appear to be hindrances in this technological world. In the midst of new, unadorned habitats, man himself ends up being a disturbance. Conceived as mass entertainment for what Siegfried Kracauer called "Pläsirkasernen" (pleasure barracks),[10] this caustic performance highlights the dialectic between progress and loss that characterized the New Objectivity era, especially during the phase of economic stability between 1924 and 1929. While the fascination with technical inventions was growing rapidly, accelerating the modernisation of German society, the negative consequences of this cold order were becoming increasingly apparent. Under this functional and utilitarian regime, what happened to people with their particularities, dreams and desires? As Peter

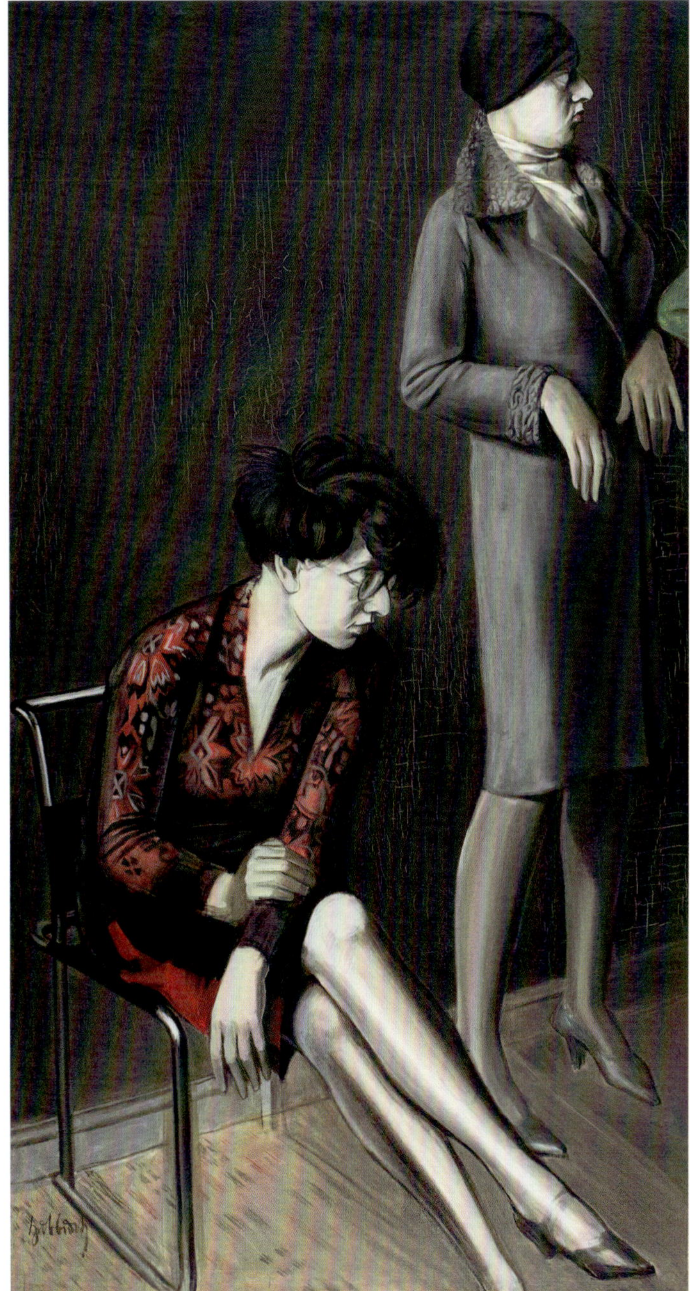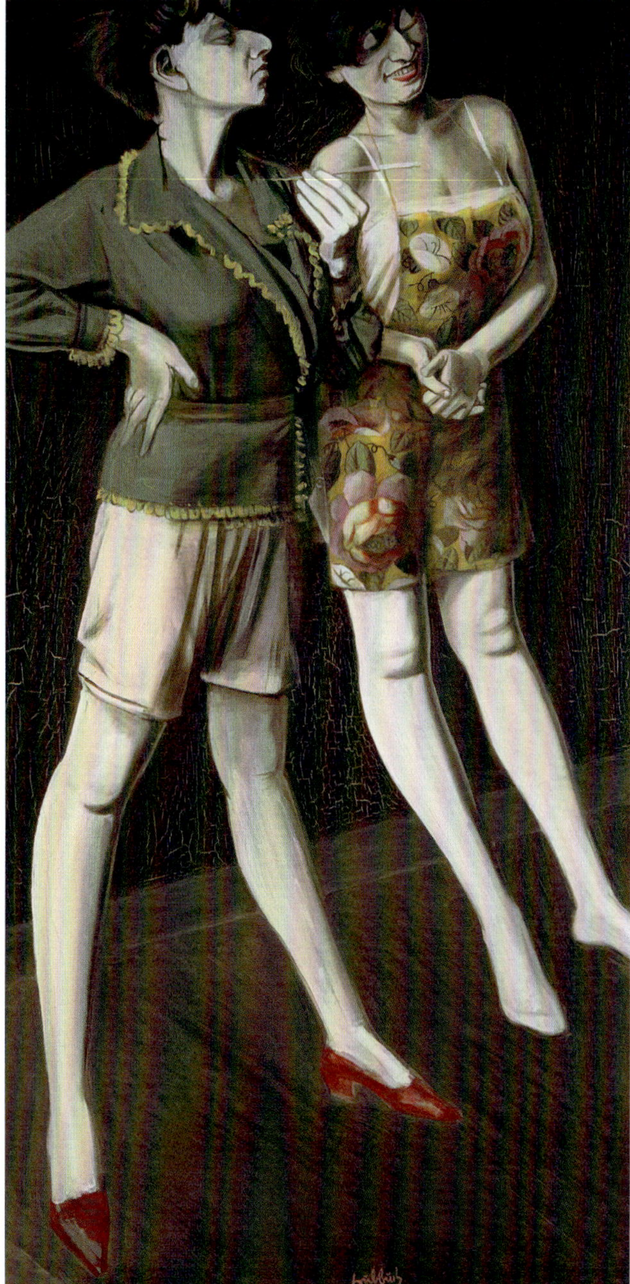

KARL HUBBUCH *Zweimal Hilde I* (Twice Hilde I), 1929
Zweimal Hilde II (Twice Hilde II), c. 1929

Sloterdijk writes: "The Weimar Republic is one of those historical phenomena through which we can best study how the modernization of a society has to be paid for. Enormous technical achievements are exchanged for an increasing uneasiness, in the unculture; conveniences of civilization for the feeling of meaningless."[11]

The most vehement plea in favour of this new modern world came, not surprisingly, from an architect, the Swiss Hannes Meyer, who, a year before joining the Bauhaus, published a powerful text with the programmatic title "Die neue Welt"[12]

(The New World) in 1926. Striking a visionary note, he proclaims the death of yesterday's world: bohemia, *Stimmung* (atmosphere), "the brushstrokes of chance," are all gone. The author considers the idea of embellishing the real environment with an artist's interpretation as pretentious. Instead, he writes, the home should be machine-like, standardised, so that all needs can be met by assigning equal resources to each individual. From now on, it is the collective that will take precedence. In dreaming of Esperanto-speaking world citizens, the Marxist architect was espousing the utopian

impulse, born of the post-war
revolutionary upheavals, to
shape life itself. This "objectification of man" inspired all the
avant-gardes, in particular the
Bauhaus, of which Meyer became director in 1928.[13] It found a
very concrete echo in Frankfurt,
where, from 1925, the architect
Ernst May launched a vast ur-
banisation programme
involving the serial construction
of large-scale housing estates.
The ambition of this social
enterprise, known as "Das Neue
Frankfurt" (The New Frankfurt), was such that, beyond the
construction of mass housing, its
founders championed the vision
of an architecture capable of
"educating" its inhabitants. By
means of functional and egal-
itarian housing that reconciled
class antagonisms, they aspired
to bring about the advent of "a
new man."[14] Five years later,

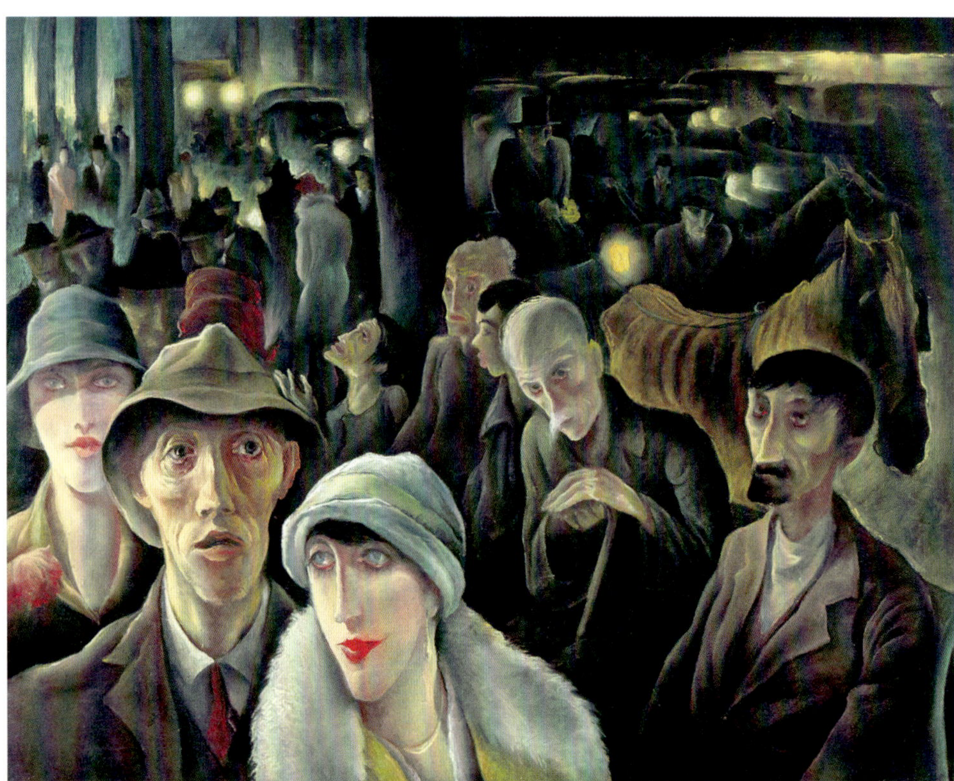

ALBERT BIRKLE *Kurfürstendamm*, 1924

however, the socialist architectural theorist Adolf
Behne wrote bitterly of another housing estate,
Dammerstock, near Karlsruhe, that, "Here [...]
man becomes an abstract housing being."[15] The
ordering of private space into uniform cells
ordaining standard actions and behaviours had
robbed man of vitality and reduced him to the
status of an object.

The reification of man thus appears as one
of the indirect consequences of these new living
environments devoid of human warmth. For left-
wing intellectuals, in a society under the growing
influence of the capitalist imperative of rationalisation, the transformation of man into a passive
entity became an essential characteristic of this
new world, even a precondition for its existence.
Max Horkheimer and Theodor W. Adorno considered technical rationality to be a fundamental
condition for the alienation of a society. The culture
industry, by standardising and mass-producing,
had, in their view, sacrificed what distinguished the
logic of the work of art from that of the societal system.[16] For the Marxist film theorist Béla Balázs, "this
New Objectivity has absolutely nothing to do with
revolution, nor with socialism, nor with the proletariat. Quite the contrary. An image of the Tay-
lorised world, it was born out of the feeling of big
capital towards life. It's the aesthetics of assembly
line work. It is the ultimate stage of that 'reification'

which Karl Marx called the greatest curse of bourgeois capitalism." The Hungarian author goes on to
explain that Marx describes this "reification" "as the
'ghostly reality' that all manifestations of life in capitalist society take on, with the result that the essential
fact, that they are relations between men, is hardly
recognisable." Balázs concludes that man "becomes
a mechanised part inserted into a mechanical system hostile to life and is deprived of his individuality.
This is objectification."[17]

The analyses put forward by critics of a tendency may sometimes prove particularly acute. A
Marxist reading helps us to understand the extent to
which the achievements of the New Objectivity were
both conditioned and disturbed by this cold order.
The technique of montage, which continued to interest filmmakers such as Walter Ruttmann and writers
such as Alfred Döblin after the beginnings of Dada,
also invaded the field of painting: literally in the case
of Karl Hubbuch, who liked to present his wife Hilde
in different postures by cutting up or pasting together his compositions, or, in a more figurative sense,
with a painter like Albert Birkle who, by eliminating
all relationships between passers-by on the Kurfürstendamm, conceived a heterogeneous typology of
Berlin society. Like Otto Dix and Gert Heinrich
Wollheim, Birkle no longer depicts an organic whole,
but rather a mosaic-like association of unrelated figures. Pinned down by the cold gaze of the painter (or

photographer), with the precision of an entomologist, the portraiture receives the same treatment as the utensils and green plants in the still lifes that New Objectivity artists liked to represent in large numbers. Always isolated, even when grouped together, the figures as well as the objects, in the crystalline clarity of their vacuum, come across as the spectres of an alienated world, where domestic things are transformed into commodities, where individuals no longer feel anything for each other. In this new world, "nickel-plated so that it shines and seduces," Ernst Bloch observed a void that was based on deceit: "Inanimation of life, beings and things becoming commodities is polished up as it was in order, indeed order itself,"[18] he concluded.

Horkheimer and Adorno would later call this lack of human warmth "bürgerliche Kälte" (bourgeois coldness).[19] This is evident in neo-objective paintings and photographs inhabited by isolated subjects with distant, empty gazes, and becomes a palpable reality in the modern environment of bourgeois apartments, for example, in those of Weimar Republic celebrities such as Fritz Lang and Erwin Piscator. Interior design magazines praised the techno-functionalist style based on the imitation of machines, but regretted that in these modern glass and metal spaces, enthusiasm for technology had replaced joie de vivre and conviviality.[20] Imported from America, the fascination with the world of machines permeated the entire production of New Objectivity, from Albert Renger-Patzsch's photographs of industrial sites to Carl Grossberg's representations of factories, via the mechanised choreographies of the Tiller Girls and the technical innovations of Erwin Piscator. For some, however, this cult of the industrial world went too far and ended up bordering on the ridiculous. This was certainly the opinion of Brecht in his famous poem *700 Intellektuelle beten einen Öltank an* (700 intellectuals worship an oil tank, 1927, p. 52).[21] Brecht, a theatre and radio producer, exemplifies the ambivalent relation to technical progress and its functionalist logic. While he mocked factory photographs, which he felt failed to convey the social reality of these entities,[22] he was aware that the democratisation of culture had made great progress in Weimar society, not least thanks to the emergence of intermediality, which made it possible to combine entertainment and education, music, reviews and spoken theatre.[23] In the broadcasting industry, which continued to develop, Brecht was able to make a significant contribution to the development of a new form of culture. In 1927, he saw radio broadcasting, which was becoming more and more widespread in German households, and especially listener participation, as an opportunity for the development of "a truly democratic cause"[24] and a real lever for political emancipation. Would the cold order finally have positive effects as well?

In her best-selling novel *Gilgi, eine von uns* (Gilgi, One of Us, pp. 50-51), Irmgard Keun has her protagonist, a young stenotypist, say: "It's nice to have one's life in front of one's eyes like a well-solved arithmetical problem!"[25] Does the end of the novel, which sees the pregnant heroine leave her city to live alone in Berlin, not suggest that a coldly organised life, devoid of all sentimentality, decided by the individual alone, could be the condition for emancipation? For the writer Marieluise Fleißer, a close associate of Brecht and author of a poignant novel about a travelling saleswoman in Bavaria,[26] women must learn to accept the "Fröste der Freiheit" – literally the frosts of freedom.[27] Would a cold, objective look at the world help to better grasp the essence of reality? The increasing appearance of effeminate men and masculine women in the artistic production of the 1920s could thus be linked to the great cinematic success of the *Steinach Film* (1923). In a pseudo-scientific approach that turned men and women into guinea pigs, this highly polemical film presented the mechanisms of sexual differentiation, while at the same time promoting a rejuvenation process. It is known that it had a real influence on contemporary debates concerning sex change and the situation of transvestites.[28] Cold objectivity, even scientificity, seem to have functioned as a distancing device, making it possible to ad-

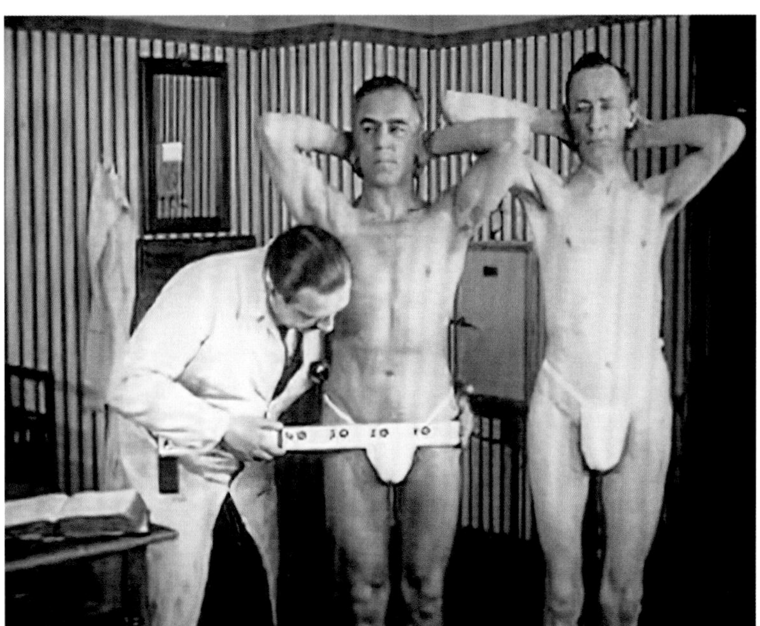

CURT THOMALLA, NICHOLAS KAUFMANN and **LEOPOLD NIERNBERGER**
Der Steinachfilm (The Steinach Film), still, 1922

dress a disturbing otherness.[29] In reality, despite its neutral façade, the film appears ambivalent. On the one hand, it seems to contribute to a trivialisation of homosexuality, which is shown without moral judgement, as a biological fact or a social phenomenon, which allows it to be represented in the arts, from Christian Schad to Jeanne Mammen; on the other hand, the *Steinach Film* reveals the humiliating treatment of homosexuals at the time, who were studied like laboratory hamsters. Showing the world as it is was still an ambiguous act. And while this approach increased the visibility of those on the margins of society, not only because of their sexual orientation but also because of their social status within the hierarchical capitalist system, the fact remains that beggars, these unemployed, peddlers, workers or modest employees were still victims crushed by the steamroller of an omnipresent rationalisation, even if they became favourite subjects for the artists of the New Objectivity.

Ambiguity was at its height. The unemotional way of looking at the contemporary world brought to the forefront those who had been left behind by technological progress, while presenting them as the subjects of the alienating productivist logic that underlay the cold order. In other words, we can measure the cynicism of wanting, in Sloterdijk's words, to overcome the "cold by the cold of art." For the German philosopher, "the post-war self is an heir without a will and almost inevitably condemned to cynicism"; one of its "great expressive attitudes" is the "cold approval of a situation that says no to the dream of our life." And the author concludes: "The Weimaraner cynics of art train themselves to play the masters of the situation when in truth the situation is one where everything is in disorder and no sovereignty is possible anymore."[30] We know how this game ended.

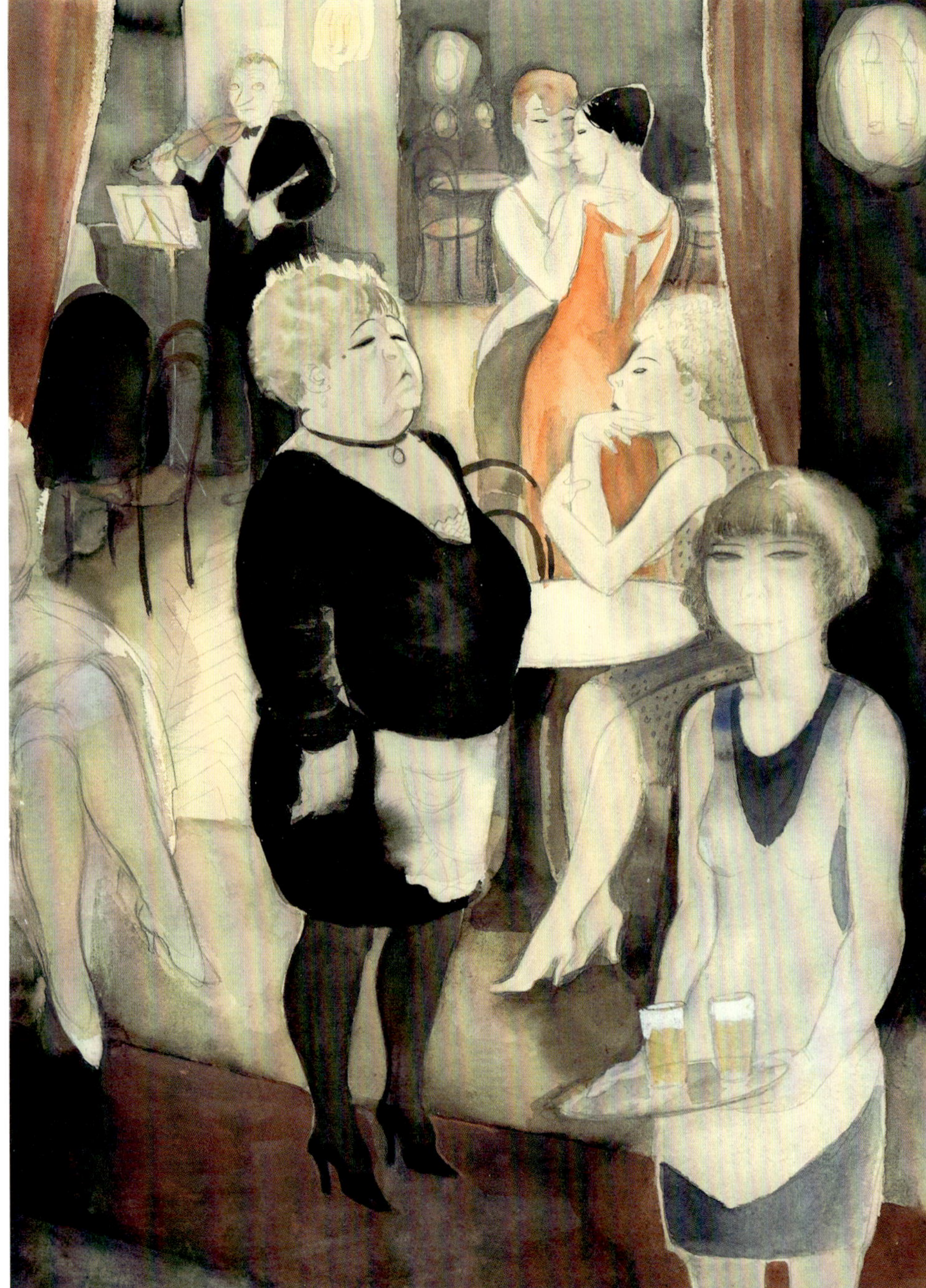

JEANNE MAMMEN *Café Nollendorf,* c. 1931

ANGELA LAMPE is a curator of modern art at the Centre Pompidou, Paris. Together with Florian Ebner, head of the photography department at the Centre Pompidou, she has curated the exhibition in Paris. Lampe is also the author of a long number of art historical books.

1. Robert Musil, *Der Mann ohne Eigenschaften*, Reinbeck bei Hamburg, Rowohlt, 1989 [1978], p. 39. English edition, *The Man Without Qualities*, translated by Sophie Wilkins, London: Picador Classic, 2017, p. 36.
2. André Warnod, "Peintres allemands," *Bulletin de la vie artistique*, 15 November 1926, p. 346. I warmly thank Marie Gispert for sending me this quotation, which marks the beginning of the diffusion of the French term "Nouvelle Objectivité."
3. Félix Bertaux, *Panorama de la littérature allemande contemporaine*, Paris: Simon Kra Éditeur, 1928, p. 253.
4. For example, Wieland Schmied's exhibition "Der Kühle Blick. Realismus der zwanziger Jahre in Europa und Amerika," (The Cool Gaze. Realism of the Twenties in Europe and America), Kunsthalle Munich, in 2001.
5. Siegfried Kracauer, "Die Wartenden," *Frankfurter Zeitung*, 12 March 1922; reprinted in *Das Ornament der Masse*, Frankfurt am Main: Suhrkamp, 1977, p. 117.
6. In Joseph Roth, "Schluss mit der 'Neuen Sachlichkeit'" (Enough of the New Objectivity), *Die literarische Welt*, 17 and 24 January 1930.
7. Helmut Lethen, *Verhaltenslehrender Kälte. Lebensversuche zwischen den Kriegen* (Behavioural lessons from the cold. Attempts to live between the two wars), Frankfurt am Main, Suhrkamp, 1994. See also the text by Catherine Wermester in this catalogue, pp. 20-25..
8. Ibid, p. 11.
9. Oskar Schlemmer, *Briefe und Tagebücher*, ed. by Tut Schlemmer (ed.) (Munich: Albert Langen/Georg Müller Verlag, 1958), p. 199.

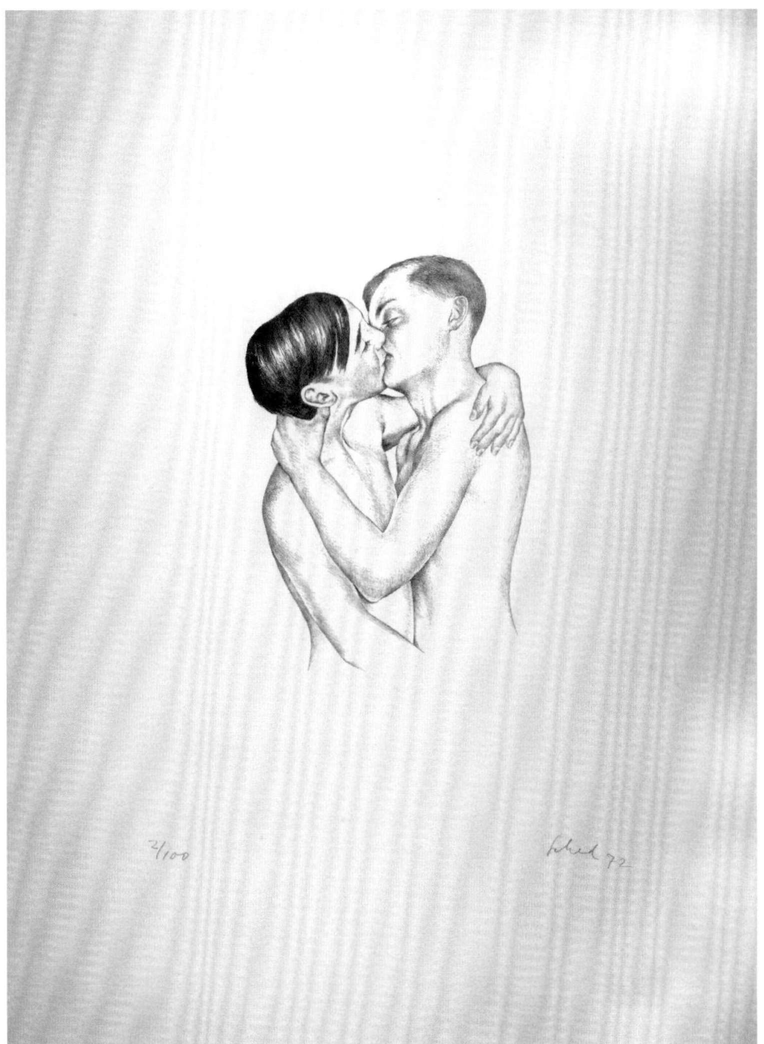

CHRISTIAN SCHAD *Liebende Knaben* (Boys in Love), 1929/1972

English translation, *The Letters and Diaries of Oskar Schlemmer*, Chicago: Northwestern University Press, 2009, p. 193.
10. Siegfried Kracauer, *Die Angestellten: Aus dem neusten Deutschland* [1929], Frankfurt am Main: Suhrkamp, 2017, p. 95.
11. Peter Sloterdijk, *Critique of Cynical Reason* [1983], translated from the German by Hans Hildenbrand, Paris, Christian Bourgois, 1987, p. 385.
12. Hannes Meyer, "Die neue Welt," *Das Werk: Architektur und Kunst*, 1926, 13th year, no. 7. English edition: "The New World," in *The Weimar Republic Sourcebook*, edited by Martin Jay and Edward Dimendberg, translated from the German by Anton Kaes, Los Angeles: University of California Press, 1994. On the relationship between New Objectivity and the Bauhaus, see Hans Joachim Dahms, "Neue Sachlichkeit in der Architekturund Philosophie der zwanziger Jahre," *Arch+*, no. 156, 2001, pp. 82-87.
13. See Éric Michaud, "Œuvre d'art totale et totalitarisme," in *La Fin du salut par l'image et autres textes*, Paris: Flammarion, 2020, pp. 394-397.
14. See Johannes Schleuning, *Die Siedlung Römerstadt in Frankfurt a.M. von Ernst May*, Hamburg: Diplomica, 2000, p. 85. See also Wolfgang Voigt, Dorothea Deschermeier, Peter Cachola Schmal (eds.), *Neuer Mensch, neue Wohnung. Die Bauten des Neuen Frankfurt, 1925-1933*, exh. cat. (Deutsches Architekturmuseum, Frankfurt am Main, 9 November 2017 – 25 February 2018), Berlin: DOM Publishers, 2019.
15. Adolf Behne, "Dammerstock," *Die Form*, no. 6, 1930, p. 264, "Hier in Dammerstock wird der Mensch zum abstrakten Wohnwesen." The author puns here on the German term *Wesen*, which could be translated as "human being" or "neutral entity."
16. Max Horkheimer and Theodor W. Adorno, *Dialektik der Aufklärung, Philosophische Fragmente* [1944], Frankfurt am Main, Fischer Verlag, 1988, p. 129. English edition: *Dialectic of Enlightenment*, translated by John Cumming, London: Verso, 1997.
17. Béla Balázs, "Sachlichkeit und Sozialismus," *Die Weltbühne*, 24 February 1928, p. 917.
18. Ernst Bloch, *The Heritage of Our Times*, translated from the German by Neville and Stephen Plaice, Cambridge: Polity Press, 1991, p. 198.
19. See Andreas Stückler, "Gesellschaftskritik und bürgerliche Kälte," *Soziologie*, 43rd year, no. 3, 2014, pp. 278-299.
20. Josef Berger, "Die Stil-Richtungen, Versuch einer Sichtung," *Innendekoration*, no. 40, 1929, p. 214.
21. Bertolt Brecht, *700 Intellektuelle beten einen Öltank an* (1927), in B. Brecht, Gesammelte Werke, vol. IV, Frankfurt am Main: Suhrkamp Verlag, 1967, pp. 316-317; reprinted in Detlev J.K. Peukert, *Die Weimarer Republik. Krisenjahre der Klassischen Moderne* [1987], Frankfurt am Main: Suhrkamp, 2018, p. 185. English edition, "700 intellectuals worship an oil tank," *The Collected Poems*, translated by Tom Kunh and David Constantine, Liverlight, 2018, n.p. See page 52 in this catalogue.
22. Sabina Becker, Experiment Weimar. *Eine Kulturgeschichte Deutschlands, 1918-1933*, Darmstadt, Wissenschaftliche Buchgesellschaft, 2018, p. 381. Siegfried Kracauer similarly contests the veracity of the reports, because for him "one hundred reports from a factory do not add up to the reality of the factory [...] reality is a construction" (quoted from D. Peukert, *Die Weimarer Republik. Krisenjahre der Klassischen Moderne*, op. cit., p. 170).
23. S. Becker, *Experiment Weimar...*, op. cit., p. 421.
24. Ibid., p. 376.
25. Irmgard Keun, *Gilgi, eine von uns* [1931], Berlin: Ullstein, 2020, p. 71. See p. 50-51 in this catalogue
26. Marieluise Fleißer, *Mehlreisende Frieda Geier. Roman vom Rauchen, Sporteln, Lieben und Verkaufen*, 1931, republished as Eine Zierde für den Verein, 1972. See p. 53 in this catalogue.
27. Helmut Lethen, *Verhaltensweisen der Kälte*, op. cit., p. 183.
28. Christine N. Brinckmann, Reiner Herrn, "Von Ratten und Männern. DER STEINACH-FILM," *montage AV. Zeitschrift für Theorie und Geschichte audiovisueller Kommunikation*, 14th year, no. 2, 2005, pp. 78-100. https://doi.org/10.25969/ mediarep/225
29. On the subject of otherness, especially racial, see Dorothy Price, Camilla Smith, "Weimar's Others. Art History, Alterity and Regionalism in Inter-War Germany," *Art History*, September 2019, pp. 628-651.
P. Sloterdijk, Critique of Cynical Reason, op. cit, p. 478.

The list of works follows the themes of the exhibition and includes the following categories: paintings, design objects, works on paper, photographs and films. The list of works reflects only the documentary material reproduced in this catalogue and not the content of the entire exhibition.

PORTRAITS

JULIUS BISSIER
Selbstbildnis eines Bildhauers, 1928 [s. 9]
Self-Portrait of a Sculptor
Oil on canvas, 85.8 × 69.2 cm
Städtische Museen Freiburg, Museum für Neue Kunst, Freiburg im Breisgau

OTTO DIX
Der Kaufmann Max Roesberg, Dresden, 1922 [s. 23]
The Businessman Max Roesberg, Dresden
Oil on canvas, 94.3 × 63.8 cm
The Metropolitan Museum of Art, purchase, Lila Acheson Wallace Gift, 1992 (1992.146)

Bildnis der Journalistin Sylvia von Harden, 1926 [front cover and p. 21]
Portrait of the Journalist Sylvia von Harden
Oil and tempera on wood, 121 × 89 cm
Centre Pompidou, Musée national d'art moderne, Paris, purchase, 1961

Bildnis des Philosophen Max Scheler, 1926
Portrait of the Philosopher Max Scheler
Oil on wood, 100 × 69.5 cm
University of Cologne

Rothaarige Frau (Damenporträt), 1931 [p. 11]
Red-haired Lady (Female Portrait)
Mixed media on wood, 60.8 × 36.6 cm
Kunstsammlungen Chemnitz – Museum Gunzenhauser, property of Stiftung Gunzenhauser

CARL GROSSBERG
Selbstbildnis, 1928 [end-paper, front]
Self-Portrait
Oil on wood, 70 × 60 cm
Private collection, Germany

GEORGE GROSZ
Porträt des Schriftstellers Max Herrmann-Neiße, 1925 [p. 5]
Portrait of the Author Max Herrmann-Neiße
Oil on canvas, 100 × 101.5 cm
Kunsthalle Mannheim

Junge Spanierin, 1917 [p. 17]
Young Spanish Woman
Oil on canvas, 65.5 × 50.8 cm
Museum Ludwig, Cologne, acquisition from the Haubrich Foundation 1950

GUSSY HIPPOLD-AHNERT
Trude (Bildnis der Schwägerin Trude), 1932 [p. 14]
Trude (Portrait of Sister-in-Law Trude)
Oil on plywood, 48 × 34 cm
Sammlung Frieder Gerlach, Konstanz

KARL HUBBUCH
Zweimal Hilde I, 1929 [p. 117]
Twice Hilde I
Oil on canvas, 150 × 77 cm
Bayerische Staatsgemälde-sammlungen, Munich, Pinakothek der Moderne

Zweimal Hilde II, c. 1929 [p. 117]
Twice Hilde II
Oil on canvas on Masonite, 150 × 77 cm
Museo Nacional Thyssen-Bornemisza, Madrid

GRETHE JÜRGENS
Stoffhändler, 1932 [p. 16]
Textile Merchant
Oil on canvas, 52.5 × 40.5 cm
Sprengel Museum Hannover, permanent loan from Land Niedersachsen, Hannover

ISSAI KULVIANSKI
Mein Töchterchen Kiki, 1927 [p. 17]
My little Daughter Kiki
Oil on canvas, 127 × 97 cm
Berlinische Galerie – Museum of Modern Art, Photography and Architecture

LOTTE LASERSTEIN
Russisches Mädchen, c. 1928 [p. 14]
Russian Girl
Oil on wooden panel, 32 × 23 cm
Collection of Linda Sutton & Roger Cooper, London

CARLO MENSE
Bildnis H. M. Davringhausen, 1922
Portrait of H. M. Davringhausen
Oil on canvas, 86.5 × 59.5 cm
Museum Ludwig, Cologne, Haubrich Foundation 1946

Don Pepe, 1924 [p. 11]
Oil on canvas, 87 × 64 cm
Städtische Galerie im Lenbachhaus und Kunstbau München, Munich

WILLI MÜLLER-HUFSCHMID
Akademiemodell, c. 1922 [p. 12]
Academy Model
Oil on paper on plywood, 67 × 54 cm
Galerie Berinson, Berlin

LOTTE B. PRECHNER
Epoche, 1928
Epoch
Oil on canvas, 105 × 85.5 cm
Friedrich-Ebert-Stiftung e.V., Germany

FRANZ RADZIWILL
Einer von den Vielen des XX. Jahrhunderts, 1927 [p. 15]
One of the Many from the Twentieth Century
Oil on wood, 56.5 × 43.8 cm
LWL-Landesmuseum für Kunst und Kultur. Westfälisches Landesmuseum, Münster, acquired with the support of the Federal State of North Rhine-Westphalia

ANITA RÉE
Bildnis Hildegard Heise, 1927 [p. 14]
Portrait of Hildegard Heise
Oil on canvas, 40.6 × 35.6 cm
Hamburger Kunsthalle, gift from Jürgen Hinrichsen, Argentina, 1995

Bildnis Otto Pauly, c. 1927 [p. 16]
Portrait of Otto Pauly
Oil on canvas, 64.5 × 49.2 cm
Hamburger Kunsthalle, gift from private collection, 2012

CHRISTIAN SCHAD
Maria und Annunziata 'vom Hafen', 1923 [p. 12]
Maria and Annunziata 'From the Harbour'
Oil on canvas, 67.5 × 55.5 cm
Museo Nacional Thyssen-Bornemisza, Madrid

Anna Gabbioneta, 1927 [p. 13]
Oil on canvas, 76.7 × 55.4 cm
Private collection, courtesy Richard Nagy Ltd., London

Lea Bondi, 1927
Oil on wood, 58 × 47 cm
mumok – museum moderner kunst stiftung ludwig wien, acquired 1965

RUDOLF SCHLICHTER
Margot, 1924 [p. 10]
Oil on canvas, 1105 × 75 cm
Stiftung Stadtmuseum Berlin

GEORG SCHRIMPF
Kinderbildnis, 1925
Portrait of a Child
Oil on canvas, 56 × 48 cm
Staatliche Museen zu Berlin, Nationalgalerie

WALTER SCHULZ-MATAN
Der Fayencesammler, 1927 [p. 24] The Faience Collector
Oil on canvas, 142 × 100 cm
Münchner Stadtmuseum, Munich

Bildnis des Dichters Oskar Maria Graf, 1927
Painting of the Poet Oskar Maria Graf
Oil on paper on plywood, 90 × 74 cm
Landesmuseum für Kunst und Kulturgeschichte Oldenburg

LEONORE MARIA GRÄFIN STENBOCK-FERMOR
Porträt Hildegard Schroeder (Konzertpianistin), 1930 [p. 19]
Portrait of Hildegard Schroeder (Concert Pianist)
Oil on canvas, 45 × 40 cm
Stiftung Stadtmuseum Berlin

AUGUST SANDER

Unless otherwise stated, the photographs are vintage gelatin silver prints and belong to Die Photographische Sammlung / SK Stiftung Kultur, Cologne.

STAMM-MAPPE [PORTFOLIO OF ARCHETYPES]

Der erdgebundene Mensch, 1910
The Man of the Soil
24.1 × 17.4 cm
Die Photographische Sammlung / SK Stiftung Kultur, Cologne / Permanent loan of the Town of Herdorf

Bauernpaar – Zucht und Harmonie, 1912
Farming Couple – Propriety and Harmony
27.2 × 20 cm
Die Photographische Sammlung / SK Stiftung Kultur, Cologne / Permanent loan of the Town of Herdorf

Bauernpaar – Zucht und Harmonie, 1912
Farming Couple – Propriety and Harmony
25.3 × 18.8 cm
Die Photographische Sammlung / SK Stiftung Kultur, Cologne / Permanent loan of the Town of Herdorf

Der erdgebundene Mensch, 1912
The Woman of the Soil
23 × 16 cm
Die Photographische Sammlung / SK Stiftung Kultur, Cologne / Permanent loan of the Town of Herdorf

Die Familie in der Generation, 1912
Three Generations of the Family
15.4 × 22.5 cm
Die Photographische Sammlung / SK Stiftung Kultur, Cologne / Permanent loan of the Town of Herdorf

Die Stürmerin oder Revolutionärin, 1912
The Fighter or Revolutionary
26.1 × 19 cm
Die Photographische Sammlung / SK Stiftung Kultur, Cologne / Permanent loan of the Town of Herdorf

Der Philosoph, 1913
The Philosopher
24.4 × 18.1 cm
Die Photographische Sammlung / SK Stiftung Kultur, Cologne / Permanent loan of the District of Altenkirchen

Der Weise, 1913
The Sage
23.9 × 17.9 cm
Die Photographische Sammlung / SK Stiftung Kultur, Cologne / Permanent loan of the Town of Herdorf

Die Philosophin, 1913
The Philosopher
26 × 18.9 cm
Die Photographische Sammlung / SK Stiftung Kultur, Cologne / Permanent loan of the Town of Herdorf

Die Weise, 1913
The Sage
24.1 × 17.2 cm
Die Photographische Sammlung / SK Stiftung Kultur, Cologne / Permanent loan of the Town of Herdorf

Die Frau im fortgeschrittenen Intellekt (Intellektuelle), 1914
The Woman of Progressive Intellect (Intellectual)
24.9 × 17.8 cm
Die Photographische Sammlung / SK Stiftung Kultur, Cologne / Permanent loan of the Town of Herdorf

Der Stürmer oder Revolutionär, 1925
The Fighter or Revolutionary
24.1 × 17.9 cm
Die Photographische Sammlung / SK Stiftung Kultur, Cologne / Permanent loan of the Town of Herdorf

GROUP I
DER BAUER [THE FARMER]

PORTFOLIO 1
DER JUNGBAUER [THE YOUNG FARMER]

Konfirmandin, 1911
Confirmation Candidate
24.5 × 18 cm

Jungbauern, 1914
Young Farmers
23.1 × 16.9 cm

Bäuerliche Braut, 1920-1925 [p. 27]
Rural Bride
Modern print from 1995, 26 × 19.3 cm

Bauernmädchen, 1925
Country Girls
28.5 × 21.3 cm

Haustochter, 1926
Home Help
29.4 × 21.4 cm

PORTFOLIO 2
DAS BAUERNKIND UND DIE MUTTER [THE FARMER'S CHILD AND THE MOTHER]

Mutter und Tochter. Bauern- und Bergmannsfrau, 1912
Mother and Daughter. Farmer's Wife and Miner's Wife
25.9 × 19.1 cm

Bauernkinder, ca. 1913
Farm Children
21.5 × 15.6 cm

Bauernkind, 1919
Farmer's Child
27.4 × 21 cm

PORTFOLIO 3
BAUERNFAMILIE [THE FARMER'S FAMILY]

Bauernfamilie zwischen Au und Wissen, 1911-1912
Farming Family between Au and Wissen
22.6 × 27.9 cm

Bauernfamilie, 1913-1914
Farming Family
21.4 × 28.2 cm

PORTFOLIO 4
DER BAUER – SEIN LEBEN UND WIRKEN [THE FARMER– HIS LIFE AND WORK]

Bauernkapelle, 1913
Country Band
15.8 × 22.6 cm
Die Photographische Sammlung / SK Stiftung Kultur, Cologne / Permanent loan of Sparkasse KölnBonn

Preisträger, 1927
Prize-winners
27.3 × 18.7 cm

PORTFOLIO 5
BAUERNTYPEN [FARMING TYPES]

Herrenbauer, 1924
Gentleman Farmer and Wife
23.9 × 19.1 cm

Holzfäller, 1931
Woodcutter
28.6 × 21 cm

Bauer, 1931-1932
Farmer
29.1 × 22.4 cm
Die Photographische Sammlung / SK Stiftung Kultur, Cologne / Permanent loan of Sparkasse KölnBonn

PORTFOLIO 6
DER KLEINSTÄDTER [THE SMALL-TOWN DWELLER]

Kleinstadtbürger, Monschäuer, 1926
Middle-class Couple, Monschau
Modern print from 1992, 18.7 × 22.8 cm

PORTFOLIO 7,
DER SPORT [SPORT]

Mitglied eines Bauernturnvereins, 1912
Member of a Rural Gymnastics Club
28.4 × 19 cm

Sportflieger, 1920-1928
Aviator
Modern print from 1992, 25.9 × 18.9 cm

Boxer, 1929
Boxers
22.7 × 14.7 cm

Jockey, c. 1930
28.3 × 21.4 cm

GROUP II
DER HANDWERKER [THE SKILLED TRADESMAN]

PORTFOLIO 8
DER HANDWERKSMEISTER [THE MASTER CRAFTSMAN]

Berliner Tapezierermeister, 1929
Master Upholsterer, Berlin
23 × 17 cm

Konditor, 1928 [p. 37]
Pastry Cook
23.8 × 14 cm

Schuhmachermeister, 1925
Master Shoemaker
28.3 × 22.2 cm

Schlossermeister, 1928
Master Locksmith
23.1 × 14.5 cm

PORTFOLIO 9
DER INDUSTRIELLE [THE INDUSTRIALIST]

Der Metzgergeselle, 1911-1914
The Butcher's Apprentice
28.8 × 21.6 cm

Großindustrieller [Kommerzienrat Arnold von Guilleaume], 1927
Industrial Magnate [Commercial Counsellor Arnold von Guilleaume]
21.5 × 16.6 cm

Der Industrielle, 1929
The Industrialist
23 × 16.4 cm

PORTFOLIO 10
DER ARBEITER – SEIN LEBEN UND WIRKEN [THE WORKER – HIS LIFE AND WORK]

Arbeiterfamilie, 1912
Working-class Family
17.9 × 22.5 cm
Die Photographische Sammlung / SK Stiftung Kultur, Cologne / Permanent loan of Sparkasse KölnBonn

Landproletarierkinder, 1914
Working-class Country Children
Modern print from 1992,
19 × 23 cm

Proletariermutter, 1926 [p. 29]
Working-class Mother
22 × 16 cm

Straßenarbeiter im Ruhrgebiet, c. 1928 [p. 29]
Workmen in the Ruhr Region
Modern print from 1997,
25.9 × 18.3 cm

Handlanger, 1928 [p. 28]
Bricklayer
19.9 × 13.4 cm

Bauernknechte, 1929
Farmhands
28.6 × 20.8 cm

Berliner Kohlenträger, 1929
Berlin Coalheaver
23.7 × 16.9 cm

PORTFOLIO 11
ARBEITERTYPEN – PHYSISCH UND GEISTIG [WORKING TYPES – PHYSICAL AND INTELLECTUAL]

Arbeiterrat aus dem Ruhrgebiet, 1929
Workers' Council from the Ruhr Region
15.7 × 22.3 cm

Kommunistischer Führer [Paul Frölich], 1929
Communist Leader [Paul Frölich]
22 × 15.1 cm

Revolutionäre [Alois Lindner, Erich Mühsam, Guido Kopp], 1929
Revolutionaries [Alois Lindner, Erich Mühsam, Guido Kopp]
22.1 × 16.5 cm

Landarbeiter, c. 1945
Country Worker
29.2 × 22.7 cm

Geistesarbeiter des Proletariats [Else Schuler, Tristan Rémy, Franz Wilhelm Seiwert, Gerd Arntz], c. 1925
Proletarian Intellectuals [Else Schuler, Tristan Rémy, Franz Wilhelm Seiwert, Gerd Arntz]
26.9 × 21.4 cm
Die Photographische Sammlung / SK Stiftung Kultur, Cologne / Permanent loan of Sparkasse KölnBonn

PORTFOLIO 12
DER TECHNIKER UND ERFINDER [THE TECHNICIAN AND INVENTOR]

Betriebsingenieur, 1924
Production Engineer
23.5 × 15.9 cm

Erfinder und Dadaist [Raoul Hausmann], 1929
Inventor and Dadaist [Raoul Hausmann]
Modern print from 2001,
26 × 18.9 cm

Ingenieur und Werbeleiter, c. 1935
Engineer and Advertising Manager
28.2 × 22.6 cm

GROUP III
DIE FRAU [THE WOMAN]

PORTFOLIO 13
DIE FRAU UND DER MANN [WOMAN AND MAN]

Großkaufmann mit Gattin, 1923
Wholesale Merchant and Wife
19.5 × 20.2 cm

Malerehepaar [Marta Hegemann und Anton Räderscheidt], c. 1925
The Painter Anton Räderscheidt and his Wife Marta Hegemann
18.5 × 12.5 cm

Malerehepaar [Tata und Heinrich Hoerle], c. 1925
The Painter Heinrich Hoerle and his Wife Tata
17.9 × 19.5 cm

Malerehepaar [Martha und Otto Dix], 1925 [p. 41]
The Painter Otto Dix and his Wife Martha
Modern print from 1998,
20.6 × 24.3 cm

Architektenehepaar [Dora und Hans Heinz Lüttgen], 1926
The Architect Hans Heinz Lüttgen and his Wife Dora
Modern print from 1996,
20.4 × 24.1 cm

Bürgerliches berufstätiges Ehepaar, 1927
Professional Middle-class Couple
Modern print from 1992,
26 × 19.3 cm

Der Dadaist Raoul Hausmann [mit Hedwig Mankiewitz und Vera Broïdo], 1929
The Dadaist Raoul Hausmann [with Hedwig Mankiewitz and Vera Broïdo]
23 × 17 cm

PORTFOLIO 14
DIE FRAU UND DAS KIND [WOMAN AND CHILD]

Meine Frau in Freud und Leid, 1911 [p. 39]
My Wife in Joy and Sorrow
28.3 × 21.7 cm

Bürgerkinder, 1925 [p. 40]
Middle-class Children
21.5 × 15 cm

Mutter und Tochter [Martha Dix mit Tochter Nelly], 1925
Mother and Daughter [Martha Dix with Daughter Nelly]
Modern print from 1993,
26 × 16.8 cm

Mutter und Tochter [Helene Abelen mit Tochter Josepha], c. 1926 [p. 29]
Mother and Daughter [Helene Abelen with Daughter Josepha]
Modern print from 1993,
25.9 × 19.7 cm

Bürgerkind, 1926
Middle-class Child
Modern print from 1992,
25.9 × 18.7 cm

Junge Mutter, bürgerlich, 1926
Young Mother, Middle-class
Modern print from 1992,
19 × 20.6 cm

Geburtstagsfeier [unten Mitte Sigrid Sander], 1927
Birthday Party [below center Sigrid Sander]
17.5 × 20.4 cm

PORTFOLIO 15
DIE FAMILIE [THE FAMILY]

Witwer, 1914 [p. 29]
Widower
27.1 × 17.9 cm

Bürgerliche Familie, 1923
Middle-class Family
24 × 16 cm

Geschwisterpaar, 1928
Brother and Sister
19 × 17.1 cm

PORTFOLIO 16
DIE ELEGANTE FRAU [THE ELEGANT WOMAN]

Junge Frau, 1922
Young Woman
Modern print from 1992,
26 × 17.7 cm

Dame der Gesellschaft, 1923
Society Lady
23.4 × 17.5 cm

Frau eines Schriftstellers und Studienrats, 1923
Wife of a Writer and High School Teacher
22.5 × 16.5 cm

Frau eines Architekten [Dora Lüttgen], 1926
Architect's Wife [Dora Lüttgen]
23.7 × 17.8 cm

Frau eines Malers [Helene Abelen], 1926-1927 [p. 18]
Painter's Wife [Helene Abelen]
Modern print from 1992,
25.9 × 18.8 cm

PORTFOLIO 17
DIE FRAU IM GEISTIGEN UND PRAKTISCHEN BERUF [THE WOMAN IN INTELLECTUAL AND PRACTICAL OCCUPATION]

Krankenschwester, 1911-1914
Nurse
28.8 × 21.4 cm

Rotkreuzschwester, 1924
Red Cross Nurse
28.7 × 22.5 cm

Malerin [Marta Hegemann], c. 1925 [p. 18]
Painter [Marta Hegemann]
25.2 × 20.5 cm
Die Photographische Sammlung / SK Stiftung Kultur, Cologne / Permanent loan from a private collection

Gymnastiklehrerin, 1925 [p. 30]
Gymnastics Teacher
Modern print from 1992,
26 × 17.7 cm

Photographin, 1927
Photographer
22.4 × 15.5 cm
Die Photographische Sammlung / SK Stiftung Kultur, Cologne / Permanent loan from a private collection

Kontoristin, c. 1928 [p. 30]
Office Worker
Modern print from 1992,
26 × 19.5 cm

Bildhauerin [Ingeborg von Rath], 1929
Sculptress [Ingeborg von Rath]
23.2 × 16.1 cm

Sekretärin beim Westdeutschen Rundfunk in Köln, 1931 [p. 18]
Secretary at West German Radio in Cologne
29 × 22 cm

GROUP IV
DIE STÄNDE [CLASSES AND PROFESSIONS]

PORTFOLIO 18
DER STUDENT [THE STUDENT]

Werkstudenten, 1926
Working Students
16.5 × 21.4 cm

Corpsstudent, 1925
Fraternity Student
23 × 17 cm

PORTFOLIO 19
DER GELEHRTE [THE SCHOLAR]

Philosoph [Max Scheler], 1926
Philosopher [Max Scheler]
Modern print from 2000,
26 × 18.9 cm

Der Kunstgelehrte [Karl Schäfer], 1926
The Art Scholar [Karl Schäfer]
28.4 × 21.4 cm

Philosophiestudent [Erich Sander], 1926
Student of Philosophy [Erich Sander]
28.5 × 21 cm

PORTFOLIO 20
DER BEAMTE [THE OFFICIAL]

Polizeibeamter. Der Herr Wachtmeister, 1925 [p. 38]
Police Officer
22.5 × 15.7 cm

Staatsanwalt, 1929-1931
Public Prosecutor
27.6 × 23.1 cm

Gerichtsdiener, 1932
Court Usher
29 × 17.5 cm

PORTFOLIO 21
DER ARZT UND APOTHEKER [THE DOCTOR AND PHARMACIST]

Der Arzt [Carl Robert Schlayer], 1929
The Doctor [Carl Robert Schlayer]
23 × 16 cm

Der Kräuterheilkundige, 1929
The Herbalist
21.5 × 14.5 cm

Apotheker, c. 1930
Pharmacist
29.7 × 18.3 cm

PORTFOLIO 22
DER RICHTER UND RECHTSANWALT [THE JUDGE AND THE ATTORNEY]

Der Notar, 1924
The Notary
27 × 17.9 cm

Rechtsanwalt, 1932
Attorney
28 × 20 cm

Winkeladvokat, 1952
Amateur Advocate
28.4 × 21.7 cm

PORTFOLIO 23
DER SOLDAT [THE SOLDIER]

Oberst, c. 1916
Colonel
28.9 × 21.4 cm

Pensionierter Major, c. 1930
Retired Major
23.8 × 17.7 cm

Fahnenjunker, c. 1944
Officer Cadet
Modern print from 1997,
26 × 18.8 cm

PORTFOLIO 23A
DER NATIONALSOZIALIST [THE NATIONAL SOCIALIST]

SA-Sanitätshauptsturmführer, c. 1935
Chief medical officer of the SA (Sturmabteilung)
17 × 12.1 cm

SS-Hauptsturmführer, 1937
SS Captain
Modern print from 1999,
25.9 × 17.3 cm

Angehöriger der Hitler-Jugend, 1938
Member of the Hitler Youth
Modern print from 2000,
25.9 × 18.7 cm

Junger Nationalsozialist, 1941 [p. 42]
Young National Socialist
Modern print from 1999,
25.9 × 17.5 cm

PORTFOLIO 24
DER ARISTOKRAT [THE ARISTOCRAT]

Großherzog, c. 1930
Grand Duke
27.8 × 19.5 cm

PORTFOLIO 25
DER GEISTLICHE [THE CLERGYMAN]

Frau Pastor, c. 1920
Pastor's Wife
28.6 × 21.8 cm

Katholischer Geistlicher, 1927 [p. 31]
Catholic Priest
23.6 × 17 cm

Evangelischer Geistlicher, 1928
Protestant Minister
28.9 × 23.5 cm

Stadtmissionare, 1930
Urban Missionaries
26.5 × 20.8 cm

PORTFOLIO 26
DER LEHRER UND PÄDAGOGE [THE TEACHER AND EDUCATOR]

Der Herr Lehrer, 1910
The Schoolmaster
22.9 × 17.5 cm

Rektor, 1910
Headmaster
28 × 22 cm

Dorfschullklasse, 1912
Village School Class
16.4 × 23.1

Junglehrer, c. 1928
Young Teacher
28.6 × 19.8 cm

PORTFOLIO 27
DER KAUFMANN [THE BUSINESSMAN]

Der junge Kaufmann, 1927
Young Businessman
Modern print from 1992,
25.7 × 16.4 cm

Kunsthändler [Sam Salz], 1927 [p. 31]
Art Dealer [Sam Salz]
Modern print from 1995,
26 × 18.8 cm

Streichholzverkäufer, 1927
Match-seller
20.4 × 24.3 cm

Bankier [Johann Heinrich von Stein], 1930
Banker [Johann Heinrich von Stein]
28 × 21.1 cm

PORTFOLIO 28
DER POLITIKER [THE POLITICIAN]

Abgeordneter (Demokrat), 1927 [p. 31]
Member of Parliament (Democrat)
20.8 × 14.3 cm

Kommunist [Jean Winterich], 1927-1928
Communist [Jean Winterich]
22.9 × 15 cm

Beigeordneter (Sozialdemokrat) [Johannes Meerfeld], 1928
Town Councillor (Social Democrat) [Johannes Meerfeld]
26.6 × 17.6 cm

Politiker der Linken [rechts Erich Mühsam], 1929
Left-wing Revolutionaries [right Erich Mühsam]
Modern print from 2001,
26 × 17.6 cm

Politikerin [Rosi Wolfstein-Frölich], 1929
Politician [Rosi Wolfstein-Frölich]
Modern print from 2000,
26 × 17.5 cm

Führer der Kommunistischen Partei Deutschlands – Opposition, KPDO [Heinrich Brandler], c. 1931
Leader of the Communist Party of Germany (Opposition), KPDO [Heinrich Brandler]
28.7 × 17.6 cm

**GROUP V
DIE KÜNSTLER [THE ARTISTS]**

**PORTFOLIO 29
DER SCHRIFTSTELLER
[THE WRITER]**

*Schriftsteller und
Literaturkritiker [Dettmar
Heinrich Sarnetzki], 1924-1926*
Writer and Literary Critic
[Dettmar Heinrich Sarnetzki]
22.2 × 16.3 cm
Die Photographische Sammlung
/ SK Stiftung Kultur, Cologne /
Permanent loan of Sparkasse
KölnBonn

*Schriftsteller [Karl August
Wittfogel], 1926*
Writer [Karl August Wittfogel]
23.5 × 17.1 cm

Arbeiterschriftsteller, 1928
Working-class Writer
Modern print from 2001,
26.2 × 18.3 cm

**PORTFOLIO 30
DER SCHAUSPIELER
[THE ACTOR]**

*Filmschauspielerin und
Kunstreiterin [Cilly Feindt],
c. 1927*
Film Actress and Trick Rider
[Cilly Feindt]
29 × 23.1 cm

*Der Tenor [Leonardo
Aramesco], c. 1928*
The Tenor [Leonardo Aramesco]
29.1 × 22.1 cm

Fahrender Komödiant, 1928-1930
Touring Player
29.2 × 20.6 cm

*Mitglieder der Piscator-Bühne,
1929*
Members of the Piscator Theater
23 × 26.5 cm

**PORTFOLIO 31
DER ARCHITEKT
UND BAUKÜNSTLER
[THE ARCHITECT]**

*Der Architekt [Hans Poelzig],
1929 [p. 31]*
The Architect [Hans Poelzig]
23.2 × 15.9 cm

*Architekt [Emil Fahrenkamp],
1930*
Architect [Emil Fahrenkamp]
22.6 × 16.3 cm

*Architekt [Richard
Riemerschmid], 1930*
Architect [Richard Riemerschmid]
27.3 × 16.4 cm

**PORTFOLIO 32
DER BILDHAUER
[THE SCULPTOR]**

Bildhauer [Hans Schmitz], 1923
Sculptor [Hans Schmitz]
28 × 20.5 cm

*Maler und Bildhauer
[Otto Freundlich], c. 1925*
Painter and Sculptor
[Otto Freundlich]
28.5 × 20.4 cm

**PORTFOLIO 33
DER MALER [THE PAINTER]**

Maler [Jankel Adler], 1924
Painter [Jankel Adler]
28 × 19.5 cm

Maler [Otto Dix], 1924
Painter [Otto Dix]
21.6 × 16.5 cm

*Maler [Franz Wilhelm Seiwert],
1924*
Painter [Franz Wilhelm Seiwert]
28.8 × 22.4 cm

*Maler [Gottfried Brockmann],
1924*
Painter [Gottfried Brockmann]
Modern print from 1999,
26 × 19 cm

*Maler [Anton Räderscheidt],
1926 [back cover and p. 68]*
Painter [Anton Räderscheidt]
21.9 × 16.8 cm

Maler [Gerd Arntz], 1926
Painter [Gerd Arntz]
27.9 × 19 cm

*Maler [Heinrich Hoerle], 1928-
1932 [p. 69]*
Painter [Heinrich Hoerle]
Modern print from 1995,
26 × 20.3 cm

**PORTFOLIO 34,
DER KOMPONIST
[THE COMPOSER]**

*Dirigent [Wilhelm Furtwängler],
1924-1927*
Conductor [Wilhelm
Furtwängler]
29.4 × 22.8 cm

*Der Komponist [Paul Hindemith],
c. 1925*
The Composer [Paul Hindemith]
28.8 × 20 cm

*Komponist [Richard Strauss],
1925*
Composer [Richard Strauss]
22.4 × 16.6 cm

Komponist [Ernst Toch], 1926
Composer [Ernst Toch]
21.9 × 16.7 cm

**PORTFOLIO 35
DER REPRODUZIERENDE
MUSIKER [THE PERFORMING
MUSICIAN]**

Kaffeehausmusiker, c. 1919
Café Musician
Modern print from 1995,
26 × 18.3 cm

*Cellist [Emanuel Feuermann],
1923*
Cellist [Emanuel Feuermann]
28.7 × 21.3 cm

*Der Pianist [Max van de Sandt],
1925*
The Pianist [Max van de Sandt]
29 × 22.6 cm

Lautenspielerin, c. 1926
Lutenist
29 × 23 cm

**GROUP VI
DIE GROSSTADT [THE CITY]**

**PORTFOLIO 36
DIE STRASSE – LEBEN UND
TREIBEN [THE STREET AND
STREET LIFE]**

Straßenmusikanten, 1922-1925
Street Musicians
28.7 × 22.3 cm

Bärentreiber in Köln, 1923
Showman with Performing Bear
in Cologne
22.9 × 18.1 cm

*Reichspräsident Paul
von Hindenburg und
Oberbürgermeister Konrad
Adenauer, 1926*
President Paul von Hindenburg
and Mayor Konrad Adenauer
24.5 × 19 cm

*Demonstration der
„Roten Front", 1927*
"Red Front" Demonstration
Modern print from 1997,
18.7 × 26 cm

Straßenmusiker, 1928
Street Musician
27.5 × 20.7 cm

Straßenphotograph, c. 1930
Street Photographer
28.2 × 21.7 cm

**PORTFOLIO 37
FAHRENDES VOLK –
JAHRMARKT UND ZIRKUS
[TRAVELING PEOPLE –
FAIR AND CIRCUS]**

*Mädchen im Kirmeswagen,
1926-1932 [p. 33]*
Girl in Fairground Caravan
Modern print from 1993,
26 × 19.7 cm

*Platzanweiserinnen, 1926-1932
[p. 32]*
Usherettes
Modern print from 1993,
26 × 18.9 cm

Zirkusartisten, 1926-1932
Circus Artistes
23.4 × 29.2 cm

Zirkusarbeiter, 1926-1932 [p. 32]
Circus Workers
28 × 21.1 cm

Zirkusleute, 1926-1932
Circus People
Modern print from 1993,
26 × 18.7 cm

Bonbonverkäufer, 1930
Candy Seller
Modern print from 1993,
26 × 18.7 cm

Inder und Manager, 1930
Indian with Manager
27.2 × 20 cm

*Schausteller „Haut den Lukas",
1930*
"Test your Strength" Showman
29 × 21 cm

**PORTFOLIO 38
FAHRENDES VOLK
– ZIGEUNER UND
LANDSTREICHER
[TRAVELING PEOPLE –
GYPSIES AND TRANSIENTS]**

*Türkischer
Mäusefallenverkäufer,
1924-1930*
Turkish Mousetrap Salesman
27.8 × 20.5 cm

Landstreicher, 1929 [p. 34]
Vagrants
27.9 × 21.1 cm

Vagabunden, 1929-1930
Vagabonds
28.3 × 20.9 cm

Zigeuner, c. 1930 [p. 34]
Gypsy
Modern print from 1993,
26 × 18.5 cm

Zigeunerprimas, c. 1930
First Violinist in Gypsy Band
24.6 × 18.7 cm

Jerusalempilger, 1930
Jerusalem Pilgrim
28 × 20 cm

**PORTFOLIO 39
VON DEN FESTLICHKEITEN
[FESTIVITIES]**

Maskenball, 1926
Fancy-dress Ball
28.6 × 19.2 cm

Stahlhelmtreffen, 1927
Stahlhelm Gathering
17.1 × 23 cm

Karneval, 1928
Carnival
Modern print from 2001,
25.9 × 16.7 cm

*Aschermittwoch, before
February 1929*
Ash Wednesday [Architect
Hans Heinz Lüttgen with
Unknown]
Modern print from 2000,
26 × 17.3 cm

**PORTFOLIO 40
JUGEND DER GROSSTADT
[CITY YOUTH]**

Kaisergeburtstagsfeier, 1915
Kaiser's Birthday Celebration
Modern print from 1999,
19 × 25.7 cm

Jugendbewegung, 1923
Youth Movement
21.8 × 16.5 cm

Gymnasiast, 1926
High School Student
22 × 11.9 cm

Lyzealschülerin, 1928
High School Girl
21.5 × 14.8 cm

*Junger Photograph
[Gunther Sander], 1929*
Young Photographer
[Gunther Sander]
22 × 16.6 cm
Die Photographische Sammlung
/ SK Stiftung Kultur, Cologne /
Permanent loan of Sparkasse
KölnBonn

Bergmannskinder, c. 1930
Miner's Children
Modern print from 1992,
26 × 18.7 cm

Arbeiterkinder, c. 1930
Worker's Children
Modern print from 1999,
26 × 18.8 cm

*Kinder in der Schemmergasse
in Köln, 1930*
Children in Schemmergasse
in Cologne
20.7 × 27.5 cm

**PORTFOLIO 41
DIE DIENENDEN [SERVANTS]**

Putzfrau, 1928
Cleaning Woman
28.3 × 20.8 cm

Schankkellner, 1928
Bartender
23 × 16.9 cm

Kaffeehausmädchen, 1928-1929
Café Waitress
23.5 × 11.4 cm
Die Photographische Sammlung
/ SK Stiftung Kultur, Cologne /
Permanent loan of Sparkasse
KölnBonn

Dienstmann, c. 1929
Porter
28.9 × 19.9 cm

Hotelpersonal in Hamburg, 1929
Hotel Staff in Hamburg
28.2 × 22.7 cm

Herzoglicher Diener, c. 1930
Duke's Manservant
28.8 × 20.5 cm

Conférencier, 1930
Compère
27.1 × 13.6 cm

**PORTFOLIO 42
TYPEN UND GESTALTEN DER
GROSSTADT [TYPES AND
FIGURES OF THE CITY]**

*Boheme [Willi Bongard,
Gottfried Brockmann], 1922-1925*
Bohemians [Willi Bongard
and Gottfried Brockmann]
17.3 × 22.4 cm

*Photograph [August Sander],
1925 [p. 36]*
Photographer [August Sander]
23.6 × 17.2 cm

Asylbewohner, 1926-1930
Asylum Inmate
28.8 × 19.3 cm

Asylbewohner, 1926-1930
Asylum Inmate
28.2 × 21.1 cm

Berginvalide, 1927-1928 [p. 34]
Disabled Miner
23 × 16 cm

Kriegsinvalide, c. 1928
Disabled Ex-Serviceman
23 × 16.7 cm

Arbeitslos, 1928
Jobless
23.3 × 15 cm

*Abgebauter Seemann, 1929
[p. 34]*
Unemployed Sailor
29.3 × 22.2 cm
Die Photographische Sammlung
/ SK Stiftung Kultur, Cologne /
Permanent loan of Sparkasse
KölnBonn

*Raoul Hausmann als Tänzer,
1929*
Raoul Hausmann as Dancer
Reproduction, print from digital
file of original photograph
(gelatin silver print),
22.5 × 15 cm
Berlinische Galerie – Museum
of Modern Art, Photography
and Architecture

**PORTFOLIO 43
MENSCHEN, DIE AN MEINE
TÜR KAMEN [PEOPLE WHO
CAME TO MY DOOR]**

Gerichtsvollzieher, c. 1930
Bailiff
29.5 × 17.1 cm

*Almosenempfänger, 1930
[p. 35]*
Welfare Recipient
22.9 × 12 cm

Bettlerin, 1930 [p. 35]
Beggar
23.4 × 11.9 cm

Bettlerin, 1930
Beggar
24.9 × 13.9 cm

Hausierer, 1930
Peddler
22.7 × 16.4 cm

**PORTFOLIO 44
VERFOLGTE [THE PERSECUTED]**

Verfolgter, c. 1938
Victim of Persecution
28 × 22.8 cm

Verfolgte, c. 1938
Victim of Persecution
28.2 × 22.2 cm

Verfolgte, c. 1938
Victim of Persecution
28.7 × 22.6 cm

Verfolgte, c. 1938
Victim of Persecution
Modern print from 1996,
25.9 × 18.1 cm

**PORTFOLIO 44A
POLITISCHE GEFANGENE
[POLITICAL PRISONERS]**

*Politischer Häftling [Erich Sander],
1943*
Political Prisoner [Erich Sander]
29.3 × 21.7 cm

Politischer Häftling, 1943
Political Prisoner
Modern print from 2001,
24.9 × 20 cm

**PORTFOLIO 44B
FREMDARBEITER
[FOREIGN WORKERS]**

Fremdarbeiter, 1941-1945
Foreign Worker
Modern print from 2001,
25.9 × 19.6 cm

Fremdarbeiter, 1941-1945
Foreign Worker
Modern print from 2001,
26.1 × 19.6 cm

**GROUP VII
DIE LETZTEN MENSCHEN
[THE LAST PEOPLE]**

**PORTFOLIO 45
IDIOTEN, KRANKE,
IRRE UND DIE MATERIE
[IDIOTS, THE SICK,
THE INSANE AND MATTER]**

Kleinwüchsige, 1906-1914
Midgets
18 × 20 cm

*Blinde Kinder beim Unterricht,
1921-1930*
Blind Children at their Lessons
Modern print from 2002,
25.7 × 18.9 cm

Blinde Mädchen, 1921-1930
Blind Girls
Modern print from 1995,
26 × 18.5 cm

Kretin, 1924
Cretin
22.1 × 16 cm

Blinde, 1921-1930
Blind People
Modern print from 1995,
26 × 20.4 cm

Blinder Bergmann und Blinder Soldat, 1921-1930 [p. 43]
Blind Miner and Blind Soldier
28.7 × 22.8 cm

Blindgeborene Kinder, 1921-1930
Children Born Blind
Modern print from 1995,
26.1 × 19 cm

Die Pflegemutter, 1921-1930
The Foster Mother
Modern print from 1995,
26 × 19.7 cm

Alter Bauer, 1931-1932
Old Farmer
27.8 × 21.6 cm

THEATRE, LITERATURE AND MUSIC

MAX BRAND
Maschinist Hopkins, Vereinigte Stadttheater, Duisburg, 1929
Machinist Hopkins
Stage photo from the premiere of the opera,
unknown photographer
9 × 12 cm
Theatre Collection,
University of Cologne

Maschinist Hopkins, Vereinigte Stadttheater, Duisburg, 1929
Machinist Hopkins
Stage photo from the premiere of the opera,
unknown photographer
10 × 12 cm
Theatre Collection,
University of Cologne

Maschinist Hopkins, Vereinigte Stadttheater, Duisburg, 1929 [p. 48]
Machinist Hopkins
Stage photo from the premiere of the opera,
unknown photographer
17.6 × 23.9 cm
Theatre Collection,
University of Cologne

FRANZ ALOÏS FLACHSLANDER
Poster for the staging of the opera *Jonny spielt auf* [Jonny Strikes Up] by Ernst Křenek at Städtische Oper in Berlin, 1927 [p. 45]
Photo of a photo collage, 1
7.7 × 23.8 cm
Theatre Collection,
University of Cologne

GEORGE GROSZ
Drei Karten spielende Gefangene, Arrestlokal, 1928
Three Prisoners Playing Cards, Detention
Sketch for projection in the play *Die Abenteuer des braven Soldaten Schwejk* [The Good Soldier Švejk] by Erwin Piscator
Ink on paper, 65 × 84 cm
Stiftung Stadtmuseum Berlin
Facsimile

Gefängniskapelle, 1928 [p. 47]
Prison Chapel
Set drawing for *Die Abenteuer des braven Soldaten Schwejk* [The Good Soldier Švejk] by Erwin Piscator
Watercolour and ink on paper,
47.5 × 64 cm
Theatre Collection,
University of Cologne

PAUL HINDEMITH, BERTOLT BRECHT
Das Lehrstück, Deutsche Kammermusik Baden-Baden Festival, 28/7 1929
The Lesson
Stage photo from the premiere, modern print from 2004, unknown photographer
24 × 18 cm
Fondation Hindemith,
Blonay (CH)

Das Lehrstück: Clownszene, Deutsche Kammermusik Baden-Baden Festival, 28/7 1929
The Lesson: Clown Scene
Stage photo from the premiere, modern print from 2004, unknown photographer
17.8 × 12.8 cm
Fondation Hindemith,
Blonay (CH)

Das Lehrstück, 1931
The Lesson
Stage photo from the dress rehearsal, modern print from 2004, unknown photographer
12.8 × 17.8 cm
Fondation Hindemith,
Blonay (CH)

MARTIN HÖHLIG
Berlin im Licht, 1928:

Europa Dance Pavilion in Stresemannstraße
Modern print, 16.5 × 22.3 cm

Radio Tower and House of the Radio Industry
Modern print, 22.5 × 16.5 cm

Flagship Store for "Leibniz Keks", Kurfürstendamm 26a

Advertising Column at Großen Stern
Modern print, 23.4 × 17.1 cm

"Columbia" Dance Cabaret, Kurfürstendamm 217
Modern print, 16.7 × 22 cm
Stiftung Stadtmuseum Berlin

"Florida" Dance Hall, probably Budapester Straße 18
Modern print, 16.5 × 22.2 cm
Stiftung Stadtmuseum Berlin

ERNST KŘENEK
Jonny spielt auf, Städtische Oper, Berlin, 1927 [p. 46]
Jonny Strikes Up
Stage photo from the opera, unknown photographer
11.8 × 15.7 cm
Theatre Collection,
University of Cologne

Jonny spielt auf, Stadttheater, Hamburg, 1927
Jonny Strikes Up
Stage photo from the opera, unknown photographer
13 × 18 cm
Theatre Collection,
University of Cologne

Jonny spielt auf, Landestheater, Darmstadt, 1928
Jonny Strikes Up
Stage photo from the opera, unknown photographer
17.7 × 23.9 cm
Theatre Collection,
University of Cologne

TRAUGOTT MÜLLER
Stage set drawing for the theatre version of *Hoppla, wir leben!* [Hoppla, We're Alive!] by Erwin Piscator, Piscator-Bühne, Theater am Nollendorfplatz, Berlin, c. 1927
Mixed media: photo, tempera and ink on paper,
20.8 × 30.3 cm
Institut für Theaterwissenschaft der Freien Universität Berlin, Theaterhistorische Sammlungen, Traugott Müller Estate

Montage for projection on the scene for the theatre version of *Hoppla, wir leben!* [Hoppla, We're Alive!] by Erwin Piscator, Piscator-Bühne, Theater am Nollendorfplatz, Berlin, c. 1927
Mixed media: photo, tempera and ink on paper, 49.7 × 67.8 cm
Institut für Theaterwissenschaft der Freien Universität Berlin, Theaterhistorische Sammlungen, Traugott Müller Estate

ERWIN PISCATOR
Die Abenteuer des braven Soldaten Schwejk, Piscator-Bühne, Theater am Nollendorfplatz, Berlin, 1928
The Good Soldier Švejk
Stage photo with silhouettes drawn by George Grosz: Švejk en route to admissions headquarters, unknown photographer, 21 × 38.5 cm
ullstein bild collection
Facsimile

Die Abenteuer des braven Soldaten Schwejk, Piscator-Bühne, Theater am Nollendorfplatz, Berlin, 1928 [p. 47]
The Good Soldier Švejk
Stage photo with silhouettes drawn by George Grosz, on a stage equipped with a treadmill, unknown photograph, 6 × 15 cm
Akademie der Künste, Berlin
Facsimile

ERWIN PISCATOR, ERNST TOLLER
Hoppla, wir leben [Hoppla, We're Alive!], Act II, Scene 5: Election Scene, Piscator-Bühne, Theater am Nollendorfplatz, Berlin, 1927
Stage photo by Sasha Stone
Modern print, 16.8 × 23 cm
Institut für Theaterwissenschaft der Freien Universität Berlin, Theaterhistorische Sammlungen, Traugot Müller Estate

Hoppla, wir leben [Hoppla, We're Alive!], Act IV, Scene 1: Prison, Piscator-Bühne, Theater am Nollendorfplatz, Berlin, 1927
Stage photo by Sasha Stone
Modern print, 16.7 × 22.40 cm
Institut für Theaterwissenschaft der Freien Universität Berlin, Theaterhistorische Sammlungen, Traugot Müller Estate

JOHANNES SCHRÖDER
Set design for the opera *Maschinist Hopkins* [Machinist Hopkins] by Max Brand, Vereinigtes Stadttheater, Duisburg, c. 1929 [p. 48]
Charcoal and tempera on paper, 65 × 90 cm
Theatre Collection,
University of Cologne

Set design for the opera *Maschinist Hopkins* [Machinist Hopkins] by Max Brand, Vereinigtes Stadttheater, Duisburg, c. 1929
Crayon on paper, 67 × 89 cm
Theatre Collection,
University of Cologne

MISCHA SPOLIANSKY (composer), MARCELLUS SCHIFFER (librettist)
Es liegt in der Luft, Komödie am Kurfürstendamm, Berlin 1928 [p. 57]
It's in the Air
Stage photo with Margo Lion and Marlene Dietrich,
21.7 × 15.8 cm
Stiftung Stadtmuseum Berlin
Facsimile

Medley from the revue *Es liegt in der Luft* [It's in the Air], part 1 and 2, 1928
[lyrics reproduced p. 57]
Audio recording
Duration: c. 3:30 min.
Electrola GmbH, Nowawes and Berlin
Deutsche Nationalbibliotek, Leipzig, courtesy Mischa Spoliansky Music

KURT WEILL (composer), BERTOLT BRECHT (text)
Audio recording from the world premiere of *Die Dreigroschenoper* [The Threepenny Opera], Theater am Schiffbauerdamm, Berlin, 1928
Moritat von Mackie Messer [Prelude: The Ballad of Mackie Messer] sung by Harald Paulsen
Duration: 2:20 min.
Private collection

Die Dreigroschenoper, Theater am Schiffbauerdamm, Berlin, 31 August 1928
The Threepenny Opera
Stage photo, unknown photographer, 23.4 × 15.8 cm
Theatre Collection,
University of Cologne

Die Dreigroschenoper, Theater am Schiffbauerdamm, Berlin, 31 August 1928
The Threepenny Opera
Stage photo, unknown photographer, 30 × 24 cm
Theatre Collection,
University of Cologne

Die Dreigroschenoper, Theater am Schiffbauerdamm, Berlin, 31 August 1928
The Threepenny Opera
Stage photo, unknown photographer, 18.1 × 12.9 cm
Theatre Collection,
University of Cologne

Die Dreigroschenoper, Theater am Schiffbauerdamm, Berlin, 31 August 1928
The Threepenny Opera
Harald Paulsen as Macheath
Stage photo, unknown photographer, 23.4 × 17.3 cm
Theatre Collection,
University of Cologne

EGON WILDEN
Drawing for the set design of the opera *Jonny spielt auf* [Jonny Strikes Up] by Ernst Křenek, Vereinigte Stadttheater Barmen-Elberfeld, 1928
Watercolour on paper,
23.1 × 24.5 cm
Theatre Collection,
University of Cologne

Drawing for the set design of the opera *Jonny spielt auf* [Jonny Strikes Up] by Ernst Křenek, Vereinigte Stadttheater Barmen-Elberfeld, 1928
Ink, watercolor and crayon on paper, 20 × 24.5 cm
Theatre Collection,
University of Cologne

Drawing for the set design of the opera *Jonny spielt auf* [Jonny Strikes Up] by Ernst Křenek, Vereinigte Stadttheater Barmen-Elberfeld, 1928
Ink, watercolor and crayon on paper, 20 × 32.6 cm
Theatre Collection,
University of Cologne

Drawing for the set design of the opera *Jonny spielt auf* [Jonny Strikes Up] by Ernst Křenek, Vereinigte Stadttheater Barmen-Elberfeld, 1928
Ink, watercolor and crayon on paper, 23 × 25 cm
Theatre Collection,
University of Cologne

STILL LIFE

IVAN BABIJ
Rechenstilleben, 1924 [p. 65]
Still Life with Abacus
Mixed media on wood,
36 × 46.5 cm
Kunsthalle Mannheim

ELLA BERGMANN-MICHEL
Wo wohnen alte Leute?, 1931
Where Do Elderly People live?
35 mm film, black/white, silent
Duration: 13 min.
DFF – Deutsches Filminstitut und Filmmuseum,
Frankfurt am Main

BERNHARD DÖRRIES
Frühstücksstillleben, 1927 [p. 63]
Breakfast, still life
Oil on Masonite, 51.2 × 69.8 cm
Sprengel Museum Hannover, permanent loan from Niedersächsisches Landesmuseum, Hannover

FRANZ XAVER FUHR
Stillleben (Gummibaum), c. 1925 [p. 61]
Still Life (Rubberplant)
Oil on canvas, 51 × 66 cm
Kunsthalle Mannheim

HEIN GORNY
Pelikan Zeichenblöcke, c. 1930 [p. 65]
Pelikan drawing pads
Gelatin silver print,
23.2 × 17.5 cm
Galerie Berinson, Berlin

ALEXANDER KANOLDT
Stillleben mit Gitarre, 1926 [p. 61]
Still Life with Guitar
Oil on canvas, 75 × 88 cm
Staatsgalerie, Stuttgart, permanent loan from Freunde der Staatsgalerie 1935-2008, and since 2013

FRANZ LENK
Stillleben mit gelber Tüte, 1927 [p. 64]
Still Life with Yellow Bag
Mixed media on canvas,
51 × 43.5 cm
Kunsthalle Mannheim

Amaryllis, 1930 [p. 62]
Egg tempera on canvas on wood, 66 × 44 cm
Staatliche Museen zu Berlin, Nationalgalerie

WERNER MANTZ
Front page, WDR's programme, 1928 [p. 63]
Gelatin silver print, black/white, 22.4 × 16.5 cm
Centre Pompidou, Musee national d'art moderne, Paris

HANS MERTENS
Stillleben mit Hausgeräten, 1928 [p. 64]
Still Life with Kitchen Utensils
Oil on canvas, 65 × 70 cm
Sprengel Museum Hannover, permanent loan from Niedersächsisches Landesmuseum, Hannover

HERBERT PLOBERGER
Stillleben mit Flasche, 1928
Still Life with Bottle
Oil on canvas, 43 × 53 cm
Private collection, Southern Germany

ALBERT RENGER-PATZSCH
Brasilianischer Melonenbaum von unten gesehen, 1923 [p. 62]
Brazilian Melon Tree Seen from Below
Gelatin silver print, 22.2 × 17.1 cm
Galerie Berinson, Berlin

Dahlia variabilis. Asteraceae, 1923 [p. 62]
Gelatin silver print, 23.2 × 17 cm
Galerie Berinson, Berlin

Gläser, 1926-1927
Glasses
Gelatin silver print, 17.1 × 22.9 cm
Galerie Berinson, Berlin

Fingerhut, 1928 [p. 63]
Foxglove
Gelatin silver print, 23.1 × 16.6 cm
Centre Pompidou, Musée national d'art moderne, Paris, purchase, 1993

Aufnahme für Katalog und Hauszeitschrift für Schocken Söhne 1929
Photograph for Catalogue and Internal Publication of Schocken Söhne
Gelatin silver print,
26.9 × 37.4 cm
Galerie Berinson, Berlin

Kolben, Jenaer Glaswerke Schott, 1934
Glass Flasks, Jenaer Glaswerke Schott
Gelatin silver print, 22.8 × 17 cm
Galerie Berinson, Berlin

GEORG SCHOLZ
Kakteen und Semaphore, 1923
[p. 59]
Cactuses and Signal Masts
Oil on panel, 69 × 52.3 cm
LWL-Landesmuseum für Kunst
und Kultur, Westfälisches
Landesmuseum, Münster

WILLY ZIELKE
Osram Glühlampen, c. 1933
Osram Incandescent Bulbs
Gelatin silver print,
22.8 × 16.9 cm
Galerie Berinson, Berlin

Stillleben (Kaktus und Orange),
c. 1930 [p. 60]
Still Life (Cactus and Orange)
Gelatin silver print, 11.9 × 8.9 cm
Galerie Berinson, Berlin

STANDARDISATION

GERD ARNTZ
Zwölf Häuser der Zeit, 1927
[p. 70]
Twelve Houses of Our Time
12 woodcuts on Japanese Paper,
variable dimensions
Private collection, Southern
Germany

MARCEL BREUER
Klubsessel B 3, 1925 [p. 78]
Club Armchair B 3
Steel tubes with nickel coating
and seat in Eisengarn cotton,
71.8 × 78.1 × 71.1 cm
Centre Pompidou, Musée
national d'art moderne, Paris,
purchase, 1993

*Hocker für die Bauhauskantine
B 9*, 1925
Stool for the Bauhaus
canteen B 9
Tubular steel and wood,
varnished, 5.4 × 45.3 × 36.2 cm
Vitra Design Museum,
Weil am Rhein

B 9-9c, 1925 [p. 77]
Tubular steel and wood,
lacquered, 60.5 × 66 × 40.5 cm
Vitra Design Museum,
Weil am Rhein

Piscator Stuhl, 1927
Piscator Chair
Steel tubes, chrome-plated
and seat in Eisengarn cotton,
84 × 45 × 54 cm
Centre Pompidou, Musée
national d'art moderne, Paris

Bauhaus Schreibtisch B 21, 1928
[p. 79]
B 21 Bauhaus Typewriter Desk
Chrome-plated steel and wood,
black lacquer, 69.5 cm / 51.5 cm
× 102 cm × 46 cm
Designmuseum Danmark

WALTER GROPIUS
Residential Area Dessau Törten,
street view, houses from
the improved 1927 model,
built 1928 [p. 75]
Gelatin silver print, 11.8 × 17 cm
Bauhaus-Archiv / Museum
für Gestaltung, Berlin
Reproduction

HEINRICH HOERLE
Selbstbildnis, c. 1931 [p. 69]
Self-Portrait
Oil on canvas, 41 × 29 cm
Bröhan Design Foundation,
Berlin

ERNST MAY
Siedlung Römerstadt, 1927-1929
Residential Area Römerstadt
Model 1:500, by Moritz Frank,
Anna Severin, Rosana Wiens &
Lea von Wolfframsdorff, 2019
Wood, 274 × 68.5 cm
Deutsches Architekturmuseum,
Frankfurt am Main

ANTON RÄDERSCHEIDT
Haus Nr 9, 1921 [p. 67]
House No. 9
Oil on panel, 66 × 54.4 cm
Private collection

*Junger Mann mit gelben
Handschuhen*, 1921 [p. 68]
Young Man with Yellow Gloves
Oil on wood, 27 × 18.5 cm
Galerie Berinson, Berlin

**CARL-HERMANN RUDLOFF,
ERNST MAY**
Römerstadt, am Forum, c. 1929
Photograph by Paul Wolff
Gelatin silver print, 9 × 14 cm
Ernst-May Gesellschaft,
Frankfurt am Main

Römerstadt, Im Burgfeld, c. 1929
Photograph by Max Göllner
Gelatin silver print, 9 × 14 cm
Ernst-May Gesellschaft,
Frankfurt am Main

Römerstadt, Frankfurt am Main,
Hadrianstrasse, block of flats
with street level shops, c. 1929
[p. 74]
Photograph by Hermann
Collischonn
Gelatin silver print, 11.3 × 21.5 cm
Ernst-May Gesellschaft,
Frankfurt am Main

Römerstadt, Frankfurt am Main,
c. 1930 [p. 74]
Aerial photo, unknown
photographer
Gelatin silver print, 9 × 14 cm
Ernst-May Gesellschaft,
Frankfurt am Main

FRANZ WILHELM SEIWERT
Der deutsche Bauernkrieg, 1932
[p. 72-73]
The German Peasants' War
Oil on wood, 99.5 × 150 cm
Von der Heydt-Museum
Wuppertal

DOCUMENTATION

Brochure Isotype, c. 1935 [p. 71]
Front and back pages,
14.7 × 20.7 cm (each)
Otto and Marie Neurath
Isotype Collection,
University of Reading
Facsimile

HAJNAL LENGYEL-PATAKY
Leaflet for the company
Standardmöbel, 1928 [p. 76]
Furniture designed by Marcel
Breuer, photos by Lucia
Moholy-Nagy, a. o.
Lithograph on paper,
47 × 62.5 cm
Museum of Modern Art, New
York, gift from Herbert Bayer
Facsimile

WALTER GROPIUS
Bauhausbauten Dessau, 1930
[p. 75]
Bauhaus Buildings Dessau
Bauhausbücher, No. 12,
23 × 36 cm
(printed by) Albert Langen,
München
Centre Pompidou, Musée
national d'art moderne,
Bibliothèque Kandinsky, Paris

RATIONALITY

ANONYMOUS
Big Zep, 2010
Series of 303 photographs
of 4 zeppelins, LZ 126, 127, 129,
and 130. Collected by Günter
Karl Bose 1924-1939
Gelatin silver prints,
variable dimensions
Centre Pompidou, Musée
national d'art moderne, Paris,
purchase, 2018

CHRISTIAN DELL
Rondella-Polo Lamp, 1929 [p. 88]
Mobile rod gliding on a central
axis of nickel coated brass.
Cast iron base and movable
shade in aluminium,
43 × 44 × 19 cm
Centre Pompidou, Musée
national d'art moderne, Paris,
donation: Société des Amis du
Musée national d'art moderne,
2003

FRANZ XAVER FUHR
Eisenbrücke, 1928 [p. 86]
Iron Bridge
Oil on canvas, 97.5 × 77 cm
Museum Folkwang, Essen

CARL GROSSBERG
Avus Berlin, 1928
Oil on wood, 44.6 × 69.5 cm
Private collection,
Southern Germany

Der gelbe Kessel, 1933 [p. 82]
The Yellow Boiler
Oil on canvas on wood,
90 × 70 cm
Von der Heydt-Museum
Wuppertal

Schwungrad mit Treibriemen,
1934 [p. 83]
Flywheel with Driving Belt
Oil on cardboard, 40 × 30 cm
Private collection

LOTTE JOHANNA JACOBI
Frau Piscator im Wohnzimmer,
1927 [p. 88]
Mrs. Piscator in the Living Room
Gelatin silver print, 17 × 23.2 cm
ullstein bild collection

HEINRICH JOST
Für Fotomontage Futura, 1929
[p. 96]
For Photomontage Futura
Promotion in the journal
Gebrauchsgraphik, Vol. 6,
No. 3, March 1929
Archiv der Massenpresse,
P. Rössler

ALICE LEX-NERLINGER
Der Flieger, c. 1930 [p. 84]
The Pilot
Photogram, 23.9 × 17.9 cm
Galerie Berinson, Berlin

Der Maschinist, c. 1930
The Machinist
Photogram, 22 × 16.5 cm
Galerie Berinson, Berlin

LUCIA MOHOLY-NAGY
*Dessau: Doppelwohnhaus
der Bauhausmeistersiedlung*,
1925-1926
Double House in the Residential
Area for the Bauhaus Teachers
Gelatin silver print, 8.3 × 11.5 cm
Centre Pompidou, Musée
national d'art moderne, Paris,
Legs de Nina Kandinsky, 1981

Bauhaus Neubau, Dessau,
1925-1926
New Bauhaus Building, Dessau
Gelatin silver print, 9 × 14 cm
Centre Pompidou, Musée
national d'art moderne, Paris,
Legs de Nina Kandinsky, 1981

Bauhaus Neubau, Dessau,
Werkstattenbau, 1925-1926
New Bauhaus Building, Studios
Gelatin silver print, 9 × 14 cm
Centre Pompidou, Musée
national d'art moderne, Paris,
Legs de Nina Kandinsky, 1981

Bauhaus Interieur, c. 1925-1926
Bauhaus Interior
Gelatin silver print, 9 × 14 cm
Centre Pompidou, Musée
national d'art moderne, Paris,
Legs de Nina Kandinsky, 1981

Bauhaus Interieur, c. 1925-1926
Bauhaus Interior
Gelatin silver print, 9 × 14 cm
Centre Pompidou, Musée
national d'art moderne, Paris,
Legs de Nina Kandinsky, 1981

Bauhaus Interieur, c. 1925-1926
Bauhaus Interior
Gelatin silver print, 9 × 14 cm
Centre Pompidou, Musée
national d'art moderne, Paris,
Legs de Nina Kandinsky, 1981

MARTIN MUNKACSI
Flat of Fritz Lang, 1932-1933
Gelatin silver print, 27.3 × 20 cm
ullstein bild collection

Flat of Fritz Lang, Fritz Lang
at his Desk, at Home in Berlin,
c. 1932-1933
Gelatin silver print, 27.3 × 20 cm
ullstein bild collection

MAX RADLER
Der Radiohörer, 1930 [p. 85]
The Radio Listener
Oil on canvas, 63 × 49 cm
Städtische Galerie im
Lenbachhaus und Kunstbau
München, Munich

Station SD/2, 1933 [p. 87]
Oil on panel, 64 × 84 cm
Galerie Berinson, Berlin

ALBERT RENGER-PATZSCH
Isolatorenkette, 1925 [p. 94]
Insulator Chain
Gelatin silver print,
27.3 × 37.5 cm
Galerie Berinson, Berlin

Maschinenkupplung, 1925
Machine Coupling
Gelatin silver print, 17 × 22.9 cm
Galerie Berinson, Berlin

Triebwerk einer Lokomotive,
1925
Locomotive Engine
Gelatin silver print, 17 × 21.2 cm
Galerie Berinson, Berlin

*Nockenwelle einer
Dampfmaschine*, 1927 [p. 83]
Camshaft of a Steam Engine
Gelatin silver print,
17.3 × 23.1 cm
Galerie Berinson, Berlin

Ohne Titel, c. 1928
Untitled
Gelatin silver print, 13 × 17.2 cm
Centre Pompidou, Musée
national d'art moderne, Paris,
purchase, 1986

Zeche „Zollverein 12" in Essen,
1929 [p. 93]
The Mine "Zollverein 12" in Essen
Gelatin silver print,
22.6 × 16.7 cm
Galerie Berinson, Berlin

Gute Hoffnungshütte, 1934
[p. 92]
The Steel Mill of Good hope
Gelatin silver print,
22.5 × 16.5 cm
Galerie Berinson, Berlin

PAUL RENNER
Futura, Die Schrift unserer Zeit,
1926-1927 [p. 97]
Futura, the Font of our Time
Typography collage on
cardboard, 29 × 22.2 cm
Klingspor Museum,
Offenbach am Main
Facsimile

WALTER RUTTMANN
*Berlin: Die Sinfonie
der Großstadt*, 1927
Berlin: Symphony of a Great
City
35 mm film, black/white, silent
Duration: 77:15 min.
Centre Pompidou, Musée
national d'art moderne, Paris,
purchase, 1984

*Fox Europa Produktion
Berlin: Die Sinfonie der
Großstadt* by Walter Ruttmann,
1927 [p. 90]
Berlin: Symphony
of a Great City
6 photo collages advertising
the film, variable dimensions
Theatre Collection,
University of Cologne

**RICHARD SCHADWELL,
MARCEL BREUER**
Telephone, the Frankfurt Model,
with handset, 1929 [p. 88]
Bakelite, metal and textile,
24 × 14 × 16 cm
Museum Angewandte Kunst,
Frankfurt am Main

OSCAR SCHLEMMER
Abstrakte Figur, Freiplastik G,
1921-1923/1961
Abstract Figure, Sculpture
in the Round G
Nickle-plated bronze,
105 × 65 × 20 cm
Louisiana Museum of Modern
Art, Humlebæk, long-term
loan: Collection of C. Raman
Schlemmer

Fünf Profilköpfe, 1921
Five Heads in Profile
Ink on paper, 27. 8 × 20.3 cm
Louisiana Museum of Modern
Art, Humlebæk, donation:
The Joseph and Celia Ascher
Collection, New York

GEORG SCHOLZ
Bahnwärterhäuschen, 1920
[p. 113]
Signalman's Cabin
Tempera and oil on paper
63 × 83 cm
Kunstpalast, Düsseldorf

FRANZ SCHUSTER
Chair for the Ernst-May-House,
c. 1929
Wood, wicker and parchment,
81 × 51 × 50 cm
Ernst-May Gesellschaft,
Frankfurt am Main

FRITZ SCHÜLER
Der Mensch als Industriepalast,
1926
Man as Industrial Palace
Poster as supplement to "Das
Leben des Menschen", Vol. 3,
Stuttgart, Kosmos Verlag,
95 × 47 cm
Collection Thilo von Debschitz,
Wiesbaden

**MARGARETE SCHÜTTE-
LIHOTZKY**
Die Frankfurter Küche, 1926
The Frankfurt Kitchen from
the Ernst-May Development
Bornheimer Hang,
Pestalozzistraße, Frankfurt
am Main
Equipped kitchen,
mixed media, 8 m²
Centre Pompidou, Musée
national d'art moderne, Paris,
purchase, 2022

Die Frankfurter Küche, 1927 [p. 89]
The Frankfurt Kitchen in the
exhibition "Die neue Wohnung
und ihr Innenausbau mit
Sonderschau des Frankfurter
Hausfrauenvereins"
Photograph: Hermann
Collischonn, 22.2 × 16.4 cm
Werkbundarchiv – Museum
der Dinge, Berlin

SASHA STONE
*11 Teile, aus denen moderne
Büromöbel zusammengesetzt
sind*, c. 1926
11 elements constituting
a modern desk
Gelatin silver print, 21 × 15.7 cm
ullstein bild collection

*Keine Nervosität im modernen
Büro durch Gedächtnisuhr
„Memor", die einen durch
eine Weckvorrichtung an alle
Termine erinnert*, c. 1926
No Nervousness in the
Modern Office Thanks to the
Memory Clock Reminding of all
Appointments with an Alarm
Gelatin silver print, 22.4 × 16.9 cm
Museum Folkwang, Essen

*Lohnbuchhaltung mit Goerz-
Rechenapparat – früher mit
14 bis 20 Buchhaltern*, c. 1926
Payroll Using Goertz-calculator –
Previously the Job of 14
to 20 Accountants
Gelatin silver print,
17.20 × 19.50 cm
ullstein bild collection

*Zeitersparnis durch phonetische
Ordnung der Kartei*, c. 1926
Time Saving Through
Phonetic Records
Gelatin silver print, 22.5 × 16.9 cm
ullstein bild collection

*Wohnung Piscator. Esszimmer
mit Wandbuffet*, c. 1928
Piscator's Flat. Dining room
with wall sideboard
Gelatin silver print, 16.5 × 21.4 cm
ullstein bild collection

Ohne Titel [Einsteinturm (FIFO)],
1928
Untitled [Einstein Tower (FIFO)]
Gelatin silver print,
23.5 × 17.3 cm
Centre Pompidou, Musée national
d'art moderne, Paris, purchase
supported by
Yves Rocher, 2011

*Sitzecke im Wohnzimmer
(Das Heim Piscators)*, 1928
Sitting corner in the living room
(the Piscator home)
Gelatin silver print,
16.5 × 21.4 cm
ullstein bild collection

UMBO
*Der rasende Reporter
(Egon Erwin Kisch)*, 1926 [p. 91]
The Racing Reporter
Authorised photo of original
photo collage, gelatin silver print
28.5 × 20.5 cm
Bauhaus-Archiv / Museum
für Gestaltung, Berlin
Facsimile

**KURT WEILL, PAUL
HINDEMITH, BERTOLT
BRECHT**
*Der Lindbergh-Flug /
Der Ozeanflug*, 1929
The Lindbergh Flight /
The Flight Across the Ocean
Historical recording
Duration: 19:02 min.
(extract: 2:31 min.)
Fondation Hindemith, Blonay

DOCUMENTATION

ANONYMOUS
Arbeiterinnen am Fließband,
1932 [p. 81]
Female Workers at the
Production Line
Photograph, black/white
Scherl / Süddeutsche Zeitung
Facsimile

ANONYMOUS
*Die Alfred-Jackson-Girls.
Ein reizvolles
Verkehrshindernis*, 1928
The Alfred Jackson Girls.
A Charming Roadblock
Gelatin silver print,
12.2 × 16.4 cm
Stiftung Stadtmuseum Berlin
Facsimile

ANONYMOUS
The First Female Graduates
From the Oldest Grammar
School in Berlin, Zum Grauen
Kloster, 1928 [end-paper, front]
Gelatin silver print,
ullstein bild collection
Facsimile

ANONYMOUS
Auto-Magazin, no. 18, July 1929
[p. 84]
Journal
Archiv der Massenpresse,
P. Rössler

ANONYMOUS (PATHETONE)
Dancing Time, 1933
35 mm film, black/white,
with sound
Duration: 1:15 min.
British Pathé

ATLANTIC PHOTO GMBH
*Die Alfred-Jackson-Girls.
Ein Tausendfüssler*, 1928 [p. 94]
The Alfred Jackson Girls.
A Millipede
Gelatin silver print, 16.6 × 12 cm
Stiftung Stadtmuseum Berlin
Facsimile

**CARL MARIA HOLZAPFEL,
KÄTE STOCKS, RUDOLF
STOCKS**
*Frauen fliegen. 16 deutsche
Pilotinnen in ihren Leistungen
und Abenteuern*, 1931 [p. 84]
Women Fly. 16 Pilots, Their
Achievements and Adventures
Book
Archiv der Massenpresse,
P. Rössler

KEYSTONE VIEW CO.
Die Tiller-Girls sind da!, 1926
[p. 2-3]
The Tiller Girls Are Here!
Gelatin silver print, 13 × 18 cm
Stiftung Stadtmuseum Berlin
Facsimile

OSWALD VOH
Das Leben, Vol. 8, No. 9,
March 1931 [p. 84]
Journal
Archiv der Massenpresse,
P. Rössler

PAUL WOLFF
Die Frankfurter Küche, 1927
The Frankfurt Kitchen
35 mm film, black/white, silent
Duration: 8 min.
DFF – Deutsches Filminstitut
und Filmmuseum,
Frankfurt am Main

*Die Frankfurter
Kleinstwohnung*, 1928
The Small Frankfurt Flat
35 mm film, black/white, silent
Duration: 6 min. (extract: 3 min.)
DFF – Deutsches Filminstitut
und Filmmuseum,
Frankfurt am Main

TRANSGRESSIONS

ALBERT BIRKLE
Kurfürstendamm, 1924 [p. 118]
Pastel on cardboard, 68 × 87 cm
Kunstsammlung
Oberschwäbische
Elektrizitätswerke (OEW) /
Landkreis Sigmaringen

WILLIAM DAVIS
*Valeska Gert, „Berlin
Unterwelt"*, 1934 [p. 104]
Valeska Gert, "Berlin
Underworld"
Gelatin silver print, 29 × 20 cm
Theatre Collection,
University of Cologne

**HEINRICH MARIA
DAVRINGHAUSEN**
Der Träumer, 1919 [p. 107]
The Dreamer
Oil on canvas, 120 × 120.8 cm
Hessisches Landesmuseum
Darmstadt

KATE DIEHN-BITT
Selbstbildnis als Malerin, 1935
[p. 99]
Self-Portrait as Painter
Oil on wood, 100 × 70 cm
Kunsthalle Rostock

OTTO DIX
Lustmord, 1922 [p. 106]
Sex Murder
Lithograph on paper,
43.5 × 46.8 cm
Otto Dix Stiftung, Vaduz

Szene II (Mord), 1922 [p. 106]
Scene II (Murder)
Watercolour on paper
65 × 50 cm
Otto Dix Stiftung, Vaduz

**CARL FROELICH,
LEONTINE SAGAN**
Mädchen in Uniform, 1931
Girls in Uniform
35 mm film, black/white,
with sound
Duration: 96 min. (extract)
Courtesy of Films sans
frontières, Paris

OTTO GRIEBEL
Zwei Frauen, 1924 [p. 102]
Two Women
Watercolour on cardboard,
63.8 × 45 cm
The George Economou
Collection

HERBERT HOFFMANN
Transvestiten im Eldorado,
Berlin, 1928-1933 [p. 102]
Transvestites in Eldorado
Gelatin silver print,
22.5 × 27.5 cm
ullstein bild collection

KARL HUBBUCH
Der Lustmord, 1930 [p. 106]
The Sex Murder
Oil on canvas, 69 × 78 cm
Collection Frank Brabant,
Wiesbaden

LOTTE JOHANNA JACOBI
Valeska Gert, „Boxen", 1927
[p. 104]
Valeska Gert, "Boxing"
Gelatin silver print, 23 × 14.5 cm
Theatre Collection,
University of Cologne

RUDOLF KUZELOWSKY
Marton. Travestie-Künstler,
c. 1925 [end-paper, back]
Marton. Transvestite Artist
Photo montage, 28.9 × 22.7 cm
Stiftung Stadtmuseum Berlin
Facsimile

JEANNE MAMMEN
Valeska Gert, 1928-1929 [p. 104]
Oil on canvas, 60 × 44 cm
Berlinische Galerie – Museum
of Modern Art, Photography
and Architecture

An der Schießbude, 1929
At the Shooting Gallery
Watercolour and graphite
on vellum, 44.5 × 36 cm
The George Economou
Collection

Langweilige Puppen, 1929
[p. 100]
Boring Dolls
Watercolour and graphite on
paper mounted on cardboard
38.4 × 28.6 cm
The George Economou
Collection

Brüderstrasse (Zimmer frei),
1930 [p. 100]
Brüderstrasse (Free Rooms)
Watercolour, ink and graphite
on vellum, 47.5 × 34.5 cm
The George Economou
Collection

Arabische Tänzerin, c. 1930
Arabic Dancer
Lithograph on paper,
66 × 45 cm
Berlinische Galerie – Museum
of Modern Art, Photography
and Architecture

Auf der Strasse (Nutten), c. 1930
On the Streets (Prostitutes)
Lithograph on paper,
46.2 × 35 cm
Berlinische Galerie – Museum
of Modern Art, Photography
and Architecture

Café Nollendorf, c. 1931 [p. 120]
Watercolour and Indian ink
over pencil on paper,
47.5 × 35 cm
Private collection

Trinkerin, c. 1934
Drunk
Indian ink pen on paper,
27.6 × 23.4 cm
Berlinische Galerie – Museum
of Modern Art, Photography
and Architecture

ELLI MARCUS
Versammlung, 1934 [p. 104]
Reunion
Gelatin silver print,
23.8 × 12.5 cm
Theatre Collection, University
of Cologne

GEORG WILHELM PABST
Die Büchse der Pandora, 1928
Pandora's Box
35 mm film, black/white, silent
Duration: 133 min.
(extract: 2:42 min.)
Tamasa Distribution, Paris

ANTON RÄDERSCHEIDT
Selbstbildnis, 1928 [p. 102]
Self-Portrait
Oil on canvas, 100 × 80 cm
Paris Musées / Musée d'Art
Moderne de Paris

CHRISTIAN SCHAD
Liebende Knaben, 1929/1972
[p. 121]
Boys in Love
Lithograph after a drawing
from 1929, 30 × 23.5 cm
Museen der Stadt
Aschaffenburg – Christian
Schad Stiftung, Aschaffenburg

Adonis-Diele, 1930/1976
Lithograph after a drawing
from 1930, 40.5 × 30 cm
Museen der Stadt
Aschaffenburg, Christian Schad
Stiftung, Aschaffenburg

Die Melancholische, 1931
The Melancholy
From the series "5
Temperamente"
Lithographic crayon on paper,
23.3 × 16.8 cm
Museen der Stadt
Aschaffenburg – Christian
Schad Stiftung, Aschaffenburg

RUDOLF SCHLICHTER
*Der Künstler mit zwei
erhängten Frauen*, c. 1924
The Artist with Two
Hanged Women
Watercolour and pencil
on paper, 46 × 34.5 cm
The George Economou
Collection

Damenkneipe, c. 1925 [p. 101]
Ladies' Pub
Watercolour and Indian ink
on paper, 60 × 50.2 cm
Private collection

FRANZ WILHELM SEIWERT
Freudlose Gasse, 1927 [p. 103]
The Joyless Street
Oil on canvas, 65.5 × 80 cm
Galerie Berinson, Berlin

**CURT THOMALLA,
NICHOLAS KAUFMANN,
LEOPOLD NIERNBERGER**
Der Steinachfilm, 1922 [p. 119]
The Steinach Fim
Documentary, black/white, silent
Duration: 73 min. (extract)
Bundesarchiv, Film: 4938 /
Friedrich-Wilhelm-Murnau-
Stiftung

GERT WOLLHEIM
Ohne Titel (Paar), 1926 [p. 105]
Untitled (Couple)
Oil on canvas, 100.3 × 74.9 cm
The Jewish Museum, New
York, gift from Charlotte Levite
in memory of Julius Nassau,
1990-130

Reiterin und Clown, 1928
Horsewoman and Clown
Oil on canvas, 100 × 119 cm
Museum Kunstpalast,
Düsseldorf

THE DOWNSIDE

ALBERT BIRKLE
Der Bahnwärter, 1927
The Signalman
Oil on cardboard,
102.5 × 71.6 cm
Private collection,
Southern Germany

HANS BALUSCHEK
Sommerabend, 1928
Summer Evening
Oil on canvas, 120 × 151 cm
Berlinische Galerie – Museum
of Modern Art, Photography
and Architecture

SLÁTAN DUDOW
*Zeitprobleme. Wie der
Arbeiter wohnt*, 1930
The problems of Our Time.
How the Labourer Lives
35 mm film, black/white, silent
Duration: 17 min.
Bundesarchiv, Film: 20070

GEORGE GROSZ
Dame im Café, 1916
Lady in a Café
Indian ink on paper,
26.5 × 24 cm
Louisiana Museum of Modern
Art, Humlebæk, donation:
The Joseph and Celia Ascher
Collection, New York

Lohnabzug, 1918 [p. 110]
Wage Reduction
Indian ink on paper,
48.5 × 31 cm
Louisiana Museum of Modern
Art, Humlebæk, donation:
The Joseph and Celia Ascher
Collection, New York

Ausbeuter, 1919 [p. 110]
Exploiter
Indian ink on paper, 50 × 37 cm
Louisiana Museum of Modern
Art, Humlebæk, donation:
The Joseph and Celia Ascher
Collection, New York

Hochofen, 1925
Blast Furnace
Indian ink on paper
65 × 52.2 cm
Louisiana Museum of Modern
Art, Humlebæk, donation:
The Joseph and Celia Ascher
Collection, New York

HANS GRUNDIG
Am Stadtrand, 1926 [p. 111]
On the Outskirts of the City
Oil on canvas, 80.5 × 120 cm
Staatliche Museen zu Berlin,
Nationalgalerie

HEINZ HAMISCH
*Arbeitsloser Hafenarbeiter
(Max Barthel)*, 1932 [p. 109]
Unemployed Docker (Max
Barthel)
Oil on cardboard, 6.4 × 50.3 cm
Lindenau-Museum Altenburg

HEINRICH HAUSER
Feldarbeit Ruhrgebiet, c. 1930
Field Work in the Ruhr District
Gelatin silver print, 12.7 × 17.7 cm
Galerie Berinson, Berlin

WILHELM LACHNIT
Schwangeres Proletariermädchen,
1924/26 [p. 111]
Pregnant Working-class Girl
Oil on canvas, 60.4 × 50.3 cm
Lindenau-Museum Altenburg

MARTIN MUNKACSI
*Arbeiter beim Verlassen
des Werkes*, 1930
Workers Leaving the Factory
Gelatin silver print, 16.7 × 23 cm
ullstein bild collection

OSKAR NERLINGER
An die Arbeit, 1930 [p. 112]
To Work
Tempera sprayed on canvas,
121 × 81 cm
Kulturstiftung Sachsen-Anhalt,
Kunstmuseum Moritzburg Halle
(Saale) M0101410

Straßen der Arbeit, 1930 [p. 112]
Work Roads
Tempera on cardboard,
79.5 × 159 cm
Stiftung Stadtmuseum Berlin

FRANZ ROH
Ohne Titel, c. 1930
Untitled
Gelatin silver print, 16 × 22.6 cm
Galerie Berinson, Berlin

RUDOLF SCHLICHTER
Schwachsinnige II, 1923-1924 [p. 111]
Mentally Impaired II
Graphite on paper,
59.4 × 45 cm
Centre Pompidou, Musée national
d'art moderne, Paris, purchase,
1997

**ROBERT SIODMAK, EDGAR
GEORGE ULMER**
Menschen am Sonntag, 1930
People on Sundays
35 mm film, black/white, silent
Duration: 74 min.
(extract: 1:36 min.)
Deutsche Kinemathek, Berlin.
Label 20070

KARL VÖLKER
Industriebild, c. 1924 [p. 110]
Image of a Factory
Oil on canvas, 93 × 93 cm
Kulturstiftung Sachsen-Anhalt,
Kunstmuseum Moritzburg Halle
(Saale) M0101528

Bahnhof, 1924-1926 [p. 114-115]
Railway Station
Oil on wood, 110 × 165 cm
Kulturstiftung Sachsen-Anhalt,
Kunstmuseum Moritzburg Halle
(Saale) M0100293

Die Arbeitermittagspause, c. 1928
The Workers' Lunch break
Oil on cardboard, 75 × 105 cm
Deutsches Historisches Museum,
Berlin, Kg 63/42

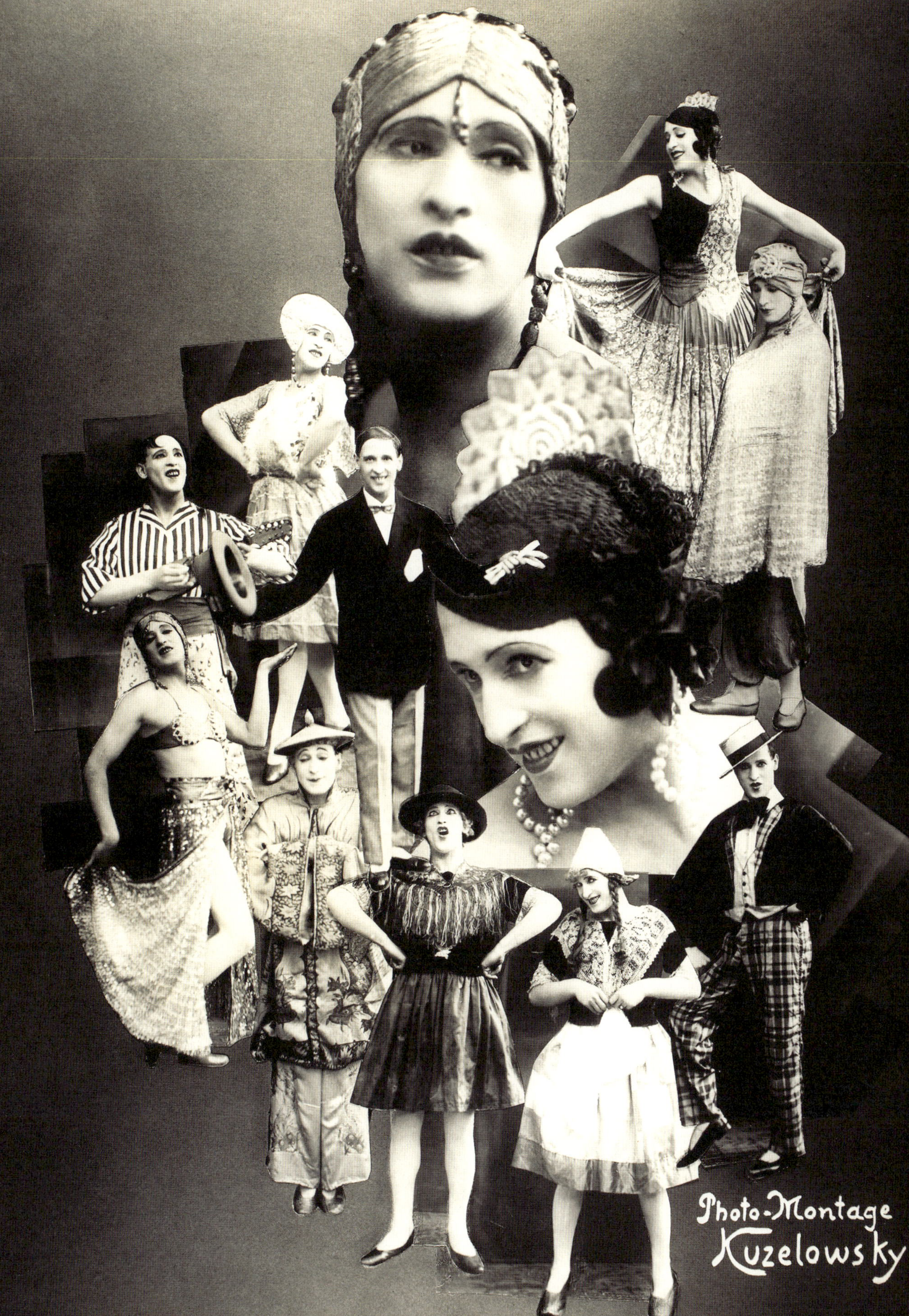
Photo-Montage
Kuzelowsky

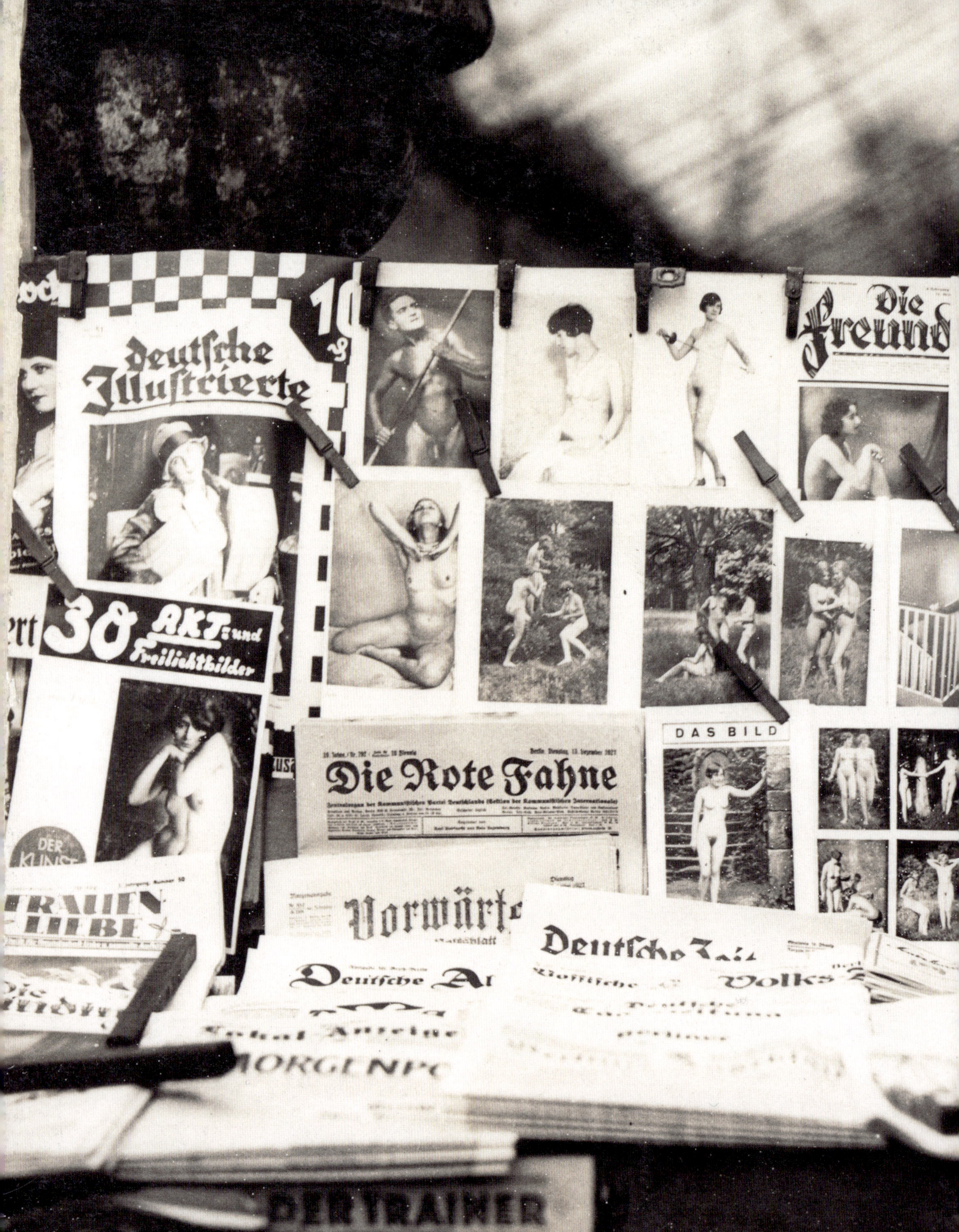
Die Freund
deutsche Illustrierte
30 AKT und Freilichtbilder
DER KLING
FRAUEN LIEBE
Die Rote Fahne
Vorwärts
Deutsche Zeit
MORGENPO
DAS BILD
DERTRAINER